# Sweet Is the Word

### Reflections on the Book of Mormon—
### Its Narrative, Teachings, and People

## Marilyn Arnold

Covenant Communications, Inc.

Published by Covenant Communications, Inc.
American Fork, Utah

Printed in the United States of America
First Printing: April 1996

01 00 99 98 97 96   10 9 8 7 6 5 4 3 2 1

ISBN 1-55503-925-1

# Dedication

*For Mother and Dad, the goodliest of parents.*

# Acknowledgments

A good many people have offered encouragement and support over the several years that this book has been simmering in my head, hands, and computer, though admittedly on the back burner for long stretches of time. Those who saw it launched, my colleagues at Brigham Young University, especially in the Graduate Office, deserve particular thanks. More recently, Erma Stott, Bonnie Ballif-Spanvill, and Heather Hansen read the completed draft with a helpful critical eye and genuine enthusiasm. And finally, the book has been blessed by the sensitive editing of JoAnn Jolley at Covenant, who caught the vision of this project from page one of the manuscript. Every writer should be as fortunate. Beyond all these to whom I owe personal thanks, however, is President Ezra Taft Benson, who urgently pled some years ago that we (I) return to the Book of Mormon, not only to reread it, but to study it with a humbled heart. And absolutely beyond calculation is my debt to the ancient prophets who faithfully engraved a sacred history for us in this day, and preserved it, along with the writings of their predecessors. Also incalculable is my debt to Mormon and Moroni for abridging, protecting, and adding to the record, and to Joseph Smith for faithfully translating and publishing it. And to the Lord for giving it to us.

# Contents

# Introduction

More than other scripture, the Book of Mormon can be read and appreciated by ordinary people with no special training or historical background, so long as they are humbly seeking the Spirit's understanding. Nevertheless, the book is not "easy" to read, in the sense that a popular novel is easy to read, because it is many-layered and structurally complex. As a reader and teacher of literature, I have often needed to write about a book in order to collect my thoughts about it. In the end, I have been compelled to do the same for the Book of Mormon.

I am not a scriptural scholar, and I have not called on the scholars to assist my reading. This essay is, very simply, my personal response to the book. My earnest hope is that what I have written will contribute in some small way to the reader's own study of the Book of Mormon, regardless of age or previous experience with the book. At every reading, the book offers new ideas and possibilities, presenting meanings and connections that had somehow eluded me previously. What the reader finds here, therefore, is not a finished product, but an essay in process. Truly, one is never really done with scripture. In my old age, I will probably regret having "rushed" the manuscript to press after only four or five years of writing and rewriting.

The Book of Mormon is, quite frankly, the most challenging and compelling text I have ever tried to explicate, the most densely rich and rewarding text I have ever read. It is assuredly not fiction, though it has narrative, character, and conflict; it cannot simply be called poetry, though it is full of poetic devices and forms; it would not qualify strictly as history, though it chronicles a people through their thousand-year existence. The Book of Mormon resembles all of these but is none of them. The Book of Mormon is scripture. That means that the book literally, unflinchingly, claims to publish the words of divinely inspired prophets in ancient America from roughly 600 B.C. to 400 A.D.

For those unfamiliar with the record, I offer some basic information by way of introduction. One aspect of the book's complexity is the fact that it chronicles two eras and two peoples. The group called Nephites after their first prophet-monarch and record keeper, Nephi, left Jerusalem six centuries before the birth of Jesus Christ and sailed to what is now the American continent, very likely landing somewhere in its midsection, or Mesoamerica. Later, the Nephites merged with a second group who left Jerusalem at approximately the same time. These colonizers were preceded by a much earlier group of old-world immigrants, the Jaredites. Although the two peoples settled in the same general area, their paths did not cross until the earlier civilization was virtually extinct. And it was nearly ten centuries after Nephi began the central narrative before the record reached its chief abridger, Mormon. When Mormon finished his work, he gave the record to his son Moroni, who added writings of his own, including his abridgment of the Jaredite record. Moroni then sealed the plates and buried them in the ground. A little far-fetched to the scriptural novice, perhaps, but not totally unimaginable. Ancient writings do occasionally surface in archaeological digs, and various findings in Mexico and Central America argue for a rather advanced ancient civilization there, some of it suggesting a strong Hebrew influence.

That same Nephi, son of the aging prophet Lehi, bears fervent testimony to the divine origin of the words he painstakingly inscribes on a set of gold plates fashioned for that purpose. Speaking to "all ye ends of the earth" (2 Nephi 33:13), Nephi admonishes his latter-day readers to "hearken unto these words and believe in Christ. . . . And if ye shall believe in Christ ye will believe in these words, for they are the words of Christ, and he hath given them unto me. . . ." Nephi further testifies that in the end, when "you and I shall stand face to face before his bar," "Christ will show unto you, with power and great glory, that they are his words" (2 Nephi 33:10-11).

When a person speaks this way, and there is nothing in it for him because he will be long dead when what he is writing comes to light, it is hard not to take him seriously. In a thought-provoking essay titled "The Message in the Bottle," the late Walker Percy, a physician turned novelist, describes us earthlings as castaways on an island, waiting for "news from across the seas" (146), that is, from God.[1] When that news comes, Percy says, it comes by an appointed "newsbearer," an apostle whose "credential . . . is simply the gravity of his message: 'I am called by God; do with me what you will, scourge me, persecute me, but my last words are my first; I am called by God and I make you eternally responsible for what you do against me'" (147).

In this context, Nephi's concluding words, engraved on metal plates in approximately 545 B.C., seem especially important:

> . . . I speak unto you as the voice of one crying from the dust: Farewell until that great day [of judgment][2] shall come.
>
> And you that will not partake of the goodness of God, and respect the words of the Jews [the Bible], and also my words, and the words which shall proceed forth out of the mouth of the Lamb of God [when he comes in person], behold, I bid you an everlasting farewell, for these words shall condemn you at the last day.
>
> For what I seal on earth, shall be brought against you at the judgment bar; for thus hath the Lord commanded me, and I must obey. Amen. (2 Nephi 33:13-15)

As a believing Catholic, Walker Percy affirms "the apostolic character of Christianity" (148), and his concluding words on the subject might be applied without serious distortion to Nephi and other Book of Mormon prophets, though it is doubtful that Percy ever heard of Nephi:

> But what if a man receives the commission to bring news across the seas to the castaway and does so in perfect sobriety and with good faith and perseverance to the point of martyrdom? And what if the news the newsbearer bears is the very news the castaway had been waiting for, news of where he came from and who he is and what he

---

[1] The Percy essay to which I refer appears in a book by the same name (New York: Farrar, Straus and Giroux, 1980, pp. 119-49). Specific page numbers are noted parenthetically in the text.

[2] Throughout this essay, the bracketed substitutions or additions to quotations are apparent in the context from which the quotations are drawn. I add them only for clarification.

must do, and what if the newsbearer brought with him the means by
which the castaway may do what he must do? Well then, the castaway
will, by the grace of God, believe him. (149)

A person could look upon the Book of Mormon as one such
"message in the bottle," as priceless divine news from across the
seas. Moreover, it has been delivered in our time by a man whose
commission earned him martyrdom. Such heaven-sent news,
according to Percy, is not news to a swallow or to an "unfallen
man" because these are "at home in the world and no castaway."
Neither is it news to "a fallen man who is a castaway but believes
himself to be at home in the world, for he does not recognize his
own predicament. It is only news to a castaway who knows himself to be a castaway" (148).

Indeed, those who have no intimations of immortality, who
have no sense of a heavenly homeland from which they are separated, may well find in the Book of Mormon no news that they
care to read. The fact that they do not care to read it, however,
does not make it one whit less vital to the welfare of their eternal
souls. To ignore the eternal soul is not to erase it. On the other
hand, those who know or suspect themselves to be castaways may
find in the Book of Mormon the very news from across the seas
for which they have watched and even hungered. In the end of the
book, the last Nephite prophet bears the same testimony borne by
his predecessor nearly a thousand years earlier. Moroni, wandering and alone, all his people slain in cruel wars, testifies before
burying the record to preserve it for later peoples that "God shall
show unto you, that that which I have written is true" (Moroni
10:29).

So certain is Moroni of the truths contained in the record
abridged and handed down to him by his father, Mormon, and in
the sections he added, that he challenges the reader to submit the
words to a test. Addressing the reader directly, though "speaking
out of the dust" as one who knows he precedes all his readers by
many centuries, Moroni makes a bold promise:

> And when ye shall receive these things, I would exhort you that ye would ask God, the Eternal Father, in the name of Christ, if these things are not true; and if ye shall ask with a sincere heart, with real intent, having faith in Christ, he will manifest the truth of it unto you, by the power of the Holy Ghost. (Moroni 10:4)

With all my heart, I confirm that he will, that he has.

The process by which "these things" have arrived in our hands today, to be read and pondered and put to such a test, is nothing short of miraculous. And for that reason, skepticism abounds, especially among those who have not read the book "with a sincere heart, with real intent, having faith in Christ." Mark Twain's good-natured but naive young self, in his mock autobiographical western narrative *Roughing It,* finds the Book of Mormon miraculous only in the fact that Joseph Smith managed to stay awake while he wrote it. The book, young Twain declares, is chloroform in print. Twain's youthful fictitious self, we remember, is wrong about a lot of other things, too.

It is very easy to dismiss the Book of Mormon unread; it is almost impossible to dismiss the Book of Mormon under the conditions Moroni prescribes. My many non-Mormon friends and colleagues across the country are too kind to say so, but I am sure that some of them wonder how anyone with extensive academic training and experience can believe the so-called "Joseph Smith story" and accept the Book of Mormon as authentic scripture. They love me in spite of this almost endearing lapse, this intellectual glitch, that makes me something of an anomaly in the tough-minded, though not ungentle, world we share. And so, in some sense, I write this essay for them as well as for me, so that they will understand the foundations of my faith. I also write it for my Mormon friends, those who have not yet been swept away by the miracle of the book and those who have. May the latter find new reason to celebrate it.

But I write this essay mainly because I must, while I am able, verbalize somehow what I think the Book of Mormon says. I must find words to express what it is about the book that lights fires in my mind, that moves me to tears, and that always, always strengthens my faith and leaves me absolutely certain of its authenticity. I say these things, knowing that I could easily be misunderstood by those who, not realizing that they are castaways, have no interest in news from across the seas. I invite any who know or suspect themselves to be castaways to read on.

Throughout his record, Nephi declares that his words and the words of his successors will come forth from the dust through the hands of "the Gentiles." These words will speak to the seed of his father's branch of the house of Israel and to all the earth. Most of Nephi's own direct descendants, he knows, will be destroyed; but some of the descendants of two of his older brothers, Laman and Lemuel, and those who join with them will survive and eventually receive the record. Before Nephi's time, the ancient prophet Isaiah also appears to have foreseen the emergence of a buried record containing the words of a long-deceased people: "And thou shalt be brought down, and shalt speak out of the ground, and thy speech shall be low out of the dust, and thy voice shall be, as of one that hath a familiar spirit, out of the ground, and thy speech shall whisper out of the dust" (Isaiah 29:4). Several verses later Isaiah seems to pick up the idea again, rather abstractly alluding to the burial of prophetic voices, but then making reference to a specific latter-day incident regarding a sealed book.[3] It surprises me that Isaiah would have foreseen so specific, and seemingly minor, an event, and yet there it is in his writings.

The unfriendly reception of the Book of Mormon as a spurious and unnecessary second book of Christian scripture is also anticipated in revelation to Nephi. The Lord reproves those who assume that one book of scripture renders another unnecessary: "Wo be unto him that shall say: We have received the word of God, and we need no more of the word of God, for we have enough" (2 Nephi 28:29). He chides future Christians for sup-

---

[3] See Isaiah 29:11-12, and Nephi's clarification of Isaiah's prophecy in 2 Nephi 27:9,10,15-20. See also Joseph Smith History 1:64-65 for an account of the fulfillment of that prophecy.

posing that the Bible "contains all my words" (2 Nephi 29:10), and for treasuring the word of God in the Bible but rejecting the Nephite record containing more of his word: "Wherefore murmur ye, because that ye shall receive more of my word?" (2 Nephi 29:8). This, he implies, is cause for celebration, not complaint. Moreover, the irony of a Gentile Christian world rejecting the Jewish people while embracing as its only legitimate scripture a Bible written by Jews[4] is not lost on the Lord:

> And because my words shall hiss forth—many of the Gentiles shall say: A Bible! A Bible! We have got a Bible, and there cannot be any more Bible.
> But thus saith the Lord God: O fools, they shall have a Bible; and it shall proceed forth from the Jews, mine ancient covenant people. And what thank they the Jews for the Bible which they receive from them? Yea, what do the Gentiles mean? . . .
> Thou fool, that shall say: A Bible, we have got a Bible, and we need no more Bible. Have ye obtained a Bible save it were by the Jews? (2 Nephi 29:3-4, 6)

The Lord also indicates that there will be several records; wherever his people are, he will instruct them and they will write. Furthermore, the various groups—Jews, Lehites, "the other tribes of the house of Israel" and "all nations of the earth" (2 Nephi 29:12)—will one day have each other's records. That will constitute a knowledge explosion the likes of which the world has never seen.

One part of that explosion occurred when the translated record we know as the Book of Mormon was first published in 1830. Having been buried by the living Moroni in about 421 A.D., the record engraved on gold plates was left for someone to recover it and translate it. Since no human being for centuries knew where it was, immortal beings had to intercede if the record—and the full gospel of Jesus Christ which the record contained—were to be

---

[4] The word "Jew" or "Jews" is used in the Book of Mormon and throughout my essay to designate a people. It carries no more connotations than a word like "Nephite" or "Israelite," and should be read as a neutral term.

restored to the earth. Apparently the time was ripe in nineteenth century America, where religious freedom was a constitutional principle if not a consistent practice. Joseph Smith, a young man with no academic training but with a fine intelligence, an exceptional spiritual sensitivity, a pure heart, and an honest hunger for truth, was chosen as the mortal instrument through whom the restoration of the record and the gospel would occur. A promising choice, when we think about it. One does not, as the Lord has said elsewhere, put new wine in old bottles (which in the first century A.D. were made of animal skin and could not be reused; see Matthew 9:17 or Mark 2:22).

Here was a young man, suited by his devotion, intellect, and humility to write what the Holy Ghost would prompt him to write. An older, more accomplished person might have been less willing to be totally directed by the Spirit. And Moroni, he who had buried the records, was the immortal being who guided young Joseph through several years of periodic instruction and then delivered the plates into his hands, temporarily, for translation. A miraculous event? Yes, indeed—but leading a young man to a set of ancient records and assisting him to translate them would scarcely tax the powers of the Lord of miracles.

In his prophecy of the restoration of the gospel of Jesus Christ in latter days, Isaiah is clearly aware of the significance of the event:

> . . . behold, I will proceed to do a marvellous work among this people, even a marvellous work and a wonder: for the wisdom of their wise men shall perish, and the understanding of their prudent men shall be hid. . . .
> And in that day shall the deaf hear the words of the book, and the eyes of the blind shall see out of obscurity, and out of darkness. (Isaiah 29:14,18)[5]

---

[5] Like the Bible, the Book of Mormon uses words like "men" and "brethren" generically to mean both female and male.

The Lord did indeed cause the physically deaf to hear and the physically blind to see. But how much greater is the miracle described here—the miracle that gives hearing to the spiritually deaf and sight to the spiritually blind. And that is the real miracle of the Book of Mormon, though being excavated from a hillside under divine guidance and translated into English from reformed Egyptian was amazing enough. What is remarkable, too, is that the record was kept and passed on through a thousand years of geographical transfers, civil turbulence, deadly wars, and cosmic cataclysms. It was neither lost nor destroyed, and the only Nephite survivor of the last great Nephite-Lamanite battle was the person who had the record in his possession.

What, then, is this book, foreseen to come forth in our time by prophets on two continents? Above all, it is a miraculous and eloquent testament of the reality and divinity of Jesus Christ and of his atoning sacrifice and resurrection. Like the Bible, it has many contributing writers; but unlike the Bible, it has undergone only one basic translation from the original text. The unbroken translation, of course, was divided into chapters and verses when it was published. All subsequent editions derive from that first translation, including renderings in dozens of languages. Here is the gospel of the Lord Jesus Christ, in all its simplicity and splendor, as taught to and by ancient prophets of the house of Israel who inhabited lands now called the Americas. This is the essence of Mormonism; this is the sweet word, the sweetest of words. Characteristics and practices the world has typically associated with Mormonism—strict health codes, moral fidelity, emphasis on family—are indeed important. Prominent as they are, however, they are not exclusively "Mormonism"; Mormons do not have a corner on such ideals, but share them with conscientious people everywhere. What distinguishes Mormons from people of other faiths, in addition to their belief in living prophets and continuous revelation, is their belief in the Book of Mormon. That book is nothing less than a sublime witness of Jesus Christ, the Son of God. On its authenticity The Church of Jesus Christ of Latter-day Saints stands or falls.

*1*

## 1 Nephi 1-6: Beginnings of a People and a Record

Even though the Book of Mormon is modeled after the brass
plates (history and scriptures roughly equivalent to the Old
Testament) in the Nephites' possession, I find the Book of
Mormon far more accessible than the Bible. The first Nephi did
us all a favor in determining to write in plain language himself and
to instruct his successors to do the same. Considering that Nephi
dearly loved—and what's more, actually understood—the highly
metaphoric, elusive writing of Isaiah, it is our good fortune that
he did not expect us to match his theological and educational
preparation. Consequently, although the Book of Mormon is
inevitably stamped by its time and its writers, the book is guided
by a clear sense of audience and purpose. Written for and to
latter-day readers, it is comfortably direct and candid; and it is less
imbedded with historical allusion and cultural apparatus than the
Old, and even the New, Testaments.

Nonetheless, the Book of Mormon is like the Old Testament
in that it follows a more or less continuous narrative that tracks
the lives and teachings of several large, dominant figures, for the
most part prophets and devout political or religious leaders. As the
record's initiator and its most prolific contributor, Nephi may well
be the pre-eminent Book of Mormon figure. Indeed, he authors
two large sections and defines the book's purposes and form. But
more than that, he is a giant in the faith and a physically imposing, intellectually dynamic leader. By sheer force of personality,
and under appointment of God, Nephi institutes and maintains
religious and civil authority where anarchy and barbarism could
easily have flourished. Even as he narrates events in which his family members are the only players, Nephi inadvertently traces his
own destined emergence as a prophet-monarch.

Like many first-person narratives (*Moby Dick* and *Huckleberry*

*Finn*, for example), Nephi's account opens with a frank introduction of himself and his intent:

> I, Nephi, having been born of goodly parents, therefore I was taught somewhat in all the learning of my father; and having seen many afflictions in the course of my days, nevertheless, having been highly favored of the Lord in all my days; yea, having had a great knowledge of the goodness and the mysteries of God, therefore I make a record of my proceedings in my days. (1 Nephi 1:1)

Nephi packs a lot of information into that one sentence—including his gratitude for good parentage, his testimony of God, and his resolve to keep a religious record of his own life and times. As it turns out, those three subjects anticipate the first chapter of Nephi's account, which treats his father's prophetic calling, the reality and glory of the Father and the Son, and the importance of the written record.

Nephi wastes no time in personally attesting to the record's authenticity: "And I know that the record which I make is true; and I make it with mine own hand; and I make it according to my knowledge" (1 Nephi 1:3). Were we to encounter such a statement in a piece of prose fiction, we would be well-advised to exercise a little skepticism, because first-person narrators are famous for their unreliability. Readers of fiction are required to appraise the controlling authorial voice behind the narrator in order to uncover the narrator's true nature and thus discern the truth or non-truth of the account. Genuine scripture, of course, is different from fiction, especially in that the focus is on truth itself rather than on plot or character. The mortal narrator is secondary to the doctrine, and the controlling authorial voice is assumed to be God.

Still, some readers are impatient with Nephi as a narrator because his account appears heavily biased in his own favor and tinctured with self-righteousness. Most of us are put off by a sibling or peer who is immune to the foibles and lapses that flaw our own characters. As Mark Twain wryly observed in Pudd'nhead

Wilson's calendar, few things are more irksome than the inescapable presence of a good example. It would seem that by Nephi's reckoning, his older brothers, Laman and Lemuel, can do no right while he can do no wrong. To appreciate the power of the first-person narrator in shaping a story, one need only consider how Nephi would have fared in the account if Laman or Lemuel had been the record keeper. Despite Nephi's physical stature, he must have seemed to them an insufferably pious upstart, stuffed with foolish notions and impossible expectations. His fictional counterpart is usually the sort of character who is headed for a well-deserved and instructive tumble. The unfolding of this particular nonfictional narrative, however, validates Nephi, not only as a virtuous truth-teller, but also as an exemplar who is possessed of great human sympathy, patience, and humility. Nephi is not a hypocrite, nor does he get his come-uppance. Furthermore, the text confirms that, if anything, Nephi has been overly generous about Laman and Lemuel. They are moral weaklings, and they are liars and murderers besides. God, after all, is the most reliable of authorial voices, and Nephi is his mouthpiece.

Having succinctly mapped out the territory, Nephi returns to his first point of mention, his "goodly parents." Just five sentences into his astonishing record, Nephi elects to introduce a spectacular vision experienced by his father Lehi, a holy prophet. It strikes me that a record keeper concerned for his credibility might not provide such grand fodder for skeptics before he had uttered six sentences. Nephi, however, speaks with the calm assurance of one who knows both himself and his God. The steadiness of his nature and conviction is reflected in the resolute execution of the repeated parallel structures cited in verse 3 above—"I know . . . and I make . . . and I make." Not only does Nephi launch his account with a supernatural occurrence, but he devotes half of what becomes his introductory chapter to the matter of Lehi's divine manifestations.

Undoubtedly, Nephi has several purposes in so quickly taking up the matter of Lehi's vision. The revelatory events do confirm Lehi's prophetic calling, but they also attest immediately to the reality of God the Father and his Son, Jesus Christ, the actual authors of the record. Moreover, it is through this visionary experience that Lehi learns of Jerusalem's imminent destruction. The vision, then, initiates the journey away from Jerusalem and sets the stage for the birth of a new nation; and it indirectly initiates the record as well. Lehi sees God and his angels, and then the Son descending in glory. Thus, just nine verses into his account Nephi makes visible the resplendent figure of Jesus Christ, who is to be the center and focus of the entire record. Lehi's vision is Nephi's entry to the subject of the Messiah, and he can brook no delays. Incidentally, Lehi learns of Jerusalem's impending doom from a book the Son hands him in his vision. The Lord could have instructed Lehi verbally, but he elects instead to teach Lehi through the written word, in that very act underscoring the importance of physical records.

Chapters 2 through 5 of 1 Nephi are largely narrative describing the departure of Lehi and his family from Jerusalem into the wilderness bordering the Red Sea, and the acquisition of the brass plates from a devious, irascible Jewish nobleman and priest named Laban. The plates contain, by Nephi's tabulation, "the five books of Moses," Jewish history and prophecies "down to the commencement of the reign of Zedekiah" (including teachings of Jeremiah), and Lehi's genealogy back to Joseph of Egypt (see 1 Nephi 5:11-14). Laman and Lemuel, worldly men who are attached to the wealth and comforts of their home in Jerusalem, are understandably unhappy with their father, whom they regard as a foolish visionary. If inclined to judge Laman and Lemuel harshly, even this early, we might consider what our own reactions would be in similar circumstances. Would we rejoice if an elderly family member, whose judgment we question anyway, were suddenly to announce that God had directed him to gather the clan and head into untracked territory?

These considerations notwithstanding, we can still see in this incident huge differences among the responses of Lehi's family members. Already sown are the seeds of rebellion that in Laman and Lemuel would fester into violence and cruelty. The pair openly dispute Lehi's prophecy that Jerusalem will be destroyed, and Nephi privately makes a disturbing comparison in which he likens them to "the Jews who were at Jerusalem, who sought to take away the life of my father" (1 Nephi 2:13). Despite his advanced age, Lehi rises to the occasion; empowered by the Spirit, he confounds his two eldest sons, temporarily winning their obedience. Nephi, who will himself be a prophet, and his older brother, the reliable Sam, are different. Filled with "great desires to know of the mysteries of God," Nephi cries "unto the Lord; and behold he did visit me, and did soften my heart that I did believe all the words which had been spoken by my father; wherefore, I did not rebel against him like unto my brothers" (1 Nephi 2:16). We should not, however, miss Nephi's reference to the need of his own heart to be softened. But unlike Laman and Lemuel, he had the good sense to pray for personal confirmation of his father's revelation.

Nephi takes his concern for his brothers to the Lord, and the Lord answers with the startling news that Nephi will "be led to a land of promise; yea, even a land which I have prepared for you" (1 Nephi 2:20). Nephi also learns what must have been unsettling in the extreme to a younger brother: if faithful, he will "be made a ruler and a teacher over thy brethren" (1 Nephi 2:22). And if those brothers are rebellious, the Lord says, they will be cut off and cursed. Should Nephi's descendants prove unfaithful, his brothers' descendants "shall be a scourge unto thy seed, to stir them up in the ways of remembrance" (1 Nephi 2:24). Here, then, is a capsule preview of the history of Book of Mormon peoples. It is a lot for a young man to absorb.

With that brief but unnerving glimpse into his own prophetic destiny, the young Nephi returns dutifully to his father's tent, there to learn that the Lord has a more immediate requirement. Nephi and his brothers are to return to Jerusalem to obtain the brass records in Laban's possession. It is risky business, and though Laman and Lemuel are unwilling, Lehi knows he can count on Nephi. His response is one of the oft-quoted passages in Mormondom, a guideline for many a striving Latter-day Saint:

> I will go and do the things which the Lord hath commanded, for
> I know that the Lord giveth no commandments unto the children of
> men, save he shall prepare a way for them that they may accomplish
> the thing which he commandeth them. (1 Nephi 3:7)

We may think that this promise applies only to major religious
assignments or callings, but the phrase "no commandments" tells
me that the Lord gladly assists any and every willing mortal to
obey any and every commandment, large or small. Presumably,
then, he will "prepare a way" for us to obey even the more abstract
injunctions—those that are not task specific but relate to character, that demand of us humility, faith, and charity.

It is worth noting that on the brothers' first attempt to secure
the plates, they follow democratic procedures. They "consult one
with another" (1 Nephi 3:10) and cast lots to see who will
approach Laban. Laman, on whom the lot falls, gamely tries to get
the plates from an implacable Laban but ends up fleeing from
Laban's wrath. After Laman's experience, all but Nephi are ready
to scuttle the project. In words that are surprisingly assertive,
Nephi steps forward and persuades his brothers to try again: "As
the Lord liveth, and as we live, we will not go down unto our
father in the wilderness until we have accomplished the thing
which the Lord hath commanded us" (1 Nephi 3:15). Then, as if
remembering that he is, after all, the youngest brother, he takes a
milder tone, gently reminding the others of their father's
prophecy, and of Lehi's willingness to obey the Lord's command
at the cost of his entire fortune. Nephi reminds them, too, that
the durable metal records they seek are essential to their cultural
survival, allowing them to "preserve unto our children the language of our fathers" in addition to the words "of all the holy
prophets . . . since the world began" (1 Nephi 3:19-20).

The strategy on the second trip into Jerusalem is to buy the
records from Laban, exchanging all of Lehi's riches for the brass
plates. When that plan, too, is foiled, Laman and Lemuel vent
their anger by taking a rod to Nephi and Sam. An angel interrupts
their sport with still more unpleasant news: "... the Lord hath

chosen him [Nephi] to be ruler over you, and this because of your iniquities" (1 Nephi 3:29). As might be expected, heavenly orders to circumvent customary birth order make life more difficult for Nephi. Treading as lightly as possible on his brothers' wounded egos, Nephi urges them to make another try for the plates, reminding them that Laban and his guards are no match for the Lord. The angel's visit has made one thing clear, however: Nephi is now in charge, and this time there is no casting of lots. Nevertheless, Nephi's obedience is certainly neither blind nor mindless. In fact, he reasons with the Spirit in the hope that the directive to kill Laban will be rescinded. Far from correcting Nephi for raising concerns, the Spirit explains to him that sometimes extreme measures are necessary, in this instance to preserve the faith of a whole nation. At stake is not only the Lehites' inheritance in the land of promise, but their very existence. People soon forget uncodified laws, and the Lord has warned that if they fail to keep the commandments written in the Law of Moses, they will perish. The plates simply must be obtained, and they are.

A written record such as Nephi acquired, and such as he would himself write, has great value to any nation; but to the Lehites it is priceless. The brass plates will play a major role in the establishment and preservation of Nephite society in the promised land. I may seem to belabor the point, but these people will soon be wrenched from their ancestral roots and cast into a strange, uninhabited land where they will be totally isolated from other human beings and civilizations. Sailing they know not where, and permanently leaving behind the whole accumulation of civilized society, they will have to rely on memory (which can shift and falter), on divine revelation, and on written records to tell them who they are and what God's purposes are for them. No one else in the world will even know they exist.

Soon enough, the followers of Laman and Lemuel will provide compelling evidence of what can happen to a people cut loose from the anchor of history and statute. Looking ahead, we see that Laman's people, in forfeiting their tangible heritage, lose their standard for language, ethics, morality, and culture. Without records, Nephi's people might also lose their sense of purpose, and perhaps even their humanity. The past is valuable for many things, but especially as a guarantor of continuity, a stabilizing prospectus for the future. If Nephi even vaguely perceives a similar purpose for the record he is preparing, that would be reason enough for him to write it.

Chapter 5 leaves no doubt, either, that Lehi treasures the record on the brass plates, for personal as well as communal reasons. To obtain it, he was willing to put his sons at risk and to incur the severe displeasure of their mother. The ceremonial rejoicing on the sons' safe return is as much for the record as for the sons. The brass plates are particularly important, too, as Nephi explains in 2 Nephi 25, because they will serve as an educational model for his people. Contemporary Judaism, which Nephi says has seriously perverted religious practice, will not do. Using the brass plates as both his intellectual and his theological link to the past, Nephi intends to develop his own instructional forms. Throughout his ministry, Nephi will teach constantly from the brass plates and exhort his younger brother Jacob to do the same. Then, too, the plates will provide a useful witness that he is proclaiming the doctrine taught by his holy predecessors, and that he is indeed teaching the word of God.

Chapter 6 is brief, but it evidences Nephi's thematic concentration on records as he explains further his intent for his own writings. Nephi engages the matter of the record again in chapter 9 and still again, in greater detail, in chapter 19. He explains that he is keeping two sets of records, the larger one basically historical ("an account of the reign of the kings, and the wars and contentions of my people"), the smaller one sacred ("for the more part of the ministry," 1 Nephi 9:4). The latter, which duplicates some of the sacred materials in the larger record, was specifically commissioned by the Lord after the first was well along, for a purpose unknown to Nephi at the time. Nephi calls both records the plates of Nephi.[1]

---

[1] For a full account of the reasons for the second record, see section 10 of the Doctrine and Covenants. It would seem that in directing Nephi to make a second record, the Lord was in part anticipating the loss of a sizeable section of translated manuscript, a section that contained a representation of Lehi's discourses. The latter-day revelation indicates that what was lost was only an abridgment, while Nephi's firsthand account was preserved. To have allowed Joseph Smith to retranslate the lost pages would have been to abet the enemies who sought to trip him up.

Many centuries later, Mormon also made a set of plates, on which to inscribe his abridgment of the materials on the larger plates. Apparently, the large plates of Nephi, which contained the writings of Nephi's successors (beginning with the book of Mosiah)² in addition to his own historical record, were not available to Joseph Smith. Nor did he have access to a sealed portion of the record, which seemingly contained the glorious writings of the first Jaredite prophet (see Ether 3:25-27). Joseph was entrusted to translate the plates of Mormon, which contained the small plates of Nephi (the religious record up until the book of Mosiah) and Mormon's abridgment of the large plates (the combined religious and historical record from the book of Mosiah through 4 Nephi). Nephi knew that sacred texts are "of great worth, both to the body and the soul" (1 Nephi 19:7). We might profit from pondering the worth of sacred texts "to the body," a curious but compelling idea.

---

² Nephi's immediate successors squeezed what they could of sacred history onto the small plates.

*2*

## 1 Nephi 7-15: Nephi's Vision

Chapter 7 of 1 Nephi chronicles the first serious conflict between Nephi and his older brothers, thus foreshadowing the great chasm that eventually splits the Lehite group. Chapters 8 through 22 detail gloriously stirring visions experienced by both Lehi and Nephi, and they chart Nephi's growth into one of the mightiest mortals ever to speak with and for God. Prophets have always been misunderstood, and Nephi is no exception. Even though their own father is a prophet, Laman and Lemuel seem unable to comprehend the prophetic role. They are especially loath to view their younger brother as God's appointed spokesman. Senseless of their participation in a larger drama, the brothers see only the moment and its material realities. Nephi, on the other hand, rejoices in the high calling of Moses and the prophecies of Isaiah, and he recognizes that he and his family are, and will continue to be, living fulfillment of those prophecies. Furthermore, Nephi will not be put off. So long as the family is together, he reads Isaiah to his brothers, trying to lengthen their perspective and build their faith in prophets (but probably annoying them all the more).

It seems quite natural that in the face of his brothers' persecution and scorn, Nephi would turn for support to Isaiah, his earnest and eloquent mentor, his model and forerunner. Isaiah's writings become priceless to this displaced sojourner who finds himself permanently detached from everything else he has known; who writes urgently for the benefit of a much later people; and who, like his predecessor, bears the often thankless responsibility of stirring a forgetful people to a remembrance of their fathers and their God. Like no one else, Isaiah described the peril of a people who disregard the commandments.

But if one aspect of being a prophet is laboring under an

agonizing burden of responsibility, another aspect is feeling the power of God coursing through one's brain and sinews. It is receiving messages from across the seas; it is seeing visions and communicating with the Spirit and with heavenly messengers. While his family is still in the nearby wilderness, Lehi has just such a lofty experience—a vision of the tree of life. Although Nephi has said that he will give the writings of Lehi little space in the smaller sacred record, he seems irresistibly drawn to his father's prophetic experiences and utterances.[1] In fact, 1 Nephi 8 is largely devoted to Lehi's recounting of his remarkable vision.

Lehi's justifiable anxiety about his less-than-valiant sons, Laman and Lemuel, is imaged in his dream; and afterward he preaches to them with great earnestness. None of this is lost on Nephi, who resonates to his father's extraordinary experiences and utterances. Nephi records his father's prediction of the captivity and later return of many of Jerusalem's inhabitants, but his attention is riveted on the prophesied "Messiah, . . . a Savior of the world" who will come "six hundred years from the time that my father left Jerusalem" (1 Nephi 10:4). Greatly moved by his father's words, Nephi hungers to "see, and hear, and know of these things, by the power of the Holy Ghost" (1 Nephi 10:17). Whatever his brothers think, Nephi knows of a surety that the heavens are not closed. The vision will be his.

To appreciate the difference between secondhand and first-hand experience, one need only set Nephi's retelling of his father's vision against his vibrant description of his own. Nephi records the actual words uttered by both the Spirit and the angel of his vision, offering a dynamic immediacy that is missing from the Lehi account.[2] For example, in speaking of the tree, Lehi is reported to have said, "And it came to pass that I beheld a tree, whose fruit was desirable to make one happy" (1 Nephi 8:10). Compare Nephi's lilting description of the tree he saw himself:

---

[1] Nephi's plan at the moment is "to give an account upon these plates of my proceedings, and my reign and ministry" (1 Nephi 10:1). The word "reign" indicates Nephi's awareness of his political role.

[2] Nephi's account of his father's vision in Jerusalem, however, is more stirring and immediate, more reliant on Lehi's language. It has the qualities of a firsthand account (see 1 Nephi 1:7-15).

> ... the Spirit said unto me: Look! And I looked and beheld a tree; and
> it was like unto the tree which my father had seen; and the beauty
> thereof was far beyond, yea, exceeding of all beauty; and the whiteness
> thereof did exceed the whiteness of the driven snow. (1 Nephi 11:8)

Where the account attributed to Lehi simply sketches out the
basic components of Lehi's dream, Nephi's reconstruction of his
own experience is grandiose, full of fire and wonder. There is
another difference, too. As Nephi's record represents it, Lehi does
not make a direct link between his prophecy of the Messiah and
his vision of the tree of life, the river of water, the rod of iron, and
the spacious building filled with the wicked. Christ, however, is
the pivotal center of Nephi's entire experience; the vision of the
tree teaches of him. In fact, Nephi is told outright that after he has
seen the tree his father saw, he shall witness Christ and "bear
record that it is the Son of God" (1 Nephi 11:7). Nephi's vision
confirms Lehi's and establishes even more convincingly that the
principal theme and purpose of the Book of Mormon is to bear
record of Jesus Christ. The vision is clearly a turning point for
Nephi.

Lehi apparently did not ask to know the interpretation of his
own magnificent vision. Perhaps he had known already and
needed no further manifestation. But when the Spirit asks Nephi
what he desires after seeing the vision of the tree, he responds
immediately: "To know the interpretation thereof" (1 Nephi
11:11). The Spirit exclaims, "Look!" and disappears (1 Nephi
11:12). Nephi's answer is a vision, orchestrated by an angel, of the
coming Messiah who in his redeeming mission is love incarnate.
The vision teaches Nephi a grand and unforgettable doctrine, that
the meaning of the tree of life is "the love of God, which sheddeth
itself abroad in the hearts of the children of men" (1 Nephi 11:22).
One tiny preposition holds the key to this passage: the word "in."
If the word "to" were substituted for "in," the passage would suggest only the dispensing of love *from* God *to* mortals. The word
"in," however, suggests that God's love is also inside mortals and
works *through* them. This love of God, Nephi tells the angel of his

vision, "is the most desirable above all things." The angel exclaims in glad reply, "Yea, and the most joyous to the soul" (1 Nephi 11:22-23).

Nephi's vision of the coming Messiah merits careful reading for its fine simplicity of expression and its illumination of Lehi's vision of the tree of life. The Savior is indeed the embodiment of divine love, the source and emblem of everlasting life, whose fruit is mortal happiness and immortal salvation. As the angel questions Nephi, we sense not only the glory of the miracle, but also the humility with which Nephi receives it:

> And it came to pass that I saw the heavens open; and an angel came down and stood before me; and he said unto me: Nephi, what beholdest thou?
>
> And I said unto him: A virgin, most beautiful and fair above all other virgins.
>
> And he said unto me: Knowest thou the condescension of God?
>
> And I said unto him: I know that he loveth his children; nevertheless, I do not know the meaning of all things. (1 Nephi 11:14-17)

In Nephi's unfolding vision lies the fuller meaning of his father's, and he sees the infant Christ, "the Lamb of God, yea, even the Son of the Eternal Father!" in his mother's arms (1 Nephi 11:21). He also sees Christ's baptism, ministry, and crucifixion—his healing and triumph, and then his being "lifted up upon the cross and slain for the sins of the world" (1 Nephi 11:33). The language movingly captures the divine nature of the Savior and the exalted character of Nephi's experience. The eleventh chapter of 1 Nephi is best appreciated if read aloud.

Chapter 12 is largely a foretelling of events that will be recorded by later annalists, the increasing wars and contentions among the Lehites in the new land, and the cataclysmic events that will mark the Savior's crucifixion and precede his ministry among the Nephites. Chapter 13 contains fascinating prophecies for the modern reader, who can recognize the rather specific fulfillment of many of them. For example, Nephi sees the divinely inspired "discovery" of America and the Gentile conquest of that land. He also sees the revolutionary war, and refers quaintly to the British as "mother Gentiles" (Nephi 13:17).

Nephi then sees a book, obviously the Bible, which the angel of his vision painstakingly explains will initially "go forth from the Jews in purity unto the Gentiles." With the advent of the devil's church, however, the book will be considerably diminished, causing "an exceedingly great many [to] stumble" (1 Nephi 13: 24-29). The chapter also contains hopeful promises, both for the Gentiles and for the seed of surviving Lamanites. One of the most hopeful, delivered by an angel in the Lord's own words, prophesies the coming forth of the Book of Mormon. Modesty is no consideration as the book powerfully and candidly foretells itself, becomes its own witness. After Nephi's seed perishes, the Lord says both unequivocally and lyrically,

> . . . these things shall be hid up, to come forth unto the Gentiles, by the gift and power of the Lamb.
> And in them shall be written my gospel, saith the Lamb, and my rock and my salvation.
> . . . and whoso shall publish peace, yea, tidings of great joy, how beautiful upon the mountains shall they be. (1 Nephi 13:35-37)

Surely Nephi's heart sang as he heard these words. He must have begun to understand that the things to be "hid up" were in the record he was keeping, and that the Lord had far-reaching purposes in directing him to make a sacred as well as a secular record of his people. We remember that earlier, an obedient Nephi had begun making a record before he knew the Lord's reasons for requiring it, and now the Lord is splendidly enlightening him.

In vision, Nephi actually sees the Bible carried from the Gentiles to the remnant of his brothers' seed, along with "other books" (1 Nephi 13:39) which are undoubtedly the Nephite writings. These other books, the angel says, "shall establish the truth of the first, . . . and shall make known the plain and precious things which have been taken away from them." They shall also inform the world "that the Lamb of God is the Son of the Eternal

Father, and the Savior of the world" (1 Nephi 13:40). The angel's words are vitally important because they clarify the purpose of the Book of Mormon in establishing the truth of the Bible, and in restoring to the gospel published there the things missing from the time-altered biblical text. The Book of Mormon, therefore, neither replaces nor supplements the Bible. It makes scripture whole again. And the ultimate purpose of the Book of Mormon is to bring people to Christ that they might be redeemed. In Christ's first coming, the angel explains, he appeared to the Jews and then the Gentiles. But his second coming will reverse the order: ". . . the last [the Gentiles] shall be first, and the first [the Jews] shall be last" (1 Nephi 13:42).

The first eight verses of 1 Nephi 14 set the stage for the next phase of Nephi's vision, which is described in distinctly Old Testament fashion (see verses 9-17), consistent with Nephi's textual model. He witnesses the latter-day opposition between two great forces battling for the souls of humankind—the "great and abominable church" of the devil, which has large numbers and great dominion, and "the church of the Lamb of God" (1 Nephi 14:9-10), which is widespread and well armed with God's might but has only small dominion. This is an important point, for although the gospel is to reach all quarters of the earth, Nephi sees that the Lord's people will be vastly outnumbered by Satan's church. Of incidental interest is the angel's earlier use of a familiar metaphor, a "great pit," to describe the destination of the devil's followers. To that metaphor he attaches an engaging little addendum: the pit "shall be filled by those who digged it" (1 Nephi 14:3; see also Ecclesiastes 10:8). A modern parallel to that idea suggests that we must sleep in the beds we make.

Nephi is also shown "a man . . . dressed in a white robe," "one of the twelve apostles of the Lamb," who "shall see and write" things Nephi is forbidden to record, particularly things "concerning the end of the world" (1 Nephi 14:19-22). This figure is obviously John the Revelator, whom "the Lord God hath ordained" to record such things (1 Nephi 14:25). An attentive reader of the Book of Mormon is likely to notice that Nephi and his successors,

while writing extensively and repeatedly of events preceding
Christ's second coming, do not write of the end of the world. The
Book of Mormon does not treat that subject—not because Nephi
and others have not experienced apocalyptic visions, but because
they are forbidden to record them. Perhaps John the Revelator
bears that responsibility alone, for this time, and even he couches
his prophecies in metaphors that mask their meaning. These passages further imply that anyone who speaks or writes prophecy
relating to the end of the world must receive a special calling to do
so. The restrictions on such prophecy also suggest that latter-day
peoples should not be unduly absorbed in these matters.

It is impossible to reduce to a few words so magnificent and
pandemic a vision as Nephi beholds. The directness of his style
almost belies the vision's comprehensiveness. Nephi leads the
reader through the experience as he himself was led, and the
angel's repeated ecstatic "Look!" becomes an injunction to the
reader also, to open spiritual eyes. In just a few lines, Nephi captures the essence of the Savior's earth life. Most moving, perhaps,
is his utter incredulity that the world would presume to judge "the
Son of the everlasting God" (1 Nephi 11:32). The paradox of the
Son's being slain by the very people his death would redeem is not
lost on Nephi, who sees the event more than 600 years before it
occurs.

After radiant visions and immortal conversation, Nephi soars
into full realization of his prophetic calling. He had been valiant
before, and obedient to his earthly father, and he knew that God
had tapped him on the shoulder. But it is this visionary event that
propels him to his incontrovertible destiny as a prophet. The experience itself, however, has been exhausting, and when he returns to
find his brothers disputing over the meaning of their father's
prophecies and vision, Nephi is vexed with them, especially so
because they have neglected the obvious: they have not asked the
Lord for enlightenment. Still, when Laman and Lemuel seek the
meaning of the olive tree, and the tree of life in Lehi's vision,
Nephi accommodates them in careful detail.

Thus, verses 12 through 20 of 1 Nephi 15 are given to Nephi's explanation of the olive tree in Lehi's prophecy. Essentially, they amplify the brief commentary recorded in 1 Nephi 10:12-14, emphasizing the scattering of the house of Israel and their latter-day restoration to belief in Jesus Christ as the promised Messiah. Wonder of wonders, after Nephi speaks "many words" to his stubborn brothers, they are momentarily "pacified and did humble themselves before the Lord" (1 Nephi 15:20). And when the unusually submissive brothers ask the meaning of "the river of water which our father saw," Nephi volunteers a piece of information that delightfully characterizes Lehi, and at the same time distinguishes between a highly visionary father and a more exacting son. Nephi says that the water was "filthiness," but that his father's mind was "so much . . . swallowed up in other things that he beheld not the filthiness of the water," the "awful gulf, which separated the wicked from the tree of life, and also from the saints of God" (1 Nephi 15:26-28). Even Sariah, we remember, murmured against her sometimes impractical husband, and Laman and Lemuel mocked him; but Nephi, while acknowledging Lehi's sometimes dreamy distraction, is never anything but respectful toward his father. Paternal honor is a prominent mark of Nephi's character, one that eminently distinguishes Nephi from his older brothers.

Nephi's observation that the filthy river symbolizes the "hell . . . prepared for the wicked" (1 Nephi 15:29) catches his brothers' attention. Here is something to which they can relate. And what they want to know—no surprise—is whether hell's torment is designed for the mortal body in this life or for the soul in the next. In other words, how much time do we have, and how much will it hurt? My own cynicism would probably have produced a guffaw at this point, but Nephi patiently answers his brothers without derision, making an important doctrinal point. The application, he says, is actually "both temporal and spiritual," because the spiritual being is judged for "works which were done by the temporal body in [each mortal's] days of probation" (1 Nephi 15:32). Temporal and spiritual are thus inexorably linked, and without repentance the wicked are lost forever.

Laman and Lemuel seem determined to differentiate between the temporal and spiritual, for they ask again in the opening verses of chapter 22 if the things Nephi is reading to them will be realized in the realm of the spirit or the realm of the flesh. Earthbound intellects seem to have difficulty comprehending that in the eternal scheme of things, spirit and body cannot be regarded as independent entities. Like spoiled children, Laman and Lemuel whine at Nephi's "hard" words. Nephi knows they are hard, and reasons that "the guilty taketh the truth to be hard, for it cutteth them to the very center" (1 Nephi 16:1-2). Nevertheless, he does not back down or modify his message, but firmly tells Laman and Lemuel that if they were righteous they would not be complaining that the truth is hard. Temporarily conscience-stricken, the brothers respond to Nephi's teachings and exhortations, and his hopes rise. But, as we shall see, their reformation is as short as their tempers.

## 3

## 1 Nephi 16-22: Emergence of a Prophet

It becomes clear in chapter 16 why Ishmael's family and Zoram are engaged to accompany Lehi's family in their flight from Jerusalem: an even number of marriage partners must be provided. The young people, as they do today, seem to match up according to their degree of steadfastness in the faith, with the less diligent marrying each other. While the group is dwelling in a valley given the name Lemuel, Lehi receives divine instructions to journey into the wilderness. Although at this time Lehi does not indicate that he knows where the promised land is, or when he is to depart for it, the parallel with Moses and his people is beginning to emerge. And whatever the Lord's purposes were for the extended wilderness migration in Moses' time, a lengthy preparatory wilderness experience (eight years in all) for Lehi's urban family makes a lot of sense. Certainly, the wilderness years teach the Lehites to survive by their wits and to rely on the Lord, and those years undoubtedly make them physically strong enough to endure a long sea journey and the rigors of colonizing a rugged frontier.

Chapter 16 mainly recounts the group's various wanderings, difficulties, and encampments, guided according to their faithfulness by an astonishing brass ball "of curious workmanship" (1 Nephi 16:10) that appears before Lehi's tent the morning after his revelation. Several centuries later, the prophet Alma describes the device to his son Helaman, calling it a "Liahona, which is, being interpreted, a compass" (Alma 37:38). The group dynamics surrounding the incident of Nephi's broken bow deserve mention as Laman and Lemuel, along with some of Ishmael's children, and even Lehi, begin to murmur. Later on, Ishmael's death triggers still another round of complaint, and the Lord intervenes to chastise the troublemakers. We should note that even though Nephi has led out in obtaining the brass plates and has received a glorious vision, and perhaps a prophetic call, he has not yet assumed official leadership of the company. Lehi, although humbled for his murmuring, is still *the* prophet and patriarch, still the oracle, and Nephi goes to him for direction in finding game. The Lord's voice tells Lehi, not Nephi, to "look upon the ball, and behold the things which are written" (1 Nephi 16:26).

Chapter 17 makes it clear that the wilderness experience is a physically strengthening one for the group. Their journey is basically eastward, toward the sea, though as Nephi says in unconsciously vivid language, they have to "wade through much affliction in the wilderness" (1 Nephi 17:1) before they reach an area they call Bountiful, by the seashore. The women bear children and become "strong, yea, even like unto the men," all of them thriving "upon the raw meat" (1 Nephi 17:2) which the Lord causes to "become sweet," and to need no cooking (1 Nephi 17:12). He looks after their temporal sustenance as he had for their ancestors under Moses. Both groups are guided by divine technology, though the means are different; and both groups are fed through divine intervention, though the Lehites are required to kill, snare, or grow their own food. There is no manna for them. All in all, the Lehites are required to exercise more initiative, and their solutions are more practical, probably because ultimately they will need more stamina. Indeed, crossing the ocean in a homemade sailing vessel is more taxing than crossing the Red Sea on dry land.

After the "space of many days" (1 Nephi 17:7) in Bountiful, Nephi receives a highly significant call which comes directly to him, not to his father; the voice of the Lord awakens him and summons him to the mountain. He arises immediately and goes, and the manner of Nephi's response is as important as the instruction he receives. To begin with, Nephi does not go to the mountain and then wait idly for the Lord to approach him; rather, he goes there and "crie[s] unto the Lord" (1 Nephi 17:7). He becomes the willing receptor, pleading with the Lord to instruct him. Nephi learns that he is to build a ship for a sea journey. Does he protest that he has no materials, no tools, no ability? Does he expect the Lord to produce a ship for him? No. What Nephi requests is help in finding *ore* so that he can *make* the *tools* he will need to construct a ship according to the Lord's instructions. To the extent possible, Nephi will use his own ingenuity, skill, and muscle to accomplish the assigned task.[1]

That Nephi has grown in mental and spiritual stature is evident in the way he finally answers his brothers' derisive taunts as he prepares to construct the ship. (The brothers are prompted in part by sloth; their desire is "that they might not labor." See 1 Nephi 17:18.) Surely, on the surface their complaints seem justified. Their wives and children have suffered in the wilderness, needlessly they suppose, when they might have been enjoying a nice home and all of civilization's amenities. Nephi knows that their drastic change in circumstances has been trying, but when his brothers argue that their countrymen in "Jerusalem were a righteous people" who "kept the statutes and judgments of the Lord, and all his commandments, according to the law of Moses" (1 Nephi 17:22), and that Lehi was overly critical of them, Nephi has heard enough. Instead of buckling, or explaining, or pleading, Nephi lets fly with an impromptu sermon.

Implying that the Lord would sustain him as he had Moses, Nephi reminds his brothers that the Israelites "hardened their hearts and blinded their minds, and reviled against Moses and . . . God" (1 Nephi 17:30), just as Laman and Lemuel are doing. It is one's righteousness, not one's blood, Nephi declares in so many words, that wins favor with God. Their fathers, he says, would not "have been more choice" than those they displaced after crossing the river Jordan if the displaced had been righteous (1 Nephi 17:34). Nephi also offers an insightful definition of a "chosen" or covenant people when he says that the Lord loves "those who will have him to be their God" (1 Nephi 17:40). That is, in one sense

---

[1] It is interesting to compare Nephi's response with that of the brother of Jared when he was building and outfitting ships for an earlier journey to the new world (see my discussion of the early chapters of the book of Ether). The Lord does not have to teach Nephi, as he did the brother of Jared, that he is to use his own abilities and resources in the process. Nephi seems to have assumed it without being told.

they *are* chosen because they *have* chosen.

The parallels Nephi draws between his family and the host of Israelites in Moses' charge are intended to induce Nephi's brothers to repent. Nephi is briefly conciliatory, pointing out that even though Moses' people "did harden their hearts from time to time, and they did revile against Moses, and also against God," they were still "led forth by his matchless power into the land of promise" (1 Nephi 17:42). But these same covenant people have in succeeding generations become wicked, he adds, and are headed for destruction. Boldly sharpening his verbal sword, Nephi alludes to "the Jews [who] also sought to take away [Lehi's] life" when Lehi warned them of impending destruction. Then, advancing from inference to accusation, he thrusts this daring and damning charge at his older brothers: ". . . yea, and ye also have sought to take away his life; wherefore, ye are murderers in your hearts and ye are like unto them" (1 Nephi 17:44).

We should not underestimate the significance of this moment, for it seems to mark Nephi's first overt rebuke of his older brothers. In any event, this is a bolder Nephi than he who once was patiently forbearing with his brothers, who silently "grieved because of the hardness of their hearts" and "cried unto the Lord for them" (1 Nephi 2:18). This is a stronger Nephi than he who endured "many hard words" and many strokes of the rod at the hands of his older brothers, to the point that an angel interfered in his behalf. Although Nephi had stood up to his brothers before, in insisting that they return to Jerusalem for the brass plates, only now does he exercise full prophetic authority. On that earlier occasion his expression softened immediately after his assertion, and he used the rhetoric of gentle persuasion rather than of command:

> let us be faithful
> let us go down
> it must needs be
> it is wisdom in God

As he himself said, ". . . after this manner of language did I persuade my brethren" (see 1 Nephi 3:15-21). And his manner did not soon change as he urged his brothers to make still a third attempt to obtain the brass plates:

Let us go up again
let us be faithful
let us go up
let us be strong like unto Moses
Now behold ye know that this is true
wherefore can ye doubt?
Let us go up (see 1 Nephi 4:1-3)

This is the language of a righteous and duty-bound son and brother, not an endowed and commanding spokesman for God. Sometime later—though still before his vision—as Nephi tried to quiet the rebellion in the ranks, he still spoke solely as a brother, not as an appointed prophet. In fact, he judiciously acknowledged his brothers' seniority, hoping to shame them; and though using stronger language than before, he cushioned his criticism in the rhetoric of question rather than assertion:

Behold ye are mine elder brethren, and how is it that ye are so hard in your hearts, and so blind in your minds, that ye have need that I, your younger brother, should speak unto you, yea, and set an example for you?

How is it that ye have not hearkened unto the word of the Lord?

How is it that ye have forgotten that ye have seen an angel of the Lord?

Yea, and how is it that ye have forgotten what great things the Lord hath done for us, in delivering us out of the hands of Laban, and also that we should obtain the record?

Yea, and how is it that ye have forgotten that the Lord is able to do all things according to his will, for the children of men, if it so be that they exercise faith in him? Wherefore, let us be faithful to him. (1 Nephi 7:8-12)

Nephi might as well have spared the diplomacy. His brothers responded to his exhortations by angrily seizing and binding him.

Even though he knew by this time that "the Holy Ghost giveth authority that I should speak these things" (1 Nephi 10:22), he was not yet the Nephi who had seen a magnificent vision.

But now, some years later, Nephi is done with cajoling and pleading. Seeming to realize that a prophet and leader of a people of destiny cannot tolerate such wickedness, he steps forth as the verbal instrument of God, addressing his brothers in all the power and authority of his calling. No longer does he chastise them indirectly, through questions; no longer does he use the tentative language of persuasion. In plain speech, he calls Laman and Lemuel murderers in their hearts. Instead of asking, as he might have done earlier, "Why are ye swift to do iniquity but slow to remember the Lord your God?" he lists their iniquities in direct address, beginning each with an accusing "ye":

> Ye are swift to do iniquity but slow to remember the Lord your God. Ye have seen an angel, and he spake unto you; yea, ye have heard his voice from time to time; and he hath spoken unto you in a still small voice, but ye were past feeling, that ye could not feel his words; wherefore, he has spoken unto you like unto the voice of thunder, which did cause the earth to shake as if it were to divide asunder. (1 Nephi 17:45)

When the Spirit speaks, we must "feel his words" rather than hear them with physical ears. To be "past feeling," therefore, is to be deaf to the Lord's words delivered through the Spirit.[2] Past pure feeling, indeed, Laman and Lemuel are enraged rather than humbled by Nephi's words, and they approach him with the intent "to throw [him] into the depths of the sea." But Nephi, empowered by God, speaks to them in a prophet's voice:

> In the name of the Almighty God, I command you that ye touch me not, for I am filled with the power of God, even unto the consuming of my flesh; and whoso shall lay his hands upon me shall wither even

---

[2] In his epistle to the Ephesians, Paul also speaks of those who are "past feeling," having "given themselves over unto lasciviousness" (4:19).

as a dried reed; and he shall be as naught before the power of God, for
God shall smite him. . . .

And I said unto them: If God had commanded me to do all
things I could do them. If he should command me that I should say
unto this water, be thou earth, it should be earth; and if I should say
it, it would be done. (1 Nephi 17:48, 50)

Perhaps for the first time, this querulous, back-sliding pair recognize that the person addressing them is not simply their pious sibling. So forcefully does Nephi speak, and with such authority, that
Laman and Lemuel are

confounded and could not contend against me; neither durst they lay
their hands upon me nor touch me with their fingers, even for the
space of many days. Now they durst not do this lest they should
wither before me, so powerful was the Spirit of God; and thus it had
wrought upon them. (1 Nephi 17:52)

For the moment, Laman and Lemuel are believers, impressed
even further by the fact that when Nephi stretches his hand
toward them in a conciliatory gesture, the Lord gives them a
shake, just to remind them of what he could do if he chose.
Nothing if not capricious, these two are as insensible in their
repentance as they are in their rebellion. All smiles and humility,
they profess now to "know of a surety that the Lord is with thee,
for we know that it is the power of the Lord that has shaken us."
Nephi observes dryly that the pair then "fell down before me, and
were about to worship me, but I would not suffer them, saying: I
am thy brother, yea, even thy younger brother" (1 Nephi 17:55).
With just an edge of disdain in his voice, Nephi tells his brothers
to direct their devotions to the Lord, not to him, and to honor
their parents rather than him. Although he hopes for the best,
Nephi recognizes that it may be merely the show of power that
impresses his captious brothers, and that their "repentance" is in
part a shallow fascination with the supernatural.

Nevertheless, for the time being the two are cooperative,
which is a great improvement by anybody's measurement. They at

least go through the motions of worship; and they even help Nephi in the shipbuilding enterprise. Significantly, I think, when the word comes from the Lord that the group is to set sail, it comes through Lehi, not Nephi. Lehi is still the patriarch, the ranking authority; and although Nephi has had to assume leadership in operational matters, and has received a good deal of personal guidance and instruction, revelation for the group as a whole still comes through hierarchical channels. In fact, it even appears that the emigrants load themselves and their provisions— basically fruit, seeds, meat, and honey—by a system of seniority. Nephi says that "we did go down into the ship, every one according to his age" (1 Nephi 18:6).

Laman's and Lemuel's newfound religiosity is not as hardy as the ship they have helped build, and at sea it quickly wears off. The situation is of the sort that puts great strain on a record keeper, particularly one who is not given to exaggeration or self-pity. I can sense Nephi channeling his words into deliberate understatement when he might justifiably employ volumes of reproachful, denunciatory rhetoric. At some point in the voyage, when the more wanton passengers begin making merry, Nephi blandly observes that they are "lifted up unto exceeding rudeness," and that they "speak with much rudeness" (1 Nephi 18:9). These are the words of Nephi the annalist. Nephi the speaker, as his verbal utterances demonstrate, can be as forceful and direct as the occasion requires; but when he merely describes situations, he sometimes flattens his expression. For example, in response to this "rude" behavior, Nephi writes only that he speaks "with much soberness" to the offenders who, of course, are not about to be ruled by "our younger brother" (1 Nephi 18:10).

As if binding their own consciences, Nephi's brothers and their cohorts tie him with cords and treat him "with much harshness" (1 Nephi 18:11). "Much harshness" hardly does justice to the event, but it is typical of Nephi's understatement in this portion of the record. If Nephi had quoted his spoken words, and theirs, too, we can be sure that, solemn or not, the language would have had more bite. Nephi does not dwell on these events, nor on the long sea journey, in this sacred record. He is careful to mention, however, that while on land he often went to the mountain to pray, and that even while bound by painful cords for four days at sea, he praised God "all the day long" (1 Nephi 18:16). Clearly, Nephi is no ordinary man.

Just in passing, I note that when the group finally arrives in the promised land, after almost a year at sea, they find "beasts in the forests of every kind, both the cow and the ox, and the ass and the horse, and the goat and the wild goat, and all manner of wild animals" (1 Nephi 18:25). Nephi plainly distinguishes among the ordinary domestic animals and the wild animals the group encounters. It occurs to me that some of the "domestic" animals may derive from errant Jaredite flocks. The book of Ether states that the Lord instructed the brother of Jared to take pairs of domestic animals in the eight vessels the Jaredites prepared for passage to the new world (see Ether 1:41), and also "food for their flocks and herds" (Ether 6:4). If, in fact, the Lehites found progeny of such flocks and herds when they arrived, it appears that at least some animals had wandered south out of Jaredite lands to the north. Their presence explains why the Lehites were not instructed to bring such animals with them.

After the group reaches the promised land in the western hemisphere, Nephi's position as prophet and teacher is axiomatic. Lehi is growing more feeble, and Nephi is required to play an ever expanding role. Once Nephi has explained the business of the plates to the modern reader, whom he addresses directly, he moves swiftly to the central concern of all Christian prophets, which is testifying of the Lord and Savior Jesus Christ. Nephi makes a deft transition from things of considerable worth, such as the contents of sacred records, to the thing of ultimate value, "the very God of Israel." He facilitates the shift by twice using the phrase "trample under their feet" and then explaining his metaphor:

> For the things which some men esteem to be of great worth, both to the body and soul, others set at naught and trample under their feet. Yea, even the very God of Israel do men trample under their feet;

> I say, trample under their feet but I would speak in other words—they
> set him at naught, and hearken not to the voice of his counsels.
> (1 Nephi 19:7)

It is as if Nephi catches himself using figurative language and
quickly reverts to plain talk.

Verses 8 through 18 of 1 Nephi 19 develop the sacred theme,
as Nephi foresees and testifies personally of his Lord and Savior.
He alludes repeatedly in these verses to previous prophets, naming Zenock, Zenos, and Neum, as well as the more familiar Moses
and Isaiah. In verse 10 he meticulously documents three sources
in succession, each testifying to the sacrifice of the Savior and each
providing a distinct sequential detail. Nephi presents the three in
parallel infinitive phrases, indicating that "the God of Abraham,
and of Isaac, and the God of Jacob" would yield himself "into the
hands of wicked men, [1] to be lifted up, according to the words
of Zenock, and [2] to be crucified, according to the words of
Neum, and [3] to be buried in a sepulchre, according to the words
of Zenos" (1 Nephi 19:10). Perhaps Nephi uses the rhetoric of
prophets, and the corroborating testimony of prophets, to establish his own prophetic role, and to underscore the importance and
value of prophets for the modern reader.

The verses that follow constitute almost a montage of well-
crafted prophetic statements, some of warning and some of jubilation. We should be alert to the fact that these verses resound
with Nephi's attributions to past prophets, witnessing to the truth
of their utterances as they witness to the truth of his. The concluding verse of 1 Nephi 19 is an heraldic introduction ("hear ye")
to Isaiah 48 and 49, which Nephi reads aloud to his brothers and
copies into his own record (see 1 Nephi 20 and 21):

> Wherefore I spake unto them, saying: Hear ye the words of the
> prophet, ye who are a remnant of the house of Israel, a branch who
> have been broken off; hear ye the words of the prophet, which were
> written unto all the house of Israel, and liken them unto yourselves,
> that ye may have hope as well as your brethren from whom ye have
> been broken off; for after this manner has the prophet written.

And in this manner, too, Nephi reminds his people who he is, who they are, and for whom he speaks. It is vital that they know that the prophecies in the brass plates are for them. Certainly, Nephi also hopes to school his people in the special and rare character of the prophetic calling. They must first believe that a prophet speaks for God, and second, that Nephi is a prophet. Otherwise, they might heed him or not, at their whim.

It seems unlikely that Nephi would randomly select the particular chapters of Isaiah that he writes into his record, and in this case, that he reads to his brothers for their reluctant edification. (Be it known, too, that I find small comfort in the fact that Laman and Lemuel are as baffled by Isaiah as I am.) In the chapters Nephi interjects here, Isaiah is addressing the house of Jacob (Israel), who need instruction, he says, because "thou art obstinate, and thy neck is an iron sinew, and thy brow brass" (1 Nephi 20:4; Isaiah 48:4). Now there is a splendid double metaphor for pride: sinew of iron and brow of brass. It is more dynamic, even, than the stiff-neckedness often alluded to in the Book of Mormon. It is also a fortuitous characterization of Nephi's older brothers. What is more important, perhaps, these two chapters describe the calling of Isaiah to be the Lord's oracle.

The call is specifically described in 1 Nephi 21 and Isaiah 49, but only after Isaiah identifies his audience. He seems to speak to and of the Lehite castaways as well as the lost tribes, and Nephi must hope that his brothers will see the application: "Hearken, O ye house of Israel, all ye that are broken off and are driven out, because of the wickedness of the pastors of my people; yea, all ye that are broken off, that are scattered abroad. . . . Listen, O isles, unto me, and hearken ye people from far" (v. 1). Significantly, the first sentence of the quoted passage, the part that must allude to Book of Mormon peoples and other scattered Israelites, does not appear in the King James Isaiah.

Isaiah clearly sees himself commissioned to pierce the conscience of Israel ("he hath made my mouth like a sharp sword," v. 2), but with the express purpose of facilitating the gathering and restoration. Nonetheless, much of this chapter is a joyful, poetic celebration of the anticipated restoration of Israel to its rightful place—a good choice, in any case, for Nephi to read aloud and to inscribe on metal for the ages. Surely, he wants his brothers to hear about the Lord's promises to Israel (including the Lehites); but he also wants the reality of the prophetic calling to penetrate their stubborn skulls. This is obviously a sensitive issue with Nephi and his brothers, and Nephi attempts to teach them indirectly, through Isaiah, something about his father's and his own holy calling.

The final chapter of 1 Nephi is essentially Nephi's interpretation of the prophecies he has just read aloud from the brass plates. Nephi has a subtext, however—his personal testimony that a prophet is called of God and speaks precious truth. When his brothers ask again about the distinction between things temporal and spiritual—this time if the prophecies Nephi has read have spiritual but not temporal significance—Nephi reemphasizes the inseparability of the two realms. Prophets perform a spiritual role in prophesying of temporal things: ". . . for by the Spirit are all things made known unto the prophets, which shall come upon the children of men according to the flesh" (1 Nephi 22:2).

Throughout his concluding chapter, Nephi authenticates his own prophetic calling with references to the prophets who preceded him and to prophecies regarding the house of Israel. Seeming to elevate the prophetic role by quoting the passage in which Moses speaks of the coming Lord as "a prophet . . . like unto me" (1 Nephi 22:20), Nephi adds his own prophetic declaration of testimony, promising that when Christ gathers his children, "there shall be one fold and one shepherd; and he shall feed his sheep, and in him they shall find pasture" (1 Nephi 22:25). The phrase "in him they shall find pasture" is a lovely variation on a familiar psalmic theme.

Twice in this chapter, Nephi speaks of the time when Satan will have "no (more) power over the hearts of the people" (1 Nephi 22: 15,26). The expression suggests, certainly, that Satan has power only when we give our hearts to him, only when we allow him place. We sometimes speak of Satan's being "bound" during the years of millennial peace. It seems clear to me, from passages such as this, that his "bonds" will be the immunity of our hearts to his influence rather than any particular exercise of force against him. Righteousness will simply render him helpless. Righteousness works that way for individuals now; imagine its power to contain Satan when all give their hearts to Christ.

Constrained from speaking further, Nephi concludes by testifying that the writings on the brass plates are true, and by describing his prophet predecessors as witnesses to the words he and his father have spoken. Thus, as remarkable as is the journey of Lehi's family from Jerusalem, through many years and miles of wilderness and eventually across the sea to a new world, it is perhaps no more remarkable than Nephi's personal journey from deferential younger brother to sovereign prophet. The distance Nephi travels is revealed in the nature and content of his discourse, and is especially evident in the distinct change in his manner of speaking and teaching after his magnificent vision.

## 4

## 2 Nephi 1-4: Lehi's Discourses and Nephi's Psalm

Throughout Nephi's writings, the reader is aware that he is the record's controlling consciousness, that he selects content and assigns priorities to it. Nephi feels the strictures of limited space, but he still includes a sampling of what he seems to regard as worthy discourses of his father Lehi and his brother Jacob. It is particularly fortunate that Nephi represents the words of Lehi; otherwise, the reader might be inclined to dismiss this venerable patriarch as merely a visionary well past his prime—the nominal head of his family but incapable of real leadership.

The first three chapters and part of the fourth in 2 Nephi are devoted exclusively to Lehi's remarkable prophecies and teachings. In these chapters Lehi affirms Nephi's prophetic calling, counsels his two eldest and two youngest sons, utters sagacious prophecies, and teaches the doctrine of Jesus Christ—all in self-possessed, inspired language. It is fitting that as he nears the end of his earthly life, Lehi speaks at length of the glorious inheritance pledged for his seed in this choice new land. Lehi's own fate is of no concern to him, for he knows he is redeemed. He has "beheld [God's] glory" and is "encircled about eternally in the arms of his love" (2 Nephi 1:15). Could any safety be more sweetly conceived?

A conviction of divine love informs Lehi's faith and undergirds the weighty doctrine that falls from his lips as he begins to instruct his first-born son in the wilderness, Nephi's valiant younger brother Jacob. If some have supposed an intellectual decline in Lehi, this discourse, in the form of a patriarchal blessing, should disabuse them of that misconception. It should also further indicate Lehi's esteem for Jacob, and young Jacob's unusual spiritual maturity. What fairly leaps from the page is

Lehi's consummate grasp of the gospel of Jesus Christ, the essence of which he articulates with relevance and purity. So compact and self-contained is the second chapter of 2 Nephi that I am sorely tempted to quote the whole of it. Lehi speaks first of humanity's redemption, from both temporal death (we have inherited mortal bodies that will die) and spiritual death (we sin and thereby cut ourselves off from the Lord). The former "is free" (2 Nephi 2:4); the latter is freely offered to "those who have a broken heart and a contrite spirit" (2 Nephi 2:7).

It might appear that Lehi digresses when in verse ten he turns to the matter of opposition. But this is not, I insist, the meandering of a failing intellect. Rather, it is the thoughtful introduction of a related doctrinal strand whose integration with the doctrine of salvation must be understood. After judgment, in which "the ends of the law" must be met, Lehi explains, the punishment affixed to violated law is administered. That punishment, though we may not have realized it, is a manifestation of opposition, the result of choices for evil rather than good. It stands, Lehi says, in opposition to the blessing, or "happiness," promised to the faithful by virtue of the Atonement. Thus, by relating the concept of punishment inversely to the doctrine of redemption, Lehi introduces the doctrinal principle of opposition. That principle constitutes the foundation of mortal agency, the freedom to make choices and be held accountable for them. If there is no opportunity to make informed choices between good and evil (that is, no personal moral agency), good has no meaning, God ceases to exist, the whole purpose of creation is thwarted, judgment is pointless, and the Atonement never happens. For how could one sin, and thus need a Savior, or how could one act righteously, if there were no opposing courses to choose between? Paradoxically, it is virtue that gives definition to sin, and sin to virtue. The balanced opposition in Lehi's rhetoric (if not this, . . . then not this either) conveys the message, too:

> For it must needs be, that there is an opposition in all things. If not so, . . . righteousness could not be brought to pass, neither

wickedness, neither holiness nor misery, neither good nor bad. . . .

And if ye shall say there is no law, ye shall also say there is no sin. If ye shall say there is no sin, ye shall also say there is no righteousness. And if there be no righteousness there be no happiness. And if there be no righteousness nor happiness there be no punishment nor misery. And if these things are not there is no God. And if there is no God we are not, neither the earth; for there could have been no creation of things, neither to act nor to be acted upon; wherefore all things must have vanished away. (2 Nephi 2:11-13)

In all creation, Lehi concludes, "it must needs be that there was an opposition; even the forbidden fruit in opposition to the tree of life; the one being sweet and the other bitter" (2 Nephi 2:15). The antithetical construct works in two ways—through the opposing fruit symbolization which Lehi introduces, and through the opposing fall and redemption which the symbolization implies. Lehi then makes the compelling intellectual leap. To be human is to have choice: "Wherefore, the Lord God gave unto man that he should act for himself." Exclamation point. Lehi continues, "Wherefore, man could not act for himself save it should be that he was enticed by the one or the other" (2 Nephi 2:16).

Having alluded to the garden, Lehi turns to the primal tempter and his vital role in the operation of the principle of opposition. Lehi scrupulously qualifies his statement because his information about the origin of unrighteous opposition comes not from personal revelation, but secondhand, from the brass plates:

And I, Lehi, according to the things which I have read, must needs suppose that an angel of God, according to that which is written, had fallen from heaven; wherefore, he became a devil, having sought that which was evil before God. (2 Nephi 2:17)

Satan's temptation of Adam and Eve in the Garden of Eden, Lehi explains, initiated them to the principle of opposition. And, I think, in addition to the choice for posterity, part of their decision was the choice to live henceforth with opposition. They must have understood that without it, there would have been no opportunity for the character development and wisdom that come from wrestling with righteous and sinful alternatives, and living with the consequences of individual decisions. Existence without opposition would be bland at best, according to Lehi. A perpetual Garden of Eden may sound inviting on days when "the thousand natural shocks that flesh is heir to" (*Hamlet* III:1) seem like a million, but Lehi knew it would be no good. Not only would Adam and Eve "have had no children," but "they would have remained in a state of innocence, having no joy, for they knew no misery; doing no good, for they knew no sin" (2 Nephi 2:23).

In some sense, Eve's and Adam's loss of innocence came with their confronting the principle of opposition. Satan presented them with a choice they would not have considered on their own. The Lord had actually given them two options ("thou mayest choose for thyself"), but as proffered, the forbidden option was not attractive in the least because he was patently honest about the outcome ("thou shalt surely die," Moses 3:17). Satan's deceptive option, however (to "be as gods, knowing good and evil," Moses 4:11), had great appeal and thus became tempting. Unlike Satan, the Lord never tempts or deceives.

In reality, untested innocence—lack of knowledge—does not equate to joy, but to the opposite. Knowledge equates to joy. Lehi sums it up masterfully: "Adam fell that men might be; and men are, that they might have joy" (2 Nephi 2:25). For many years I considered that striking passage in isolation, thinking only that it meant the Lord desired our happiness. Well, it does mean that. But the particular joy alluded to here is the joy we can know only by encountering evil, seeing it for what it is, rejecting it—or failing that, repenting of it—and thereby qualifying for redemption. In its allusion to the Fall, the passage confirms the necessity of opposition, which enhances joy when we make righteous choices. Indeed, the opposition that led to the Fall enabled both our being and our subsequent redemption. It also inaugurated the sorrow that enables us to know joy.

Scholars have spoken often about John Milton's doctrine of "the fortunate fall" in *Paradise Lost*, but Lehi had insights that extend beyond Milton's extraordinary and surely inspired perception. For Lehi understood not only that the Messiah would redeem mortals, but also that the plan of salvation freed them to make choices, that agency allows mortals to choose whether or not they will be saved from spiritual death. The Savior pays the price of their redemption if they elect to follow him. Lehi constructs his argument with great care, weaving the threads of opposition, Fall, repentance, and agency into the fabric of Jesus Christ's redeeming sacrifice, the plan of salvation.

Many use the term "free agency" when we might more accurately speak of "freeing agency," or the agency that frees. With grace and clarity, Lehi celebrates the freedom implicit in the doctrine of agency:

> And the Messiah cometh in the fulness of time, that he may redeem the children of men from the fall. And because that they are redeemed from the fall they have become free forever, knowing good from evil; to act for themselves and not to be acted upon, save it be by the punishment of the law at the great and last day, according to the commandments which God hath given. (2 Nephi 2:26)

"To act for themselves and not to be acted upon." That is what it means to have choice, to look at the alternatives and select the noble or the ignoble, knowing that the ultimate consequences of our choices are grand in scale. Frightening as that seems, we would not like to think that what we do is of no concern to God. Lehi also teaches that the unrepentant sinful will lose agency in the end, for they will "be acted upon" in the administration of punishment. By giving ourselves to sin, and thus to Satan, who stands in opposition to the freedom of agency and personal choice (for which principle the war in heaven was fought), we willfully forfeit the eternal gift of agency.

I think it no accident, either, that Lehi chooses to teach the doctrine of opposition in Jacob's blessing. Jacob's whole life has been and will be a drama of opposition, and Lehi wants this sensitive son to understand opposition's important purpose. In the end, Lehi begs all his sons, not just Jacob, to "choose eternal life" rather than "eternal death," to choose not to give "the spirit of the devil power to captivate, to bring you down to hell" (2 Nephi 2:28-29). He closes by juxtaposing his own pure intent, "I have none other object save it be the everlasting welfare of your souls" (2 Nephi 2:30), against the devil's evil intent.

At the conclusion of this important gospel discourse, Lehi turns to his small son, Joseph, and begins to speak of other Josephs—he who was sold into Egypt and he who in the latter days would bring forth the record of Lehi's seed. Chapter 3 of 2 Nephi, an extremely important text, requires careful reading to keep the pronouns and the various Josephs straight, but we are aided by remembering that Lehi is quoting at some length from the prophecies of Joseph who was carried into Egypt. The ancient Joseph foresaw a latter-day prophet of his own seed and name, as well as the joining of the biblical and Nephite records.[1]

For me, the "simpleness of [the] words" (2 Nephi 3:20) in the Book of Mormon is not a lack of rhetorical sophistication and power, but rather, as I suggested in the beginning, an accessibility, a happy intelligibility. Although less metaphorical, less "fancy," than much of the Old Testament, the book has its own quiet grandeur. Lehi's prophecy of the latter-day Joseph is as moving as that of his ancestor:

> And there shall rise up one mighty among them, who shall do much good, both in word and in deed, being an instrument in the hands of God, with exceeding faith, to work mighty wonders, and do that thing which is great in the sight of God, unto the bringing to pass much restoration unto the house of Israel, and unto the seed of thy brethren. (2 Nephi 3:24)

Indescribable thoughts and feelings must have thrilled through Joseph Smith when he translated references to himself from the

---

[1] It is helpful to compare 2 Nephi 3:16-17 with Joseph Smith's translation of Genesis 50:24-38. Joseph Smith included prophetic utterances of the ancient Joseph that do not appear in the King James translation of Genesis.

lips of God's ancient spokesmen.

Upon concluding his words to Joseph, old Lehi turns finally to the children of Laman, Lemuel, and Ishmael, warning them but also blessing their seed with longevity. To the faithful Sam, Lehi promises that his seed "shall inherit the land" and be numbered with Nephi's seed (2 Nephi 4:11). Sam's blessing is brief, and no specific father's blessing is recorded for Nephi. If Nephi received a formal blessing, he did not elect to include it on the small plates. Shortly after pronouncing these blessings, Lehi dies.

Although Nephi has experienced high peaks of spiritual emotion and power, when his father dies he succumbs momentarily to self-doubt and despair. Surely, he is feeling the loss of his father's wisdom and influence, the burden of solitary leadership, and the fear of his older brothers' wrath. He takes great comfort, however, in the scriptures, in which his "soul delighteth," and "in the things of the Lord"; and his "heart pondereth" these things "continually" (2 Nephi 4:15-16). At such a time as this, one can be overcome with the magnitude of one's own imperfections; and Nephi is no exception. Although not one to spread his suffering out for public view, in a rare moment of tender personal disclosure, he composes a psalm to describe his discouragement and his recovery from it. We should recognize, however, that by choosing a formulaic poem as his vehicle, Nephi distances himself from the reader. The form allows him to order and objectify his feelings (see 2 Nephi 4:17-35). It aids him as he works through a deep sense of his own unworthiness—an outgrowth of his grief and burden—and takes heart in the knowledge that the Lord is with him.

A lovely composition very likely patterned after David's psalms, Nephi's poem begins in a confessional manner as he contemplates his mortal weaknesses:

> Nevertheless, notwithstanding the great goodness of the Lord, in showing me his great and marvelous works, my heart exclaimeth: O wretched man that I am! Yea, my heart sorroweth because of my flesh; my soul grieveth because of mine iniquities.

I am encompassed about, because of the temptations and the sins which do so easily beset me.

And when I desire to rejoice, my heart groaneth because of my sins; nevertheless, I know in whom I have trusted. (2 Nephi 4:17-19)

The word "nevertheless" in verse 19 signals a turn from contemplation of weakness and sorrow to numeration of the Lord's sustaining blessings. The lovely passage following it must be read aloud:

My God hath been my support; he hath led me through mine afflictions in the wilderness; and he hath preserved me upon the waters of the great deep.

He hath filled me with his love, even unto the consuming of my flesh.

He hath confounded mine enemies, unto the causing of them to quake before me.

Behold, he hath heard my cry by day, and he hath given me knowledge by visions in the nighttime.

And by day have I waxed bold in mighty prayer before him; yea, my voice have I sent up on high; and angels came down and ministered unto me.

And upon the wings of his Spirit hath my body been carried away upon exceedingly high mountains. And mine eyes have beheld great things, yea, even too great for man; therefore I was bidden that I should not write them. (2 Nephi 4:20-25)

And this, mind you, is the expression of a man who regards himself as inept with the written word. The next verse indicates another turn as Nephi again considers his failings, which seem especially grievous to him in view of the Lord's constancy. He offers a useful insight, suggesting that in yielding to temptation, we grant Satan power over us. Then, still in the manner of the psalmist, he resolves to cast off his wretchedness:

Awake, my soul! No longer droop in sin. Rejoice, O my heart, and give place no more for the enemy of my soul.

Do not anger again because of mine enemies. Do not slacken my strength because of mine afflictions.

> Rejoice, O my heart, and cry unto the Lord, and say: O Lord, I will praise thee forever; yea, my soul will rejoice in thee, my God, and the rock of my salvation. (2 Nephi 4:28-30)

We see in this psalm a side of Nephi that his brothers probably never knew. It is a private, disquieted side that Nephi may have seen mirrored in David's duality—David who was a sinner as well as a psalmist and a king, but David who always confessed his dependence on God. Although David's may have seemed the more celebrated assignment, both men labored to unite a people and rule a temporal kingdom by means of religious law.

It is well to remember that even though we speak of the Book of Mormon as "latter-day" scripture because of its publication date, Nephi was a contemporary of several Old Testament prophets. He must have seen in the Psalms language that described his own circumstances and feelings; but in adopting the form, he does more than mimic the psalmist's content. Whereas in some instances the psalmist's primary aim, whether the psalmist was David or another, may have been simply to make a poem, Nephi's intent is to express his anguish and to regain assurance of the Lord's abiding presence and mercy. He cherishes the writings of the prophet Isaiah above all other scripture, but here he takes for his model the simplicity of the psalm rather than the high color of Isaiah's poesy.

Notwithstanding the poetic conventions Nephi employs, much of his psalm is individual and particular to him. True, he echoes the psalmist in speaking of his afflictions in the wilderness and his preservation on "the waters of the great deep" (see Psalm 18:16, for example), but the psalmist's references may not have the specific personal applications we recognize in Nephi's. His references to grievous afflictions in the wilderness, for instance, are not the psalmist's customary metaphorical abstractions. And on the long sea journey his life was in actual peril, though more from the ire of his brothers than from the fury of the elements. Even Nephi's rather conventional reference to the confounding of enemies is keenly real, because his deadliest enemies are the brothers of his flesh. Additionally, in alluding to visions and the ministrations of angels, both of which are psalmic conventions (see Psalms 89:19 and 91:11-12), Nephi corroborates particular incidents in his narrative. He also specifically mentions his struggle against the temptation to resent his enemies; that may well have been his greatest test of character.

Although Nephi would never admit to having poetic gifts, and even prides himself on being prosaic, his writing belies his modesty. The effective use of parallel structures and balanced rhetoric, for example, which simplify rather than complicate his expression, seems second-nature to him:

> he hath led me
> he hath preserved me
> He hath filled me
> He hath confounded mine enemies
> he hath heard my cry by day, and he hath given me knowledge by
> visions in the nighttime

Nephi nicely offsets "day" with "nighttime" in one verse (v. 23), and then in the next, he picks up the phrase "by day" (v. 24) and repeats it, visually connecting his parallel series to what follows, even as he alters the structure.

Nephi's sincerity is unimpeachable, but he concludes his psalm with an eloquent prayer that is less individual and more conventional than the lines that precede it. He pleads with the Lord to redeem and deliver him, again demonstrating true poetic sensibility by employing word and structural repetition: "O Lord, wilt thou redeem my soul? Wilt thou deliver me out of the hands of mine enemies? Wilt thou make me that I may shake at the appearance of sin?" (2 Nephi 4:31). In verse 32, he demonstrates unusual rhetorical skill:

> May the gates of hell be shut continually before me, because that my heart is broken and my spirit is contrite! O Lord, wilt thou not shut the gates of thy righteousness before me, that I may walk in the path of the low valley, that I may be strict in the plain road!

Here Nephi employs parallelism and repetition, but to effect reversal rather than merely to achieve rhythm or to create incremental building blocks. He pleads first that "the gates of hell be shut" before him, and then asks the Lord not to "shut the gates of [his] righteousness" before him. Nephi perceives two kinds of gates, one evil and one good, and asks that the evil gate be shut and that the good not be shut. Then he concludes with structural repetitions that justify his desire:

> that I may walk
> that I may be strict

Such repetitions continue in verse 33 as Nephi entreats the Lord to protect and guide him, first repeating the phrase "O Lord, wilt thou," next shortening it to "Wilt thou," and then altering it to "that thou." Nephi also knows that the repeated word achieves coherence and emphasis. The last sentence of verse 33 picks up the word "way(s)" from the first sentence and repeats it three times, as Nephi asks the Lord to clear his way and "hedge up" his enemies' ways. In verse 34 he uses the word "trust" five times, twice as a verb and three times as a noun:

> O Lord, I have trusted in thee, and I will trust in thee forever. I will not put my trust in the arm of flesh; for I know that cursed is he that putteth his trust in the arm of flesh. Yea, cursed is he that putteth his trust in man or maketh flesh his arm.

This is the writing not only of one sensitive to language and skilled in poetic forms, but also of one wholly aware that he is composing a poem of and for his Lord. The fact that Nephi writes only one confessed "poem" in his sacred record may suggest that he inherited the bias of the synagogue that preferred the Law to the Psalms, and even regarded the latter as inferior scripture. In any case, Nephi more than balances his personal lyric with lengthy excerpts from Isaiah and references to Moses. It was, after all, the Law of Moses that Nephi taught his people, a law that would prevail, he said, until Christ himself came with his completing gospel. In this lovely poetic moment, however, we see another side of Nephi—not only the man who is a prophet, but also the prophet who is a man.

To no one's surprise, with the restraining hand of Lehi gone, Laman and Lemuel indulge their baser natures, becoming a frightening and constant threat to both the general peace and Nephi's life. Although Nephi underplays the ensuing family split, skimming over it in a few short verses, the grief behind his words reveals an excruciating event. The split becomes, in very fact, a symbolic enactment of the polar opposition Lehi had described so eloquently in counsel to his son Jacob. As a result of this early family division, the social and political history sketched in the Book of Mormon is mainly a chronicle of conflict between Nephites and Lamanites, as the antagonists came to be called.

With this rupture comes a curse on the families and followers of Laman and Lemuel, a curse foreseen by both Lehi and Nephi. The matter of a curse being visited on a people is a difficult concept for the modern mind to digest. We have seen the evils of class distinctions based on skin color, and we believe in a God self-described as no respecter of persons. Since my own understanding of curses is sorely limited, what follows is simply a personal effort to reconcile these realities with a seemingly contradictory reality, a divinely inflicted curse in the form of modified skin color. My own bias against distinctions based on skin color will be apparent.

Although Jacob later speaks of "the cursing which hath come upon their skins" (Jacob 3:5), my reading of Nephi's account gives me an additional impression. Granted, Nephi makes it clear that "the Lord God did cause a skin of blackness to come upon" those associated with Laman and Lemuel (2 Nephi 5:21), but he does not say that this was the only, or even the direst, application of the curse. Rather, the sorest aspect of the curse appears to be that they were "cut off from the presence of the Lord" (2 Nephi 5:20), that the Spirit withdrew from them. The Spirit's withdrawal is indeed a terrible curse, "and because of their cursing which was upon them they did become an idle people, full of mischief and subtlety" (2 Nephi 5:24). Surely, it is the Spirit's absence, rather than the skin's pigmentation, that accounts for such a moral decline.

The darkening of the skin, I believe, served mainly to make a physical distinction between the two groups, one that would discourage intermingling of the righteous with the wicked and thus prevent a similar spiritual degradation among the children of Nephi's group. Many centuries later, the matter is discussed again in the record of the prophet Alma. The dark skin of the Lamanites is spoken of as "the mark which was set upon their fathers, which was a curse upon them because of their transgression and their rebellion against their brethren" (Alma 3:6). This sounds as though the "mark" of dark skin itself was the only curse. But consider verse 7, which seems to describe the curse and the mark of the curse as two separate things, the mark coming subsequent to the curse: "And their brethren sought to destroy them, therefore they were cursed; and the Lord God set a mark upon them. . . ." Verse 8 explains further that the change in skin color "was done that their seed might be distinguished from the seed of their brethren, that thereby the Lord God might preserve his people, that they might not mix and believe in incorrect traditions which would prove their destruction." It is false beliefs that corrupt, not blood.

It is important to remember, too, that the cursed families are intended to be "loathsome" to Nephi's people only until "they shall repent of their iniquities" (2 Nephi 5:22); and Nephi foresees the eventual lifting of the curse. Speaking of the time when "the book" (the Book of Mormon) will be carried "forth unto the remnant of our seed" (2 Nephi 30:3), meaning the descendants of the Lamanites, Nephi prophesies that these people "shall be restored unto the knowledge of their fathers, and also to the knowledge of Jesus Christ, which was had among their fathers" (2 Nephi 30:5). Furthermore, he says,

> And then shall they rejoice; for they shall know that it is a blessing unto them from the hand of God; and their scales of darkness shall

begin to fall from their eyes; and many generations shall not pass away among them, save they shall be a pure and a delightsome people. (2 Nephi 30:6)

Here, clearly, the darkness of the curse is spiritual darkness, figurative "scales" over the eyes. The whiteness Nephi spoke of earlier, and the purity and delightsomeness he speaks of here, refer to the diligence and inner radiance that accompany spiritual light. We should remember, too, that in the end the greater blessing, that of survival and restoration, comes not to the descendants of Nephi, who had the light and discarded it, but to the descendants of Laman and Lemuel, who temporarily lost the light. Even Jacob warns the Nephites to "revile no more against [the Lamanites] because of the darkness of their skins," admonishing his people to "remember your own filthiness" rather than that supposed of the Lamanites, who inherited both their dark skins and their hatred for the Nephites from their rebellious fathers (Jacob 3:9). The subject presents dilemmas not easily resolved.

## 2 Nephi 5-11: Jacob's Sermon

In response to the Lord's warning, the families of Nephi, Nephi's sisters, Sam, Jacob, Joseph, Zoram, and others of the faithful "flee into the wilderness" (2 Nephi 5:5). After journeying for many days, they pitch their tents in a place Nephi's followers insist on naming after him. There, under Nephi's leadership and the statutory guidance of the Law of Moses, they begin to prosper, to frame a civilization, and to manufacture arms for their defense. The technical skills Nephi developed during the ship-building process come in very handy, for he teaches his people to work with wood and metals. Nephi regards himself as his people's "ruler" and "teacher" (2 Nephi 5:19), but he refuses the title of king. His language is tentative as he describes a less than joyful status quo: ". . . we lived after the manner of happiness" (2 Nephi 5:27). "After the manner of happiness" hardly equates to living happily ever after.

We are told little about Joseph, except that he and Jacob are consecrated as "priests and teachers" (2 Nephi 5:26). But Jacob, who is to be guardian of the record after Nephi, and who adds seven chapters to it, has apparently become a dynamic spiritual leader in his own right. Although Jacob defers to Nephi as a matter of course, he is blessed with great faith as well as enviable spiritual and intellectual gifts of his own. Nephi is fortunate to have him, and it is a tribute to Jacob that Nephi includes one of Jacob's sermons in his own record. (Of course, Jacob is speaking and quoting Isaiah at Nephi's behest, which might have influenced Nephi's decision.) The occasion is important, and the sermon is major, for it extends into a second day and occupies chapters 6 through 10 of 2 Nephi.

Jacob's introduction at the beginning of his sermon offers a fleeting insight into his character. The younger brother may have

been overshadowed by Nephi's colossal presence, but he opens
with the confident statement of a man who knows his charge:

> . . . I, Jacob, having been called of God, and ordained after the man-
> ner of his holy order, and having been consecrated by my brother
> Nephi, unto whom ye look as a king or a protector, and on whom ye
> depend for safety, behold ye know that I have spoken unto you
> exceedingly many things. (2 Nephi 6:2)

Curiously, although Jacob acknowledges Nephi's hand in his
ordination, he speaks of Nephi primarily as a political leader,
someone the people look to "as a king or protector" and "depend
[on] for safety." If Jacob had a role in political governance, it is not
disclosed. Jacob attributes some of his text to an angel, but Isaiah
is his principal source in the early part of his sermon. There, Jacob
deftly interweaves his own and the angel's messages with lines
from Isaiah (see 2 Nephi 6:16-18; Isaiah 49:24-26), smoothing
the transitions until the figurative language of verse 18 signals a
distinct return to Isaiah.

Chapter 7, a short chapter which essentially repeats Isaiah 50,
unconsciously underscores the pre-eminent role of a prophet as
Isaiah speaks with the voice of the Messiah. In powerful, imperative language he issues a wake-up call to Israel. Three verses begin
with the command to "Awake, awake" (9, 17, 24), three begin
with "Hearken unto me" (1, 4, 7), and the final verse admonishes
Jerusalem to "shake thyself from the dust" (25). After reading at
length from Isaiah, Jacob launches into his own subject (chapter
9). A gifted orator, Jacob appears to take considerable pleasure in
language and its possibilities, and this discourse requires a lot of
the reader. Perhaps he is following a homiletic pattern he discovered in the brass plates, for his argument is highly organized and
carefully constructed. His subject, however, could not be more
elemental: the plan of salvation whereby fallen humanity can
return to dwell with God.

To present that subject, Jacob employs Isaiah's prophecies of
the restoration of Israel to its promised lands and blessings. In his

skillful hands, Israel's restoration becomes a type for the restoration of human souls to their heavenly home, a connection I would not have thought to make. When Jacob introduces his thesis in verse 4, he describes a spiritual rather than a temporal future: ". . . our flesh must waste away and die; nevertheless, in our bodies we shall see God" (2 Nephi 9:4). The echo of Job 19:26 is unmistakable here—"And though after my skin worms destroy this body, yet in my flesh shall I see God"—suggesting that some version of the book of Job was among the writings in Nephi's possession. This is the sort of memorable, quotable line that would appeal to Jacob, who himself enjoyed turning a good phrase. Like many Old Testament writers, he is able to enunciate a penetrating truth in precise, comely language that hangs in the mind. In this instance, the line is the essence of his message and a striking distillation of the Christian gospel.

The doctrine may be basic, but it is not easy to articulate, nor to understand. Infected with the English teacher's rage for explaining, I simply must say something about how effectively Jacob melds content and form, how what he says is enhanced by his use of language. One of Jacob's favorite devices is repetition, which he typically uses to connect separate but related ideas, or to effect an appropriate reversal. The sophistication of the practice is evident, for example, in Jacob's use of the terms "flesh" and "bodies" in the passage cited above. The reversal plays on the fact that "flesh" and "body" can mean the same thing, but here do not. Jacob also reverses the order of the Job passage, making it doctrinally more precise; the body, but not necessarily the flesh, is part of the immortal soul. Verse 5 continues the pattern, but makes "flesh" and "body" synonymous even as it shifts their application. The "body" alluded to now is Christ's; the "flesh" may be humankind's. Jacob adds a third repeater, "subject," whose application he also reverses:

> Yea, I know that ye know that in the *body* he shall show himself unto those at Jerusalem, . . . for it behooveth the great Creator that he suffereth himself to become *subject* unto man in the *flesh*, and die for

all men, that all men might become *subject* unto him. (2 Nephi 9:5; emphases added)

In fact, all three repeated words have dual applications, one to human beings and the other to the Creator, thereby figuratively uniting their separate destinies. Again using repetition and conjunction, Jacob takes the word "die" from verse 5 and employs it as "death" in verse 6—in 5 it applies to the Creator, in 6 to humanity—linking the two deaths pertinent to "the merciful plan of the great Creator." In the Savior's death and resurrection lies the "power of resurrection" from death for fallen mortals. The word "fall" or "fallen" appears three times in verse 6.

The power of resurrection does not reside in mortals, Jacob declares, nor can they save themselves from the consequences of their sins. Only "an infinite atonement" (2 Nephi 9:7), an atonement performed by a divine, eternal being (see Alma 34:10) endowed with the power of resurrection, can overcome death of both the body and the spirit. Then, applying the words "subject" and "fall" in still a different way, Jacob warns that if there were no resurrection and atonement, mortal souls would be *subject* to the *fallen* deceiver, forever "shut out from the presence of our God" (2 Nephi 9:9). This is surely a state more grimly permanent than being temporarily "cut off from the presence of the Lord" (2 Nephi 9:6) as a result of the fall from Eden.

Jacob makes an important distinction between the death of the body, or temporal death, and the death of the spirit, or spiritual death. I note that the verb and the pronoun referring to the united spirit and body are singular, suggesting one entity rather than two: ". . . the spirit and the body *is* restored to *itself* again" (2 Nephi 9:13; emphases added). In contemplating this remarkable plan, Jacob can scarcely contain his jubilation:

O the greatness and the justice of our God! (2 Nephi 9:17)
O the greatness of the mercy of our God, the Holy One of Israel! (2 Nephi 9:19)
O how great the holiness of our God! (2 Nephi 9:20)

He then turns his attention specifically to the matter of the soul's salvation. The requirements are simply stated and easily understood: repentance, baptism, faith, and unflagging endurance. Despite their simplicity, however, these principles are all-encompassing and extremely demanding. Simplicity is not a synonym for ease. And Jacob hastens to explain that the merciful exemption for those ignorant of the law does not apply to his fully informed listeners.

The reader can sense the tempo quickening and the mood intensifying as Jacob delineates the groups who will not qualify for redemption. At the top of his list are the prideful learned:

> O the vainness, and the frailties, and the foolishness of men! When they are learned they think they are wise, and they hearken not unto the counsel of God, for they set it aside, supposing they know of themselves, wherefore, their wisdom is foolishness and it profiteth them not. And they shall perish. (2 Nephi 9:28)

It would be hard to define intellectual pride more succinctly and memorably than this. Jacob is not arguing against learning, but against the pride it might lead to. His next statement more than vindicates learning itself: "But to be learned is good if they hearken unto the counsels of God" (2 Nephi 9:29).

Jacob is no softer on the wealthy than on the learned, for they, too, are often swallowed up in pride, though of a different sort:

> But wo unto the rich, who are rich as to the things of the world. For because they are rich they despise the poor, and they persecute the meek, and their hearts are upon their treasures; wherefore, their treasure is their god. And behold, their treasure shall perish with them also. (2 Nephi 9:30)

That passage contains another of Jacob's memorable lines: "their treasure is their god." It would appear from Jacob's choice of subjects that even in this fledgling society, people were beginning to separate into social and economic classes.

Jacob then leaves the learned and the rich for the moment and turns his attention to other endangered species, listing them in a rapid-fire series of parallel structures:

> And wo unto the deaf that will not hear; for they shall perish.
> Wo unto the blind that will not see; for they shall perish also.
> Wo unto the uncircumcised of heart, for a knowledge of their iniquities shall smite them at the last day.
> Wo unto the liar, for he shall be thrust down to hell.
> Wo unto the murderer who deliberately killeth, for he shall die.
> Wo unto them who commit whoredoms, for they shall be thrust down to hell.
> Yea, wo unto those that worship idols, for the devil of all devils delighteth in them. (2 Nephi 9:31-37)

There is a lesson in Jacob's words that he may not have considered. It concerns the speed with which mortals can grow careless about things that really matter. Jacob is speaking to people who in just a few decades have apparently grown rapidly in both numbers and iniquity. Thirty years ago they were a small band who fled to preserve their lives and their religion, and now Jacob is addressing them as one might a group of seasoned sinners.

Jacob has indicated some rather frightening consequences of sin—destruction and hell, to name two—but even those scarcely equal the anguish of the sinners' confrontation with the God they have denied: ". . . wo unto all those who die in their sins; for they shall return to God, and behold his face, and remain in their sins" (2 Nephi 9:38). All will be resurrected, sinful and righteous alike, to face God at the judgment seat. All who have encountered the Christian gospel but have not repented and followed the Savior will be stung with the heartbreaking realization of what has been lost. The immensity of their folly, the stupidity of their failure to believe and repent, will crush in upon them as, just this once, they look upon the glorious countenance that will then be denied them forever. The agony of such a moment is beyond comprehension. The spiritually blind and deaf will suddenly see and hear, and the din of the revelation will be unbearable.

Having reached the crest of his idea, Jacob shifts to a gentler mode, pleading with his people. In one memorable sentence, he articulates his theme: ". . . to be carnally-minded is death, and to be spiritually-minded is life eternal" (2 Nephi 9:39). All inventories of the sinful and the righteous are subsumed in these two concepts, the carnal mind and the spiritual mind. Jacob implores his listeners to follow the straight and narrow course that leads to "the keeper of the gate" who "is the Holy One of Israel; and he employeth no servant there; . . . the Lord God is his name" (2 Nephi 9:41). Those who have thought to be greeted by St. Peter may be in for a surprise, too.

Continuing his metaphor of the gate, Jacob warns in an intentional reprise that the gate will be closed to persons prideful over their learning and riches. Those of us who have seen firsthand the strutting of the arrogant—and may have strutted a little ourselves—cannot help thinking that on this point, especially, Jacob speaks to a latter-day audience as well as to a congregation of his peers in the sixth century before Christ came in the flesh. Most of us are unlikely to commit murders or armed robberies, but we may well suffer from an overblown sense of self-importance.

At this moment Jacob does a startling thing, almost a shocking thing. He removes his outer garments and shakes them before the eyes of his congregation. This strikes me as a highly dramatic gesture, though not entirely out of character for a person of Jacob's considerable oratorical abilities. Although Paul also similarly shakes his "raiment" (see Acts 18:18), such an act, by contrast, would be totally out of character for Nephi. I have struggled to assess the tone of the words that accompany this gesture, and confess that I once imagined Jacob histrionically flinging off his cloak to underscore the highly pitched climax of his sermon. Now, however, it does not seem so to me. The words Jacob speaks as he shakes his garments may be disturbing, but they are not frenzied. These words, in English, at least, contain many hard consonant sounds, sounds that must be spoken slowly, that cannot be uttered in rapid succession. After repeated readings, I hear Jacob speaking in low, deliberate tones to a hushed congregation, tones that cut to the quick more effectively than a high-pitched harangue. The accelerated tempo and the crescendo of Jacob's earlier words are juxtaposed against the quiet solemnity of this emphatic moment. With awful intensity he speaks:

> O, my beloved brethren, remember my words. Behold, I take off my garments, and I shake them before you; I pray the God of my salvation that he view me with his all-searching eye; wherefore, ye shall know at the last day, when all men shall be judged of their works, that the God of Israel did witness that I shook your iniquities from my soul, and that I stand with brightness before him, and am rid of your blood. (2 Nephi 9:44)

The only response I can imagine is a deafening silence.

In retrospect I can see that Jacob accomplishes three purposes, all of them symbolic, in removing and shaking his robes. First, he figuratively opens his soul to God's "all-searching eye." Second, he symbolically shakes his congregation's iniquities from his own soul. And third, he offers his listeners a symbolic suggestion to free themselves from Satan's bondage by shaking off his chains. Once the climactic moment has passed, Jacob moves toward his conclusion with two lovely verses from Isaiah, gently urging his listeners to "come . . . to the waters" to quench their spiritual thirst, and begging them not to "spend money for that which is of no worth, nor your labor for that which cannot satisfy" (2 Nephi 9:50-51; Isaiah 55:1-2). Again, I note how easily he interposes the words of Isaiah into his sermon. Both men are rhetoricians of the first order.

Jacob's sermon on the plan of salvation is now essentially finished, and Nephi does not record the second part, or sequel, to that sermon in its entirety. The fragment we have, however, contains two new pieces of information. Jacob makes no issue of it, and we could easily miss the first in reading this passage: "Wherefore, as I said unto you, it must needs be expedient that Christ—for in the last night the angel spake unto me that this should be his name—should come among the Jews. . ." (2 Nephi 10:3). Prior to this moment, the name "Christ" has not been used in the Book of Mormon; and evidently Jacob, rather than Nephi, is first to receive the revelation about it. In previous sections of the book, and in the Old Testament, too, Jesus is designated by titles such as Lord, Son, Holy One of Israel, Lamb, and Messiah; but only after Jacob's revelation is he called Christ in the Book of Mormon. The name appears frequently in the New Testament, of course, but that text originates much later.

The other piece of information occurs in 2 Nephi 10:18, where Jacob reports the Lord's vow to "soften the hearts of the Gentiles" (in the land of promise) toward the house of Israel, to the end that "the Gentiles shall be blessed and numbered among the house of Israel." It seems that in accepting Christ as their Lord, the Gentiles become his covenant people, too. Later, Nephi also comments on who God's covenant people are and will be, confirming Jacob's prophecy that the Lord will one day covenant with the Gentiles and warning that unrepentant Jews may lose their covenant status (see 2 Nephi 30:2).

Finally, although Jacob accuses and exhorts his listeners, he must also have detected the same underlying sadness among them that he feels in himself—an aggrieved sense of isolation, perhaps even a feeling that God, too, had forgotten them. All of these exiles must have wondered, despairingly at times, what was to become of them. Perhaps it is in part to bring comfort and a sense of identity and belonging that Jacob and Nephi speak frequently and at length about membership in the house of Israel, and about promises made to these people and their posterity. The future holds hope, despite the bleakness of the present. Sensitized by his own privation, Jacob seems to be searching for personal consolation when he urges his people to remember their "merciful God," to

lay aside our sins, and not hang down our heads, for we are not cast off; nevertheless, we have been driven out of the land of our inheritance; but we have been led to a better land, for the Lord has made the sea our path, and we are upon an isle of the sea. (2 Nephi 10:20)

Jacob takes comfort, too, in the fact that, according to scripture, the Lord forgets none of the Israelite groups who have left the old world and crossed the seas. He may be referring to prophecies about the Jaredites and the Mulekites, as well as to the Lehites and the lost tribes of Israel (see 2 Nephi 10:21-22).

Having rehearsed for his listeners their temporal promises and blessings, Jacob concludes by reminding them, again in memorable language, of their spiritual blessings, specifically agency and salvation from both temporal and spiritual death. He touches a theme already articulated by his father, one that will be echoed by others: our eternal destiny is ours to choose. Jacob also urges his listeners to "reconcile" themselves to the "will of God" rather than "to the will of the devil and the flesh" (2 Nephi 10:24). Significantly, his definition of the rivalry places the will of the devil and the will of the flesh on the same side of the equation. Jacob's final words are a lovely benediction:

> Wherefore, may God raise you from death by the power of the resurrection, and also from everlasting death by the power of the atonement, that ye may be received into the eternal kingdom of God, that ye may praise him through grace divine. Amen. (2 Nephi 10:25)

Although the teachings reported in chapter 10 are sermon fragments, the earlier discourse comprising chapter 9 seems to me whole and complete in itself. It may well be a segment of a larger treatise, but its coherent development suggests more than a collection of isolated passages. Conversely, most of the material Nephi excerpts from the second day's sermon had already been voiced eloquently by Isaiah. And it is to Isaiah that Nephi will soon turn as another witness to the words he and Jacob have spoken. Nephi also states with calm certitude that both he and Jacob have personally seen the Lord Jesus Christ.

Before quoting a large section of Isaiah, however, Nephi pauses to address the reader directly, to bear fervent personal testimony of "the coming of Christ," of whom all things given from the beginning, including the law of Moses, are types (2 Nephi 11:4). Three times in three verses (2 Nephi 11:4-6), Nephi uses the phrase "my soul delighteth in" to express his joy in his Savior, his gladness in "proving" that Christ will indeed come (and he now uses that holy name which Jacob had introduced). This is a man who loves to teach the gospel of Christ—and Christ is the motif that gives the whole fabric of the Book of Mormon its character.

# 6

## 2 Nephi 12-33: Nephi's Final Discourses

With only minor variations, chapters 12 through 24 of 2 Nephi replicate chapters 2 through 14 of Isaiah. This is the largest block of Isaiah's writings that Nephi inscribes into his own record. Since it is not my purpose to explicate biblical text, I make only a few brief observations about the contents of these superbly written discourses. The chapter summaries in Isaiah and 2 Nephi indicate the subjects treated, and the reader should note that they predict both pain and felicity—a dire political future for Judah, and also the Messiah's birth and the millennium of peace that will follow his second coming. These chapters contain some of Isaiah's most moving poetry, attesting to Nephi's aesthetic judgment as well as his doctrinal acuity. Incidentally, the following passage, which opens the Isaiah section, was chosen to adorn the pioneer monument at the mouth of Emigration Canyon east of Salt Lake City: "And it shall come to pass in the last days, when the mountain of the Lord's house shall be established in the top of the mountains, and shall be exalted above the hills, and all nations shall flow unto it" (2 Nephi 12:2; Isaiah 2:2). The Wasatch Mountain range leaping skyward behind the monument adds validating force to Isaiah's words.

Later, Isaiah describes with disquieting accuracy the major character flaws of latter-day peoples—worldliness, materialism, and pride. This particular passage blends them tidily into one: "Their land is also full of idols; they worship the work of their own hands, that which their own fingers have made" (2 Nephi 12:8; Isaiah 2:8). I wonder how many of our civilization's "toys" Isaiah saw. He singles out "the daughters of Zion" (*not* the daughters of infidels) for particular condemnation; they are flirtatious, they adorn themselves with lavish jewelry and clothing, and they are, in name at least, members of Christ's church (see 2 Nephi 13-14; Isaiah 3-4). Then, through a parable of the Lord's vineyard, Isaiah issues a warning of impending destruction for the house of Israel. He shifts abruptly in chapter 6 (2 Nephi 16), however, to his own personal call to prophecy, the famous visionary account of an angel cleansing him by touching a live coal to his lips.

Chapter 17 (Isaiah 7) foretells a besieged Judah, but tucked in the center of that gloomy forecast is a lovely passage familiar to all of Christendom: "Behold, a virgin shall conceive, and shall bear a son, and shall call his name Immanuel" (v. 14). Chapter 19 (Isaiah 9) revisits the theme, heralding, with poetry irresistible to Handel, the joyous infusion of Messianic light: "For unto us a child is born, unto us a son is given; and the government shall be upon his shoulder; and his name shall be called, Wonderful, Counselor, The Mighty God, The Everlasting Father, The Prince of Peace" (2 Nephi 19:6; Isaiah 9:9).

Chapter 21 (Isaiah 11) sketches a comely picture of millennial bliss after the Lord's righteous judgment. These are the gladsome images we eagerly call up in our imaginings of Christ's reign after wickedness has been defeated—the wolf and the lamb, the leopard and the kid, the calf and the lion dwelling tranquilly together. For me, verse 9 describes the sweetest prospect of all: "They shall not hurt nor destroy in all my holy mountain, for the earth shall be full of the knowledge of the Lord, as the waters cover the sea." The appealing phrase "full of the knowledge of the Lord" suggests not only that all will know the Lord, but also that the knowledge contained in his magnificent mind will permeate the earth and be available to all its inhabitants.

Rereading these chapters, I marvel again at Isaiah's mastery of the language and his incomparable artistry. He writes verse after verse that is at once powerful and exquisite. No wonder Nephi venerated him. Chapter 24 (Isaiah 14) is triumphal, prophesying Israel's gathering and the defeat of both Lucifer and Babylon. Isaiah understands completely Lucifer's deadliest failing, his unbridled ambition: "For thou hast said in thy heart: I will ascend into heaven, I will exalt my throne above the stars of God; . . . I will ascend above the heights of the clouds; I will be like the Most High" (vs. 13-14). In the end, Isaiah foresees that Lucifer shall meet scorn from those he sought to rule. The prophet chooses a fitting image, the "narrow" look, to depict Satan's reduced circumstances: "They that see thee shall narrowly look upon thee, and shall consider thee, and shall say, Is this the man that made the earth to tremble, that did shake kingdoms?" (2 Nephi 24:16; Isaiah 14:16).

As moving as the Isaiah chapters are, it is the chapters following them that touch me most deeply, those in which Nephi delivers his final message to his people and to us. In some sense, however, Nephi uses Isaiah as a springboard for his own prophetic utterances. His words reinforce Isaiah's, but they are delivered "according to my plainness," minus Isaiah's poetic embellishments, so "that no man can err" (2 Nephi 25:7). Having finished his lengthy borrowing, Nephi serves notice that the prophetic voice is now his. Nevertheless, he is confident that Isaiah's prophecies "shall be of great worth unto them in the last days; for in that day shall they understand them; wherefore, for their good have I written them" (2 Nephi 25:8). His view of our interpretive abilities may be overly generous, but I confess that, set in the context of his enthusiasm, the Isaiah passages are somehow more navigable than I have found them in the Bible. And if Nephi seems to repeat himself in his stirring prophecies of the Messiah and the latter-day restoration of the gospel, it is probably at least partly because his record spans several decades.

There are some sterling moments in Nephi's final discourses, moments made luminous by his maturity in the gospel and his inviolate integrity. His unique gift for expressing the profound in simple terms is evident when he alludes to the source of our salvation:

> For we labor diligently to write, to persuade our children, and also our brethren, to believe in Christ, and to be reconciled to God; for we know that it is by grace that we are saved, after all we can do. (2 Nephi 25:23)

With the same directness, Nephi justifies the Law of Moses as a precursor to Christ's saving gospel. Unquestionably, the center of Nephi's life is the Savior, Jesus Christ, and he achieves an almost unconscious rhythmic elegance in reaching for simple words to convey his devotion:

> And we talk of Christ, we rejoice in Christ, we preach of Christ, we prophesy of Christ, and we write according to our prophecies, that our children may know to what source they may look for a remission of their sins. (2 Nephi 25:26)

From this point on, Nephi tables his narrative and speaks almost exclusively in prophetic terms. The resurrected Lord, he announces, will visit this new land and introduce a new kind of law, framing it even as he speaks to his people, present and future. Christ's birth in the Holy Land will be accompanied by wondrous signs, but his death will trigger such cataclysmic destruction that Nephi's vision of it wracks his soul. Nevertheless, he does not question God's justice; he makes a point of affirming it. His compassion and humane understanding are as large as his faith.

Still, in alluding to the Gentiles in the last days, Nephi demonstrates a capacity for satire that matches his rhetorical agility. He foresees that in their foolish pride, the Gentiles will have "built up many churches" wherein "they put down the power and miracles of God, and preach up unto themselves their own wisdom and their own learning, that they may get gain and grind upon the face of the poor" (2 Nephi 26:20). Nephi deftly balances contrastive phrases, playing on the prepositions "up" and "down": "built up . . . churches," "put down God," and "preach up . . . themselves." He also employs a powerful metaphor of cruelty in the phrase "grind upon the face of the poor"; the word "grind" suggests the twisting and grinding action of a boot heel on an insect, or the wearing action of a grinding wheel or mill, and the word "upon" echoes previous uses of "up," but inverts its meaning.

Warning against the devil, this champion of plain speech has no difficulty finding an impressive figure or other trick of language to serve his purposes. But whatever the device Nephi employs, it is always to the point, as with his vivid metaphor for the devil's entrapping deceit: ". . . he leadeth [his followers] by the neck with a flaxen cord, until he bindeth them with his strong cords forever" (2 Nephi 26:22). Whatever entices becomes a permanent fetter. Seeking, by contrast, to accentuate the Lord's liberating constancy, Nephi asks a series of rhetorical questions:

> Behold, doth he cry unto any, saying: Depart from me? (2 Nephi 26:25)
> Behold, hath he commanded any that they should depart out of the synagogues, or out of the houses of worship? (2 Nephi 26:26)
> Hath he commanded any that they should not partake of his salvation? (2 Nephi 26:27)
> Behold, hath the Lord commanded any that they should not partake of his goodness? (2 Nephi 26:28)

Nephi answers each of his own questions with an emphatic "Behold, I say unto you, Nay," roundly demonstrating that the Lord never—repeat, *never*—deceives or abandons those who follow him. Furthermore, he loves all persons equally, denying "none that come unto him," regardless of color, status, or gender; "all are alike unto God" (2 Nephi 26:33). This is an important concept, for it states unequivocally that the covenant people have no exclusive entitlement to the Lord's love.

Nephi covers a wide array of subjects in his counsel, from latter-day "priestcrafts" (2 Nephi 26:29) to charity. He also restates some of the Lord's more exacting commandments to his children, naming several of the ten given to Moses. Where the wording varies from that of Exodus 20, the effect is to place increased emphasis on our human obligation to love one another. The Book of Mormon text, for example, substitutes the word "envy" for "covet," envy suggesting a more personal, less generic emotion than covetousness. And, instead of using the phrase "bear false witness," the Book of Mormon text forbids mortals to "have malice," which seems to get at the very root of gossip. Nephi also declares that mortals are forbidden to "contend one with another"

(2 Nephi 26:32), intimating that quarrelsomeness, and perhaps even over-competitiveness, undermine character and produce enmity. Nephi saw enough of envy, malice, and contention in his own family to know their capacity for destruction. In citing the Lord's decrees, he pleads for generosity and kindness in human relationships.

Chapter 27 is given exclusively to prophecies of the last days, both Isaiah's and Nephi's, with a decided emphasis on the book that is to be brought forth through the Lord's designated prophet as the heart of the restored gospel. Here also is the astounding revelation that the sealed portion of the book will one day come forth to be figuratively "read upon the house tops . . . by the power of Christ" (2 Nephi 27:11). Further, Nephi prophesies the publication of other records of other peoples, declaring that "all things shall be revealed . . . which ever have been among the children of men, and which ever will be even unto the end of the earth" (2 Nephi 27:11). His clear and detailed perception of these events, including the Lord's precise instructions to Joseph Smith, attests to his extraordinary intellectual and spiritual powers. He observes that once Joseph has read the section of the record intended for his eyes (and ours), and "obtained the witnesses," he is to "seal up the book again" so that the Lord "may preserve the words" Joseph has not read until the Lord chooses to bring them forth (2 Nephi 27:22). These verses are vitally important, for they state unequivocally that the Lord intends to bring out, "in mine own due time" (2 Nephi 27:20), additional scripture unread by Joseph. Verse 23 suggests that such an event is contingent upon the faith of mortals.[1]

It appears that in the chapters following the Isaiah borrowings, Nephi is writing one continuous discourse, but doing it in several phases. Chapters 28 and 29 rehearse the same general subjects as the chapters that precede them; but in these chapters, fol-

---

[1] Much later, Mormon attests that the opening of the records is contingent upon latter-day acceptance of his abridgment (see 3 Nephi 26:9-11).

lowing Isaiah's practice, Nephi shifts into first person to signify that he is uttering the Lord's words. He describes with great vigor and dexterity Satan's activities, and he issues warnings to latter-day peoples. Some "will [Satan] pacify, and lull them away into carnal security, that they will say: All is well in Zion; yea, Zion prospereth, all is well—and thus the devil cheateth their souls and leadeth them away carefully down to hell" (2 Nephi 28:21). Nephi's language proficiency is apparent as he links seemingly conflicting words to shock his reader to attention. The ordinarily positive "security" and the seemingly harmless "lull" take on a sinister cast in the presence of the word "carnal" and the deceiver, Satan. Nephi achieves a similar effect by using the word "carefully" to describe a guided tour to hell.

Nephi elaborates further about the devil's duplicity, cautioning that while he sedates and pacifies some, "others he flattereth away, and telleth them there is no hell; and he saith unto them: I am no devil, for there is none—and thus he whispereth in their ears, until he grasps them with his awful chains, from whence there is no deliverance" (2 Nephi 28:22).[2] This is not the writing of a man inept with words, regardless of his protests to the contrary. Prophetic inspiration has intensified Nephi's style, and his ominous warnings echo Isaiah: "Therefore, wo be unto him that is at ease in Zion! Wo be unto him that crieth: All is well" (2 Nephi 28:24-25). Here, certainly, is prophecy to ponder. Why will it be dangerous to be "at ease in Zion," to assume and announce that "all is well"? Perhaps because danger must be perceived before it can be averted, whether the danger be physical or spiritual.

There is hazard, too, Nephi adds, in assuming that the Bible provides sufficient scripture. The Lord promises that those who are receptive to additional instruction will receive more knowledge. Conversely, those "that shall say, We have enough, from them shall be taken away even that which they have" (2 Nephi

---

[2] In our time, the gifted Christian fictionist of the grotesque, Flannery O'Connor, says in dead earnest, attributing the thought to Baudelaire: "The devil's greatest wile ... is to convince us that he does not exist." *Mystery and Manners* (New York: Farrar, Straus and Giroux, 1962, p. 112.)

28:30). The Lord's language, and the point he is making as Nephi renders it here, bear enough resemblance to the wording he would later use in the parable of the talents that the passage illuminates the parable. If we see it that way, the talents could represent, in one of their meanings, the varying degrees of knowledge and wisdom. Nephi concludes the chapter with a figure that emphasizes the Lord's merciful yearning toward mortals: ". . . for mine arm is lengthened out all the day long, saith the Lord God of Hosts" (2 Nephi 28:32). The central message of these chapters is that the Lord intends for all of God's children to have his word—the same word.

Chapter 29, from which I quoted in the introduction to this essay, repeats with even greater intensity the Lord's utterances to Nephi about the record and its crucial role, in terms of both belief and a rightful inheritance, in the restoration of the house of Israel. In chapter 30, Nephi returns to his own voice to prophesy of latter-day events, especially those relating to the "carrying forth" of the "sealed up" book "unto the remnant of our seed" (2 Nephi 30:3). With prophecies such as these in holy scripture, The Church of Jesus Christ of Latter-day Saints is bound to proclaim the restored gospel with vigor among Native and Latin Americans. Remnant peoples and Jews alike, Nephi says, shall embrace the truth (see 2 Nephi 30:6,7). Then, blending Isaiah's prophecies with his own, and traversing from warnings of destruction to blissful images of millennial peace, he prepares to inscribe his closing words.

Of the many splendid passages in the writings of Nephi, none surpasses his discourse on the doctrine of Christ set forth in chapter 31 of 2 Nephi. Resuming a more personal stance as loving leader and brother to this much expanded group of castaways, he outlines and discusses four basic aspects of the Christian gospel presented earlier by Jacob: faith, repentance, baptism, and endurance to the end. As he enlarges the meaning of these four, he adds another: baptism by fire, or the gift of the Holy Ghost. By so doing, he introduces the four basic principles and ordinances of the gospel later put forth by Joseph Smith in the Articles of

Faith. In these and in other things, Nephi says, the Savior's mortal life is the pattern—a rather surprising expectation when one stops to think of it, for the Savior is not to be born for another five and a half centuries. Jesus Christ, of course, is no stranger to Nephi, and his people know of Christ through prophecy. But Nephi writes mainly for later peoples blessed with accounts of the Savior's already-accomplished earthly ministry.

Speaking as though the events of Jesus' life in the Holy Land had already occurred—for indeed, he has seen them in vision—Nephi asks a logical question: ". . . wherein [did] the Lamb of God . . . fulfill all righteousness in being baptized by water? Know ye not that he was holy?" That is, why would a perfect being require baptism? Nephi answers his own question. In baptism, the Savior offers a witness of his humility and personal obedience to the Father's will, thereby becoming the ultimate exemplar. On the occasion of his baptism, Jesus also received the Holy Ghost, in this, too, showing "the children of men the straitness of the path, and the narrowness of the gate, by which they should enter, he having set the example before them" (2 Nephi 31:6-9). Through his example, therefore, Jesus emphasized the exact and irrevocable nature of divine commandments.

The Savior's injunction to "Follow thou me" resounds through the chapter, and Nephi links it to the keeping of the Father's commandments: "Wherefore, my beloved brethren, can we follow Jesus save we shall be willing to keep the commandments of the Father?" (2 Nephi 31:10). Nephi then moves to the core of his final discourse, which encompasses all he has said and adds the sublime promise of the Holy Ghost's companionship: ". . . the voice of the Son came unto me, saying: He that is baptized in my name, to him will the Father give the Holy Ghost, like unto me; wherefore follow me, and do the things which ye have seen me do" (2 Nephi 31:12). Even the mortal Jesus received that gift. Succeeding verses set forth the same admonition, to follow him.

Obviously moved by the doctrine, Nephi grows increasingly eloquent as he starts to echo the voice of the Son. For instance, in verse 13 he begins quite deliberately, but as he expounds more of the doctrine and its implications, his language becomes more intense and rhythmic. I quote it all, making special note of his insistence that following the Savior exacts commitment to the gospel's basic principles and ordinances—faith, repentance, baptism, and the reception of the Holy Ghost:

> Wherefore, my beloved brethren, I know that if ye shall follow the Son, with full purpose of heart, acting no hypocrisy and no deception before God, but with real intent, repenting of your sins, witnessing unto the Father that ye are willing to take upon you the name of Christ, by baptism—yea, by following your Lord and your Savior down into the water, according to his word, behold, then shall ye receive the Holy Ghost; yea, then cometh the baptism of fire and of the Holy Ghost; and then can ye speak with the tongue of angels, and shout praises unto the Holy One of Israel. (2 Nephi 31:13)

The first half of the sentence tells what is required ("if ye shall . . ."), and the second half enumerates the blessings to the faithful ("then . . ."). At the midpoint is the word "yea," which is repeated as promises are added in steps. Despite the center rotation, the passage is one long sentence, its larger form suggesting unbroken acceleration toward a climactic moment.

As with most scripture, the passage carries insights that are only dimly perceived in a first reading. Consider, for example, the phrase "following your Lord and your Savior down into the water," which seems to require immersion as the Savior's designated mode of baptism. Additionally, the last lines of the passage suggest that one exceptional outcome of baptism by fire is the ability to speak as angels do. That is a tantalizing thought, but Nephi postpones elaboration. Instead, he reports the words of both Father and Son, including the Father's assurance that "he that endureth to the end, the same shall be saved" (2 Nephi 31:15). Most of us have at least a vague notion of what the often-repeated phrase "endure to the end" means. The first thought that pops into my mind, "gut it out," does not become an English teacher, but it conveys the general notion. Nephi has a better idea: ". . . unless a man shall endure to the end, *in following the example of the Son* of the living God, he cannot be saved" (2 Nephi 31:16; emphasis added). Nephi intimates here and throughout the chapter that to endure to the end is to follow the Savior's example unceasingly.

While the Holy Ghost is acknowledged in Christian doctrine everywhere, Nephi accords the third member of the Godhead a significance not generally understood. He had stated in verse 13, cited above, that following baptism one receives "the baptism of fire and of the Holy Ghost," but in this, too, he delays explanation for several verses. After one enters "the gate" of "repentance and baptism by water," Nephi says, "then cometh a remission of your sins by fire and by the Holy Ghost" (2 Nephi 31:17). Once we have experienced a symbolic death, burial, and resurrection through the ordinance of baptism by water, the Holy Ghost participates in the cleansing process (see also Moroni 6:4). The mention of cleansing fire recalls, too, the burning coal touched to the lips of Isaiah.

Subsequent verses describe another function of the Holy Ghost, that of witness and teacher. For Nephi, and for believing Mormons and probably many others, the Holy Ghost is not only the Comforter Jesus promised his disciples, but also the agent of inspired testimony, knowledge, and guidance leading to salvation—the holy being who attends us, prompting us to gospel understanding and actions, and enlightening our minds. Addressing the subject again in chapter 32, Nephi at last explains his statement about speaking "with the tongue of angels." Through a series of "wherefores," he guides his readers to an understanding of the role the Holy Ghost is to play in their lives:

> Do ye not remember that I said unto you that after ye had received the Holy Ghost ye could speak with the tongue of angels? And now, how could ye speak with the tongue of angels save it were by the Holy Ghost?
>
> Angels speak by the power of the Holy Ghost; wherefore, they speak the words of Christ. Wherefore, I said unto you, feast upon the words of Christ, for behold, the words of Christ will tell you all things what ye should do. (2 Nephi 32:2-3)

But, Nephi says, one must *ask* for understanding.

The Holy Ghost's function also includes prompting God's children to pray, to overcome pride, and to seek direction constantly. Nephi instructs his readers not to "perform any thing unto the Lord save in the first place ye shall pray unto the Father in the name of Christ, that he will consecrate thy performance unto thee, that thy performance may be for the welfare of thy soul" (2 Nephi 32:9). This is an interesting concept: our worship and our service to the Lord are to be accompanied by prayer so that he may consecrate them, not to *his* good, or the church's good, but to ours. What we consecrate and offer to him turns around to bless us. Nephi's moving statement about what is required of one who enters the gate reveals not only the character of the man, but also his sensitivity to language. It is one of the loveliest passages in all scripture:

> Wherefore, ye must press forward with a steadfastness in Christ, having a perfect brightness of hope, and a love of God and of all men. Wherefore, if ye shall press forward, feasting upon the word of Christ, and endure to the end, behold, thus saith the Father: Ye shall have eternal life. (2 Nephi 31:20)

Is there a finer phrase anywhere than "perfect brightness of hope"?

In my introduction, I quoted Nephi's official farewell, the final verses of chapter 33. The opening verses of that chapter appropriately cap his teachings about the Holy Ghost, and at the same time squarely state his position: "But I, Nephi, have written what I have written, and I esteem it as of great worth. . ." (2 Nephi 33:3). This is one man's humble yet sure witness to the worth of the thing he has lived his life for: the gospel of Jesus Christ. That gospel, so far as it is known at this time, is contained in the writings the testifier has inscribed. It will be added to only by the Savior in person.

As Nephi prepares to close his record, he composes what resembles a solemn personal creed. Although not specifically addressed to his readers, it is clearly intended for their eyes:

I glory in plainness; I glory in truth; I glory in my Jesus, for he hath redeemed my soul from hell.

I have charity for my people and great faith in Christ that I shall meet many souls spotless at his judgment-seat.

I have charity for the Jew—I say Jew, because I mean them from whence I came.

I also have charity for the Gentiles. But behold, for none of these can I hope except they shall be reconciled unto Christ, and enter into the narrow gate, and walk in the strait path which leads to life, and continue in the path until the end of the day of probation. (2 Nephi 33:6-9)

This man Nephi, against unspeakable odds, maintained the faith and taught the doctrine. He was the message bearer for what became a large and often unruly band of castaways, teaching them news from across the seas, that is, news from their Maker. And from first to last, over half a century, he taught undeviatingly a consistent doctrine: the doctrine of the Lord Jesus Christ. His teachers were his father, the ancient prophets of Israel, and the Lord himself, in his own being and voice and through angels and the promptings of the Holy Spirit. This same Nephi, who grew to become a great prophet in his own right, was also the political leader who almost singlehandedly fashioned a civilization out of a wild and desolate land, an ocean away from the known world. The magnitude of his accomplishment and his faith leaves me rather dazed. What is more, he maintained his perspective, humbly seeing to the good of his people rather than caring for his own advancement or comfort. Surely, it is no affectation when Nephi voices fear for his people near the end of his record:

For I pray continually for them by day, and mine eyes water my pillow by night, because of them; and I cry unto my God in faith, and I know that he will hear my cry.

And I know that the Lord God will consecrate my prayers for the gain of my people. (2 Nephi 33:3-4)

It is a rare monarch whose greatness is defined as much by the strength of his faith and the depth of his humility as by his political and civic accomplishments. When such a person speaks, it is imperative that we listen.

# The Book of Jacob

The next section in the Book of Mormon, comprising only seven chapters, is written by Nephi's younger brother, Jacob, whom we met earlier through his sermon on the plan of salvation. Clearly, he is second only to Nephi in the religious hierarchy of Nephite governance. Jacob is something of an enigma, a complex and gifted man who seems both sure and unsure—sure in his duty, sometimes unsure in his ability to perform it. I have labored to understand him and can only make a few intuitive guesses. At first, and even second, glance Jacob seems a letter-of-the-law man, rather rigid and exacting in his expectations both of himself and of his people. Perhaps it seemed so to me because of Jacob's unfailing desire to do right and to fulfill his calling irreproachably. That early impression, I have come to realize, needs adjustment.

Nonetheless, there is an almost painful earnestness about Jacob, even a somberness that suggests a deep, abiding melancholy. Undoubtedly, his nature to some extent reflects his circumstances; Jacob was born in the wilderness and never saw the civilized world. He suffered physical deprivation as a child, and while still very young he was packed on a boat and forced to sail for many days to a new land, an untamed territory where hardship and loneliness must have scarred his days and perhaps his soul. The boy Jacob was also aware of the hatred Laman and Lemuel bore toward Nephi, and this malevolence wounded him. On the boat, for example, he watched his parents nearly die of grief over the cruelty of their eldest sons. Nephi wrote that "Jacob and Joseph also, being young, having need of much nourishment, were grieved because of the afflictions of their mother" (1 Nephi 18:19). "Having need of much nourishment" suggests a good deal more than the physical need for food. Emotional nourishment

was at least as critical for these youngsters. In pronouncing a blessing on Jacob, we remember, Lehi acknowledged that his son had
"suffered afflictions and much sorrow," but promised that God
would "consecrate thine afflictions for thy gain" (2 Nephi 2:2).
There is in these observations a recognition of Jacob's unusual sensitivity, his natural inclination to feel keenly the effects of events
and circumstances. Further, the sort of beginning Jacob experienced can leave a permanent mark on the mind, and an adulthood that offers only increased burdens and intensified conflict
would do little to relieve his heavy heart.

One of the most poignant moments in the Book of Mormon
is the self-revealing, almost heartbreaking conclusion to Jacob's
record. First, he speaks of a disappointing failure to return his
brothers and their followers to the fold: ". . . many means were
devised to reclaim and restore the Lamanites to the knowledge of
the truth; but it all was vain, for they delighted in wars and bloodshed, and they had an eternal hatred against us, their brethren"
(Jacob 7:24). I can hear the anguish in the words, "their
brethren," and in his description of his brothers only a verse later
as "enemies" of his people. The tone of lament in Jacob's single-
sentence farewell defines his life and his nature more tellingly than
any mere description of the man could accomplish:

> . . . I conclude this record, declaring that I have written according to
> the best of my knowledge, by saying that the time passed away with
> us, and also our lives passed away like as it were unto us a dream, we
> being a lonesome and a solemn people, wanderers, cast out from
> Jerusalem, born in tribulation, in a wilderness, and hated of our
> brethren, which caused wars and contentions; wherefore, we did
> mourn out our days. (Jacob 7:26)

I urge the reader to repeat those mournful phrases, letting words
like "passed away," "a dream," "lonesome," "solemn," "wanderers," "cast out," "tribulation," "wilderness," "hatred," and "mourn
out our days" reverberate in the consciousness. Only profound
sadness would produce the chilling sentiment that life has been
more like a dream than an actual experience; only a man who had

walked hand in hand with grief would speak of mourning out life's days. Jacob is a castaway both physically and emotionally, and those of us who live warmly and well can little comprehend his feelings.

It is perhaps not out of character that Jacob would elect to elucidate the "mystery" of a scattered Israel's eventual acceptance of Christ as its Lord by quoting seventy-seven long verses from the writings of Zenos (who was represented in the brass plates, but not in the King James Bible). Nephi, of course, had quoted long sections from Isaiah, but he did it in confident admiration of his mentor and not out of self-doubt or failure of nerve. With Jacob, I am not so sure; he almost seems uncertain of his ability to explain the doctrine to his latter-day readers. He will, he says, address the matter of Israel's return to its Lord, "if I do not, by any means, get shaken from my firmness in the Spirit, and stumble because of my over anxiety for you" (Jacob 4:18). Apparently Jacob is shaken from his firmness, for he defers to Zenos's allegorical symbolization of the matter. In fact, Jacob consigns the whole of chapter 5, nearly a third of his total inscription, to the Zenos interpolation, a remarkable deed in light of his earlier rationale for the record's brevity: ". . . I cannot write but a little of my words, because of the difficulty of engraving our words upon plates" (Jacob 4:1).

Jacob prophesies only that "the things which this prophet Zenos spake . . . must surely come to pass" (Jacob 6:1), leaving the burden of the argument to Zenos. But then, as if inspirited by the Zenos text, he adds his own quite wonderful summary of Zenos's discourse. Jacob sidesteps the task, yes, but rather happily so, for otherwise we would have missed a small masterpiece. Zenos likens Israel to the tame olive trees in the Lord's vineyard and the Gentiles to the wild ones.

The borrowing from Zenos is perhaps indicative that at times, Jacob simply felt overwhelmed by the responsibility that fell upon his shoulders after Nephi's death. Perhaps Nephi, too, had begun to recognize the burgeoning task of Nephite leadership, for he decided that a king should succeed him in his secular role—this despite Jacob's earlier prophecy that in the latter days, at least, there would be no kings in the promised land (see 2 Nephi 10:11). Nephi's civil successor is not named on the small plates, but it is not Jacob. The latter assuredly has the faith and the character to be a spiritual leader, but perhaps not the forcefulness or the prowess to be a political leader as well. What Jacob might lack in brawn and majesty, however, he more than compensates for in conscience and devotion. Three times in the first several verses of his writings, he speaks of his obligation to keep a record of things he considers "most precious" (Jacob 1:2). Perhaps humility leads him to record little of his own preaching—a portion of only one sermon—and not a whole lot of revelation and prophecy. Most of his writings are directed to his posterity and to later peoples who would read his words.

Jacob venerates Nephi, and with good reason; but he probably suffers by comparison in his own eyes. He pays tribute to Nephi, again, curiously, acknowledging the people's love for Nephi as a "great protector" and powerful temporal leader (Jacob 1:10) without mentioning his spiritual leadership. Jacob is different—a good man but a troubled man, troubled not only over his older brothers' animosity, but also over the increasing wickedness of the Nephite people. And he regrets having to chastise them for it. Never forgetting his commission but fearful of coming up short, he speaks of his desire to be "diligent in the office of my calling" (Jacob 2:3), referring repeatedly to his heavy responsibility:

> . . . ye yourselves know that I have hitherto been diligent in the office of my calling; but I this day am weighed down with much more desire and anxiety (Jacob 2:3)
>
> it grieveth my soul (Jacob 2:6)
>
> it grieveth me (Jacob 2:7)
>
> it burdeneth my soul (Jacob 2:9)

notwithstanding the greatness of the task, I must do according to the
strict commands of God (Jacob 2:10)

the word of God burdens me (Jacob 2:23)

Twice Jacob repeats the words he uttered when he shook his
garments in an earlier sermon, words that he insists absolve him
of responsibility for the sins of those he teaches. Only someone
who feels responsibility acutely would keep repeating absolution
for himself. Many years later, King Benjamin and Paul use the
same expression, but with considerably less emphasis. Still, I find
it a bit odd that in the beginning of a stinging sermon of reproach,
Jacob would say that "as yet, ye have been obedient unto the word
of the Lord, which I have given unto you" (Jacob 2:4). Certainly,
all have not been obedient, or he would not be delivering this
address. Maybe the ultra-conscientious Jacob in some sense
regards the Nephites' moral lapses as his personal failure. The following three passages appear in rather quick succession, and they
speak directly to the point I am making here:

> And we [Jacob and Joseph] did magnify our office unto the Lord,
> taking upon us the responsibility, answering the sins of the people
> upon our own heads if we did not teach them the word of God with
> all diligence; wherefore, by laboring with our might their blood might
> not come upon our garments; otherwise their blood would come
> upon our garments, and we would not be found spotless at the last
> day. (Jacob 1:19)

> Now, my beloved brethren, I, Jacob, according to the responsi-
> bility which I am under to God, to magnify mine office with sober-
> ness, and that I might rid my garments of your sins, I come up into
> the temple this day that I might declare unto you the word of God.
> (Jacob 2:2)

> Yea, it grieveth my soul and causeth me to shrink with shame
> before the presence of my Maker, that I must testify unto you con-
> cerning the wickedness of your hearts. (Jacob 2:6)

Why is it that the Jacob of the sermon quoted in Nephi's writings

seems stronger and surer than the Jacob we generally encounter in
his own selection of writings? I find myself greatly admiring the
skilled craftsman of the first sermon, but loving more the anxious
and compassionate individual of his own record—perhaps
because the later Jacob seems less aware of his gifts, rhetorical and
otherwise, and more afraid of disappointing his Lord. In a word,
I can relate to the man who is searching, like the rest of us, for
confidence and certitude. But the Jacob of the first sermon, that
unwavering prophet with extraordinary understanding and
insight, that verbal craftsman who can reason brilliantly and make
words fairly sing, is also present in the book of Jacob, notably in
the sermon fragment that constitutes chapter 2.

The occasion of the sermon is a meeting of church membership in the temple. Jacob's intent is first to warn against pride—
especially pride associated with close-fisted wealth—and then to
chastise the men in his congregation for their callous promiscuity.
Although Jacob begins this difficult assignment with eleven verses
of preparatory warm-ups, when he catches stride he speaks boldly
and impressively. It is not timidity, however, that delays Jacob in
broaching his delicate subject, but sensitivity to the feelings of
some dear people in his congregation. His words are not simply a
passing courtesy, for Jacob agonizes over the matter, alluding to it
again and again. In verse 7, for example, Jacob regrets having to
use "much boldness of speech" in reproving the Nephite men
because of the hurt it will inflict on their "wives and . . . children,
many of whose feelings are exceedingly tender and chaste and delicate." They have come, he says, to hear "the word which healeth
the wounded soul" (Jacob 2:8), but he cannot speak that word.
Instead, he must "enlarge the wounds of those who are already
wounded" and "pierce" the "souls and wound" the "delicate
minds" of "those who have not been wounded" (Jacob 2:9; see
also Jacob 2:35). I do not recall ever hearing anyone speak in quite
this way; Jacob's empathy has a lesson for us all.

Jacob warms to the task by denouncing pride, an easier subject to introduce in mixed company. Still, I think he chooses to
speak of infidelity at a gathering of families so that the guilty par-

ties will be shamed by the presence and visible anguish of their wives and children. Jacob speaks with power and grace, as one who indeed represents God. He also tells his brothers in the church that they have no business reviling the Lamanites, for the latter observe the law of marital fidelity and will therefore be preserved "and one day . . . become a blessed people" (Jacob 3:6). Apparently on that one point the Lamanites win continuance; it is obviously no trifling matter to the Lord. Moreover, unless the Nephites repent, Jacob says, at the judgment seat "their skins will be whiter than yours" (Jacob 3:8). Here, too, skin color is used symbolically to denote the blessedness associated with merited divine companionship.

Despite his heavy burden, and his occasional surrender to melancholy, Jacob never loses his sense of purpose or his faith. There is a quiet, even forward-looking, eloquence in his words when he writes of the record to readers he will not see in this life. Jacob wants us to know that faith flourished even among a group of endangered exiles in a remote corner of the world, that he and his people, like the prophets before them, "knew of Christ, and we had a hope of his glory many hundred years before his coming." Although exiles, they "search the prophets, and . . . have many revelations and the spirit of prophecy." Most important, they "obtain a hope" and an unshaken faith. "We truly can," Jacob states, "command in the name of Jesus and the very trees obey us, or the mountains, or the waves of the sea" (Jacob 4:4,6). Their latter-day counterparts might well emulate such faith.

Jacob conveys splendidly his sense of the Lord's power and mystery. These passages of pure poetry must be read and reread:

> Behold, great and marvelous are the works of the Lord. How unsearchable are the depths of the mysteries of him; and it is impossible that man should find out all his ways. . . .
>
> For behold, by the power of his word man came upon the face of the earth, which earth was created by the power of his word. (Jacob 4:8-9)

Jacob is a man of keen intellect, as his insight into Israel's rejection and murder of its prophets, and ultimately of the Messiah, demonstrates. Because of blindness, he prophesies, Israel will fall, and his assessment of that blindness is enlightening. (He speaks in the past tense for readers in the distant future.) Israel's people, Jacob says, erred by seeking "for things that they could not understand," and their "blindness came by looking beyond the mark" (Jacob 4:14). In wanting to probe the mysteries that lie beyond their ability to comprehend, the Israelites will miss both God's wisdom over the ages and the miracle of his Son ministering in their own foreground. They will miss their Messiah, "the stone upon which they might build and have safe foundation" (Jacob 4:15).[1]

As I review my early notes about Jacob, I see that I, too, looked beyond the mark, seeking to find a characterization that fit my previous notions of the man. One of my notes reads like this: "We all know people like Jacob—wonderful, righteous, hardworking, thoroughly dependable—but not very relaxed, and not very tolerant." (How could I have missed his compassion?) Another note reads: "Sees himself as an authority figure." (How could I have missed his humble uncertainty?) But as I tried to write of Jacob in this way, the text kept deserting me. Thank goodness for the integrity of a text that simply would not tolerate the direction I was trying to take it. In returning to the book of Jacob still again, I have found a human being as well as a prophet, a man who repeatedly addresses future readers as "my beloved," a man wanting desperately to do well and fearful of doing ill, a man of tender feelings and a superabundant sense of responsibility for others.

I have also found a man of great rhetorical, intellectual, and spiritual gifts. Without question, Jacob could be mighty in speech when the occasion called for it, as evidenced in this injunction to

---

[1] I note that the text unconsciously uses the term "stone" rather than the accustomed biblical "rock," suggesting again the independence of the Book of Mormon translation.

his reader in some future day:

> Behold, will ye reject these words? Will ye reject the words of the prophets; and will ye reject all the words which have been spoken concerning Christ, after so many have spoken concerning him; and deny the good word of Christ, and the power of God, and the gift of the Holy Ghost, and quench the Holy Spirit, and make a mock of the great plan of redemption, which hath been laid for you? (Jacob 6:8)

Only one gifted in language would speak of "quenching" the Holy Spirit, and then two verses later subtly reinforce that figure by describing the flames of the lake of fire and brimstone ("which lake . . . is endless torment") as "unquenchable." Those who willfully quench the Spirit's fire will ultimately find a fire they cannot quench—the fire of hell.

In addition to his engravings on the plates reserved for religious matters, Jacob or others kept a rather extensive history of the Nephite people (see Jacob 7:26). Still, he represented only briefly his own religious discourses while quoting lengthily from Zenos and adding the story of a repentant Antichrist named Sherem. To the end, Jacob is both stirring and perplexing. The story of Sherem is the closest he comes to relating personal experience, for Sherem had sought out Jacob to dissuade him from belief in Christ. Sherem was a "learned" and cunning deceiver whose skill in language netted him considerable influence among the Nephites, and he addresses Jacob with feigned familiarity as "Brother Jacob" (Jacob 7:6). Jacob, however, who "truly had seen angels" and "had heard the voice of the Lord speaking unto me in very word, . . . could not be shaken" (Jacob 7:5). In fact, it is Sherem who is shaken. Jacob adds a few concluding paragraphs, admitting that overall his "writing has been small." His farewell, however, is not without charm: "Brethren, adieu" (Jacob 7:27).

## Concluding Books of the Small Plates

It is time for a few housekeeping matters. The next several sections of the Book of Mormon are very short, and the record passes

quickly through several hands. Nephi had turned the plates over
to his younger brother Jacob in 544 B.C., fifty-five years after
Lehi and his family left Jerusalem; thus the books of Jacob
through Omni span the years from 544 B.C. to anywhere from
279 B.C. to 130 B.C. Evidently, the plates Nephi prepared for
religious inscriptions were nearly filled by the time he finished his
own writings on them. Jacob's additions to the religious record on
the small plates of Nephi are not lengthy, and the writers who followed him wrote very briefly, some scarcely at all. With the books
of Enos, Jarom, and Omni, therefore, the exclusively religious
record ends; and the large plates of Nephi, heretofore devoted
mainly to secular history, combine religious and secular writings
in one record. Mormon explains all of this in an insert at the end
of the book of Omni.

Nephi's injunction to reserve the small plates for writings of
religious significance appears to have reached the ears of Jacob's
son, Enos, who received the record from his father. His book is
short, but it details an intensely spiritual experience, "the wrestle
which I had before God" (Enos 1:2). It is difficult to envision so
lengthy and fervent a prayer as Enos offers. While hunting in the
forest, he is filled with a desire to make his life right with God.
With hungering soul he kneels and cries to his Maker "in mighty
prayer and supplication," unceasingly "all the day long" and into
the night (Enos 1:4). Most of us do not have that kind of stamina,
being more disposed toward the failing suggested by the book title
*How to Pray and Stay Awake*. The difference between ordinary
prayers and the strenuous, soul-wrenching cries Enos utters is
apparent in phrases such as these:

> I did pour out my whole soul (Enos 1:9)
> while I was thus struggling in the spirit (Enos 1:10)
> I prayed unto him with many long strugglings (Enos 1:11)
> I . . . prayed and labored with all diligence (Enos 1:12)

Each of his requests is answered, but none more gratifyingly than
his prayer for his own soul:

> And there came a voice unto me, saying: Enos, thy sins are for-
> given thee, and thou shalt be blessed.
> And I, Enos, knew that God could not lie; wherefore, my guilt
> was swept away. (Enos 1:5-6)

The deeper we read into the Book of Mormon, the more we become conscious of pride as a distinct problem among the Nephites. From all appearances, nothing short of the direst threats of destruction kept them on course. Even though Enos reports that the Nephites were taught by "exceedingly many prophets" (Enos 1:22) and lived in a civilized manner, tilling the land and keeping domestic beasts rather than eating raw game as the Lamanites did at that time, they were, he says, a "stiffnecked peo- ple, hard to [make] understand" (Enos 1:22).

Given the people's propensity to disregard the law and the prophets, it is no surprise that Jarom, the son of Enos, would allude even in his short account to legal as well as divine ramifica- tions of violating religious statutes. First, Jarom begs off writing "the things of my prophesying" and "my revelations" on the grounds that those preceding him have already said it all. And then, while granting that many Nephites have kept the faith, Jarom finds it merciful of God not to have "swept" most of this bunch "off from the face of the land" (Jarom 1:3). Some stay in line, Jarom seems to suggest, because "the laws of the land were exceedingly strict" (Jarom 1:5). I'll bet they were. With the found- ing fathers gone and the attention of the people turning more and more toward worldly pleasures and riches, the inclination of an anxious leadership would be to tighten the reins on an increasingly slippery populace. Mormon's reading of King Benjamin's efforts to establish righteous peace confirms that strict enforcement of reli- gious laws was standard practice later on, too, for false prophets and teachers were "punished according to their *crimes*" (Words of Mormon 1:16; emphasis added).

In the beginning, the book of Omni serves mainly to identify a succession of record keepers. Jarom's son Omni, who confesses to being a good soldier but "a wicked man" (Omni 1:2), passes the record to his son Amaron, who delivers some rather startling news: ". . . the more wicked part of the Nephites were destroyed" (Omni 1:5) as the Lord had forewarned, presumably in warfare with the Lamanites. After noting that the righteous were spared, Amaron turns the record over to his brother Chemish, who merely testifies that he saw Amaron write in the record "with his own hand" before delivering it to Chemish. Chemish's son, Abinadom, also a warrior, declines to write more than a few words, indicating that another record is being kept and that "sufficient" (Omni 1:11) revelations and prophecies have already been written. But Abinadom's son, Amaleki, has something to say.

A precipitous event occurs while Amaleki superintends the record. Like Nephi several generations earlier, the Nephite prophet Mosiah receives a warning from the Lord that he and his righteous followers are to flee for safety from the land of Nephi into the wilderness. The Lord leads them into a land populated with another group of people, originally contemporaries of Lehi and Nephi, who had managed to escape from Jerusalem when the city was taken captive by Babylonia. These people have been dubbed Mulekites by modern readers, after Mulek, seemingly the only son of King Zedekiah known to have escaped the carnage. They call their land Zarahemla, after their leader.[2]

The reader's challenges are just beginning, for Amaleki also mentions a man named Coriantumr, the only survivor of still another group of people who crossed the sea to this land many centuries earlier—at the time of the tower of Babel. Mosiah, Amaleki says, interpreted a set of engravings on "a large stone," engravings which "gave an account of one Coriantumr, and the slain of his people" (Omni 1:20-21), the Jaredites. This same Coriantumr was found by the people of Zarahemla, and he "dwelt with them for the space of nine moons" (Omni 1:21). Amaleki

---

[2] Many escaped into surrounding countries during this siege. Some scholars have suggested that since the Phoenicians were able seamen, this particular group might have engaged Phoenician vessels and sailors for their voyage. Mulek would have been only a child at the time. See John L. Sorenson, "The 'Mulekites,'" *Brigham Young University Studies* 30 (Summer 1990):6-22.

also tells of Nephite expeditions back to the home area evacuated by Mosiah and his followers, but I will save that for later discussion.

For now, let it be said that Mosiah and his group join with the Mulekites, teaching them the language that the Mulekites had lost because they had not brought records with them. The Nephite immigrant Mosiah is made king over the combined peoples, who hereafter call themselves Nephites, although their center of governance is the Mulekite city of Zarahemla. It appears that the Mulekites, who readily adopt the Nephite name and traditions, as well as the Nephite prophet, were hungry for both spiritual and political leadership. Mosiah is eventually succeeded by his righteous and extraordinary son, Benjamin. A childless Amaleki passes the small plates bearing the religious record to King Benjamin who, Mormon says, "put them with the other plates, which contained records which had been handed down by the kings" (Words of Mormon 1:10), the latter being the historical records on the large plates of Nephi.

Mormon explains in his insert that he came across this batch of small plates after he had prepared his abridgment of the large plates. Finding the contents of the religious record "pleasing" (Words of Mormon 1:4), he chose to combine "this small account of the prophets, from Jacob down to the reign of this king Benjamin, and also many of the words of Nephi" (Words of Mormon 1:3) with the record he was preparing. Mormon's actual abridgment, then, begins with the book of Mosiah.

## 8

## Mosiah 1-6: Benjamin, a Righteous King

The book of Omni serves well as a prelude to the opening chapters of the book of Mosiah, chapters which focus on the princely King Benjamin and his teachings. Once King Benjamin, by applying "all the might of his body and faculty of his whole soul" (Words of Mormon 1:18), has soundly defeated the Lamanites in battle and rid the land of false teachers and false Christs, his reign is a peaceful and fruitful one. With the priceless brass plates now in their possession, the people of Zarahemla relearn the language and wisdom of their fathers. The quality of the man Benjamin is obvious in his stirring address to the people of Zarahemla. We have little else of Benjamin, but that address is proof enough that he was a splendid ruler and human being.

The time is approximately 124 B.C., 476 years after Lehi left Jerusalem. Benjamin is growing old and wishes to appoint his son, the second Mosiah, to succeed him as king. Desiring also to give his people counsel and a distinguishing "name that shall never be blotted out, except it be through transgression" (Mosiah 1:11-12), he calls them together in a vast outdoor congregation. Like Nephi before him, and possibly the first Mosiah too, Benjamin is a mighty prophet-monarch, possessed of a magnificent heart and a penetrating mind. His opening statement, which is enhanced by crisp monosyllables and repeated parallel structures, demonstrates his gift for sturdy, yet pliable prose:

> . . . I have not commanded you to come up hither to trifle with the words which I shall speak, but that you should hearken unto me, and open your ears that ye may hear, and your hearts that ye may understand, and your minds that the mysteries of God may be unfolded to your view. (Mosiah 2:9)

The repetitions build in steps as Benjamin asks that his people listen first to hear his words, second to understand their meaning, and third to recognize their eternal significance.

This address has unusual importance because it is Benjamin's final message to his people and represents the accumulated wisdom of his years. I scramble for adjectives sufficient to describe Benjamin. Words like "serene," "wise," "large-hearted," "noble," and "generous" come to mind, but even in concert they do not fully comprehend the man. It occurs to me that Benjamin's own assessment of his role anticipates revered Renaissance concepts of the divinely appointed magistrate, the ideal prince, or king. Although few of Shakespeare's historical models exemplified that ideal, his audience knew what it was and measured their theatrical monarchs by its code. Shakespearean scholar Hardin Craig articulates the ideal in his description of the great dramatist's character, Henry V. Craig praises Henry as a "prudent and conscientious" ruler, one in whom "the duties of kingship and not its frivolities" are manifest. Henry is "just and unflinching in the enforcement of law and discipline. He is a man of most pronounced devotion to great objects outside of himself, modest, humble, honest, religious, sympathetic with all classes of men. . . ."

The description fits King Benjamin as well as it fits Henry. Craig points out that behind these traits is "the most important theme in the social and political thinking of the Renaissance, namely, the ideal prince." Magistrates, Craig continues, were expected to uphold a high "standard of righteousness."[1] During the Renaissance, educated people made a study of statesmanship, and one of the most influential books of the time, Sir Thomas Elyot's *The Governour* (1531), taught the ideal. More familiar, perhaps, is Machiavelli's opposite, self-serving prototype in *The Prince*. Elyot's list of the virtues that characterize the noble governor or magistrate—benevolence, justice, faith, fortitude, patience,

---

[1] Hardin Craig, ed., *The Complete Works of Shakespeare* (Chicago: Scott, Foresman and Company, 1961, p. 738).

courage, continence, sapience (wisdom), understanding (intelligence)—could well be applied to King Benjamin.

With modesty and humility, though certainly also with intent to instruct publicly the son who will succeed him, Benjamin verbalizes his philosophy of kingly governance. Justice and service, not personal gain, have been his object; for a king, though only human, "like as yourselves" (Mosiah 2:11), is a paradigm of service to constituents who should likewise "labor to serve one another" (Mosiah 2:18). Then Benjamin adroitly shifts from the matter of temporal king and kingdom to the more salient matter of heavenly king and kingdom, and from the somewhat temporal matter of service to the more spiritual matter of gratitude and obedience. If you owe me thanks for my service, he reasons, how much more thanks do you owe to "your heavenly King" (Mosiah 2:19). Perhaps his advanced years have made Benjamin singularly conscious of physical weakness and human powerlessness. He repeatedly reminds his people that they are "eternally indebted" to God, who "lends" them the very breath by which they live (Mosiah 2:34, 21), whether they be kings or subjects of kings.

Following his opening remarks and counsel, Benjamin offers insight on several doctrinal matters, the first being the soul's consignment to hell. Benjamin teaches that sin presupposes knowledge, and that the sinner elects his own hellish fate, voluntarily withdrawing from the Spirit in this life and the next. The unrepentant person who makes willful choices for evil "contrary to his own knowledge" of God's law, "drinketh damnation to his own soul" (Mosiah 2:33). It is the knowing that makes a mortal liable, and it is transgressing despite the knowing that drives a person away from God. Benjamin also gives significant new meaning to the proverbial lake of fire and brimstone traditionally seen as hell. The torment he pictures is not environmental, but internal; and the guilty soul, unable to bear the proximity of God, removes itself from his presence. Returning to this point a little later, Benjamin describes consignment to hell as the enacted realization of one's personal "guilt and abominations," a realization that drives one to "shrink" from the Lord's presence. He speaks of fire and brimstone not as a physical phenomenon, but as a figure of speech, a simile, to depict the torment of lost souls: "And their torment *is as* a lake of fire and brimstone, whose flames are unquenchable, and whose smoke ascendeth up forever and ever" (Mosiah 3:25,27; emphasis added).

The end of chapter two marks a natural division in Benjamin's address as he turns to his principal subject, a subject rather different from the central concerns of his great predecessor, Nephi. Although Nephi had seen and brilliantly described a vision of the Messiah, and would later teach of Christ with great power, most of his earlier prophetic utterances were strongly influenced by his inescapable ties to Jerusalem, the home of his youth, and to prophecies of its impending destruction. His father Lehi and the brass plates, which contained numerous warnings to Jerusalem and prophecies of Israel's scattering and gathering, were Nephi's schoolmasters. Benjamin, on the other hand, follows Nephi by several centuries. He is a citizen of the new world, and of Zarahemla, and he has no personal memory of Jerusalem and its prophets. He is familiar with the contents of the brass plates and values them highly, but their influence on him is less pronounced than it had been on the castaways Nephi and Jacob. When Benjamin prophesies in his farewell address, it is not of Jerusalem and Israel but of the subject of Nephi's vision—the Savior's impending birth and ministry.

Nearly all of chapter 3 repeats "the glad tidings of great joy" (Mosiah 3:3) delivered to Benjamin by an angel. Those joyful tidings proclaim the redemptive miracle of the Savior's atoning sacrifice. The concern here, as in Benjamin's earlier statement on the matter, is not with redemption from physical death, which applies universally through the power of the resurrection. Rather, the concern is with redemption from spiritual death, which requires repentance and obedience from those who know the law. Peter speaks of the unconverted being taught the gospel in spirit prison, and Joseph F. Smith saw a vision clarifying Peter's statement (see 1 Peter 3:18-20; Doctrine and Covenants 138). But the angel and Benjamin teach that the truly believing and repentant need not enter spirit prison at all. The remission of sins can occur in mortality. Even those who precede the Savior may know him through the teachings of prophets and thereby "receive remission of their sins, and rejoice with exceedingly great joy, even as though he had already come among them" (Mosiah 3:13).

The miracle of redemption unfolds before our eyes as we read of the transformation of King Benjamin's people. Pierced to the soul by the ineffable truths they have heard, and having "viewed themselves in their own carnal state" (Mosiah 4:2), this great multitude, as a body, surrender the natural being and humble themselves before God. They sink to the earth, crying in one voice,

> O have mercy, and apply the atoning blood of Christ that we may receive forgiveness of our sins, and our hearts may be purified; for we believe in Jesus Christ, the Son of God, who created heaven and earth, and all things; who shall come down among the children of men. (Mosiah 4:2)

Heaven's glad response is on record:

> . . . after they had spoken these words the Spirit of the Lord came upon them, and they were filled with joy, having received a remission of their sins, and having peace of conscience, because of the exceeding faith which they had in Jesus Christ who should come. . . . (Mosiah 4:3)

Benjamin stresses the role of humility in such a transformation, the recognition of one's fallen state and one's dependence upon God's goodness and power and wisdom. The redemptive transformation itself, and a continuing remission of sins, however, require unwavering belief in God and all that such belief entails. Verse 9 of Mosiah 4 states it bluntly—"Believe in God"—and each succeeding explanatory injunction carries an implicit antecedent: To believe in God is to. . . . Reading the injunctions with that antecedent clarifies what belief means:

> (To believe in God is to) believe that he is, and that he created all things, both in heaven and in earth;

(To believe in God is to) believe that he has all wisdom, and all power, both in heaven and in earth;

(To believe in God is to) believe that man doth not comprehend all the things which the Lord can comprehend;

(To believe in God is to) believe that ye must repent of your sins and forsake them, and humble yourselves before God; and ask in sincerity of heart that he would forgive you. (Mosiah 4:9-10)

Benjamin sums it up: Believing in God is "com[ing] to the knowledge of the glory of God." True belief, then, is a good deal more than mere acknowledgment that God exists. Benjamin eloquently urges his people to

retain in remembrance, the greatness of God, and your own nothingness, and his goodness and long-suffering towards you, unworthy creatures, and humble yourselves even in the depths of humility, calling on the name of the Lord daily, and standing steadfastly in the faith of that which is to come. . . . (Mosiah 4:11)

I see nothing here to suggest that we should spend much energy pursuing an elevated self-image.

Humility, paradoxically, leads to exalted joy in this life and the next. The very antithesis of self-aggrandizement, humility is the key to "always retain[ing] a remission of your sins" and to growing "in the knowledge of the glory of him that created you" (Mosiah 4:12). According to Benjamin, other virtues naturally follow humility. For example, the humble "will not have a mind to injure one another, but to live peaceably" (Mosiah 4:13). Furthermore, they will care for their children and teach them not to "transgress the laws of God," and to "love . . . and to serve one another" rather than to "fight and quarrel" (Mosiah 4:14-15).

This admonition leads Benjamin to another subject: the obligation to give succor and sustenance to the needy. This is his last word of counsel, and it comprises the final fifteen verses of Mosiah 4. Enjoining his hearers not to turn the beggar out, Benjamin warns them against the self-justifying excuse that the poor and afflicted have earned their misfortune. I hear the same rationalizations today, particularly from those who oppose public assistance to the homeless or jobless. We have, I think, little personal responsibility for the honesty and motives of those who seek help, but we have considerable responsibility for what is in our own hearts. If others lack integrity, that is their problem; but if we lack charity, that is our problem. The person who argues that the disadvantaged have brought their woes on themselves, Benjamin declares, "hath great cause to repent." If he fails to repent, "he perisheth forever" (Mosiah 4:18).

That is strong language, and Benjamin means every word. He follows it with a truth that cuts to the quick: "For behold, are we not all beggars? Do we not all depend upon the same Being, even God, for all the substance which we have. . . .?" (Mosiah 4:19). Benjamin reminds his people that even now they have been calling on God, "begging for a remission of your sins," and that God has not "suffered that ye have begged in vain" (Mosiah 4:20). With impeccable logic, he then delivers the clincher:

> And now, if God, who has created you, on whom you are dependent for your lives and for all that ye have and are, doth grant unto you whatsoever ye ask that is right, in faith, believing that ye shall receive, O then, how ye ought to impart of the substance that ye have one to another. (Mosiah 4:21)

I suspect, too, that in one sense multiplying our talents (as in the parable) means neither hoarding our wealth nor seeking to increase it mainly for our own comfort and indulgence—which is the same as hoarding—but multiplying its beneficial effects among a great many people. Like Benjamin, the parable also reminds us that our talents, including our wealth, are the Master's and not ours in the first place.

Then Benjamin makes an explicit and perhaps unexpected connection between giving sustenance to the poor and retaining a remission of sins: "And now, . . . for the sake of retaining a remission of your sins from day to day, that ye may walk guiltless before God—I would that ye should impart of your substance to the poor, every man according to that which he hath. . . ."[2] This is not a connection most of us would readily make, but Benjamin clearly specifies what is required, mentioning spiritual succor as well as temporal—"feeding the hungry, clothing the naked, visiting the sick and administering to their relief, both spiritually and temporally" (Mosiah 4:26).

Finally, lest any mistake his intent, Benjamin cautions his people to perform their charitable service "in wisdom and order; for it is not requisite that a man should run faster than he has strength" (Mosiah 4:27). Always, he is the wise governor, the ideal king, cautioning against excess and imprudence at the same time that he urges to good works. Few of us, I suspect, err in the direction of excessive charity. In his closing words, which are to the point and yet all-inclusive, Benjamin warns the people that only faith, right action, and obedience will sustain them.

The next chapter (chapter 5) of the book of Mosiah recounts one of the choice moments in Book of Mormon history. It is a moment to savor, to read again and again. King Benjamin's people have been deeply touched by his counsel and by the Spirit of the Lord, through which he has spoken to them. At the conclusion of his address, when he sends among them to learn if they have believed his words, they respond in jubilant chorus, confirming that they have cast off the natural being and have indeed become saints through the atonement of Jesus Christ. In their joyous shout we see the possibility for ourselves:

> And they all cried with one voice, saying: Yea, we believe all the words which thou hast spoken unto us; and also, we know of their surety and truth, because of the Spirit of the Lord Omnipotent, which has wrought a mighty change in us, or in our hearts, that we have no more disposition to do evil, but to do good continually. (Mosiah 5:2)

---

[2] Paul makes a similar connection between caring for the needy and retaining a remission of sins in his second epistle to the Corinthians: "...he [the cheerful giver] hath given to the poor: his righteousness remaineth for ever" (9:9).

Here is a documented manifestation of the redeeming miracle—the great change of heart which may be the loveliest, sweetest, most moving experience an ordinary mortal can know, an experience felt physically as well as emotionally and spiritually. It is the quintessential human drama, since time immemorial the story at the very core of the world's most enduring literature. Charles Dickens' beloved old Scrooge is only one of countless mortals, real and imaginary, who have gained regenerative insight into their own souls. The happy truth at the root of human experience, the wellspring of faith and hope—and yes, of charity too, as Benjamin suggested earlier—is that self-knowledge and blessed change are possible, that mortal mistakes need not drag us into hopeless despair. The Savior has paid the price and met the demands of justice, if we but humble ourselves in true repentance and ask the Father's forgiveness.

The joy King Benjamin's people feel is an expression of the spiritual rejuvenation that accompanies a mighty change of heart. In their gladness and faith they covenant to obey the Lord the rest of their lives, and in Benjamin's gladness at their response he proclaims their rebirth as Christ's offspring:

> And now, because of the covenant which ye have made ye shall be called the children of Christ, his sons, and his daughters; for behold, this day he hath spiritually begotten you; for ye say that your hearts are changed through faith on his name; therefore, ye are born of him and have become his sons and his daughters. (Mosiah 5:7)

Benjamin now asks his people to do one more, very important thing: ". . . take upon you the name of Christ" (Mosiah 5:8). Emphasizing repeatedly the importance of Christ's spiritual children bearing his name, Benjamin exhorts his people "to retain the name written always in your hearts" so that "ye hear and know the voice by which ye shall be called, and also, the name by which he shall call you" (Mosiah 5:12). Given the significance Benjamin attaches to calling the faithful by the name of Christ, it is not surprising that some members of The Church of Jesus Christ of

Latter-day Saints prefer to be known by that full title and not by abbreviations.

Chapter 6 of Mosiah is a brief transitional interlude. It informs the reader that Benjamin recorded "the names of all those who had entered into a covenant with God to keep his commandments" (Mosiah 6:1), and that "there was not one soul, except it were little children" (Mosiah 6:2), who did not make that covenant. Benjamin also "consecrated his son Mosiah to be a ruler and a king over his people" and "appointed priests to teach" them (Mosiah 6:3).

Benjamin died three years later, we are told, and Mosiah was a good and righteous king. Like his father, he worked for his living, "that thereby he might not become burdensome to his people" (Mosiah 6:7). There was no ruffling of the peace for three years.

## 9

# Mosiah 7-17: The Zeniff Record and Abinadi's Faith

The next chapters of Mosiah introduce chronological and logistical complications into the record, largely because of population movements and a variety of settlements that grew into nations. The second Mosiah, grandson of the first Mosiah and son of King Benjamin, is now the principal keeper of the main record on the large plates of Nephi (the small plates are full). Occasionally, however, more than one record keeper prepared an account of the same events; and when Mormon chooses to include supplementary accounts and summaries in his abridgment, the record doubles back on itself. Even if there were no other evidence for the authenticity of the Book of Mormon, the intricacies of these chapters should convince the most skeptical of readers. A narrative jumbled this way would tax even an accomplished fictionist, and a literary novice like Joseph Smith would have been lost before he began. If at the very least these ancient people had remained stationary, Mormon's task would have been simpler, too.

We have already witnessed two migrations—Nephi's and Mosiah's—since the Lehite settlement in the new world; we have been introduced to the fact that an earlier civilization has flourished and expired in this same new world; and we have learned of a heretofore unknown but contemporary civilization in a land called Zarahemla. We also learned from Amaleki, in the book of Omni, that in time a group of the most recent Nephite immigrants left Zarahemla in the hope of repossessing their homeland. Their story, which is told in the record of Zeniff, their leader, comprises chapters 9 through 22 of the book of Mosiah. The last part of their narrative, however, overlaps the history being kept by the second Mosiah. Thus the Zeniff record breaks the main chronological thread, but it clarifies matters Amaleki had mentioned earlier.

I am picking up the story in Zarahemla, some years after Zeniff and his group have set out for Lehi-Nephi. Quite predictably, as time passes a number of those who remain begin to wonder what has become of Zeniff and his people. "They wearied" King Mosiah (Mosiah II) "with their teasings" (Mosiah 7:1) to the point that he allows sixteen strong men, under the able leadership of Ammon, to go in search of them. (This Ammon is not to be confused with the later Ammon who is instrumental in the great conversion of the Lamanite nation). After wandering in the wilderness for many days, they find the people they seek, but are brought captive before a wary King Limhi, grandson of Zeniff. Limhi rejoices when he learns who they are, for he and his people are in bondage to the Lamanite king, and Limhi hopes that his Nephite brethren will deliver them. Still another adventure entangles the narrative when Limhi indicates that earlier he had sent a group to seek help from Zarahemla. Missing Zarahemla, these explorers had stumbled onto the ruins of the much older Jaredite civilization, in the homeland of Coriantumr, its last survivor.

As if matters were not confusing enough, the Book of Mormon presents three different accounts of the expedition (actually there were two expeditions; the first aborted) initiated by Zeniff, and three different portrayals of the man Zeniff. The three provide an interesting study in point of view. The first account is by Amaleki, who seems bitter toward Zeniff, perhaps understandably so, because his brother disappeared in the Zeniff venture. Amaleki describes Zeniff as "a strong and mighty man," but also "a stiffnecked man" who "caused a contention" among the first group to leave Zarahemla (see Omni 1:28). In fact, Amaleki reports, all but fifty were slain in the fray, and those fifty returned to Zarahemla. There they organized a new party and set out again for Lehi-Nephi. Amaleki would fault a prideful Zeniff and blame him for provoking the quarrel that led to bloody civil strife.

The second account is that of Zeniff's grandson, King Limhi. We might expect him to bias his report in Zeniff's favor, but he remains quite neutral. According to Limhi, Zeniff was "over-zealous to inherit the land of his fathers," and I suspect that over-zealousness made him vulnerable to "the cunning and craftiness of king Laman."[1] The guileful Laman, Limhi says, had yielded land to the settlers "for the sole purpose of bringing this people into subjection or into bondage" (Mosiah 7:21-22).

The third account is that of Zeniff himself. From Zeniff's record (see Mosiah 9), it appears that the first group included a sizeable company of armed men who made an encampment in the wilderness. As Zeniff tells it, he was not the highest authority of the group, nor did he wrongfully cause friction among his comrades. In any case, when Zeniff endeavors to "spy out" the Lamanite forces, he sees enough "good among them" (Mosiah 9:1) that he changes his mind about destroying them. On this point, Zeniff says, "I contended with my brethren in the wilderness, for I would that our ruler should make a treaty with them; but he being an austere and a blood-thirsty man commanded that I should be slain." Zeniff then describes his rescue from a bloody internal battle, a sad affair in which "father fought against father, and brother against brother, until the greater number of our army was destroyed in the wilderness." The survivors returned to Zarahemla "to relate that tale" to the widows and children of the slain (Mosiah 9:2). This considerable setback did not deter Zeniff from his original purpose, however, and he set out again. Zeniff exonerates himself on the grounds that his benevolence toward the Lamanites led his own spiteful commander to order his death and precipitate mutiny among the troops.

All biases aside, it appears that once Zeniff was established in his ancestral homeland, he ruled in righteousness. His ill-advised treaty with King Laman to acquire land brought bondage, but still his people are said to have fought victoriously, numerous times, against the dissembling Laman and the son who succeeded him.

---

[1] It seems that the Lamanites took the name Laman for their kings just as the Nephites initially took the name Nephi for theirs, both after their first leaders.

Zeniff's people attribute their success in repelling forces much greater than their own to their reliance on the Lord. Making a treaty with King Laman was not Zeniff's only mistake, however; in his old age, he also conferred the kingdom on his wicked and worthless son Noah. Under the influence of a corrupt magistrate, the whole complexion of a people can change with amazing speed. Noah dismissed the righteous priests who had served under his father and appointed others who resembled himself—proud, lazy, greedy, lecherous, and idolatrous. Furthermore, Noah began to exact a heavy tax from his people, many of whom responded by copying him in apostasy and infamy.

It strikes me that the reign of King Noah stands in dramatic contrast to the administration of the righteous King Benjamin. In just a few short years the Zerahemla counterparts of these debased people would experience, under Benjamin, a great change of heart and a spiritual rebirth as children of Christ. And only recently, these very people had worshiped the Lord and defended their homes and flocks in his might. Nevertheless, out of the materialism and corruption of Noah's reign emerges a mighty prophet who will revive an old strand of faith and nourish a new line of great prophets. Faith can erode, but opposition to that erosion can beget new faith.

The mighty prophet who challenges Noah a century and a half before Christ, and pays for that challenge with his life, is Abinadi. He incurs Noah's wrath by preaching repentance and warning Noah's people that failure to repent will deliver them into the hands of their enemies. Incensed, Noah seeks to slay Abinadi, but Abinadi disappears, only to return in disguise two years later. Abinadi foretells a fiery death for King Noah, declaring cryptically that his life "shall be valued even as a garment in a hot furnace" (Mosiah 12:3).

So blind are Noah's people to their own corruptness that upon capturing Abinadi, they incredulously ask the king "what great evil" Noah has done, "or what great sins" they themselves have committed that would earn them God's condemnation or Abinadi's censure (Mosiah 12:13). Noah's priests seek to question

Abinadi "that they might cross him, that thereby they might have wherewith to accuse him" (Mosiah 12:19). But Abinadi turns the tables, confounding his accusers with their own questions. Then he delivers a memorable sermon, teaching these self-proclaimed adherents to the Law of Moses what they should have known already. In devastating reproach, he testifies to those who falsely pretend to speak and act for God. Abinadi is a figure who grabs the imagination, a lone man fearlessly challenging a corrupt king and his council of degenerate priests.

Thinking to trick Abinadi with an unanswerable question and thereby to discredit his prophetic claim, the priests ask him the meaning of a particular passage from Isaiah. The passage they cite, a lyrical proclamation of Israel's redemption at the Savior's second coming (Isaiah 52:7-10), begins, "How beautiful upon the mountains are the feet of him that bringeth good tidings; that publisheth peace" (Mosiah 12:21). Abinadi responds by taking the offensive, turning the question meant to confuse and discredit him into a pointed accusation: "Are you priests," he charges, "and pretend to teach this people, and to understand the spirit of prophesying, and yet desire to know of me what these things mean?" (Mosiah 12:25). Having caught his pompous accusers off guard, Abinadi follows his advantage relentlessly. They are supposed to be scriptural authorities, but they are ignorant of what they profess to teach. "Ye have not applied your hearts to understanding," Abinadi charges; "Therefore, what teach ye this people?" (Mosiah 12:26-27).

Abinadi's definition of wisdom as an engagement of the heart that reaches beyond knowledge to understanding offers an exceptional insight—one which Noah's priests probably miss entirely. So disconcerted are they by Abinadi's volley of reproach that they not only allow the question, but offer a defensive reply: "We teach the law of Moses" (Mosiah 12:28). Their response ensnares them in their own trap, for Abinadi then counters with a condemning question: "If ye teach the law of Moses why do ye not keep it?" He then presses his advantage with rapid-fire accusing questions: "Why do ye set your hearts upon riches? Why do ye commit whoredoms and spend your strength with harlots, yea, and cause this people to commit sin, that the Lord has cause to send me to prophesy against this people. . . ?" (Mosiah 12:29). Abinadi says, in effect, it is your wickedness that brings me here. Astutely keeping his questioners off-balance, he asks a question, then answers it before they can speak.

Never relinquishing his advantage, Abinadi challenges the priests' insupportable claim: ". . . ye have said that ye teach the law of Moses. And what know ye concerning the law of Moses? Doth salvation come by the law of Moses?" He prods them for an answer, and their response provides the opening he seeks: ". . . they answered and said that salvation did come by the law of Moses" (Mosiah 12:32). Having netted his prey, Abinadi prepares to instruct them as to the true source of salvation—and it is *not* the Law of Moses. He judiciously grants that, yes, the priests will be saved if they "keep the commandments which the Lord delivered unto Moses in the mount of Sinai" (Mosiah 12:33); and then he begins to recite these commandments to allow the priests' own doctrine to condemn them.

At this point, King Noah collects his wits and interrupts Abinadi, ordering that the madman be removed. In full control, Abinadi calmly informs the court that God will protect him until he finishes his message. Knowing that ultimately he will be executed for his faith, Abinadi warns his captors that his death will foreshadow another: ". . . what you do with me, after this, shall be as a type and a shadow of things which are to come" (Mosiah 13:10). The prophecy is fulfilled in Abinadi's martyrdom and King Noah's death, both by fire.

With his captors still at bay, Abinadi returns to Exodus 20 and recites the ten commandments delivered on Mount Sinai. Rereading these as Abinadi quotes them (Mosiah 12:35-36; 13:12-24), I realize that all ten given to Moses are encompassed in the two great commandments taught by Jesus: love of the Lord and love of neighbor (see Matthew 22:36-40; Luke 10:27-28). Commandments one through four of the Decalogue pertain to love of God:

Thou shalt have no other God before me.
Thou shalt not make unto thee any graven image.
Thou shalt not take the name of the Lord thy God in vain.
Remember the Sabbath day, to keep it holy.

Commandments five through ten pertain to love of fellow beings:

Honor thy father and thy mother.
Thou shalt not kill.
Thou shalt not commit adultery.
Thou shalt not steal.
Thou shalt not bear false witness against thy neighbor.
Thou shalt not covet.

Having exposed the priests' ignorance of the law they profess to obey and teach, Abinadi addresses their assumption that "salvation cometh by the law of Moses." The law is to be kept "as yet," he says, but "the time shall come when it shall no more be expedient to keep the law of Moses" (Mosiah 13:27). If that statement elicited surprise in the king's court, the next one probably produced audible gasps:

> And moreover, I say unto you, that salvation doth not come by the law alone; and were it not for the atonement, which God himself shall make for the sins and iniquities of his people, that they must unavoidably perish, notwithstanding the law of Moses. (Mosiah 13:28)

Abinadi knows why the Lord gave the children of Israel the Law of Moses rather than the full gospel of atonement. That flock of spiritual adolescents required a strict law of daily "performances and of ordinances" which would "keep them in remembrance of God and their duty towards him" (Mosiah 13:30). These "performances" and "ordinances" were not the actual means of salvation, but were "types" of the fulfilling gospel to be brought through a Messiah (Mosiah 13:31). I have not looked at the specific details of the law in that way before. And obviously, neither have Noah and his priests; they understand neither the law nor what it typified.

Approaching the crux of his impromptu sermon, through a channel opened inadvertently by the priests themselves, Abinadi reminds these apostates that the very Moses whom they profess to teach prophesied the Messiah's coming and the redemption of his people. After expounding on that point, Abinadi repeats the poetic and deeply moving Messianic prophecy recorded in Isaiah 53 (see Mosiah 14), thus enlisting both Moses and Isaiah from the priests' own scriptures to testify of the Savior.

Abinadi explains first that in an important sense, Christ can be considered as both Father and Son. For Christ, having been "conceived by the power of God," is a God and is thus a Father in relation to earth; but as Son "he dwelleth in the flesh," and the flesh is "subjected . . . to the will of the Father" (Mosiah 15:2-3). Abinadi next discourses on the Savior's mission, speaking of the redemption in the past tense just as Nephi, who had seen the future in vision, sometimes did. Even though Christ has not yet appeared in the flesh, Abinadi knows that the redemption "was prepared from the foundation of the world" (Mosiah 15:19); it must have seemed to him and other prophets an accomplished fact.

If Noah's priests have supposed that by this time Abinadi has forgotten their first question concerning the publishers of peace celebrated by Isaiah, they are mistaken. He now astutely connects his exposition on the Savior's atonement to that very matter. Christ's "seed" (Mosiah 15:10), that is, those who have heeded the words of his prophets, are the ones "for whom he has died" (Mosiah 15:12). And those prophets, Abinadi continues, "are they who have published peace, who have brought good tidings of good, who have published salvation" (Mosiah 15:14) wrought by "the founder of peace, yea, even the Lord" (Mosiah 15:18). An exultant Abinadi cries out, "And O how beautiful upon the mountains were their feet!" (Mosiah 15:15) He repeats the phrase again and again, applying it to prophets past, present, and future. And thus Abinadi fuses all the threads of his discourse, attaching his accusers' questions and comments to the subject of primary importance to their souls: resurrection from death and redemption from sin through Christ's atoning sacrifice.

Still undaunted, Abinadi advances to a more detailed analysis of his subject, explaining that there is to be a first resurrection of the righteous. Among them will be individuals who preceded the Messiah on earth or who died in ignorance of the law, including little children. (See Alma 40:15ff for further clarification of this doctrine.) Then, he shifts cleverly to Isaiah's prophecy of the last days and the Savior's second coming, a prophecy related to the passage that the priests had put to him for explication. Abinadi prophesies that "the time shall come that the salvation of the Lord shall be declared to every nation, kindred, tongue, and people" (Mosiah 15:28), a publishing of peace, indeed, as Isaiah had foretold. Thus Abinadi has brought his interrogators back to their initial question. But he is not through with them yet.

After teaching the doctrine of the first resurrection, Abinadi concludes with a powerful discourse on the general resurrection that is to occur after the Savior's second coming. All nations will then know who he is, and all people will be resurrected from temporal death to face judgment. The good will go "to the resurrection of endless life and happiness," the evil "to the resurrection of endless damnation, being delivered up to the devil, who hath subjected them, which is damnation" (Mosiah 16:11). I want to pause for just a moment on that last statement. Abinadi defines damnation as an individual's being handed over to the devil, by right of that individual's denial of mercy and mortal choice for subjection to the father of lies. The devil is not the chooser; he is merely the tempter and the welcoming committee.

If the priests have failed to catch Abinadi's very pointed warning, he makes it plain in summary, his words circling deftly back to his early subject: "Therefore, if ye teach the law of Moses, also teach that it is a shadow of those things which are to come" (Mosiah 16:14). And his final words encapsulate his whole purpose: "Teach them that redemption cometh through Christ the Lord, who is the very Eternal Father. Amen" (Mosiah 16:15). His closing "Amen" attests that Abinadi has delivered these words in the earnestness of sermon, prophecy, and prayer, as a testimony that would stand against his captors and executioners at the bar of judgment. He refuses to recall his words, and King Noah falteringly pronounces a death sentence upon him. Abinadi is executed, and as the flames scorch his body he again prophesies afflictions, terror, and bondage for Noah and his seed, and death by fire for Noah himself.

If it seems that Abinadi's sermon and testimony go for naught, except to witness against his executioners, it is important to recognize that among the priests who heard him speak was one who believed what he said. From this one man would spring a revival of belief among Noah's people, the escape of the righteous to Zarahemla, and a son who would become one of the mightiest prophets in Nephite history. This man who sat in Noah's court was named Alma, and he was a descendant of Nephi. He pled in vain with the king to release Abinadi, and then had to flee for his own life. During the days when he was in hiding, Alma "did write all the words which Abinadi had spoken" (Mosiah 17:4). If he had not, we would have missed one of the Book of Mormon's finest discourses.

## 10

## Mosiah 18-29: The Two Almas

The next seven chapters of Mosiah, chapters 18-24, are jam-packed and rather fast-paced. In the main, though still part of the record of Zeniff, they recount an assortment of battles, schemes, and migrations, as well as the workings of the Lord among the Nephite colonists in Lamanite territory. The high point of these chapters is the emergence of Alma and the newfound faith of the people who follow him into hiding. He is an extraordinary man, repentant for his years of blindness, selfless in teaching his people, stalwart in the faith. The description of the glorious moment when Alma seeks and receives authority from God to establish a church and perform baptisms is so vivid that the reader becomes almost a firsthand witness. Accompanied by the faithful Helam, Alma enters the water and cries, "O Lord, pour out thy Spirit upon thy servant, that he may do this work with holiness of heart" (Mosiah 18:12). Divine response is immediate:

> . . . when he had said these words, the Spirit of the Lord was upon him, and he said: Helam, I baptize thee, having authority from the Almighty God, as a testimony that ye have entered into a covenant to serve him until you are dead as to the mortal body; and may the Spirit of the Lord be poured out upon you; and may he grant unto you eternal life, through the redemption of Christ, whom he has prepared from the foundation of the world. (Mosiah 18:13)

After Alma speaks these stirring words, both Helam and he "were buried in the water; and they arose and came forth out of the water rejoicing, being filled with the Spirit" (Mosiah 18:14). Alma submerges in the water to accomplish his own baptism. Then he proceeds to baptize the others, on that occasion "about two hundred and four souls; yea, and they were baptized in the waters of

Mormon, and were filled with the grace of God" (Mosiah 18:16).

Alma is meticulous about the matter of divine authority. Since there is no mortal in the area who can bestow it upon him, he asks that it be conferred directly from God. Later, John the Baptist would receive authority the same way, and as a resurrected being he would confer that authority on Joseph Smith and his associate, Oliver Cowdery. Once Alma has received authority to perform holy ordinances, he can ordain others to assist him in baptizing and teaching his people. I note that the baptisms are performed by immersion in water, just as the baptism of Jesus would be by immersion, to typify burial in death and ascent from the grave in resurrection. Later, Jesus himself would teach the Nephites the new baptismal and sacramental prayers they were to use, prayers that would reflect the fact that his atoning sacrifice had been accomplished.

In all, chapter 18 of the book of Mosiah is a lovely little interlude in the chaos of conflict, hardship, and flight. For a brief moment, the small company who elude Noah and follow Alma find rich spiritual sustenance and happiness. Expounding on the oneness that must distinguish the faithful, Alma teaches them the doctrines of resurrection, redemption, and the Sabbath day; and he teaches them to love and care for one another. Significantly, "of their own free will and good desires toward God," these people practice the law of consecration, sharing their material substance, according to their abundance, with "every needy, naked soul" (Mosiah 18:28). Their priests also labor for their own sustenance. Thus, for perhaps as long as two years, Alma's people live in a blessed society, an oasis of peace. Perhaps taking a celebratory cue from the original keeper of the record, Mormon sums up this gratifying experience in lilting language:

> . . . all this was done in Mormon, yea, by the waters of Mormon, in the forest that was near the waters of Mormon; yea, the place of Mormon, the waters of Mormon, the forest of Mormon, how beautiful are they to the eyes of them who there came to the knowledge of their Redeemer; yea, and how blessed are they, for they shall sing to his praise forever. (Mosiah 18:30)

If Mormon seems to exult in the very sound of the word denoting the place of this joy, it is surely because he is named after it (see 3 Nephi 5:12).[1] Little did this small group know that the name chosen for their place of glad worship would eventually signify a mighty book of scripture, and even a dynamic latter-day faith.

Mosiah 19 traces the eventual collapse of Noah's government and his death, as Abinadi had foretold, by fire. Noah's son Limhi becomes king of the puppet Nephite government, but the Lamanite king exacts a fifty percent tribute that essentially keeps Limhi's people in bondage. Successive chapters chronicle abuses that lead to warfare, and to an expedition in search of Zarahemla that ends up, as noted earlier, in the stubble of the Jaredite civilization. The search party finds "a land which was covered with dry bones; yea, a land which had been peopled and which had been destroyed" (Mosiah 21:26). I can almost feel the grit of those bones. Assuming that they have found the remains of Zarahemla, the party returns, bringing with them a record inscribed on plates of ore. It is at this point that Ammon and his group from Zarahemla enter the scene.

Mosiah 23 and 24 reverse the chronology still one more time in order to incorporate into the larger record the account of Alma and the people who escaped with him. These chapters pull together a lot of loose ends in the narrative. But more important, they portray the birth of the democratic ideal in the new world— an ideal that will be embattled numerous times in the course of Nephite history. Alma refuses the title of king, enjoining the faithful refugees to "stand fast in this liberty wherewith ye have been made free" (Mosiah 23:13). Two generations later, young Captain Moroni will rally the Nephites with those same words. The bliss cannot last, however, and Alma's people are discovered by their enemies and returned to bondage. But with the Lord's assistance, they escape into the wilderness and find their way to a joyous reception in Zarahemla.

[1] It is said in Mosiah 18:4 that the place "received its name from the king"—possibly a Nephite king who ruled after Nephi and before Benjamin.

Thus, Zarahemla is a point of convergence for the descendants of Zeniff, who have now come full circle in both their geographic and their spiritual journeys. At last all those who call themselves Nephites—the people of the first Mosiah, the people of Zarahemla, and the followers of King Limhi and Alma—are gathered in one place under one government and church. The second Mosiah, now King Mosiah, assembles his people for a reading of the various records of the splinter groups, and his people are understandably "struck with wonder and amazement" (Mosiah 25:7) at what they hear.

We remember that when the first Mosiah, the father of King Benjamin and grandfather of the present King Mosiah, fled with the righteous from the land of Nephi and came upon Zarahemla, he was made ruler there. With him began a monarchial line that never reverted back to the descendants of Mulek and Zarahemla, even though the latter were probably far more numerous. In fact, Mormon explains, "the kingdom had been conferred upon none but those who were descendants of Nephi" (Mosiah 25:13). With this consolidation comes an extensive formalization of both religious and civil statutory government. Led by Alma as "founder" and high priest, the strong institutional church comes into being. The population has grown to the point that a well-defined structure is essential, and with Mosiah's sanction, Alma organizes several satellite congregations. Mormon is careful to explain, however, that "notwithstanding there being many churches they were all one church, yea, even the church of God" (Mosiah 25:22).

As I suggested above, this period also marks the beginning of a rather sophisticated civil government among the Nephites (I am jumping ahead, for the moment, to Mosiah 29). In the closing years of his reign, an inspired Mosiah proposes a new kind of rule, by elected judges rather than by kings. Like Alma, he has seen how one wicked monarch could canker a whole society, and he fears a repeat of Noah's perfidy under the rule of one of his own successors. The issue is particularly pressing because Mosiah's sons decline the kingship, and Mosiah is reluctant to appoint a non-heir lest an heir subsequently change his mind and contend for the throne. Kingship, he believes, has a way of corrupting the ambitious, and it might well "destroy my son" and "turn [him] again to his pride and vain things" (Mosiah 29:8-9). The word "again" tells a story of its own. Mosiah composes and distributes a lengthy treatise on the dangers of rule by kings.

Mosiah's words convince his followers that government by the voice of the people is desirable, with several levels of judges to administer civil law based on religious principles ("the judgments of God are always just, but the judgments of man are not always just," Mosiah 29:12). Mosiah articulates the ideal of responsible popular government and structures a system of checks and balances, thus anticipating the principles that would be established by America's founding fathers many centuries later. Words such as these reveal Mosiah's political acumen and wisdom:

> Now it is not common that the voice of the people desireth anything contrary to that which is right; but it is common for the lesser part of the people to desire that which is not right; therefore this shall ye observe and make it your law—to do your business by the voice of the people. (Mosiah 29:26)

Liberty and equality, with the same "rights and privileges" for all (Mosiah 29:32), are the basis of the government which Mosiah espouses, and which his people accept. Before these changes in government occur, however, Mosiah's ability to rule is tested when a new generation of unbelievers begins to persecute and to deceive church members, leading many into dissent and iniquity. Some of the troublemakers are brought before the priests for church action, with witnesses testifying to their sinful behavior.

Dealing with charges raised against church members by other church members is something new to Mosiah and to the elder Alma. "Troubled in his spirit" by the situation (Mosiah 26:10), Alma asks Mosiah to take action against serious violators of God's law. But Mosiah, scrupulously practicing separation of church and state, refuses to interfere in religious judgments, though he does make it unlawful for anyone to persecute others for their religious beliefs. The matter of violation of church law he turns back to Alma to resolve, and Alma "pour[s] out his whole soul to God" (Mosiah 26:14) for guidance.

In a lengthy reply, the Lord establishes the foundation of church governance, including the broad requirements for baptism and continuing membership. The Lord also establishes an institutional procedure for dealing with transgressors, with repentance and forgiveness of others the key to their return. Mormon underlines Alma's conscientiousness, noting that, just as Alma had recorded Abinadi's words, he now "wrote . . . down" the words spoken by the voice of the Lord. He wishes to "have them . . . that he might judge the people of that church according to the commandments of God" (Mosiah 26:33). And apparently Alma's religious judgments are strictly applied; those who repent and confess their sins are "number[ed] among the people of the church," but the names of the recalcitrant are "blotted out" (Mosiah 26:35-36). Initially, this is a time of severe trial for the church, as persecutions intensify and pressures mount against church members. Only a powerful leader could have held the church together in the face of tearing internal and external forces, and the elder Alma is such a leader. Aided by new civil and church laws forbidding persecution, and church laws decreeing "equality among all men" (Mosiah 27:3), the Nephite nation blossoms into prosperity and peace.

We can scarcely overstate the significance of Alma's emergence from the wicked society of King Noah to plant the seed of belief among a small band of exiles, and then to become the prophet-leader of an expanding church. An equally precipitous event occurs in these few chapters: the conversion of Alma's rebellious son and namesake, Alma the younger, and the four sons of Mosiah. The miraculous turnabout of these young men is one of the great dramas in Book of Mormon history. Young Alma, we are told, was "an idolatrous man" and also "a man of many words" who spoke "much flattery to the people," "stealing away [their] hearts" and "causing much dissension" (Mosiah 27:8-9). If someone with the younger Alma's considerable charisma and abundant verbal gifts were converted and enlisted in the cause of righteousness, he could be a tremendous influence for good. No wonder the Lord intervenes. As it happens, he becomes one of the giants of the record, standing alongside prophets like Nephi and Moroni.

Knowing this young man's potential destiny, the Lord sends a no-nonsense angel to interrupt Alma and his friends, the four sons of Mosiah, in their ill-conceived efforts to destroy the church. For Christians who accept the divine interception of Paul (then Saul) on the road to Damascus, this event in the Book of Mormon should not seem implausible or even unique, though it is certainly unusual. Dropped in their rebellious tracks by the angel's thunderous voice, Alma and his companions are a captive audience. Singling out Alma, the angel commands him to "arise and stand forth" (Mosiah 27:13), daring him to "dispute the power of God" while the angel stands visible before him, an emissary from that very God. He warns Alma, even if "thou wilt of thyself be cast off," to stop misleading others and "seek to destroy the church no more" (Mosiah 27:15-16). Collapsing again, an awestruck Alma can neither speak nor move.

Ordinarily, a father would not be overjoyed at the sight of his prostrate son. But the elder Alma rejoices because he knows that the Lord has heard his prayers. Young Alma's spiritual rebirth and redemption from sin are breathtakingly swift. When he regains strength and speech, his first words capture the essence of his miraculous change of heart: "I have repented of my sins, and have been redeemed of the Lord; behold I am born of the Spirit" (Mosiah 27:24). In Alma's stricken state, the Lord had taught him the meaning of spiritual rebirth, emphasizing that all human beings "must be born again; yea, born of God, changed from their carnal and fallen state, to a state of righteousness, being redeemed of God, becoming his sons and daughters" (Mosiah 27:25). "And thus," he said, "they become new creatures," eligible to "inherit the kingdom of God" (Mosiah 27:26). Benjamin and others preached the doctrine of the heart's transformation, but none with more conviction than Alma, who in a matter of days, and as a result of divine intervention, experienced that mightiest of changes. He cast off the natural man to become a son of God. Is it surprising, then, that this subject becomes a principal theme of his ministry?

In graphic diction, Alma depicts himself as a sinner "wading through much tribulation, repenting nigh unto death," rescued only because "the Lord in mercy hath seen fit to snatch me out of an everlasting burning, and I am born of God" (Mosiah 27:28). The life of a sinner, he says, is a life already fraught with the torments of hell. As if in proof, there is a hellish immediacy in Alma's portrayal of his soul's sinful state prior to conversion and redemption. The chief difference between the daily damnation of sin during mortality and the eternal damnation of the unrepentant is that the repentant mortal soul can still be "snatched" from destruction. Those who have heard the truth, however, must repent and seek forgiveness in mortality; only in mortality can they win redemption from sin through the Savior's atoning sacrifice.

Alma's words describe in balanced structural antithesis the soul's polarity before and after repentance and redemption:

> I was in the darkest abyss; but now I behold the marvelous light of God. My soul was racked with eternal torment; but I am snatched, and my soul is pained no more.
>
> I rejected my Redeemer, and denied that which had been spoken of by our fathers; but now that they may foresee that he will come, ... he will make himself manifest unto all. (Mosiah 27:29-30)

Three times Alma describes his perilous condition before conversion ("I was . . ."), and three times he shifts emphatically to the blessedness engendered from the redeeming change in his life ("but now . . ."). The last of these nearly parallel statements extends beyond Alma's own personal experience, leading his listeners to see that his condition typifies theirs, both in their peril and in their assurance of a coming Messiah who can redeem their souls. With that broadened focus, Alma bears testimony to the reality of Christ, and to the truth that one day none, especially none who obstinately presumes to "live without God in the world" (Mosiah 27:31), will be able to deny him. It is the utmost expression of vain pride to insist on living one's life independent of God, who is the source of that life.

Armed with newfound testimony, the younger Alma and the four sons of Mosiah become emissaries of God, traveling and teaching the doctrines of the kingdom in spite of heavy persecution. As he concludes this episode, Mormon is so touched by the transformation in these young men that he rejoices in language reminiscent of Abinadi and Isaiah: "And how blessed are they! For they did publish peace; they did publish good tidings of good; and they did declare unto the people that the Lord reigneth" (Mosiah 27:37).

In the closing chapters of the book of Mosiah, we learn that Mosiah's sons, who still suffer "much anguish of soul because of their iniquities," and still fear "that they should be cast off forever" (Mosiah 28:4), are granted permission to become missionaries "to their brethren, the Lamanites" in the land of Nephi. Indeed, memory of sin can sometimes remain sharp, perhaps especially for the repentant who have seen themselves with sudden disturbing clarity. While guilt may seem a burden, memory of sin—and such memory is not the same thing as guilt, I think—can be a blessing. It may, in fact, keep us on course and prompt us to good works and righteous actions, as in the case of Mosiah's sons.

Mormon leaves Mosiah's reformed sons for the moment and returns to their father, who finds himself with "no one to confer the kingdom upon" (Mosiah 28:10). As he begins to wind up the affairs of his kingdom, Mosiah entrusts Alma the younger with all the records, including his translation of the Jaredite record and the special translating instruments. The Jaredite record, of course, had greatly aroused the curiosity of the Nephites, but its gloomy unfolding caused Mosiah's people "to mourn exceedingly," even though they rejoiced in their new knowledge (Mosiah 28:18). Before his death at age eighty-two, the elder Alma confers the office of high priest upon his son, who also serves as the first chief judge of the Nephite nation. The rule of the judges commences, and Alma, we are told, "did judge righteous judgments; and there was continual peace through the land" (Mosiah 29:43). Mosiah dies at age sixty-three.

*11*

## Alma 1-5: The Power of Alma's Discourse

The book of Alma comprises a substantial sixty-three chapters at the heart of the Book of Mormon, the longest section by far and perhaps the richest doctrinally. Of the sixty-three chapters that bear the second Alma's name, forty-four are from his writings. His discourses teach with unusual eloquence and understanding the coming of Christ and the doctrine of his kingdom. They rival the beauty and power of any scripture anywhere. Distinguished by a great spirit and a superb mind, Alma somehow seems less distant than Nephi, for whom the incessant press of responsibility and imminent danger perhaps diminished the opportunities for personal reflection. And while Nephi was valiant from beginning to end, it took a messenger from heaven to set the incorrigible young Alma on a righteous course. Indeed, he never forgets how close he came to being lost forever.

Under Alma's leadership, the church becomes a large, well-superintended organization, with a network of ordained priests and teachers dispersed through numerous cities and regions. The years of his ministry are fretted by wars and by the atrocities of power-hungry individuals, but they are amazing years of church growth and prosperity nonetheless. Missionary work enjoys extraordinary success, especially among the descendants of Laman and Lemuel, and church members reach levels of spiritual understanding matched to date only by Benjamin's people at the time of their universal conversion to righteousness. Certain terms, such as "church," come into currency, offering linguistic evidence of a clearly defined institution administered through a priesthood organization that Alma calls "the holy order of God." In these pages, too, Mormon is an active presence, moralizing on events and adding his wisdom to that of the contemporary record keeper.

Plainly, Mormon is often deeply touched by what he reads; the keepers of the record are very real to him.

I sense in Alma's discourses a tone distinctly his, a tone manifest in his emphasis on matters of the heart and mind, matters of human character. He urges kindness, gentleness, and caring—charity in its loftiest possibilities. He cautions against pride and worldliness, pleading with his people to live by the Spirit. And for a time, at least, despite external rumblings, Alma's example prevails.

As the book of Alma opens in the first year of the rule of the judges, Mosiah has "gone the way of all the earth, having warred a good warfare" (Alma 1:1), or as Paul would say also, "fought a good fight" (1 Timothy 1:18; 2 Timothy 4:7). The peace is disturbed early on when an imposing but false teacher named Nehor is prosecuted for advocating priestcraft, arguing that priests and teachers "ought not to labor with their hands" but should instead "be supported by the people" (Alma 1:2-3). Nehor also teaches that all are redeemed regardless of their earthly behavior, and he brutally kills the aged and faithful Gideon who challenges him. I mention Nehor because his doctrinal descendants crop up later on, twisting human rights provisions in Nephite law to their advantage. For example, the Nehors evade justice by pretending belief in their false doctrine, "for liars were punished" while "the law could have no power on any man for his belief" (Alma 1:17). An interesting distinction. In fact, the church forbids its members to persecute anyone, in or out of the church, but it has no power to protect members from persecution at the hands of either malevolent apostates or non-members.

Once the hardhearted have withdrawn or been dismissed—a sorting out process that understandably causes "much trial" in the organization (Alma 1:23)—the body of the church becomes indeed a community of saints in which equality is the guiding principle. The "steadiness of the church" (Alma 1:29) engenders humility and generosity, and thus prosperity among its people. They are "liberal to all," regardless of age or church affiliation (Alma 1:30). Most of us are adept at articulating the ideals spelled out in these verses, but we tend to fall short in living them. On the other hand, we are several cuts above the Nephites who opposed the church, for they spent their days in such laudable enterprises as "sorceries," "idolatry," "idleness," and "babblings" (a choice word, *babblings*). They also entertained themselves with murder, theft, lechery, fancy clothes, and quarrels (Alma 1:32). Seeking to corral these destructive impulses, the government enforces the laws strictly. The insurgents go underground, and peace lasts into the fifth year of the reign of the judges.

But then a trouble-making demagogue named Amlici, of the persuasion of Nehor, aspires to be king. Bloody warfare ensues, the Amlicites mark themselves as Lamanites (and take on themselves the Lamanite curse), and Alma is wounded. These wars, we must remember, are religious wars, and church leaders fight in the front ranks. Perhaps Alma's position as chief judge also carries military obligations. The trials of war serve to awaken the irresolute "to a remembrance of their duty" (Alma 4:3), and the church baptizes 3,500 converts in one year. But by the eighth year of the judges, or 84 B.C., returning prosperity nourishes pride, arrogance, and materialism.

Several things stand out in the passages that describe the collapse of this people into pridefulness. First, Alma 4:6 speaks of "the people of the church" beginning to "wax proud" over the possessions they had acquired "by their industry," and twice (see verse 8 also) the unusual phrase "lifted up in the pride of their *eyes*" (emphasis added) is employed. The passage seems to suggest that even work, which is a good thing, can have a down side if it is done largely for material gain. Like us, perhaps, the Nephites have labored ever more strenuously to acquire ever more superfluous possessions. And since, as Thoreau has said, it is not merely our *money*, but our lives that we spend for material objects, such objects tend to become overvalued in our eyes. Moreover, the phrase "the pride of their eyes" suggests a distortion of values, an overemphasis on surface glitter and grandeur, an inclination to gratify the physical eye above all else.

Second, verse 8 also states that the scorn accompanying pride

has led to persecution of those who do not share the foolish affliction of the proud. The pride of church members begins "even to
exceed the pride of those who did not belong to the church"
(Alma 4:9), and contention within the church creates endless
problems for its leaders. Third, and worse still, perhaps, this
wickedness within the church becomes "a great stumbling-block"
to people outside it, leading the "unbelievers on from one piece of
iniquity to another" and ultimately to "destruction" (Alma 4:10-
11). The bad example of those who should be a good example is
a heavy drag on a society, even more so than the bad example of
those who make no pretense or profession of goodness.

As the social and material equality of earlier years yields to
inequality, and the proud begin "despising others, turning their
backs upon the needy" (Alma 4:12),[1] Alma "deliver[s] the judgment-seat unto Nephihah" (Alma 4:18) in order to "preach the
word of God." He sees "no way that he might reclaim [the
Nephites] save it were in bearing down in pure testimony against
them" (Alma 4:19). We should pause on the phrase, "bearing
down in pure testimony," for its uniqueness of expression and for
its suggestion that testimony can be a relentless weapon—in this
case perhaps the only effective weapon—in the war against evil.

If Alma had not relinquished the chief judgeship, we might
not have had the remarkable discourses that distinguish his
record. The people lost a great civic and military leader, but they
gained a full-time prophet. His first major discourse, delivered to
church members in the city of Zarahemla, appears in chapter 5 of
the book of Alma, where Mormon quotes directly from Alma's
"own record" (Alma 5:2). Alma begins his address as several of his
predecessors had done, by stating his name and his line of divine
authority: "I, Alma, having been consecrated by my father, Alma,
to be a high priest over the church of God, he having power and
authority from God to do these things. . ." (Alma 5:3). Sensitive

---

[1] I note that Alma, like Benjamin, ties "retaining a remission of their sins" (Alma 4:14) to active generosity toward the poor. See Mosiah 4:26.

and loving, Alma is also very strong—physically (he killed Amlici in battle and frightened off the Lamanite king), spiritually, and mentally. He speaks both tenderly and boldly, uttering splendid promises and fearsome warnings. Alma is a master of the spoken and written word, advancing his argument by several series of questions—some of them rhetorical—and by repetition of interlocking words, phrases, and images.

The opening discourse, which comprises verses 3 through 62 of Alma 5, is organized into several parts, each of which evolves from the one preceding it and anticipates the one to follow. Verses 3-5 are introductory and 6 is transitional, but all verses from 2-26 expound a principle dear to Alma: every mortal must experience a mighty change of heart, must be spiritually born of God. From this beginning, Alma issues a warning and a plea for repentance which he reinforces with personal testimony and prophecy. No paraphrase or discussion can adequately describe the verbal acuity and oratorical skills of this great man of God. And his style is so individual that it argues impressively for multiple authorship of the Book of Mormon.[2] We remember that by his own admission, Nephi was a gifted speaker, his gift deriving from the power of his personality and the workings of the Spirit in him and in his listeners. But writing, Nephi said, was another matter. Alma does not comment on his speaking or writing abilities; but the fact that he left his judgeship to devote himself to gospel instruction suggests that he knew he had the power of the word as well as of the Word.

I cannot begin to do justice to Alma 5. It simply must be read, preferably aloud. The reader must try to imagine Alma speaking to a large congregation, urging them to remember their fathers' deliverance from earthly captivity by the same hand that "delivered their souls from hell" (Alma 5:6). Alma teaches by asking questions, sometimes with answers implied in the questions,

---

[2] I mention in passing that statistical studies, in which "word prints" of Nephi and Alma have been compared, offer more objective proof than an English teacher's eye provides that the writings of Nephi and Alma come from two different persons. See John L. Hinton, "On Verifying Wordprint Studies: Book of Mormon Authorship," *BYU Studies* 30 (Summer 1990:89-108).

sometimes with instruction explicit in the questions, sometimes with answers that only he can supply. But all questions on one subject, that is, all questions in a series, are framed by the same introductory words and structures.

In urging his listeners to remember the Lord's mercies to their fathers (followers of the first Alma), Alma three times poses questions that begin, ". . . have you sufficiently retained in remembrance" (Alma 5:6). Then, he reveals in lyrical language what should have been retained in remembrance: "Behold, [the Lord] changed their hearts; yea, he awakened them out of a deep sleep, and they awoke unto God. Behold, they were in the midst of darkness; nevertheless, their souls were illuminated by the light of the everlasting word. . ." (Alma 5:7). Powerful stuff, the awakening of a soul into divine light. Alma then repeats and expands the theme, this time by a series of rapid-fire questions and answers. Even here, the poet in the man keeps bursting through the lines as though prose cannot contain him:

> And now I ask of you, my brethren, were they destroyed? Behold, I say unto you, Nay, they were not.
> And again I ask, were the bands of death broken, and the chains of hell which encircled them about, were they loosed? I say unto you, Yea, they were loosed, and their souls did expand, and they did sing redeeming love. And I say unto you that they are saved. (Alma 5:8-9)

". . . and their souls did expand, and they did sing redeeming love"—that is high poetry. Also impressive are the structural balance, the reversals ("Nay . . . Yea"), and the parallelism in the questions and answers.

But we should note, too, the word "saved" that ends verse 9. Alma hangs his next series of questions on that word. Those questions, recorded in verse 10, are really three renderings of the same question about salvation, the second and third amplifying the first and second. And the third question also teaches that there is a spiritual redemption from sin as well as a temporal redemption from death. The question asked three times in verse 10 is an important one:

> And now I ask of you on what conditions are they saved? Yea, what grounds had they to hope for salvation? What is the cause of their being loosed from the bands of death, yea, and also the chains of hell? (Alma 5:10)

Alma speaks of the "conditions," "grounds," and "cause" of salvation—in other words, what is required of mortals if the Atonement is to apply. Again, those "fathers" he alluded to earlier provide the example, particularly Alma's own father who believed the prophet Abinadi and in turn preached the word to others:

> And according to [the first Alma's] faith there was a mighty change wrought in his heart. . . .
> And behold, he preached the word unto your fathers, and a mighty change was also wrought in their hearts, and they humbled themselves and put their trust in the true and living God. And behold, they were faithful until the end; therefore they were saved. (Alma 5:12-13)

What is required, Alma says, is a mighty change of heart—and the humility, trust, and lifelong faith that accompany and follow such a change.

Whenever Alma speaks of this change, his language fairly shimmers with the beauty and wonder of it. As one who has experienced personally and dramatically a great change of heart, he knows its value. Again, the poet's voice asks three questions that are the same question, but employ three different poetic figures: ". . . have ye spiritually been born of God? Have ye received his image in your countenances? Have ye experienced this mighty change in your hearts?" (Alma 5:14). What is it to receive God's image in one's countenance? I think it is, from that moment on, actually to look like his offspring, to glow with his radiance, to shine with his goodness. And the word "received" suggests that the gift is available, but requires a receptive mind and heart.

I sense a crescendo of feeling and meaning as Alma moves into succeeding and related questions in verse 15:

> Do ye exercise faith in the redemption of him who created you?
> Do you look forward with an eye of faith, and view this mortal body
> raised in immortality, and this corruption raised in incorruption, to
> stand before God to be judged according to the deeds which have
> been done in the mortal body?

The second question above is an expansion of the first, explaining the meaning of temporal redemption, and setting the stage for instruction regarding spiritual redemption. In verse 16 Alma dramatizes the concept, entreating his listeners to project themselves into the glorious moment after judgment when Christ will claim the righteous as his own, saying: "Come unto me ye blessed. . ." (Alma 5:16).

This is one side of it, but there is another, Alma warns. Having painted a lovely picture of redemption's blessedness, Alma switches abruptly to the other possibility—the one awaiting the unrepentant. The word "or" signals the change: "Or do ye imagine to yourselves that ye can lie unto the Lord in that day . . . and that he will save you?" (Alma 5:17). The word "save" provides a link to the subject at hand; verses 17 and 18 repeat the pattern of verses 15 and 16, the second of the two dramatizing the moment of judgment, this time with heartbreaking consequences:

> Or otherwise, can ye imagine yourselves brought before the tri-
> bunal of God with your souls filled with guilt and remorse, having a
> remembrance of all your guilt, yea, a perfect remembrance of all your
> wickedness, yea, a remembrance that ye have set at defiance the com-
> mandments of God? (Alma 5:18)

It is notable, too, that Alma uses the word "remembrance" three times, making an explicit verbal link to his opening admonitions to remembrance. In this tightly knit discourse, no loose threads, no concepts and key words, escape the fabric's larger design.

The subject of this section of Alma's discourse is the soul's salvation wrought by Jesus Christ; but the focus is on what is required of the mortal who hopes to realize redemption—that is, the remission of sins that translates into spiritual salvation for the repentant. In positive terms Alma says, "I say unto you, can ye look up to God [at judgment] with a pure heart and clean hands? I say unto you, can you look up, having the image of God engraven upon your countenances?" (Alma 5:19). This radiant image is the outward manifestation of a changed heart, expressed in the same metaphor Alma had used earlier. Then, shifting to the negative possibility but retaining the linguistic pattern, Alma asks, ". . . can ye think of being saved when you have yielded yourselves to become subjects to the devil?" (Alma 5:20).

Alma answers his own question, making his reply a succinct and penetrating summary of the doctrine of redemption from sin:

> I say unto you, ye will know at that day that ye cannot be saved; for there can no man be saved except his garments are washed white; yea, his garments must be purified until they are cleansed from all stain, through the blood of him of whom it has been spoken by our fathers, who should come to redeem his people from their sins. (Alma 5:21)

Through the next few verses, Alma, like Nephi before him, again asks his listeners to consider how they will feel standing at the "bar of God" (Alma 5:22) in all their sins. With verse 26, he concludes a major section of his discourse, calling up his earlier portrayal of the joy of the penitent: "And now . . . if ye have experienced a change of heart, and if ye have felt to sing the song of redeeming love, I would ask, can ye feel so now?" (Alma 5:26).

The words "can ye feel so now" provide the link to the next section of Alma's discourse, which outlines some specific traits of character that lead to and accompany a change of heart, traits that enable one indeed to "feel so now." Following his practice of instructing through questions, Alma asks his listeners if they "have been sufficiently humble," if they are "stripped of pride," or if, to the contrary, they are "not stripped of envy," or if there is any among them "that doth make a mock of his brother, or that heapeth upon him persecutions" (Alma 5:27-30). In the next section of his discourse he pursues his subject in earnest, stressing the need for repentance if one is to obtain mercy. Pairing opposites again, he sets the voice and promise of the good shepherd against the voice and wages of the devil.

In verses 34-42, Alma skillfully weaves an intricate pattern of repeated words and phrases that keep doubling back on themselves to underline his theme. The pattern is too complex to describe in detail here, but we can observe a few things, noting especially how Alma introduces a word or phrase in one verse and then casts back from the next to pick up that word or phrase. For example, in verse 34, quoting the Lord, Alma introduces the expression, "Come unto me." Then in verse 35, he repeats the expression, but adds the instruction to "come unto me and bring forth works of righteousness." In verse 36, still quoting the Lord, he takes the last phrase of the expression and splits it in two, and then reverses its meaning by adding the word "not" to each of its two halves, warning "that whosoever *bringeth forth not* good fruit, or whosoever *doeth not the works of righteousness*, the same shall have cause to wail and mourn." Verse 37 loops back to the words "works" and "righteousness" in the phrases "workers of iniquity" and "ways of righteousness." At the same time, it introduces two new terms which will play in the next several verses.

Alma, in the Lord's voice, compares those who work iniquity to "sheep having no *shepherd*, notwithstanding a *shepherd* hath called after you and is still calling after you, but ye will not *hearken unto his voice!*" Verse 38 repeats these two new terms and adds another, the word "name," indicating that the Lord calls his people in his own name, and if some do not recognize the name by which they are called, they are not his sheep. In verse 39, Alma creates another reversal through repetition of the word "shepherd" introduced earlier: "And now if ye are not the sheep of the *good shepherd*, of what fold are ye? Behold, I say unto you, that the *devil* is your *shepherd*, and ye are of his fold. . . ." Then in verse 40, he clarifies the distinction between the two shepherds by adding that "whatsoever is *good* cometh from God, and whatsoever is *evil* cometh from the *devil*." (It is certainly no accident that except for the initial "d," the words "devil" and "evil" are identical in English.)

As he begins to wrap up his argument in verse 41, Alma returns to the notion with which he began, the notion of works, linking it to the idea of hearkening to the voice of either the good shepherd or the devil: "Therefore, if a man bringeth forth *good works* he *hearkeneth unto the voice of the good shepherd*, and he doth follow him; but whosoever bringeth forth *evil works*, the same becometh a child of the *devil*, for he *hearkeneth unto his voice*, and doth follow him." Alma concludes by introducing a powerful new term, "death," for those who choose the evil alternative, but he sets it in a context of terms he had repeated above: "And whosoever doeth this must receive his wages of him; therefore, for his wages he receiveth *death*, as to things pertaining unto *righteousness*, being *dead* unto all *good works*" (Alma 5:41-42; emphases added throughout). Alma is obviously someone who takes great care with language, who knows how to use it for optimal effect, who writes powerfully without straining or overstating.

Having worked smoothly through highly structured and insistent rhetorical patterns of questions and answers to deliver his argument, Alma suddenly changes modes. In verse 43, with the words "And now, my brethren," he downshifts to address his people in a very personal way, testifying that the things he has taught them are true. His language is full of verbal cues such as this, and even without the benefit of aural tone and inflection, we can hear his voice lower and become deliberate: ". . . I would that ye should hear me, for I speak in the energy of my soul. . ." (Alma 5:43). His calling, more than that, his commandment, "to stand and testify unto this people" (Alma 5:44), comes from God. He testifies in no uncertain terms, having "fasted and prayed many days" for the knowledge, "that I do know that these things whereof I have spoken are true" (Alma 5:45-46). Some might think that Alma's miraculous conversion spared him the trouble of earnestly striving for personal testimony. The experience turned him around, true, but it was only the beginning of knowledge. Alma makes it clear that he has paid the price to know, and now his testimony is unassailable. He knows *of himself*, he says twice.

As he prepares to prophesy, Alma bears testimony of the coming Christ with the same surety:

> I say unto you, that I know *of myself* that whatsoever I shall say unto you, concerning that which is to come, is true; and I say unto you, that I know that Jesus Christ shall come, yea, the Son, the Only Begotten of the Father, full of grace, and mercy, and truth. And behold, it is he that cometh to take away the sins of the world, yea, the sins of every man who steadfastly believeth on his name. (Alma 5:48; emphasis added)

This Alma knows, as surely as he knows anything, eighty-three years before the coming he foresees. Now, from the language of personal testimony, Alma shifts abruptly and briefly once more to the language of spokesman for God. Verse 50 registers that shift in the first line: "Yea, thus saith the Spirit. . . ." Five times in three verses Alma attributes this rather formal, impersonal, but imperative utterance to the Spirit. Even so, his prophetic message underscores the abiding theme of his discourse, repentance and the coming Lord: "Repent, all ye ends of the earth, for the kingdom of heaven is soon at hand; yea, the Son of God cometh in his glory, in his might, majesty, power, and dominion" (Alma 5:50).

Then, as swiftly as he had left it, Alma returns to his original method of instructing through interrogation. Verses 53-56 consist of parallel structures shaped by questions that begin "can ye" or "will ye still persist." Here, before changing to a yet stronger imperative mode, he rehearses the matters of character he had addressed earlier. I observe especially that he urges his congregation to "be separate," to avoid the "unclean things" of their peers whose "names shall be blotted out" (Alma 5:57). This is clearly a time of purification, of separating the righteous from the unrepentant wicked. In any society or institution, this kind of stringency tends to meet with resistance, but Alma stands firm: "I say unto you, if ye speak against it, it matters not, for the word of God must be fulfilled," and the wicked must be dismissed just as the wolf is driven out when he enters the flock (Alma 5:58-60). The challenge facing institutional leaders under such circumstances, I think, is to distinguish the evil wolf from the sometimes unruly, but not evil, members of the flock.

The final words of Alma's sermon are both rigorous and appealing, a fitting conclusion to a remarkable discourse by a speaker highly conscious of language:

> And now I, Alma, do command you in the language of him who hath commanded me, that ye observe to do the words which I have spoken unto you.
>
> I speak by way of command unto you that belong to the church; and unto those who do not belong to the church I speak by way of invitation, saying: Come and be baptized unto repentance, that ye also may be partakers of the fruit of the tree of life. (Alma 5:61-62)

Command and invite—this is the double thrust of Alma's leadership throughout his ministry.

*12*

## Alma 6-16: Missionary Labors and Discourses

Alma was greatly concerned for the people of Zarahemla, who had strayed from the doctrines and practices of the church; and chapter 6, a transitional section, reports Alma's restoration of truth and order there. We begin to appreciate the strength of the man and his verbal and organizational abilities when we realize that through his teachings and leadership, he reversed the apostasy of an entire city.

Alma's ministry takes a very different turn among the faithful people of Gideon. Gone are the pointed rhetoric, the accusing questions, and the insistent answers that characterized his discourse in Zarahemla. Although he teaches repentance and spiritual rebirth, and the need to develop fine traits of character, his predominant theme is the earthly advent of the Savior. And even when he urges repentance, he employs long, flowing sentences—the inviting language of promise rather than the harsh language of condemnation. Mormon quotes directly from Alma's record.

Alma's feelings run deep for these dear people whom he repeatedly calls "beloved," and in whom his "soul doth exceedingly rejoice" (Alma 7:26). Although at this point, interestingly, he does not know if Jesus will appear in the new world during his mortal ministry, he does know and teach many sacred "things which cannot be written" (Alma 8:1). Alma's final counsel in Gideon repeats a frequent theme in his discourses, one appropriate for even the most faithful. His words are a sure reflection of his nature:

> And now I would that ye should be humble, and be submissive and gentle; easy to be entreated; full of patience and long-suffering; being temperate in all things; . . . always returning thanks unto God for whatsoever things ye do receive. (Alma 7:23)

Alma has three purposes in journeying from city to city throughout the land: (1) to restore backsliding church members to the faith, (2) to establish a strong church organization, and (3) to bring new members into the fold. He accomplishes these things in Zarahemla, Gideon, and Melek, but Ammonihah is a different story. The people want nothing to do with him or his church. Reminding Alma that he no longer holds secular authority over them—I suspect they despise him for voluntarily relinquishing political power—they "withstood all his words, and reviled him, and spit upon him, and caused that he should be cast out of their city" (Alma 8:13). In great anguish of soul he departs, only to be intercepted by an angel—the same angel, incidentally, who had accosted Alma in his rebellious youth.

The two may be old acquaintances, but the angel's words do not offer quite the heartfelt sympathy that a suffering, defeated man might have hoped to hear: "Blessed art thou, Alma; therefore, lift up thy head and rejoice. . ." (Alma 8:15). If Alma protests this seemingly insensitive response to his misery, Mormon does not say so; and besides, the angel does not appear ready to entertain Alma's troubles. Instead of comforting him, the unsentimental messenger tells him to rejoice in his own faithfulness and get himself back to Ammonihah to "preach again" (Alma 8:16). Of particular concern to the angel is the desire of the people of Ammonihah to "destroy the liberty" (Alma 8:17) of the saints. Even in his woeful state, Alma is not a person who questions the Lord's purposes or instructions, and "he return[s] speedily to the land of Ammonihah" (Alma 8:18). I repeat, *speedily.*

Slipping into "the city by another way" (Alma 8:18), Alma meets a Nephite named Amulek who has also been visited by an angel, very likely the same fellow. In accordance with the angel's instructions, Amulek feeds and attends the ailing Alma. The latter apparently settles in gratefully and enjoys Amulek's hospitality, "tarry[ing] many days" (Alma 8:27)—perhaps too many—while, as Mormon unceremoniously observes, "the people did wax more gross in their iniquities" (Alma 8:28). The expression "wax more gross" is not in most of our vocabularies, but we get the picture.

Clearly, it is time to resume the work, for "the word came to Alma" (Alma 8:29) that he should enlist Amulek and get on with it. The fact that Amulek is now able to teach with great knowledge and power, as we shall see, suggests that the time Alma spent "tarrying" in his home was not merely "R and R," but also a time of intensive learning and preparation for Amulek. Spiritually invigorated, the two men set out "filled with the Holy Ghost" and girded with such power "that they could not be confined in dungeons" or slain (Alma 8:30-31). The Lord shields his servants.

In chapter 9, Mormon again quotes directly from Alma's record as he describes Alma's futile attempts to stir the people of Ammonihah to repentance. In addition to impending destruction, Alma prophesies the imminent arrival of "the Son of God," whose "glory shall be the glory of the Only Begotten of the Father, full of grace, equity, and truth" (Alma 9:26). My eye stops on the word "equity," which seems to add a new and important dimension to typical descriptions of the Savior's attributes. Only Alma, of all scriptorians, adds "equity" to the phrase, and he does so twice, here and in 13:9. In 5:48 Alma substitutes the word "mercy" for "equity," suggesting a link between the two qualities. Nephi and John both use the phrase "full of grace and truth" to describe the Savior, and there are several such references in Moses and the Doctrine and Covenants, as well as in Joseph Smith's translations of Genesis and Revelations. The term "equity" itself is uncommon in any case; it appears only ten times in the Old Testament and not at all in the New. Six of those ten are in Psalms, Proverbs, and Ecclesiastes. Amulek also quotes the Lord's use of the word on one occasion (see Alma 10:21). I suggest here that Alma, whether consciously or unconsciously, is emphasizing justness and fairness in the Savior's character, subtly reminding us that God is indeed no respecter of persons.

As the narrative continues, the people of Ammonihah contend with Alma, even attempting to imprison him. Chapters 10 and 11 are given to Amulek, who proves himself a fearless and outspoken advocate of godliness. Amulek begins his sermon by revealing that he is a descendant of Aminadi, he who "interpreted the writing which was upon the wall of the temple, which was written by the finger of God" (Alma 10:2). At first the reader might suppose Amulek to be referring to an Old Testament event, but in verse 3 we learn that Aminadi was a descendant of Nephi. It would appear, then, that buried somewhere in Nephite sacred history is the story of a prophet named Aminadi who, like Daniel, interpreted prophetic symbols written on a wall.

Before his conversion, Amulek had stubbornly resisted spiritual promptings, refusing to hear and accept the truth. Now confessing his hard-heartedness, he describes his conversion through angelic intercession. His incredulous listeners, presented with an unwelcome second witness to Alma's words, engage crafty lawyers to trick and trap Amulek, but he reads their thoughts and condemns them. I find Amulek extremely affecting, in his testimony, his bold exhortations, and his command of language. The more his listeners storm and protest, "the mightier [Amulek cries] unto them" (Alma 10:25). His gospel understanding, too, is amazing for a person so newly converted.

When the people of Ammonihah accuse Amulek of controverting their law, he answers as Abinadi had before King Noah's wicked priests. He has, he says, "spoken in favor of your law, to your condemnation" (Alma 10:26). The lawyers of the city, standing to lose a lot of business were Amulek to prevail, "put it into [the people's] hearts" to condemn him for speaking against their law. "The foremost" of the lawyers is a shrewd fellow named Zeezrom (Alma 10:30-31). Mormon includes in the record a fascinating dialogue between Amulek and Zeezrom, who fully expects to befuddle and humiliate Amulek in debate. In Nephite society, Mormon explains, lawyers are paid according to the number of cases they handle, so these enterprising folks incite riots and other disturbances "that they might have more employ" (Alma 11:20). Alma and Amulek are victims of this kind of activity. (Were there "lawyer jokes" in Nephite society, pray tell?)

Zeezrom may be a hotshot legal eagle, but he proves to be no match for Amulek. An "expert in the devices of the devil" (Alma 11:21)—a curious specialization, even for a shyster!—Zeezrom has only his wit to support him, while Amulek has the Holy Spirit and truth on his side. He also has the power of upright personality, conviction, and the word, all of which he convenes to outgun his assailant. Totally miscalculating Amulek's mettle, Zeezrom foolishly offers him a bribe. Then, thinking to trick Amulek into contradicting himself, he asks several questions about the nature and purposes of God. To his last question, "Is the Son of God the very Eternal Father?" (Alma 11:38), an unflappable Amulek replies that the Son is indeed Father and Creator of this earth. Without pause, Amulek bears testimony of Christ, introducing the subject of redemption from both sin and temporal death.

Perhaps nowhere in scripture is the reunion of the resurrected body with the immortal spirit expounded with more acumen and grace. Completely disarmed by the profundity of Amulek's message, the once arrogant Zeezrom visibly trembles. Amulek explains just what salvation from temporal death means:

> The spirit and the body shall be reunited again in its perfect form; both limb and joint shall be restored to its proper frame, even as we now are at this time; and we shall be brought to stand before God, knowing even as we know now, and have a bright recollection of all our guilt.
>
> Now, this restoration shall come to all, both old and young, both bond and free, both male and female, both the wicked and the righteous; and even there shall not so much as a hair of their heads be lost; but every thing shall be restored to its perfect frame, as it is now, or in the body, and shall be brought and be arraigned before the bar of Christ the Son, and God the Father, and the Holy Spirit, which is one Eternal God, to be judged according to their works, whether they be good or whether they be evil. (Alma 11:43-44)

Once body and spirit are reunited, Amulek declares, "they can die no more," nor can they "be divided; thus the whole becom[es] spiritual and immortal" (Alma 11:45).

Alma is present to hear Amulek's words and to witness Zeezrom's trembling reaction and the people's astonishment. Like the senior partner of a tag team, Alma steps into the ring the moment Amulek pauses, determined to pursue this line of argument with Zeezrom, "to establish the words of Amulek, and to explain things beyond, or to unfold the scriptures beyond that which Amulek had done" (Alma 12:1). Capitalizing on Zeezrom's new readiness to listen, a readiness born of fear and consternation, Alma frankly tells Zeezrom and all who have gathered that they have been doing the devil's work. A vanquished and sober Zeezrom, convinced that Alma and Amulek can read his thoughts, now begins to ask honest questions in earnest.

It is apparent from his questions that Zeezrom and the other residents of Ammonihah have not understood the basic doctrines of resurrection, judgment, and redemption from sin. Since God grants his children knowledge and an understanding of his mysteries "according to the heed and diligence which they give unto him" (Alma 12:9), the hard of heart receive "the lesser portion of the word" (Alma 12:10) and may be cut off from enlightenment entirely. The ignorant become the devil's captives. Alma seems to suggest that the "chains of hell" (Alma 12:11) are forged in the furnace of spiritual ignorance. Significantly, in this part of his discourse he uses the familiar first person plural ("we," "our") with his hearers, implying that his choices and judgment are the same as theirs. But he shifts to a less personal mode as he introduces a new and very important doctrine, one that Amulek had only hinted at: the doctrine of the second, or spiritual, death.

Now using the more direct, yet impersonal, language of second-person address ("I say unto *you*") and relative pronoun reference ("whosoever"), Alma explains that "whosoever dieth in his sins, as to a temporal death"—that is, without having exercised the faith and repentance that bring mercy into play through the Atonement—"shall also die a spiritual death" (Alma 12:16). And when he speaks of the lost, instead of using the more immediate and particular "we" or "you," Alma uses the indeterminate third-person "they." With the lost, he says regretfully, it "shall be as though there had been no redemption made; for they cannot be redeemed according to God's justice." And, as immortal beings, "they cannot die" (Alma 12:18). This is a perplexing doctrine to the people of Ammonihah, and another spokesman, a chief ruler named Antionah, comes forward to ask the meaning of the scripture that says, "God placed cherubim and a flaming sword on the east of the garden of Eden" to prevent Adam and Eve from eating fruit from the tree of life (Alma 12:21; Genesis 3:24). Antionah's question anticipates Alma's next subject, the plan of salvation.

Explaining the Fall and its consequences, Alma underscores the fact that if our first parents had eaten of "the tree of life at that time" (Alma 12:23), they would have achieved immortality without having first had a chance to repent, prove faithful, and receive a remission of their sins through the Savior's atonement. Thus, for the sake of their eternal souls, and in order to produce mortal offspring, they had to be prevented from eating the fruit from the tree of life. I think that this precaution confirms that Adam and Eve chose the better part when they elected to partake from the tree of the knowledge of good and evil, even though it meant the loss of the garden. God could just as well have put "cherubim and a flaming sword" to guard that tree, too, but he did not. He left it entirely accessible as the garden's centerpiece (see Moses 4:9) and made it extremely appealing (see Moses 4:12), the only barrier to it a verbal warning. He also allowed Lucifer the freedom to tempt our first parents.

We should consider, too, that at the time of tempting, Adam and Eve had no ability to discern between good and evil. As father Lehi taught in Jacob's blessing, they could do "no good, for they knew no sin" (2 Nephi 2:23). They had no knowledge of evil, nor any experience with it. Eve did not recognize Lucifer and his evil intent until *after* she had eaten the fruit. What Lucifer suggested to her, therefore, in her innocence would not necessarily seem wrong, even though the Father had forbidden it. In her world, there was no such thing as wrong, least of all the luscious fruit from a lovely tree. The Lord was willing that they partake; the choice for mortality had to be theirs.

The tree of life, however, was a different matter; in their innocence, Adam and Eve needed the Father's protection. Everlasting life at that point would have "frustrated" the "plan of redemption"

(Alma 12:26) and spelled everlasting misery for the primal pair. Mortality, on the other hand, opened the door to forgiveness and redemption, thus according Eve and Adam and all their posterity "a time to prepare to meet God" (Alma 12:24) and also to prepare for the "endless state" of existence after resurrection—something we do not always consider.

The first consequence of the infraction in Eden, then, was the plunge into temporality, and Alma triggers some interesting ideas by stating that the first pair precipitated the fall when they "transgressed the first commandments *as to things which were temporal*" (Alma 12:31; emphasis added). The passage suggests to me that our first parents, by ingesting temporal "fruit," whether literally or figuratively, produced a change that was incompatible with their non-temporal bodies and their surroundings. In any event, they made an informed and highly courageous choice for temporality and biologically vulnerable bodies. In so choosing, however, they paradoxically also became "as Gods," in the sense of having agency, of "knowing good from evil, placing themselves in a state to act, or being placed in a state to act according to their wills and pleasures, whether to do evil or to do good" (Alma 12:31). It is significant that although some of Adam's and Eve's children swerved from the righteous path, the first parents never did. They yielded to temptation only when the course of eternal progress made it necessary.

The plan of salvation, Alma teaches, presupposes a physical separation of mortals from their divine origins for a period of probation or preparation, a period in which those mortals actually define themselves by countless choices confronted and made. I think that most of us fail to realize the force of daily choices in shaping both our lives and our natures. Alma assures his listeners that the separation he describes need not be permanent. As he concludes this portion of his discourse, he shifts once more to a personal, loving appeal in the second person (see Alma 12:36), and then in first-person plural, thereby affirming that he joins these, his brothers and sisters, in the process. "Let us repent," he urges, "and harden not our hearts, that we provoke not the Lord our God to pull down his wrath upon us . . . ; but let us enter into the rest of God. . ." (Alma 12:37).

The next section of Alma's discourse relates to the Lord's ordaining of special "priests, after his holy order, which was after the order of his Son, to teach . . . the people." He asks the people to "cite your minds *forward* to the time when the Lord *gave* these commandments" (Alma 13:1; emphases added), ingeniously imploring his listeners to regard a future event as something already accomplished. It is the same with the priesthood foreordinations he discusses next; they are future events that are set in motion ahead of time, "from the foundation of the world according to the foreknowledge of God" (Alma 13:3). All are "on the same standing with their brethren" (Alma 13:5) in the beginning, having been foreordained but not predestined. There is no mention of social position or privilege.

Concluding his doctrinal instruction with a poetic exhortation declaring the gloriousness of the proclaimed "day of salvation" (Alma 13:21), Alma then makes a personal plea full of hope and promise. Conscious still, as were predecessors like Jacob, that the people to whom he speaks are "wanderers in a strange land" (Alma 13:23), he encourages them even as he counsels them to repent. Angels are declaring the coming of the Lord "unto many at this time in our land" (an unexpected disclosure!), he states, to prepare "the hearts of the children of men to receive his word at the time of his coming in his glory" (Alma 13:24). Alma seems increasingly aware that the prophesied birth of the Lord in the flesh is close. His own happy anticipation of that event spills unrestrained into his plea: "Would to God that it might be in my day; but let it be sooner or later, in it I will rejoice" (Alma 13:25). Alma would love to greet his Lord in person and participate in his ministry.

The final entreaty Mormon records of this occasion, though Alma "spake many more words unto the people, which are not written in this book" (Alma 13:31), is typical of Alma in its hopefulness and its emphasis on gentle submissiveness to divine will:

... humble yourselves before the Lord, and call on his holy name, and watch and pray continually, that ye may not be tempted above that which ye can bear, and thus be led by the Holy Spirit, becoming humble, meek, submissive, patient, full of love and all long-suffering;

Having faith on the Lord; having a hope that ye shall receive eternal life; having the love of God always in your hearts, that ye may be lifted up at the last day and enter into his rest. (Alma 13:28-29)

Although some are converted, the general populace of Ammonihah respond to this gentle message with violence and abuse. The Lord protects the lives of Alma and Amulek, and ultimately delivers them; but even so, they are bound and imprisoned and forced to witness unspeakable atrocities perpetrated upon believers. And, despite the miraculous events at the prison, the people of Ammonihah remain unconverted. Of the persuasion of the false Nehor, they are "a hard-hearted and a stiffnecked people" who do "not believe in the repentance of their sins" (Alma 15:15). The Nehors conveniently believe that repentance is unnecessary, because all will be "saved" whether they live virtuously or wickedly. Alma and Amulek travel next to Sidom, where they find people receptive to the word, and the two missionary priests have great success establishing the church.

If occasionally we forget that the Lord's servants, people like Alma and Amulek, are human beings who sacrifice in extraordinary ways for the sake of the faith, chapter 15 offers a poignant reminder. We learned some time ago that Amulek was a prominent citizen in Ammonihah before an angel visited him and Alma arrived to change his life. But we probably did not stop to count the cost of Amulek's decision to join with Alma and devote his life to teaching the gospel of Jesus Christ. Not only did Amulek suffer imprisonment, deprivation, and brutality, but he sacrificed everything he had valued up to that time—position, honor, family, friends, wealth, and property. We are quietly reminded that he had "forsaken all his gold, and silver, and his precious things, which were in the land of Ammonihah, for the word of God." Not only that, but he was "rejected by those who were once his friends and also by his father and his kindred" (Alma 15:16). I, who have been required to sacrifice little for my faith, and in fact feel the greater support from my family and many friends because of it, can never really know the depth of Amulek's suffering. Even Alma, who experienced persecution with him, did not have to deny friends and family in order to embrace the truth; and Alma still had his home in Zarahemla. There, "having established the church at Sidom" (Alma 15:17), Alma takes a spent and nearly broken Amulek, and there he "did administer unto him in his tribulations, and strengthened him in the Lord" (Alma 15:18).

The record does not make a lot of this, but I think we should not overlook such things. One does not have to read far into the Book of Mormon to encounter heroes of the first magnitude, remembering that the great mythologist, Joseph Campbell, rightly described the hero in any culture as one who lives for something other than self. Amulek is a hero in the truest sense. And it is gratifying to remember that in the beginning of their association, Amulek took a weary and driven Alma into his home and ministered to his needs. In a sense their relationship has come full circle, for Alma is now able to serve as he was served.

Chapter 16 briefly rehearses events of the three years following the return of Alma and Amulek to Zarahemla. Early in the first year, the Lamanites begin to invade Nephite territory and are beaten back—but not before they lay waste the city of Ammonihah in just one day. We recall that back in Alma 9:4, the wicked citizenry debunked Alma's prophetic powers, saying, "We will not believe thy words if thou shouldst prophesy that this great city should be destroyed in one day." There is certainly poetic justice in the fact that "in one day it was left desolate" and "every living soul . . . was destroyed" (Alma 16:9-10). Furthermore, the city suffered unspeakable desecration, for the human "carcases were mangled by dogs and wild beasts of the wilderness." "Bodies were heaped up" and "covered with a shallow covering," but "so great was the scent thereof that the people did not go in to possess the land of Ammonihah for many years" (Alma 16:10-11). I guess not. We must assume, too, that Amulek suffers yet another great grief. Surely, his family and friends are all destroyed in this massacre.

The next three years are peaceful ones among the members of the church, who are beginning to look forward in earnest to the coming of their Lord to the earth. Notably, "there was no inequality among them." They know that Christ will be born in another land, but they also now know that after his resurrection, he will appear in their land. It is a time of preparation, and "the Lord did pour out his Spirit on all the face of the land," that both the minds and the hearts of the people might be ready "to receive the word which should be taught among them at the time of his coming," and to receive it "with joy" (Alma 16:16-17).

# *13*

## Alma 17-28: The Great Lamanite Conversion

At this point, the record interrupts Alma's narrative to reverse its chronology and recount the missionary journeys and experiences of the sons of King Mosiah. These men, we remember, declined the kingship and elected to return to the land of Nephi and preach the gospel to the Lamanites. Chapters 17-26 of the book of Alma follow Mosiah's sons and their fellow laborers until their chance encounter with Alma after fourteen years' separation. It is a joyful reunion of old friends and fellow converts.

Among the defining aspects of the Book of Mormon, and the book of Alma in particular, is the manifest assumption that the mind and heart operate as one, that visionary experiences and glorious prophecies are wholly compatible with splendid intellectual gifts. Religious faith, intelligence, and stability of character are praised together. I mention elsewhere in this essay that the intellects as well as the affections of the people were being prepared for the completing doctrines that Christ would teach when he came. And now, as Alma happily greets "his brethren in the Lord," he comments on their steady intelligence. They "had waxed strong in the knowledge of the truth; for they were men of a sound understanding and they had searched the scriptures diligently, that they might know the word of God" (Alma 17:2). Being himself a person of extraordinary mental ability, Alma values that quality in his friends. And like him, by exercising faith and reason together, they have avoided the opposing extremes of secular intellectual pride and religious zealotry. Alma lauds the "sound understanding" they have acquired through their study, and then adds, "But this is not all; they had given themselves to much prayer, and fasting; . . . and when they taught, they taught with power and authority of God" (Alma 17:3). The teacher is always a learner.

The record of their labors confirms the courage of these missionaries as they set out armed only with faith, mental acuity, and weapons for obtaining food. The odds are against them as they seek "to preach the word of God" to an "indolent" and sometimes "wild and a hardened and a ferocious people; a people who delighted in murdering the Nephites" and whose "hearts were set upon riches" (Alma 17:14-15). The moment must have been a poignant one when "they separated themselves one from another, and went forth . . . every man alone" (Alma 17:17). The phrase "every man alone" sounds both lonesome and foreboding.

The narrative focuses first on Mosiah's son Ammon (not to be confused with the Ammon who had led an expedition from Zarahemla to the land of Nephi), the leader of the group. A winning sort of fellow, Ammon turns an arrest to his advantage in the land of Ishmael, gaining favor with the Lamanite king by single-handedly defeating a gang of plunderers who try to scatter and steal the royal flocks.[1] The event stirs the conscience of King Lamoni, who clearly has the idea of a supreme being, a "Great Spirit" (Alma 18:18), etched in his racial memory. Uncertain as to whether Ammon is mortal or divine, Lamoni vows to grant anything within his kingly capacity if Ammon will reveal the source of his unusual power. A pleased Ammon, who is characterized as "wise, yet harmless" (Alma 18:22), asks only that Lamoni accept his message. (A questionable word, "harmless." Ammon certainly intends Lamoni no harm, but the thieves who lost their limbs to his sword would scarcely call him harmless.)

By his own vow, Lamoni is obligated to listen, and a fascinating dialogue ensues between the two men. Ammon first teaches Lamoni the rudiments of religious belief, in the main who and what God is and where he dwells. Then Ammon expounds upon the plan of salvation, from the Creation and Fall to the coming of Christ. He also tells Lamoni of records and scriptures, and the his-

---

[1] It is apparent from this section of the Book of Mormon that many, though perhaps not all (see Alma 17:14), of the Lamanite people lived in cities and enjoyed abundant material amenities. Although "the more idle part of the Lamanites lived in the wilderness, and dwelt in tents" (Alma 22:28), the others, like Lamoni and his people, appear to have lived in permanent dwellings. Their ethic in regard to thievery and murder seems to have been different from that taught among the Nephites, however.

tory of his rebellious ancestors. Overwhelmed by the force of Ammon's words and the Spirit's confirmation, Lamoni falls into a three-day death-like trance, perhaps another symbolic type of the Savior's three-day entombment. The chapters that follow chronicle a spectacular event in Book of Mormon history, the beginning of a great Lamanite conversion to Christianity.

If we have wondered what can be accomplished in a person who has lost consciousness, Ammon provides an answer. Lamoni is "under the power of God":

> . . . the dark veil of unbelief was being cast away from his mind, and the light which did light up his mind, which was the light of the glory of God, which was a marvelous light of his goodness—yea, this light had infused such joy into his soul, the cloud of darkness having been dispelled, and that the light of everlasting life was lit up in his soul, yea, he knew that this had overcome his natural frame, and he was carried away in God— (Alma 19:6)

Complex syntax shows forth a complex event. Lamoni's experience is virtually unutterable, but his words in Alma 19:13 indicate that he has received a vision of the Redeemer. Most of us have been touched by the Spirit on occasion, and we recognize the exceptional character of that experience. But most of us have not been so moved spiritually as to be totally overcome physically, as were Lamoni and members of his household. What a scene that must have been—inert bodies everywhere. The quiet hero of the occasion is a "Lamanitish" servant woman (Alma 19:16) named Abish, a secret believer for many years.

Although many refuse to heed the words of a transformed Lamoni, many others gladly declare "that their hearts had been changed; that they had no more desire to do evil" (Alma 19:33). Thus, Ammon's narrative replays the theme of Alma's first major discourse, the great change of heart that signifies repentance and makes redemption from sin possible through the Savior's atoning sacrifice. The magnitude of the conversion and the establishment of the church in the land of Ishmael is not easily fathomed from the brief account in Alma 19, but a great deal is suggested in the passing observation that many claimed to have seen and conversed with angels (see Alma 19:34). A society in which angels regularly and openly speak with large numbers of mortals is beyond my poor powers to imagine.

Chapter 20 advances the narrative, with Ammon and Lamoni setting out for Middoni to free Ammon's brother, Aaron, and two fellow missionaries from prison. En route, Ammon and Lamoni encounter Lamoni's father, king over all the Lamanites.[2] Angered at Lamoni's traitorous sympathy for his hated enemies, Lamoni's father commands his son to kill Ammon. Lamoni refuses, and his father threatens to kill Lamoni. The incident is a good reminder of just how deep the Lamanites' hatred runs. When Lamoni's father twice refers to Nephi, our great prophet-hero, as "a liar" (Alma 20:10, 13), we are startled to see him and his descendants through antagonistic eyes. We know that Laman and Lemuel despised Nephi, but their vicious words against him do not appear in Nephi's report. Their venom, however, has festered through the centuries as succeeding generations of Lamanite offspring have been taught that Nephi was a blackguard, a villain who "robbed our fathers." And "now [Nephi's] children," the king complains, are up to his old tricks, attempting by "their lyings" and deceit to "again rob us of our property" (Alma 20:13). The incident provides another valuable exercise in point of view.

When Ammon intercedes between father and son, the incensed father turns his attack on Ammon. Vanquished as much by Ammon's greatness of spirit as by his physical strength, the defeated king offers any terms, "even to half of the kingdom" (Alma 20:23), in exchange for his life. Ammon asks only for the release of the imprisoned missionaries and freedom for Lamoni to live and rule as he sees fit. The "greatly astonished" king (Alma 20:27) opens his mind to the word and the door to the Christian gospel throughout the Lamanite world. Less fortunate than their

---

[2] The Lamanites seem to have had a system of greater and lesser kings, something unheard of in Western European history. There was certainly no model for this type of governance in Joseph Smith's experience.

brother missionary, Aaron, Muloki, and Ammah have been cast out and driven "from place to place" (Alma 20:30). Each of them ends up in Middoni where he is stripped, beaten, bound, and starved.

At this point, the record again backtracks briefly, now following Aaron's activities after he separates from Ammon. Aaron journeys first to a large and hostile city, incongruously called Jerusalem. It is inhabited by an aggregation of Lamanites and two groups of apostate Nephites, the Amalekites[3] and the Amulonites. The latter groups, true to form, have outstripped the Lamanites in wickedness and incited them to abominations they might not have contrived on their own. As Mormon, who is quick to detect irony, says, "Now the Lamanites of themselves were sufficiently hardened, but the Amalekites and the Amulonites were still harder. . ." (Alma 21:3). Aaron eventually meets up with Muloki, Ammah, and other missionaries, and together they achieve varying degrees of success and failure. No success surpasses that of Ammon and Lamoni, however. The narrative returns to Ammon as Lamoni speaks to his people of freedom, rejoicing that they now enjoy "the liberty of worshiping the Lord their God according to their desires" (Alma 21:22). The subject of human liberty and freedom of worship is a recurring theme throughout the Book of Mormon. It is a theme that will soon be thrust into extraordinary prominence.

Mormon performs some rather demanding verbal acrobatics as he tracks the various missionaries and their activities. Once again, the narrative leaves Ammon and follows Aaron and his brothers, who are "led by the Spirit to the land of Nephi" (Alma 22:1) and to the palace of Lamoni's father. Both touched and troubled by Ammon's earlier words, this great king has many questions to ask Aaron. The monarch shows extraordinary willingness to be taught, vowing that "if now thou sayest there is a God, behold I

---

[3] The first Amaleki we encountered, back in the book of Omni, was an angry man. Perhaps it is his descendants who have fallen into apostasy.

will believe" (Alma 22:7). Incredibly, this same man had only recently thought to kill his own son for so believing.

As Ammon had done in teaching the king's son, Aaron instructs the older man, reading from the scriptures and expounding the Creation, the Fall, and "the plan of redemption" (Alma 22:13). Now hungry for truth, the once antagonistic king begs to know how he might merit eternal life. He deems no sacrifice too great for such a blessing. We who regard a tithe ample sacrifice might consider what this infidel is willing to pay. He offers to "give up all that I possess," even to "forsake my kingdom," in order to experience the great change of heart that makes one a child of Christ. "Yea," he pleads, "what shall I do that I may be born of God, having this wicked spirit rooted out of my breast, and receive his Spirit, that I may be filled with joy?" (Alma 22:15). This is not a man who enjoys the comfort of sure belief; this is a man seeking testimony, a man who would give everything to know if God does indeed live, and if salvation from death and sin is possible for one such as himself. In one of the sweetest moments in all of scripture, this once proud and mighty king falls to his knees and offers a simple prayer, wrenched in tremulous words from his humbled heart:

> O God, Aaron hath told me that there is a God; and if there is a God, and if thou art God, wilt thou make thyself known unto me, and I will give away all my sins to know thee, and that I may be raised from the dead, and be saved at the last day. (Alma 22:18)

That sincere one-sentence prayer quietly makes a promise of almost incomprehensible magnitude: "I will give away all my sins to know thee." To give up sins may be a greater sacrifice than to give up kingdoms. When it comes right down to it, our favorite sins may be the very things most of us are least willing to relinquish. We want salvation, and we long for purity, but too often we do not truly wish to change, to "give away" our sins—even to know God. And when we remember that pride and worldliness are the sins perhaps most frequently decried in the Book of

Mormon, we must acknowledge our failure to match the devotion and humble desire of this mightiest of the Lamanite kings in an uncharted land nearly a century before Christ's birth.

Following the king's overpowering conversion, churches are built, teachers and priests are appointed, the gospel is taught widely, and "thousands were brought to the knowledge of the Lord" (Alma 23:5). Again, the role of records in the conversion process is stressed. The fact that Aaron reads to the king from scripture (Alma 22:12) suggests that missionaries and other teachers enjoyed ready access to contents of the brass plates that were brought out of Jerusalem by Lehi's family. These scriptures must have been available in a portable, and combustible, form if teachers of the word carried them and knew their contents. (We remember that in Ammonihah records and scriptures were burned.) The Nephite missionaries also "taught the records and prophecies" of their new-world predecessors, "which were handed down even to the present time" (Alma 23:5). The importance of sacred records, indeed, of written language, is another abiding theme in the Book of Mormon.

This massive and lasting metamorphosis of entire Lamanite cities—among them Ishmael, Middoni, Nephi, Shilom, Shemlon, Lemuel, and Shimnilon—defies description. And it all began with one man's single-minded desire to save souls, with Ammon's entering King Lamoni's service as a humble guardian of his flocks. The Amalekites ("save only one," Alma 23:14) and the Amulonites, and the Lamanites living under their apostate influence, however, do not soften their hearts. Therefore, to distinguish themselves from their unpenitent kinspeople, the converted reject the Lamanite designation and adopt the name, Anti-Nephi-Lehies.[4] Furthermore, they become "very industrious" and "friendly with the Nephites," even opening "a correspondence with them." Most significant, "the curse of God did no more follow them" (Alma 23:18).

---

[4] I suspect that this awkward title results from a term that did not lend itself readily to translation.

There are many touching moments in the Book of Mormon, but none more moving than that reported in Alma 24 where these blessed Lamanite converts, as if in one magnificent gesture, lay down their weapons and vow to fight no more, though it cost them their lives. Indeed, many do pay that price; for shortly after Lamoni's aging father confers the greater kingdom on one of his sons, the Amalekites and Amulonites begin agitating among the unconverted Lamanites, inflaming their passions against their own king and people. War is imminent, but despite their grave danger, "there was not one soul . . . that would take up arms against their brethren; nay, they would not even make any preparations for war" (Alma 24:6). Speaking to his people with the calm repose of absolute faith, the new king serenely offers thanks to God that he has forgiven them and "taken away the guilt *from our hearts,* through the merits of his Son" (Alma 24:10; emphasis added).

This passage suggests that the Atonement has the power not only to remove the actual guilt of the repentant, but also to remove the *feelings* of guilt, and to bestow peace of conscience. Nevertheless, we should not miss the fact that the repentance of these people has been an arduous process. The king repeats his reminder that "it has been all we could do to repent sufficiently before God" (Alma 24:11); clearly, he does not want his people to put their hard-won forgiveness at risk. Urging them without fanfare to renounce war and weaponry permanently, he makes a metaphorical connection between blood-stained swords and the similarly-stained lives of his people: ". . . if we should stain our swords again they can no more be washed bright through the blood of the Son of our great God, which shall be shed for the atonement of our sins" (Alma 24:13). The Lamanite king chooses an apt figure, one that attaches double meaning to the words "blood" and "stain." When swords are stained with blood, so too are the souls of those who wield them; but the blood of the Savior washes away the stains of the repentant. The people as well as their swords will retain their newfound brightness if they refrain from bloodshed. The incongruity of the king's metaphor lends it force,[5] for ordinarily, a sharp-edged instrument is brightened rather than stained by use.

Now that our swords are clean, the Lamanite pleads again, let us "bury them deep in the earth, that they may be kept bright, as a testimony that we have never used them, at the last day; and if our brethren destroy us, behold, we shall go to our God and shall be saved" (Alma 24:16). In that declaration lies the true measure of a nation's courage; to die rather than harm another, enemy or not, is a standard few moderns would comprehend. In our efforts to create ever more powerful weaponry, we have ignored the most invincible weapon of all: fearless individual integrity.

Of one mind with their leader, these reborn infidels bury all their weapons of war and make a covenant with God. It is a covenant and more; it is a creed for the saintly life:

. . . rather than shed the blood of their brethren they would give up their own lives; and rather than take away from a brother they would give unto him; and rather than spend their days in idleness they would labor abundantly with their hands. (Alma 24:18)

Such a covenant proves the total transformation of these people and gives new meaning to the word "commitment"; every aspect of their lives is forever changed. Their story is at the center of Alma's narrative, just as the change of heart it exemplifies is at the center of his doctrinal teachings. Surely Mormon, too, is aware of this significant blending of theme and event. The dramatic juxtaposition of succeeding events, however, is highly ironic; for just as these humble Lamanite converts "buried the weapons of war, for peace," so "their brethren, the [unconverted] Lamanites, made preparations for war" (Alma 24:19-20). The record confirms that when their enemies approached, these noble souls neither fought them nor ran from them, but rather "went out to meet them, and prostrated themselves before them to the earth, and began to call

---

[5] Shakespeare employs the same figure when Othello urges a group of unruly Venetians to keep their swords bright by sheathing them.

on the name of the Lord; and thus they were in this attitude when the Lamanites began to fall upon them, and began to slay them with the sword" (Alma 24:21).

A thousand and five are swiftly killed, but then the Lamanites among their attackers lose heart for such slaughter. To kill the unarmed who neither run nor fight, who freely choose to "lie down and perish," and more than that, who "praised God even in the very act of perishing under the sword" (Alma 24:23), is to reap shame rather than victory. The Amalekites and Amulonites, however, feel no such remorse. These hardened apostate Nephites continue the carnage even as many descendants of Laman and Lemuel throw "down their weapons of war" and refuse to fight, joining "their brethren, relying upon the mercies of those whose arms were lifted to slay them" (Alma 24:25). The concluding moralism for this particular chapter makes an apt observation about the nature of apostasy:

> And thus we can plainly discern, that after a people have been once enlightened by the Spirit of God, and have had great knowledge of things pertaining to righteousness, and then have fallen away into sin and transgression, they become more hardened, and thus their state becomes worse than though they had never known these things. (Alma 24:30)

The upshot of these martial campaigns is that the remaining Lamanite aggressors, angered at having turned their swords against their own people, vent their fury on the Nephite city of Ammonihah. In so doing, they unwittingly fulfill Alma's prophecy of destruction for the wicked city that had imprisoned him (see Alma 9:18-19). Furthermore, in the course of the conflicts, "almost all the seed of Amulon and his brethren, who were the priests of Noah" (Alma 25:4), are killed, as Abinadi years ago had prophesied; and the rest, according to Alma's record, are hunted even "at this day" (Alma 25:9).

The point to be made here is that in spite of murder and strife, the great revolution has begun, the upward spiraling toward belief. Additional converts are made among the once ferocious descendants of Laman and Lemuel. Mistreated by their former allies, they "join themselves to the people of God" and "bury their weapons of war." With understanding far beyond that of Abinadi's ill-informed accusers, they observe the Law of Moses, which they know to be "a type of [Christ's] coming." They will "keep those outward performances" until he comes (Alma 25:13-15).

In the wake of these uncommon events, Mosiah's missionary sons—Ammon, Aaron, Omner, and Himni—though deeply saddened at the deaths of the slain, are overjoyed at their success in teaching the Lamanite nation and bringing many thousands to belief in Christ. Ammon, however, is more than overjoyed; he is ecstatic. Remembering his happy exuberance in teaching King Lamoni and the royal household, we should not expect reticence from the likes of this irrepressible fellow. He would not even understand the word. I like him immensely and find myself smiling all over as the jubilant Ammon exults to his brothers over the conversion of the Lamanites, in a veritable whirlwind of praise and thanksgiving.

Too elated to wait for responses, Ammon fires happy questions at his brothers and then answers them himself ("Behold, I answer for you," Alma 26:3). They are rhetorical anyway, and they launch Ammon into a spirited metaphorical summary of what has been accomplished. His enthusiasm is met, however, with a gentle "rebuke" from his brother Aaron, a more sober sort of fellow. Aaron cautions, "Ammon, I fear that thy joy doth carry thee away unto boasting" (Alma 26:10). Rather than daunting the agreeable Ammon, however, Aaron's criticism seems to catapult him into an unstoppable volley of praise. In language that almost dances, he answers Aaron: "I do not boast in my own strength," he cries, "nor in my own wisdom; but behold, my joy is full, yea, my heart is brim with joy, and I will rejoice in my God." God has "loosed" the converted "from the pains of hell," he declares, "and they are brought to sing redeeming love . . . because of the power of his word which is in us" (Alma 26:11-13).

No match for this verbal cyclone, Ammon's brothers appar-

ently indulge him. I hope that they were finally caught up in the
miracle that set Ammon's heart on fire and his tongue in motion.
In truth, Ammon finds language inadequate for his gladness, but
he is not slowed by the lack:

> Therefore, let us glory, yea, we will glory in the Lord; yea, we will
> rejoice, for our joy is full; yea, we will praise our God forever. Behold,
> who can glory too much in the Lord? Yea, who can say too much of
> his great power, and of his mercy, and of his long-suffering towards
> the children of men? Behold, I say unto you, I cannot say the small-
> est part which I feel. (Alma 26:16)

Reminded of his own conversion and the knowledge that led to
repentance, Ammon asks his brothers, ". . . what natural man is
there that knoweth these things? I say unto you, there is none that
knoweth these things, save it be the penitent" (Alma 26:21). I
note that in this passage Ammon treats "the natural man" and "the
penitent" as opposites, which helps us understand scriptural references that describe the "natural man" (i.e., the impenitent) as
God's enemy.

   This is not the last we will hear of Ammon, the unsinkable,
but I simply must quote his concluding words to his brothers as
he begs them to celebrate with him: "Now have we not reason to
rejoice? Yea, I say unto you, there never were men that had so
great reason to rejoice as we, since the world began. . ." (Alma
26:35). That bit of honest hyperbole persuades me to quote the
rest of his joyful outcry, which reads like a psalm of praise:

> . . . yea, and my joy is carried away, even unto boasting in my God;
> for he has all power, all wisdom, and all understanding; he compre-
> hendeth all things, and he is a merciful Being, even unto salvation, to
> those who will repent and believe on his name.
>    Now if this is boasting, even so will I boast; for this is my life and
> my light, my joy and my salvation,[6] and my redemption from ever-

---

[6] This line echoes the first verse of Psalm 27, which begins, "The Lord is my light and my salvation," suggesting again the continuing presence and influence of the brass plates among the Nephite faithful. But as the
next sentence suggests, even the optimistic Ammon knows he is a castaway.

lasting wo. Yea, blessed is the name of my God, who has been mindful of this people, who are a branch of the tree of Israel, and has been lost from its body in a strange land; yea, . . . wanderers in a strange land.

Now my brethren, we see that God is mindful of every people, whatsoever land they may be in; yea, he numbereth his people, and his bowels of mercy are over all the earth. Now this is my joy, and my great thanksgiving; yea, and I will give thanks unto my God forever. Amen. (Alma 26:35-37)

Ammon's great physical strength is more than matched by his spiritual energy and his poetic soul. He is the kind of man whom fathers and brothers good-naturedly tease and tolerate, but whom mothers and sisters and maiden aunts adore. Ammon, bless him, is not embarrassed by emotion. It simply is not in his nature to be half-hearted about anything.

I smile again when in the next chapter this big, strapping fellow, who could fight off a whole pack of sheep rustlers, is so thrilled at reuniting with Alma, so "swallowed up in the joy of his God," that he actually swoons. Either Alma or Mormon adds knowingly, "Now was not this exceeding joy?" (Alma 27:17-18). Ammon is living rebuttal to the notion that humility and boyish enthusiasm are somehow incompatible. I suspect that the sliver of humor in the next verse is intentional: "Now the joy of Alma in meeting his brethren was truly great, and also the joy of Aaron, of Omner, and Himni; but behold their joy was not that to exceed their strength" (Alma 27:19). And we know whose joy did exceed his strength, do we not? I love that passage.

As the narrative continues, the Lamanite converts are threatened again by the frustrated Amalekites, and again "they suffered themselves to be slain" (Alma 27:3) rather than take up arms. After counseling with the Lord, it is determined that they will seek sanctuary in Zarahemla, despite their king's misgivings. From this time forward, they drop the tri-partite title "Anti-Nephi-Lehies" (to my relief, I confess) and are called the people of Ammon. These once murderous people are unimpeachable testaments to the miracle of true repentance.

Chapter 28 is a transitional chapter in which Mormon writes that a "tremendous battle" (Alma 28:2) ensues after the people of Ammon are established in Jershon. Many thousands are slain on both sides, but the Lamanites are finally driven from the land. Mormon's summary rehearses a bittersweet tale of contrasting impulses and emotions, of "sorrows, and . . . afflictions, and . . . incomprehensible joy" (Alma 28:8). These people, like most mortals, have cause to rejoice and cause to mourn. They know "sorrow because of death and destruction among men, and joy because of the light of Christ unto life" (Alma 28:14).

## 14

## Alma 29-34: Sermons on Faith and Redemption

In chapter 29, Mormon again steps aside from the narrative to quote directly from Alma's record. He includes from Alma's personal writings a poetic monologue, a hymn of praise that opens in an unusual rhetorical supplication. Apparently energized by his own success teaching the Nephites, and by the astonishing success of his friends among the Lamanites, Alma strains against the mortal limitations that prevent him from proclaiming repentance and the saving gospel to every living soul on earth.

> O that I were an angel, and could have the wish of mine heart, that I might go forth and speak with the trump of God, with a voice to shake the earth, and cry repentance unto every people!
>
> Yea, I would declare unto every soul, as with the voice of thunder, repentance and the plan of redemption, that they should repent and come unto our God, that there might not be more sorrow upon all the face of the earth. (Alma 29:1-2)

This is not a modest desire, this wish to "speak with the trump of God" in a "voice of thunder" that would "shake the earth." Perhaps startled by his own boldness, Alma quickly checks himself: "But behold, I am a man, and do sin in my wish; for I ought to be content with the things which the Lord hath allotted unto me" and not "harrow up in my desires" (Alma 29:3-4). Even as I copy Alma's words, inscribed three-quarters of a century before Christ's birth, I can almost feel his presence and comprehend his desire. At some time or other, most of us have conceived a fancy for extraordinary power—to fly, to make a perfect score in some game or examination, to enjoy perpetual youth—but few of us have wished it for Alma's altruistic reasons.

Surely, Alma writes in full awareness of the fact that as a mortal in a remote land, he can reach relatively few people. He faithfully engraves his soliloquy of faith on the metal record in his keeping, however; and perhaps it is no coincidence that an angel (Moroni, who delivered Mormon's abridged record to Joseph Smith) did indeed miraculously give Alma voice across continents and seas, in a sense fulfilling his petition. Alma's prayer was nineteen hundred years in the answering, but it has been answered nonetheless. What is the message Alma would broadcast? Mainly repentance, repentance and redemption, a subject he knows firsthand. Having been snatched from damnation himself, he understands the magnitude of the choice each mortal must make.

The preceding chapter (chapter 28), a transitional interlude depicting life's duality, anticipated Alma's next words, which are words about choice and about the polarities that shape our desires and prompt our wills. The Lord, Alma says, "granteth unto men according to their desire, whether it be unto death or unto life; . . . he allotteth unto men according to their wills, whether they be unto salvation or unto destruction" (Alma 29:4). This is just one of several places where the Book of Mormon teaches that mortals do indeed reap everlasting life or spiritual death according to their individual election of one or the other. In the next verse, Alma employs three pairs of opposites to describe life's most fundamental choice for those who have been taught the difference between good and evil:

> . . . good and evil have come before all men; he that knoweth not good from evil is blameless; but he that knoweth good and evil, to him it is given according to his desires, whether he desireth good or evil, life or death, joy or remorse of conscience. (Alma 29:5)

Then, seemingly still rather abashed at having boldly dared wish to be a trumpeting angel, shaking the earth with the word of God, Alma speaks in self-reprimand:

> Now, seeing that I know these things, why should I desire more than to perform the work to which I have been called?
> Why should I desire that I were an angel, that I could speak unto all the ends of the earth? (Alma 29:6-7)

In a very real sense, this personal discourse is Alma's soul-searching scrutiny of his own calling. His desire is to take the shining word to the whole earth, but his assignment is more circumscribed and he knows it. Readers of Alma will see that modern-day Mormons come by their missionary zeal honestly. No one could accuse either Alma or his devout Mormon heirs of reluctance to share their belief. Alma also accepts the mortal limitations of his calling, as each of us must. At the same time, he rejoices in the successful labors of Ammon and the others, who released a whole nation from the bondage of ignorance. So great is his joy, he cries, that "my soul is carried away, even to the separation of it from the body, as it were" (Alma 29:16). Such intense happiness is beyond most of us, though with Ammon it seemed perfectly natural. It is clear, too, that Alma is not describing a psychic or mystical experience. Rather, he is looking for words to express the inexpressible, to convey feelings and experiences beyond the symbolism of mortal language.

A return to the narrative in chapter 30 shows another side of Alma as he challenges and condemns an Antichrist named Korihor, who tries to argue the Nephites and the people of Ammon into disbelief. The record is careful to note that although the Nephites "were strict in observing the ordinances of God" (Alma 30:3), civil law could not touch Korihor because, thankfully, "there was no law against a man's belief." Such a law would be "strictly contrary to the commands of God" (Alma 30:7), for in Nephite society, all are to be equal under the law.

At this point Alma makes a direct reference to Joshua 24:15, saying, "For thus saith the scripture: Choose ye this day, whom ye will serve" (Alma 30:8). I find it interesting that Alma would make an explicit connection between Nephite law guaranteeing freedom of belief for all persons and the Old Testament injunction to choose between God and his adversaries. I realize now that the emphasis in that famous Joshua passage is as much on the exercise of agency as it is on the nature of the choice made. The God-given right to choose underlies whatever is chosen. By divine edict, civil

rights and personal liberty are the basis of government in any society divinely sanctioned in the land of promise, a land consecrated
for the nurturing of souls in a climate of freedom.

Under protection of law, then, Korihor attacks the basic doctrines of the church and its leaders. He tellingly reveals his base
assessment of the human soul in arguing that "every man fared in
this life according to the management of the creature," and "prospered according to his genius" (Alma 30:17). The people of
Ammon (the converted Lamanites) are not fooled by Korihor, and
neither is the high priest in Gideon. Brought at last before Alma
and the chief judge in Zarahemla, Korihor "rise[s] up in great
swelling words" (Alma 30:31)—a fitting phrase to characterize
pride. However, he is no match for the great Nephite, neither
intellectually nor spiritually. One by one, Alma demolishes
Korihor's arguments; and when Korihor foolishly repeats his
demand for a convincing sign that God exists, Alma enjoins God
to strike him dumb. On the instant, Korihor loses the power of
speech, and the chief judge cannot resist taunting him a little. "In
whom did ye desire that Alma should show forth his sign?" he
asks, adding, "Would ye that he should afflict others, to show
unto thee a sign?" (Alma 30:51). Cast out, the once arrogant
Antichrist meets an ignominious end among a group of separatists
called Zoramites. Moralizing on the incident, the text makes an
important point about the devil's reliability: "And thus we see the
end of him who perverteth the ways of the Lord; and thus we see
that the devil will not support his children at the last day, but doth
speedily drag them down to hell" (Alma 30:60). The devil is reliable only in his unreliability.

The Zoramites who make such quick work of Korihor are an
odd bunch. Not only do they engage in gang-style murder, but
they worship idols and by other means "pervert . . . the ways of
the Lord" (Alma 31:1). Alma is sorely grieved over them, and the
Nephites fear that they might "enter into a correspondence with
the Lamanites" (Alma 31:4) that would threaten Nephite borders.
Alma determines to deflect this threat by converting the
Zoramites. He knows that "the preaching of the word had a great

tendency to lead the people to do that which was just," and that, in fact, "it had had more powerful effect upon the minds of the people than the sword, or anything else" (Alma 31:5). Accustomed as our world has grown to violent persuasion, we too often forget that important truth: the *idea* is indeed more powerful than any tangible weaponry. Force may subdue and silence the vanquished, but it does not alter thinking. The only lasting victory lies in the winning of minds.

Alma sets out with Ammon, Aaron, Omner, Amulek, the converted Zeezrom, and two of his own sons, Shiblon and Corianton, hoping through "the virtue of the word of God" (Alma 31:5) to restore the Zoramites to Christianity. It will not be easy, for the missionaries find a mystifying sort of worship among the Zoramites in Antionum. These dissenters, who had once been taught the true faith, now speak of God only in weekly services, as they assemble around a tower in the center of their synagogue. In turn, they mount the tower and offer a rote prayer that articulates a strange and false doctrine. The prayer assumes, for example, that God is, was, and will be only "a spirit" (Alma 31:15); that "there shall be no Christ" (Alma 31:16); that the Zoramites are God's only elect, "a chosen and a holy people" (Alma 31:18); and that "all around us are elected to be cast by [God's] wrath down to hell" (Alma 31:17).

The perverse gratitude expressed in this prayer is not gratitude at all, but pride, pure and simple; and any people who regard themselves as holier than others, and more favored of God, have fallen into pride's deadliest trap. In particular, the Zoramites discount prophecy—more especially prophecy of the coming Christ—thanking God "that their hearts were not stolen away to believe in things to come, which they knew nothing about" (Alma 31:22). Their hearts, it turns out, are set on "their costly apparel, and their ringlets, and their bracelets, and their ornaments of gold" (Alma 31:28).

Never before have we seen Alma in such despair. He is very nearly broken-hearted that after all his labor, a group of former Nephites should be consumed by material vanity and pride and caught up in apostate doctrine. Perhaps the two go together only too well. To make matters worse, Alma's physical health is apparently flagging just now, for he confesses to being "infirm" and prays for strength to "bear with mine infirmities" (Alma 31:30). Mormon includes Alma's anguished prayer (Alma 31:26-35), seemingly word for word, as the discouraged prophet begs his Lord for personal comfort; for success for himself and his companions in their labors; and for strength, "power, and wisdom" to return "these, our brethren" (Alma 31:35), to truth. The juxtaposition of Alma's disheartened plea for comfort against his celebratory soliloquy (in chapter 29) creates a tension in the text that illustrates the very duality of human experience Alma had described earlier. That duality is nowhere more obvious than in the prophetic calling, which alternately, or simultaneously, yields both joy and pain.

Alma's prayer of grief and supplication shows another aspect of his individual nature, too—his susceptibility to sorrow as well as his capacity for joy. Alma prays not for ease in the task, but for comfort of soul, strength to bear what occurs, and "power and wisdom" to do the work of conversion. It is well to remember that the supplicant here is not an irresolute weakling. He is, rather, the mighty leader who, against immeasurable odds, established the church of God throughout the entire Nephite nation and presided over the conversion of the Lamanite nation. He is the high priest who reduced the influential Korihor to a mute beggar. He is the political powerhouse who left the highest government position in the land in order to devote full time to the work of the Lord. He is also a man bowed low by sorrow and affliction. No strangers to discouragement ourselves, we discover in this unguarded moment the Alma who is our brother.

Fortified by the Spirit for their individual labors among the Zoramites, Alma and the others begin proselyting throughout Antionum, in synagogues, houses, and streets. As Alma teaches on a hill called Onidah, a "great multitude" (Alma 32:4) of the poor surge forward, complaining that the fraternity of prideful priests and members has barred them from worship in the very synagogues they helped to build. In their compulsory humility, however, Alma sees an opportunity for instruction. The humble, he teaches, may be especially receptive to wisdom. We do not always think to connect the two, humility and wisdom, but what Alma says makes sense. Surely, arrogance is the signature of foolishness; the truly wise know their limitations and their dependence on God. There is such a thing as the flaunting of learning; there is no such thing as the flaunting of wisdom.

More blessed than the humble poor, Alma says, are those whose humility is not coerced. Using this point as a springboard, he launches into one of his finest discourses, perhaps the highlight of the whole book of Alma. Not easy reading by any means, Alma's sermon is a masterpiece of reason and composition, a splendid discussion on the nature and acquisition of faith. In a single verse Alma describes the connection between faith and spontaneous humility, which is quite different from the compulsory humility of his listeners, though both may lead to belief:

> Therefore, blessed are they who humble themselves without being compelled to be humble; or rather, in other words, blessed is he that believeth in the word of God, and is baptized without stubbornness of heart, yea, without being brought to know the word, or even compelled to know, before they will believe. (Alma 32:16)

The "stubborn of heart" accept truth only when their circumstances or the evidence of their senses obligates them to believe. This is not faith, Alma says, "for if a man knoweth a thing he hath no cause to believe, for he knoweth it" (Alma 32:18). Furthermore, *knowing* God's will and failing to do it brings greater condemnation than merely *believing* it and ignoring it.

The exercise of faith, on the other hand, requires a leap in the dark, a heartfelt desire to know, a desire that is the beginning of enlightenment. "Faith," Alma explains, "is not to have a perfect knowledge of things; therefore if ye have faith ye hope for things which are not seen, which are true" (Alma 32:21; compare Hebrews 11:1). He also makes a careful point about revelation.

Shifting from the more common, generic use of the term "man," he states rather emphatically that women and children as well as men receive divine instruction and speak the words of God.

His own words, even at this moment, Alma says, become a test of faith: "Ye cannot know of their surety at first, unto perfection, any more than faith is a perfect knowledge" (Alma 32:26). Try "an experiment upon my words," he implores; exercise just the merest "particle of faith." Alma begins at ground level, meeting the Zoramites (and the reader) where they are, asking them to give faith a chance: ". . . even if ye can no more than desire to believe, let this desire work in you, even until ye believe in a manner that ye can give place for a portion of my words" (Alma 32:27). This is surely one of the most vital concepts ever proposed for the fledgling in faith: if one desires faith, that *desire* creates a climate in which the word can thrive.

For these spiritual adolescents, Alma frames his discourse meticulously, presenting his proposed "experiment" as an extended metaphor of the planting and nurturing of a seed until it takes root and becomes a fruit-bearing tree. As in the Savior's parable recorded in Luke 8:11-15, Alma's metaphorical seed is the word of God; and the first step in Alma's experiment of faith, which is a test of the goodness of the seed, is the willingness of a seeker for truth to let the seed be planted. Unless the seed, or word, is planted, its goodness cannot be tested. But if planted, a good seed will begin to swell, "to enlarge [the] soul," "to enlighten [the] understanding," and "to be delicious" (Alma 32:28). Those who love language know that words can indeed be "delicious," almost physically savored. Alma conjectures, then, that these swelling motions will "increase your faith" even though "it hath not grown up to a perfect knowledge" (Alma 32:29). Openness to receive the seed must displace refusal.

By contemplating the contrasting behavior of good and bad seeds, the person in whom a good seed is planted can know of a surety whether or not the seed is good, Alma says, and at that point "your knowledge is perfect in that thing, and your faith is dormant; and this because ye know. . ." (Alma 32:34). The new understanding is good "because it is discernible" as light (Alma 32:35). This is a crucial observation, for evil cannot be so discerned. You have glimpsed the light, Alma assures his listeners, but your knowledge is not perfect and you must not "lay aside your faith" (Alma 32:35-36). You must now nourish the growing tree, that it may take firm root, that you may one day pluck its fruit.

This is Alma's parable of the planting of the seed, of the desire for faith that is willing to test the word by allowing its planting in the mind and heart. In one sense the parable is a metaphor for the whole Book of Mormon, which is an embodiment of the word, and which, by implication, asks that its readers put it to the test Alma outlines. Specifically, does it enlighten the mind and enlarge the soul? Alma cautions, however, that sometimes even a tree sprouting from a good seed will not take root, "not because the seed was not good, neither . . . because the fruit thereof would not be desirable; but . . . because your ground is barren, and ye will not nourish the tree" (Alma 32:39). With that compelling image of the barren ground of our own closed minds and hearts, Alma makes his point: "And thus, if ye will not nourish the word, looking forward with an eye of faith to the fruit thereof, ye can never pluck of the fruit of the tree of life" (Alma 32:40). He then turns from a negative to a positive supposition:

> But if ye will nourish the word, yea, nourish the tree as it beginneth to grow, by your faith with great diligence, and with patience, looking forward to the fruit thereof, it shall take root; and behold it shall be a tree springing up unto everlasting life. (Alma 32:41)

The word "springing" captures the upward surge of Alma's thought. I note, too, that three times in the final verses of chapter 32, he urges patience and diligence in nourishing the seed of faith and awaiting its fruits. So often, we want immediate rewards for our faith, instant miracles, blessings and certitude within the hour. This, Alma teaches, is not how faith generally works. Rather, the rewards of faith lie in "your diligence, and patience, and long-suffering, waiting for the tree to bring forth fruit unto you" (Alma 32:43).

Alma's picture of the final harvest for one who nourishes the seed of faith is pure poetry, full of alliteration, assonance, and balanced repetition:

> . . . by and by ye shall pluck the fruit thereof, which is most precious, which is sweet above all that is sweet, and which is white above all that is white, yea, and pure above all that is pure; and ye shall feast upon this fruit even until ye are filled, that ye hunger not, neither shall ye thirst. (Alma 32:42)

This rather amazing sermon, so simple in its form and so grand in its message, is a diamond of lucidity and brilliance, a dazzling treasure in its own right. It also reveals one more facet of Alma, the man and prophet: he is an artist.

Alma may have thought his sermon finished, but questions from his apparently baffled listeners lead to a rather lengthy postscript. He has been so careful, so precise, so studied in his exposition that it seems none could have failed to understand. And yet the questions come hammering back—

> . . . whether they should believe in one God, that they might obtain this fruit of which he had spoken, or how they should plant the seed, or the word of which he had spoken, which he said must be planted in their hearts; or in what manner they should begin to exercise their faith. (Alma 33:1)

I think I know how Alma must have felt. This is how my students have always behaved after I have made a lengthy and (so I think) crystal-clear explanation of the nature of the next examination or the expectations for the next paper. They are too busy framing questions to hear my instructions. Nevertheless, the questions confirm that they—my students and Alma's Zoramites—are engaged; their teacher has caught their attention.

Alma, patient Alma, backtracks to the familiar, the matter his listeners raised in the beginning: their exclusion from the synagogues because of their poverty. He had said earlier that worship was not merely a once-a-week affair in a synagogue (see Alma

32:10-11). Quoting now (as Jacob had done very early) from the ancient prophet Zenos, whose writings appeared on the brass plates but were omitted from the Old Testament as we have it, Alma teaches that worship and prayer are not limited to designated buildings or schedules, but can occur anywhere—wilderness, field, house, or closet. The prayer, however, must be intended for the ears of God, "not of men" (Alma 32:8).

Making several allusions to Old Testament prophets familiar to his listeners, Alma takes still another route to establish his point. By way of Zenos and Moses, he introduces the being whom mortals are to worship without constraints of hour or circumstance, in whom they are to exercise faith. These Zoramites need to connect their worship to Jesus Christ, and they need to understand his mission. Worship, whether in a religious building or not, is pointless if it is directed to a false god and unconnected with the Savior and his redemption. Alma wants to steer his listeners onto a new course, and he has to start at an elementary level because they do not even comprehend their deficiency. It was very different with the Lamanite kings taught by Ammon and Aaron; they knew their lack and they hungered to know the true and living God.

The word Alma wishes his Zoramite listeners to plant in their hearts, the word spoken by all the prophets, the truth that he wants them to "begin to believe," is no more and no less than the Christian gospel: ". . . the Son of God . . . will come to redeem his people," "he shall suffer and die to atone for their sins," and "he shall rise again from the dead, which shall bring to pass the resurrection, that all men shall stand before him, to be judged at the last and judgment day, according to their works" (Alma 33:22). As before, Alma declares that the choice for belief is theirs. In the end, he returns to his metaphor of the seed; he knows no better way to describe the earnest overture into faith. And now he adds a pointed reference to the Savior:

> . . . I desire that ye shall plant this word in your hearts, and as it beginneth to swell even so nourish it by your faith. And behold, it will become a tree, springing up in you unto everlasting life. And then may

> God grant unto you that your burdens may be light, through the joy
> of his Son. (Alma 33:23)

This is Alma's last recorded public sermon, but it is not his last recorded discourse. After interjecting Amulek's sermon on the same occasion, and a summary chapter as well, Mormon includes Alma's patriarchal counsel to his sons. But first, Amulek.

Amulek's sermon, recorded in Alma 34, is proof of Alma's prescribed experiment, for the word was planted and took root in Amulek's willing heart. His splendid discourse, enlivened by faith and keen doctrinal understanding, is one of the delicious fruits of that planting. Once a novice in the faith, and only recently recovered from severe emotional and physical exhaustion, Amulek has become a spiritual powerhouse and a dynamic teacher. I love this sermon as I love King Benjamin's. Arising as Alma finishes his address to the poor among the Zoramites, an inspired Amulek enjoins his listeners to "prepare your minds" (Alma 34:3) to receive the truth that "the word is in Christ unto salvation" (Alma 34:6). How frequently Book of Mormon peoples are asked to prepare their minds for instruction—and how seldom, perhaps, do their latter-day counterparts think to apply that counsel. Amulek's brilliant elucidation of the Atonement in the next eight verses is almost without parallel.

Jacob had spoken of the need for an "infinite atonement" (2 Nephi 9:7), but not until Amulek is the term defined for the reader. The "great and last sacrifice," Amulek explains, cannot be "a sacrifice of man, neither of beast, neither of any manner of fowl; for it shall not be a human sacrifice; but it must be an infinite and eternal sacrifice" (Alma 34:10). There is the key—an infinite sacrifice is a divine, not a human, sacrifice. Blending logic and inspiration, Amulek reasons that since in the realm of human possibility no man "can sacrifice his own blood which will atone for the sins of another" (Alma 34:11)—Nephite civil law, for example, explicitly "requireth the life of him who hath murdered" (Alma 34:12)—"nothing . . . short of an infinite atonement . . . will suffice for the sins of the world" (Alma 34:12). Furthermore, the "great and last sacrifice" presupposes "a stop to the shedding of blood," for with it "shall the law of Moses be fulfilled" (Alma 34:13). "The whole meaning of the law" of Moses resides in its "pointing to that great and last sacrifice," which sacrifice must and "will be the Son of God, yea, infinite and eternal" (Alma 34:14). Thus, Amulek proves, an infinite atonement is of necessity an atonement made by an immortal, eternal God.

Moving from argument to plain talk, Amulek states the doctrine, explaining how such an atonement introduces mercy into the sin-and-justice equation for those who repent and "believe on his name" (Alma 34:15). In the next verse, he says it more frankly still; only the repentant merit the mercy that overrides the demands of justice. His discourse, like that of many others in the Book of Mormon, reminds us how much the text benefits, stylistically as well as doctrinally, from the presence of the brass plates in the new world. An obvious undercurrent in the Book of Mormon, as in the Old Testament, is its celebration of the versatility and power of language. The figure describing mercy's encircling "arms of safety" (Alma 34:16) is simple yet lovely, and Amulek seems conscious of language structures as he augments his own thesis to include Alma's advocacy of worship unhampered by conventional constraints of time, place, or custom.

Amulek also teaches that prayer is not to be simply a worldly wish list; it must engage the very soul. In fact, prayer should be a habit of mind, a consciousness of the Lord's presence even when formal invocation is not on the lips. And then, echoing King Benjamin many years earlier, Amulek links the soul's salvation to the practice of charity. It seems an unlikely subject for a gathering of the poor and outcast, but his words suggest that imparting of one's material goods is only one aspect of charity, and that even those without substance to give must be charitable.

Clarifying further the doctrine of repentance, Amulek affirms that redemption from sin is contingent upon repentance and diligence in this life. For those who have been taught the doctrine, redemption cannot be won in the next life, nor are its effects delayed until then. "Now is the time and the day of your salvation,"

Amulek insists; "and therefore, if ye will repent and harden not your hearts, shall the great plan of redemption be brought about unto you" (Alma 34:31, emphasis added). He says it again in Alma 34:32 and 33. It can never be said of Amulek that he races over a point and leaves his meaning obscure. Maybe he is determined to be especially diligent with this outdoor assemblage who are bumbling through a spiritual labyrinth, forgetful of even the rudiments of their religion. There can be no redeeming repentance after death, he warns, because "that same spirit which doth possess your bodies at the time that ye go out of this life, that same spirit will have power to possess your body in that eternal world" (Alma 34:34).[1]

Much as we might relish instant improvement, the transformation from mortal to immortal being is not a transformation of character. We might weary of Amulek's seemingly endless repetitions about the consequences of "procrastinat[ing] the day of . . . repentance" (Alma 34:33, 35), but the risk of overkill is no concern to him. Hell, as Amulek describes it, is an intensified incarnation of choices made by the headstrong unrepentant in mortality. If we willfully bar the Spirit of the Lord from our consciousness and give the devil allegiance in this life, he will own us in the next, period. Amulek's final words to the Zoramites point the way home, down the path of humility, worship, gratitude, and prayer.

---

[1] This doctrine is clearly related to Alma's discussion of the concept of restoration with Corianton. See the later verses of chapter 40 and chapters 41 and 42. See also Revelation 22:11.

## 15

## Alma 35-44: Alma's Counsel to His Sons

Chapter 35 returns to the narrative, providing both summary and transition. After Alma, Amulek, and their fellow missionaries depart for Jershon, "the more popular part of the Zoramites" (Alma 35:3), including the practitioners of priestcraft, cagily assess the general response to the teachings they have heard. Finding themselves in the majority, the unbelievers promptly run the converts out of town. Exiling the believers turns out to be woefully disappointing, however, for instead of falling into deprivation and death, the converts fall into the care of the people of Ammon. These faithful saints offer refuge, giving the exiles land and sustenance in Jershon. Incensed at the happy outcome of their cruelty, the Zoramites incite the Lamanites to join them in war against their common foe.

Mormon indicates that "an account shall be given of their wars hereafter" (Alma 35:13), but just now he intends to quote directly from Alma's record, and to inscribe Alma's final patriarchal counsel to his sons. Having consecrated his life to missionary labors, and having firmly established the church in many locations, Alma grieves "that the hearts of the people began to wax hard, and that they began to be offended because of the strictness of the word" (Alma 35:15). I suspect that to the faithful, the word does not seem particularly strict, but merely defines what they would do anyway. Like the rest of us, the Nephites are "offended" mainly by counsel they do not wish to heed.

First in the text are Alma's words to his eldest son, Helaman, who may have been named after one of King Benjamin's children. As the son who is to succeed his father in church leadership, Helaman will in the end be entrusted with all the records and sacred materials in Alma's possession, including the brass plates, the plates of Nephi, and the record of the Jaredites. Alma had apparently planned that Nephihah, who followed him as chief judge, would become keeper of these priceless materials; but as Mormon mentions some time later, Nephihah "refused Alma to take possession of those records" and materials (Alma 50:38). Nephihah's refusal may be puzzling at first, but it explains Alma's lengthy, repetitious, and almost anxious instructions to Helaman with regard to the records. Because of Nephihah's refusal, Helaman evidently had to be enlisted as the record keeper with little prior preparation for that huge responsibility. Nephihah was the logical choice, and there was no question about his faithfulness, but he was not a young man. The fact that he dies just six years after Alma's final departure suggests that he may have declined Alma's request for reasons of age and health. Likely, he favored placing the care of the records on the shoulders of a younger, more robust person than himself.

In any case, Alma has to enlist and educate a new record keeper, and he gives lengthy, two-part instructions to Helaman which are recorded in chapters 36 and 37. The first part is largely a retelling in considerable detail of Alma's miraculous conversion, as a personal lesson to his son. The second is more formal—the counsel of a church leader to his successor, particularly on the matter of records and record keeping. Alma's dramatic conversion, initiated by an angel's stern rebuke, remains excruciatingly sharp in his memory; and we realize more fully here than in Mormon's previous account (see Mosiah 27) that Alma paid an agonizing price for his lesson. He was struck helpless "for three days and for three nights"—the death and resurrection pattern again—during which time he was "racked, even with the pains of a damned soul" (Alma 36:16). The knowledge he gained from the experience, Alma says, is "not of the temporal but of the spiritual" kind, and "if I had not been born of God I should not have known these things." Such blessings can never be earned; they are from God and "not of any worthiness of myself" (Alma 36:4-5).

Even now, Alma severely indicts himself as one who "murdered many of [God's] children, or rather led them away unto destruction" (Alma 36:14). The point he wishes to make, I think, is that inflicting spiritual harm on others as he did is a murderous act and must be viewed in that light. The death of a soul is infinitely more consequential than the death of a body. Alma remembers that his only desire as he lay paralyzed and voiceless, his soul tortured "with inexpressible horror," was to cease to exist, to "be banished and become extinct both soul and body, that I might not be brought to stand in the presence of my God, to be judged of my deeds" (Alma 36:14-15). But he was wrested from his torment by the recollection of his father's prophecy "concerning the coming of one Jesus Christ, a Son of God, to atone for the sins of the world" (Alma 36:17). In that instant of shattering self-knowledge, regret, and remembrance of Christ, Alma was spiritually reborn.

Alma's mind rests for a moment on the bittersweet nature of his experience—"there could be nothing so exquisite and so bitter as were my pains" and "nothing so exquisite and sweet as was my joy" (Alma 36:21). He also witnessed a glorious vision, or what seemed vision-like, in his semi-conscious state. A one-sentence description of that magnificent event satisfies Alma:

> Yea, methought I saw, even as our father Lehi saw, God sitting upon his throne, surrounded with numberless concourses of angels, in the attitude of singing and praising their God; yea, and my soul did long to be there. (Alma 36:22)

To appreciate Alma's preference for understatement, one need only consider how Ammon might have characterized the same experience. We must remember, too, that only moments before, the person who expressed this longing to be in God's presence was horrified at such a prospect. The text offers a great lesson on the effects of repentance and redemption: when the heart is changed, dread of God converts to longing for God. Additionally, the spiritually reborn are seized with a desire that others "might also be born of God, and be filled with the Holy Ghost" (Alma 36:24).

When Alma turns in chapter 37 to the matter of records, it is once more affirmed that record keeping was no casual duty for

Nephite leaders. Twice in the first two verses, Alma is said to "command" Helaman with regard to the records, historical and current. Often, especially when a mortal action is being described, the word translated as "command" in the Book of Mormon might reasonably be interchanged with a word like "admonish," "instruct," "require," or even "ask." But here, it seems to me, there is some urgency, and the word is used in a sense that approaches its modern meaning. Alma is not merely *asking* Helaman to preserve the old records and to continue an ongoing sacred history; Nephihah has declined the responsibility and Alma is *insisting* that Helaman assume it. Alma promises that "if they are kept," the plates "will retain their brightness" as will "all the plates which do contain that which is holy writ" (Alma 37:5). The promise has double meaning: if kept—that is, both preserved and added to— the records will be physically immune to rust and tarnish, and the radiance of their message will be preserved undimmed through time.

Having pressed his son on the matter, Alma good-naturedly anticipates a younger man's impatient response: "Now ye may suppose that this is foolishness in me; but . . . by small and simple things are great things brought to pass; and small means in many instances doth confound the wise" (Alma 37:6). Alma's obvious implication is that the record, whose keeping at the moment may seem to his son just one responsibility among many, will one day be an instrument of tremendous influence. Even now, Alma continues, the records in their possession "have enlarged the memory of this people," an advantage the young do not always consider. Furthermore, the records have "convinced many of the error of their ways, and brought them to the knowledge of their God unto the salvation of their souls" (Alma 37:8). Specifically, Alma mentions the role of religious records in the conversion of "many thousands of the Lamanites" (Alma 37:9, 19) and the prophesied conversion of "future generations" of Lamanites (Alma 37:19) by the same means. He also ventures to suppose that through the records "many thousands of our stiff-necked brethren, the Nephites," might come "to the knowledge of their Redeemer." But then, with typical humility, he halts his speculation, forbearing because "these mysteries are not yet fully made known unto me" (Alma 37:10-11).

In earlier readings, I have been inclined to skim the first half of chapter 37 as largely housekeeping. Lately, however, as the record's preciousness to me, personally, has increased, I have come to appreciate Alma's concern more fully. In fact, I think that few discourses in the Book of Mormon surpass this one in pure feeling. Perhaps fearing that his son might not grasp the seriousness of the assignment, Alma repeatedly alludes to the Lord's wise purposes for the record. No doubt, if any person in a long chain of record keepers had proved faithless or neglectful, there could easily have been no record at all. And, as the centuries went by, the guardianship of the record carried increasing responsibility, because there was more to be lost as well as much that might never have been born. Alma seems to foresee great trials ahead, and he wants Helaman to be prepared to face them.

Shifting gears, but not reducing speed or intensity, Alma turns to the matter of the twenty-four plates containing the history of the now extinct Jaredite nation, and their accompanying interpreting devices. We learn in Ether 3:21 and 4:1 that the Lord specifically informed the first Jaredite prophet that his visionary writings "should not come unto the world until after Christ should show himself unto his people" (Ether 4:1). Presumably, the Lord placed similar restrictions on later Jaredite writings of a very different sort, for Alma instructs Helaman to save the record but not to share certain of its details with the Nephites. It is not the wicked *deeds* of this earlier people, such as "their murders, and robbings, and their plunderings" (Alma 37:21), that are deemed dangerous in the telling. In fact, they can serve as a lesson to the Nephites. Rather, it is the insidious appeal of evil Jaredite conspiracies—"their oaths, and their covenants, and their agreements in their secret abominations; yea, and all their signs and their wonders"—that must be kept "from this people, . . . lest peradventure they should fall into darkness also and be destroyed" (Alma 37:27). Alma warns Helaman about this repeatedly.

The susceptibility of mortals to the seduction of abominable secret oaths and covenants is well known to the Lord and well documented in human history. In spite of Alma's precautions, however, such oaths eventually surface among the Nephites when the Gadianton robbers embrace them. Satan, who will welcome followers without asking for references, is the common source of these evil oaths and covenants. Alma's concern seems to validate my perception that Book of Mormon peoples were especially vulnerable to this particular kind of spiritual virus. It was devil worship on a grand scale, and I remain bewildered by its magnetism.

Having issued this warning, Alma speaks once again as a loving father whose urgency we probably cannot fully comprehend. Here is a parent trying to arm his son for a destiny perhaps only slightly less inscrutable to Helaman than to us. "O, remember, my son," Alma begins, and in so doing touches the chords of my own memory. His next words were, in my high school years, a motto for what was then called the Mutual Improvement Association (the MIA) of the Church. My companions and I could repeat them in our sleep: ". . . learn wisdom in thy youth; yea, learn in thy youth to keep the commandments of God" (Alma 37:35). No less wise are the two succeeding verses:

> Yea, and cry unto God for all thy support; yea, let all thy doings be unto the Lord, and whithersoever thou goest let it be in the Lord; yea, let all thy thoughts be directed unto the Lord; yea, let the affections of thy heart be placed upon the Lord forever.
>
> Counsel with the Lord in all thy doings, and he will direct thee for good; yea, when thou liest down at night lie down unto the Lord, that he may watch over you in your sleep; and when thou risest in the morning let thy heart be full of thanks unto God. . . . (Alma 37:36-37)

That passage is nothing less than a recipe for a happy life.

Concluding his counsel to Helaman with an admonition to follow Christ unfailingly, Alma alludes metaphorically to the special "ball, or director" (Alma 37:38) the Lord provided as a guide to Lehi and his family in the wilderness. The "Liahona," or compass, Alma says, can be seen as a type or a shadow for "the word of Christ, which will point to you a straight course to eternal bliss" (Alma 37:44). I confess that this astute metaphorical typing of the Liahona would not have occurred to me. Moreover, Alma's insight continues. After clarifying his metaphor in verse 45, Alma retains the journey motif, but shifts abruptly to a personal plea: "O my son, do not let us be slothful because of the easiness of the way" (Alma 37:46). Here he alludes again to the skeptical folly of the children of Israel, who had merely to look on the brass serpent to be healed (see Alma 33:19-23), but did not. Indeed, for us, too, the easiness of the way may be the most real danger; ease so often erodes vigilance.

Alma offers only brief counsel to his faithful son Shiblon, relating a much abbreviated account of his personal conversion. Helaman, who is to superintend the record, needs the more concentrated lesson. Alma's focus with Shiblon is clearly on traits of character, for Alma cautions him against pride, boasting, overbearance, unbridled passions, and idleness. He also urges his son to be diligent, temperate, and loving. I note, too, Alma's observation that it is in the control, rather than the indulgence, of passions that we develop the capacity for genuine love: ". . . see that ye bridle all your passions, that ye may be filled with love" (Alma 38:12). Unbridled passion is an enemy, not an expression, of love. Alma might have seen in Shiblon some character flaw, especially in the form of unrighteous pride, for his final counsel cautions against the Zoramite practice of thanking God "that we are better than our brethren" (Alma 38:14).

Alma speaks last and longest to his youngest and least steady son, Corianton, and his words betray the ache in his heart. The young man had accompanied Alma and Shiblon in their mission to the Zoramites, and chapter 39 is principally a reprimand for his misbehavior. Instead of teaching the gospel to the apostate Zoramites, Corianton boastfully forsook "the ministry" and pursued "the harlot Isabel" (Alma 39:3). Alma declares Corianton's behavior to be especially grievous because of its far-reaching effects among the Zoramites: ". . . for when they saw your conduct they would not believe in my words" (Alma 39:11). This is as true today as it was then, as every missionary knows.

Although Alma does not record Corianton's part of the dialogue, it is clear that, whatever his faults, Corianton is a thinking young man who does not ask idle questions. He is either looking for reasons to disbelieve, or he genuinely wants to *know*, and his father teaches him. Alma seems to feel a particular affection for this son over whom he has grieved so deeply. It is an odd truth that a child's very intractability seems to endear her or him all the more to a long-suffering parent, perhaps because of the parent's immense emotional and mental investment in that child. Plainly, Corianton, who has struggled with doctrine as well as with temptations of the intellect and flesh, has grieved his father. The two prongs of the struggle may well be linked, but in any case, the questions and concerns of this beloved and troubled son occasion some of Alma's most notable teachings. Why, Corianton has evidently asked, is the Savior's coming being preached with such fervor long years before the actual event? There is the matter of the mind's preparation, Alma explains, for those who will witness his coming and for those who precede and teach them. Then too, "a soul at this time [is] as precious unto God as a soul will be at the time of his coming" (Alma 39:17).

Seeing that Corianton is also "worried concerning the resurrection of the dead" (Alma 40:1), Alma explains what he has learned about this rather complex doctrine from diligent inquiries of the Lord. As always, Alma is quick to admit the gaps in his knowledge, and to differentiate between his own opinion and the sure truths taught him by an angel. Puzzled himself as to whether there shall be one or several resurrections, Alma nevertheless knows "that there is no resurrection . . . until after the coming of Christ" (Alma 40:2), and he knows that "there must needs be a space betwixt the time of death and the time of the resurrection" (Alma 40:6). That "space" is Alma's subject through much of chapter 40. Based on the angel's teachings, Alma pictures the spirits of the righteous in "paradise" during that space of time, and "the spirits of the wicked" in "outer darkness" (Alma 40:12-13).

The two groups, he says, remain in their respective temporary states "until the time of their resurrection" (Alma 40:14), when the soul and the body are reunited to face judgment.

There are two theories about the nature of a so-called "first resurrection," Alma explains—probably in response to a question from Corianton. Some have thought that the soul's temporary assignment to paradise or to a state of misery "may be termed a [first] resurrection" (Alma 40:15); others have assumed the first resurrection to be "a resurrection of all those who have been, or who are, or who shall be, down to the resurrection of Christ from the dead" (Alma 40:16). Alma favors the second theory, but he does not claim to know the specific timing of the resurrections, nor whether or not resurrection will occur simultaneously for both wicked and righteous. In his view ("I give it as my opinion," Alma 40:20), however, there definitely will be a resurrection of deceased mortals, a reuniting of souls and bodies, at the time of Christ's resurrection and ascension, or soon after.

Near the end of chapter 40, Alma introduces the word "restoration" to describe the resurrection process. Subsequently, he uses the word repeatedly, giving it unusual emphasis, forcing us to consider resurrection in terms of restoration and thereby modifying the way we perceive the event. Alma is talking about a real, not an illusory, reunion between elements that belong together: "The soul shall be restored to the body, and the body to the soul; yea, and every limb and joint shall be restored to its body; yea, even a hair of the head shall not be lost" (Alma 40:23). Moreover, according to Alma, this process "is the restoration of which has been spoken by the mouths of the prophets" (Alma 40:24). Then in chapter 41, noting that "some have wrested the scriptures, and have gone far astray" in their assumptions about the "plan of restoration," and that Corianton in particular has been "worried" about it (Alma 41:1, 2), Alma explores the concept of restoration as it relates to resurrection and judgment. In particular, he unexpectedly connects restoration and justice, declaring that restoration "is requisite with the justice of God," for justice requires "that all things should be restored to their proper order" (Alma 41:2). In so saying, he makes a stunning philosophical leap that profoundly illuminates a doctrine most Christians have assumed needs no further clarification. In just thirteen verses, through the concept of restoration, Alma extends our understanding of the resurrection, and of the Atonement and judgment as well.

The sophistication of this discourse indicates that both Corianton and Alma enjoy exceptional intellectual and spiritual gifts—gifts that dwarf the rudimentary genius of the Zoramites—and that Alma respects his son's questioning mind. Alma's words, as he begins to amplify the concept of "restoration" and relate it to the concept of justice, turn on the notion of works and the heart's desires. We will, Alma says, inherit the goodness or evil of our own deeds and motives. The passage is important in the extreme:

> . . . it is requisite with the justice of God that men should be judged according to their works; and if their works were good in this life, and the desires of their hearts were good, that they should also, at the last day, be restored unto that which is good.
> And if their works are evil they shall be restored unto them for evil. . . . (Alma 41:3-4)

I am consoled, too, by the fact that desires of the heart as well as works of the body and mind will be considered in the final accounting. And I do believe that faith is as dependent for its life on works of the mind as on works of the flesh.

Three times in verse 5 Alma uses the phrase "according to his desires," attesting emphatically that, as he had intimated in his earlier soliloquy (chapter 29), it is by personal volition ("whosoever will," Alma 41:8) that mortals "stand or fall; for behold, they are their own judges, whether to do good or do evil" (Alma 41:7). And, by implication, they are also their own judges, whether to have good restored to them, or evil. It is no accident, I think, that Alma uses the term "judge"; his subject, after all, is justice. Taking his argument a step further, Alma warns the sometimes hardheaded Corianton not to "suppose, because it has been spoken concerning restoration, that ye shall be restored from sin to happiness." And then he utters one of the oft-repeated maxims in Mormondom: "Behold, I say unto you, wickedness never was happiness" (Alma 41:10). This statement means something in isolation, true; but it means considerably more in the context of the doctrine of restoration.

As Alma expands on the truism that "wickedness never was happiness," his argument becomes more intricate and elusive. He informs Corianton that all mortals who have not cast off the natural personality and been reborn spiritually "are without God in the world, and they have gone contrary to the nature of God." To be without God in mortality, and thus to be contrary to his nature, is to live in wickedness or "in a state contrary to the nature of happiness" Alma 41:11). Does restoration, he asks, imply that "a thing of a natural state" in mortality is to be placed "in an unnatural state" in immortality, that is, "in a state opposite to its nature?" (Alma 41:12). He answers his own question with an emphatic no, clinching his argument through definition, in a series of modified parallel statements:

> . . . the meaning of the word restoration is to bring back again evil for evil, or carnal for carnal, or devilish for devilish—good for that which is good; righteous for that which is righteous; just for that which is just; merciful for that which is merciful. (Alma 41:13)

It is worth noting that Alma uses amplified structures for the four positive rewards, adding "that which is" to each. The three negative consequences have no such buffering verbal enhancements. The words hit hard and incisively. Compare "evil for evil" with "good for that which is good," for example.

Having presented the doctrine as it applies to humanity generally, Alma then makes a fatherly appeal to Corianton, explaining restoration as wages in kind for his son's (or anyone's) treatment of his fellow beings. He uses the same basic structural design as in verse 13, except that in verse 14 both halves of his statement are positive. Three of his four admonitions are concise ("deal," "judge," "do good"), while the rewards are amplified ("ye shall have . . . again"):

> Therefore, my son, see that you are merciful unto your brethren; deal justly, judge righteously, and do good continually; and if ye do all these things then shall ye receive your reward; yea, ye shall have mercy restored unto you again; ye shall have justice restored unto you again; ye shall have a righteous judgment restored unto you again; and ye shall have good rewarded unto you again. (Alma 41:14)

This passage more or less confirms what I have privately assumed for many years—that we will be judged in a large measure for how we have felt, thought, spoken, and acted toward our fellow beings.

Consequently, I find Alma's statement to be one of the most absorbing suppositions in all of Christian doctrine. At the very least, it suggests additional implications for the Savior's assurance that "with what measure ye mete, it shall be measured to you again" (Matthew 7:2). To speak of the restoration (of all things promised through the resurrection and atonement) in terms of mercy, justice, and good works returning to bless the merciful, just, and good is, in my view, to offer a remarkable insight. Alma recapitulates in plain terms: "For that which ye do send out shall return unto you again, and be restored; therefore, the word restoration more fully condemneth the sinner, and justifieth him not at all" (Alma 41:15). We see clearly now that the form restoration takes has to be a function of justice.

Alma has one more matter to discuss with his son Corianton, something else "which doth worry your mind, which ye cannot understand." It concerns "the justice of God in the punishment of the sinner," a subject Amulek had treated in his sermon to the Zoramites (see Alma 34). Corianton, Alma says, tries "to suppose that it is injustice that the sinner should be consigned to a state of misery" (Alma 42:1). Like most of us, Corianton prefers to focus on God's mercy rather than his justice, and his father painstakingly reasons that "God would cease to be God" if mercy without repentance were to "destroy the work of justice" (Alma 42:13).

This is not an easy concept to teach, and Alma attempts it by first establishing a context out of which Corianton can understand the relationships among sin, justice, and mercy.

The context Alma chooses is the plight of our first parents after they had lost Eden and had to be barred from the tree of life. To have partaken of its fruit would have meant living forever with the just consequences of their disobedience, thus frustrating "the great plan of salvation" (Alma 42:5), which was designed to overcome the effects of the Fall. Nevertheless, mercy could not justifiably take effect without repentance, nor could it prevail "except an atonement should be made" (Alma 42:15). Law, Alma tells Corianton, is necessary, since too many mortals choose not to exercise self-governance: ". . . if there was no law given against sin men would not be afraid to sin" and justice "would have no claim" on them (Alma 42:20-21).

The legal systems of free countries labor daily to arbitrate the conflicting demands of justice and mercy. The divine plan of salvation is probably the only perfect mediation between those two seemingly incompatible demands, for it "appease[s] the demands of justice, that God might be a perfect, just God," but it allows him to be "a merciful God also" (Alma 42:15). Human courts will always struggle with the matter of repentance. When is leniency, or parole, or pardon justified? Unlike human judges, God can read the heart unerringly.

Alma sums up his doctrine succinctly: ". . . there is a law given, and a punishment affixed, and a repentance granted; which repentance, mercy claimeth" (Alma 42:22). Indispensable to the plan of salvation, Alma insists repeatedly, is the repentance that justifies God in extending mercy toward mortals. Yes, surely, if (in addition to conceiving offspring) we were not sent to earth to refine our characters, to overcome our weaknesses, to learn to make decent choices, and to repent when we do not make them, then why this lengthy and complicated trial? Undoubtedly not to amass wealth, pursue fame, deplete the earth, and offend God.

It is obvious that Alma is intensely fearful for his son; we can read his concern in recurring phrases such as "my son" and "O my son." He does not rehearse the details of his own wanton and rebellious youth for the erring Corianton, as he has done for the faithful Helaman and Shiblon. His past is no secret, but perhaps he fears that Corianton might use his father's youthful turpitude to justify his own behavior. Above all, Alma hopes to convince Corianton that forgiveness and redemption are possible to "the truly penitent" (Alma 42:24). Although he warns that justice must be answered, Alma speaks more of atonement and restoration than of sin and punishment. In a nutshell, the choice is Corianton's: "If he has desired to do evil, and has not repented in his days, behold, evil shall be done unto him, according to the restoration of God" (Alma 42:28). Alma implores his son to be troubled by his sins rather than by points of doctrine, to the extent that he humbly repents. Repentance presupposes full acceptance of God's justice as well as his mercy, and an appreciation for his incredible patience with his erring children.

As a classic example of the reformed sinner himself, Alma may have a special facility for penetrating the consciousness of the weak or rebellious. In any case, Corianton seems to have responded to Alma's counsel, for very soon, the record speaks of Corianton setting out with his brothers "to declare the word" (Alma 43:1). And the aging Alma, even though he has essentially handed the reins of leadership to the next generation, "could not rest, and he also went forth" (Alma 43:1). His restless compulsion to go forth is totally in character, I might add. Missionary work is his life, his very breath; he loves to teach the gospel of Jesus Christ.

Alma's writings conclude with chapters 43 and 44, and the record kept by his eldest son, Helaman, occupies the final third of the book of Alma. Just ahead of the chapters containing Alma's patriarchal counsel to his sons (Alma 36-42), Mormon had indicated that an account of certain wars would be "given . . . hereafter" (Alma 35:13). "Hereafter" turns out to be Alma 43 and 44.

The wars of which Mormon speaks are generated from the resentment of apostate Nephite groups over the conversion of the people of Ammon (who are former Lamanites) and their finding sanctuary among the believing Nephites. The apostate Nephites—

namely, the Amalekites, Zoramites (who become Lamanites), and descendants of the wicked priests of Noah—join with the power-hungry unconverted Lamanites and prepare to make war on the Nephites. Since the people of Ammon cannot break their pacifistic vows, their defense falls upon the Nephites, who are vastly outnumbered by the Lamanite coalition. The Lamanite leader, a man named Zerahemnah (a name which looks suspiciously like a linguistic mutation of the word "Zarahemla"), craftily appoints Amalekites and Zoramites as "chief captains over the Lamanites" because they are "of a more wicked and murderous disposition than the Lamanites" (Alma 43:6). The irony is obvious here. Even so, the Lamanites bear an "extreme hatred" (Alma 43:11) toward the people of Ammon. What is this perversity in human nature that magnifies hatred toward a brother?

The commander of the Nephite armies, which have gathered in Jershon, is extremely young for such responsibility—a fiery twenty-five-year-old named Moroni. What he lacks in maturity and patience, this Moroni more than compensates for in intelligence, determination, high-mindedness, and faith. A clever strategist, he outwits his foes and defeats his enemies, against seemingly insurmountable odds. The narrative of these events is easy to follow, and I need not repeat it here. Moroni's first strategy is a stroke of genius. He protects his vastly outnumbered soldiers with "breastplates and with arm-shields, yea, and also shields to defend their heads, and . . . thick clothing" (Alma 43:19). (We wonder why no one had thought to do it before!) By contrast, the Lamanite warriors are vulnerably "naked, save it were a skin which was girded about their loins" (Alma 43:20). The Amalekites and Zoramites are clothed, but have no armor, and they are afraid to go against the well-shielded Nephite soldiers.

The point made repeatedly in the record is that this is a religious war. "The Nephites were inspired by a better cause, for they were not fighting for monarchy nor power but they were fighting for their homes and their liberties, their wives and their children, and their all, yea, for their rites of worship and their church" (Alma 43:45). From their forefathers they have learned that so long as they are "not guilty of the first offense, neither the second" (Alma 43:46), they can "defend themselves against their enemies, even to the shedding of blood if it were necessary." But they are "never to give an offense, yea, and never to raise the sword except it were against an enemy, except it were to preserve their lives" (Alma 48:14). Perhaps only the people of Ammon, who have covenanted not to raise arms at all, are more valorous. They already practice the counsel the Savior will one day teach; they turn the other cheek. Despite the Nephite policy of restraint, there are bloody and costly battles for both sides. The Nephites finally prevail, but the dead are too numerous either to count or to bury. They are simply cast into the river.

Although Moroni figures prominently in Helaman's writings, the final chapters of Alma's record provide a valuable introduction to him. It is easy to see why Mormon, in reading about Moroni, would name his own son Moroni. Such deep-seated faith and fearless, yet compassionate, leadership in extreme circumstances are exceptional in one so young. Having defeated his enemies, Moroni has no desire to destroy them, nor does he wish to enslave them.

Alma's record basically ends with chapter 44, but the first nineteen verses of chapter 45 concern Alma. It seems appropriate to mention here his final words to Helaman and his last, highly unsettling prophecy, even though Helaman rather than Alma records it. Again Alma underscores the importance of the record, this time pointedly and relentlessly questioning Helaman about his testimony and his commitment to keeping the record. Although previous record keepers have been diligent, not since Nephi have we seen such overt conscientiousness about it. Seemingly convinced at last of Helaman's steadfastness, Alma proceeds from questioning his son to delivering an important prophecy, one that he had neither inscribed into the record nor spoken to his people. He directs Helaman to write the prophecy, but its contents are not to be disclosed "until the prophecy is fulfilled" (Alma 45:9). The prophecy is impressive in its exactitude and disheartening in its content.

Alma has seen too much to trust his people's constancy, and this is the second matter that he has instructed Helaman not to publish. We remember that earlier Alma had cautioned his son against revealing the clandestine doings of the Jaredites, and now he justifiably fears the Nephites' response to a prophecy of certain annihilation: "... this very people, the Nephites, ... in four hundred years from the time that Jesus Christ shall manifest himself unto them, shall dwindle in unbelief"; and after "wars and pestilences, yea, famines and bloodshed, ... [they] shall become extinct," having fallen "into the works of darkness, and lasciviousness, and all manner of iniquities..." (Alma 45:10-12). Indeed, a volatile people who believe that they have no future may well squander the present. Nephi had voiced the same prophecy (see 2 Nephi 26:9-11) many years earlier, though he was less precise about the date than Alma, and he ascribed the Nephite fall largely to pride. Even the Nephite birthright will be lost with this great apostasy. Except for a few disciples, Alma says, those who escape destruction "shall be numbered among the Lamanites, and shall become like unto them" (Alma 45:14). Alma's dreadful prophecy is realized in full, and Mormon's son, Moroni, is its final witness.

At the conclusion of his ministry, Alma pronounces blessings upon his sons and upon the church. He also touchingly blesses "the earth for the righteous' sake" (Alma 45:15), reminding his sons that God has blessed the land for those who are righteous and cursed it for those who "do wickedly" (Alma 45:16). In this he echoes an incessant theme: God will prosper the righteous in the land, but the wicked have no such promise. Having issued his final warnings and pronounced his benedictions, Alma departs from Zarahemla, "as if to go into the land of Melek. ... he was never heard of more; as to his death or burial we know not of" (Alma 45:18). Helaman and the others assume that Alma was either "taken up by the Spirit, or buried by the hand of the Lord, even as Moses" (Alma 45:19). How readily Alma's people liken him to Moses, and how reluctantly modern skeptics entertain the possibility of new-world prophets, much less compare them to Moses.

This kind of supposition about Alma's destiny testifies not only to his extraordinary spiritual leadership and personal virtue, but also to his people's immense love and regard for him. In all, a modest man who never forgot that he once rebelled against his God and was blessedly forgiven, Alma grew to become a prophet of such character and holiness that his people had no difficulty attributing his disappearance to God's intervening embrace.

## 16

## Alma 45-63: Moroni, Champion of Liberty

Chapters 45 to 63 of the book of Alma are of a rather different sort than those that precede them. They make up the section that Mormon abridged from the record kept largely by Alma's son, Helaman, and then by Helaman's brother Shiblon after Helaman's death. The section covers twenty years, for the most part chronicling political and military conflicts against a backdrop of God's holy purposes. Some readers have found tedious the accounts of wars and battle strategies, wondering why Mormon would spend his precious strength engraving such things into his record. I can think of several possible reasons, the main one being that the Lord probably told him to, for the instruction of latter-day readers. These "war" chapters also confirm unequivocally that the principle of liberty is a divinely sanctioned ideal.

There may have been other reasons, too. As a military man himself, Mormon was obviously interested in the operations he describes, and he possibly foresaw instruction for latter-day peoples in what may be parallel conflicts of the last days. Furthermore, Mormon was captivated by the heroic figure of Moroni, with whom, though separated by centuries, he shared a vision of the divine destiny of the land of promise. Less obvious, but perhaps more compelling, is the fact that the final chapters of Alma detail the circumstances and events that brought the Nephite nation within inches of vanishing as a people. Such a vanishing could have meant the end of the record, the rescinding of Christ's plan to minister among new-world peoples, and the thwarting of the promises of latter-day gospel restoration. Could anything be more important than these chapters that narrate the struggle of a few patriots to maintain faith and freedom, both for their age and ours?

Although there are numerous references to religious concerns in this section of Alma, there are no major religious discourses. Helaman either did not include any of his own sermons in the record he kept, or Mormon elected to omit them from his abridgment. However it was, the only verbatim discourses in these chapters are Alma's prophecy of the eventual destruction of the Nephite nation (which I alluded to above) and a variety of epistles exchanged during the stresses of war. This section of the record brings home to me again, more forcefully than ever, the fragility of peace, the precariousness of life, the slender chance of lasting survival for those Nephite castaways who strove to maintain belief and order in a rather frightening world.

In nearly every conflict in every generation, the believers have been far outnumbered by those seeking to enslave or destroy them. The numerical disadvantage is especially evident in the final third of Alma, which describes the saints fortifying their cities behind huge walls, struggling with internal dissension, fighting Lamanites and apostate Nephites, and trying to keep the fires of religious and political freedom burning. As strenuous as life was for America's post-Columbian settlers, at least they were not totally separated from a world ignorant of their existence. The Nephites may have built large cities, but in many respects they lived on the edge of the wilderness, literally and figuratively. Isolated and vulnerable, they faced extinction almost continually; they had only themselves and God. And time after time, they accomplished rescue by outwitting their enemies and by importuning their God. Nonetheless, on numerous occasions they were slaughtered by the thousands. Fortification helped, of course, and there were brief periods of peace; but the spectre of impending annihilation must have cast a shadow over even their peaceful interludes. If nothing else, the nineteen chapters that conclude the book of Alma make that spectre patently real.

In Nephite society there is a cooperative division of church and civil leadership, with Helaman guiding the church (yet still leading military forces), Moroni commanding the armies (yet still supporting the church), and Pahoran serving as chief judge (yet still leading troops and supporting the church). It is a sign of the times, I think, that the main focus of the abridged record, and probably of Helaman's original record too, is on Moroni rather than Helaman or Pahoran. In 73 B.C., Helaman and his brothers, Shiblon and Corianton, make "a regulation . . . throughout the church" (Alma 45:21), presumably to safeguard it through a strong organization of priests and teachers. Moroni's task is on another front; he is to fortify and defend the Nephite nation against internal as well as external foes. There are more than enough of both, which accounts for the new emphasis on "regulation."

In these chapters, Moroni emerges as a luminous champion and symbol of freedom and faith. A gifted military strategist, he outwits and outmaneuvers his enemies countless times. But he is also a powerhouse of faith, inspiring troops and citizens alike to resist bondage with all their might and will. The overriding theme in these chapters is the God-given right of people to be free; and for Moroni, faith and liberty are inexorably linked in the doctrine of agency. Sometimes impulsive and hot-headed, yes, but never self-serving, Moroni wants only the freedom of his people. Without him, or someone like him, the Nephites of his generation would surely have been conquered and destroyed by their enemies. As in Nephi's time, the record again attests to the power of virtue seated in a single righteous individual. It also attests to "the great wickedness one very wicked man can cause to take place among the children of men" (Alma 46:9).

The first Nephite conflict detailed in this section is an internal dispute over freedom. Amalickiah, who is "desirous to be a king," emerges to test Moroni's mettle; and many of "the lower judges of the land," who are also "seeking for power" (Alma 46:4), support him. Not one to sit idly by while Amalickiah deludes the citizenry into trading their liberty for subservience to an ambitious apostate, Moroni springs into action. (Indecisiveness is decidedly not one of his character flaws.)

It is an electric moment as, full of wrath and fearless purpose, Moroni dramatically "rent his coat; and he took a piece thereof,

and wrote upon it—In memory of our God, our religion, and
freedom, and our peace, our wives, and our children" (Alma
46:12). In one sense, Moroni's pledges are quite concrete, encompassing God, country, and home. In another sense, they are
abstract, encompassing agency, peace, duty, and even memory.
After uttering a mighty prayer to God and heralding the land as
"a chosen land . . . of liberty" (Alma 46:17), Moroni brandishes
the pole bearing "his rent coat, (and he called it the title of liberty)" (Alma 46:13) and dashes "forth among the people" (Alma
46:19). Boldly he invites the brave to "enter into a covenant that
they will maintain their rights, and their religion" (Alma 46:20).
He knows that political freedom allows religious freedom to flourish. Inspired by Moroni's grand summons, the people rally, and
the upholders of liberty soon outnumber the now fleeing dissenters. The language of the passages describing these events is full
of energy and action. Whenever Moroni is on stage, we feel his
presence in the animated rhetoric of the narrative.

Although Amalickiah and a small band escape to the
Lamanites, Moroni's forces are successful in heading off most of
the defectors and bringing them back to Zarahemla. Moroni gives
this cowardly bunch two options: ". . . enter into a covenant to
support the cause of freedom" and "a free government" or "be put
to death." The irony of such a choice is not lost on Mormon, who
observes with studied understatement that "there were but few
who denied the covenant of freedom" (Alma 46:35).

Meanwhile, the power-hungry Amalickiah determines that if
he cannot be king among the Nephites, he will be king of the
Lamanites; and by various betrayals, ruses, schemes, and murders
detailed in chapter 47, he gains the Lamanite throne. Mormon
observes that, despite their Christian upbringing, Amalickiah and
his followers soon "became more hardened and impenitent, and
more wild, wicked and ferocious than the Lamanites" (Alma
47:36). It is a pattern we see again and again. The fruits of apostasy are poisonous indeed.

I think Mormon intentionally portrays Moroni and
Amalickiah as opposing symbols of good and evil, mighty adver-

saries in a contest for human souls. They represent the ageless conflict initiated in pre-mortality by Lucifer, and at issue still is human freedom, the power of choice. In chapters 46, 47, and 48, Mormon illustrates the antagonism between the two men, defining their natures by their deeds and desires. But in one verse he distills their essential polarity: ". . . while Amalickiah had thus been obtaining power by fraud and deceit, Moroni, on the other hand, had been preparing the minds of the people to be faithful unto the Lord their God" (Alma 48:7). Still, no line is more telling than the one in Alma 49:10, where Amalickiah is said to have been willing to attack the well-fortified city of Ammonihah regardless of the cost in lives, "for behold, he did care not for the blood of his people." To Amalickiah, commoners are expendable. Mormon wryly observes in the next verse, however, that "Amalickiah did not come down himself to battle" (Alma 49:11); he cares about his own blood. By contrast, Moroni abhors the shedding of blood, even that of his enemy, and he leads his troops in battle while Amalickiah protects his own skin.

Mormon admiringly describes Moroni's imaginative fortification of Nephite cities; for unlike the personally ambitious Amalickiah, Moroni invests his whole energy in the safety and preservation of his people. Mormon's description of this righteous patriot is a textbook characterization of the ideal prince mentioned earlier in connection with King Benjamin:

> And Moroni was a strong and a mighty man; he was a man of a perfect understanding; yea, a man that did not delight in bloodshed; a man whose soul did joy in the liberty and the freedom of his country, and his brethren from bondage and slavery;
>
> Yea, a man whose heart did swell with thanksgiving to his God, for the many privileges and blessings which he bestowed upon his people; a man who did labor exceedingly for the welfare and safety of his people.
>
> Yea, and he was a man who was firm in the faith of Christ, and he had sworn with an oath to defend his people, his rights, and his country, and his religion, even to the loss of his blood. (Alma 48:11-13)

When we read his scorching letter to Pahoran later, we should keep in mind this eloquent verbal portrait and not judge Moroni too harshly. Then, too, in Mormon's abridgment we see only a fraction of the man he had come to know in the unabridged record. Mormon cannot praise him enough:

> Yea, verily, verily I say unto you, if all men had been, and were, and ever would be, like unto Moroni, behold, the very powers of hell would have been shaken forever; yea, the devil would never have power over the hearts of the children of men. (Alma 48:17-18)

Short periods of peace bring welcome respite from war; but for the most part, the next chapters chronicle a series of battles and skirmishes, in all of which Amalickiah is embarrassingly out-foxed. To the "uttermost astonishment" (Alma 49:8) of the Lamanite troops, for example, Moroni fortifies all the Nephite cities with great earthen and timber walls. It is no small irony that when the Lamanites attempt to pull down the walls at the city of Noah and fill the surrounding trenches with earth from the walls, the trenches are instead "filled up in a measure with their dead and wounded bodies" (Alma 49:22). As Nephite numbers increase, new cities (including one named Moroni) are founded, and a period of peace and prosperity graces the Nephite nation.

In the next several years, however, it is internal strife, not external menace, that interrupts the peace. First, military action is required to settle land disputes and to quell an uprising of "king-men" who agitate to dethrone the chief judge, alter the law, "over-throw the free government," and install a king (Alma 51:5). This is, as Mormon says, "a critical time for such contentions" (Alma 51:9) to arise, what with Amalickiah also presenting a renewed threat from the outside. To be sure, having to march against its own people puts a democratic government in an ambiguous position. Mormon is careful to confirm (twice) that Moroni's military action against those who want to surrender their liberty to a titled monarch, and who refuse to defend their country against its external foes, is endorsed by "the voice of the people" (Alma 51:15,16).

Nevertheless, coerced liberty is a paradoxical notion, even when the cause and its leaders are honorable and just.

There are, of course, other examples of "compulsory" freedom in the history of the human race; but it is nevertheless problematic that people who wish to relinquish their freedom must be restrained from doing so and *forced* to embrace liberty. Mormon's language captures the contradiction: the defeated survivors among the king-men, he says, "were *obliged* to maintain the cause of freedom" (Alma 51:7); they "*yielded* to the standard of liberty, and were *compelled* to hoist the title of liberty upon their towers" (Alma 51:20). Moreover, they were required to fight alongside their neighbors, having been "*subject[ed]* to peace and civilization" (Alma 51:22; emphases added) by Moroni.

It is a sad commentary on the times that the king-men "were glad in their hearts" to see their old comrade, Amalickiah, coming against their countrymen (Alma 51:13), and that Moroni has to wage war against dissenting Nephites before he can confront the external enemy. In extreme circumstances, when a nation is facing annihilation, perhaps freedom can be preserved for the larger body only if the freedom of dissent is denied to its citizens. A difficult situation at best. Troubling, too, is the fact that 4,000 Nephite king-men are slain, and their leaders "cast into prison, for there was no time for their trials at this period" (Alma 51:19). Expediency sometimes rules in dangerous times; ultimate national survival is at stake here, and Moroni knows it. Amalickiah is amassing a great army, and if the Nephites divide into factions or abandon democratic principles, their nation will fall.

I see in the internal struggle between Nephite freemen and king-men a prefiguration of the American civil war. In that conflict, too, which was also played out on western soil, half a nation was forced to remain in the union and compelled to accept the concept of freedom for all members of its society. We should likewise remember that in the American revolutionary war, a good many loyalists to the crown were "forced" into accepting freedom from royal rule.

An opportunistic Amalickiah makes his move in the midst of the Nephite civil turbulence. Amalickiah must be very confident, for Mormon notes a bit sardonically that this time "even Amalickiah did himself come down, at the head of the Lamanites" (Alma 51:12). Perhaps hoping to end the warfare, Teancum daringly assassinates Amalickiah as he sleeps; but the battle of wits and blows continues under Amalickiah's brother Ammoron. Anyone interested in military tactics will find chapter 52 fascinating.

In chapter 53, Mormon interrupts the main narrative to describe the entry into the war of 2,000 young warriors from the people of Ammon, noble sons of the converted Lamanites who had made and kept pacifistic vows. Not bound by their fathers' promises, these valiant youths present themselves and covenant "to fight for the liberty of the Nephites, yea, to protect the land unto the laying down of their lives" (Alma 53:17). Though tender in years and woefully inexperienced, the "two thousand stripling soldiers" (Alma 53:22) turn the tide in a number of battles. Later, in an epistle to his commander, Helaman tells Moroni why they fought so gallantly and why none were killed:

> Now they never had fought, yet they did not fear death; and they did think more upon the liberty of their fathers than they did upon their lives; yea, they had been taught by their mothers, that if they did not doubt, God would deliver them.
> And they rehearsed unto me the words of their mothers, saying: We do not doubt our mothers knew it. (Alma 56:47-48)

This is one of the rare moments in scripture when women are singled out for their knowledge and faith. It is well to remember, too, that these are women of Lamanite lineage. Among the people of Ammon, the women must have been the primary instructors of the young in matters of doctrine and character. In these splendid young men, who carry their mothers' teachings in their hearts, lies the stuff of a national epic. Helaman reports in his letter that these youths "fought as if with the strength of God," and on one occasion they fell upon the Lamanites with such power that the frightened "Lamanites deliver[ed] themselves up as prisoners of war" (Alma 56:56). We sometimes forget that even the very young, if "their minds are firm, and they do put their trust in God continually" (Alma 57:27), can serve in extraordinary ways.

Two other epistles precede Helaman's in the record. One is a fiery letter from Moroni to Ammoron, prompted by the latter's request for a prisoner exchange, and the other is Ammoron's incensed reply. On the surface, Moroni's contentious letter scarcely seems serviceable as its advertised "stratagem to obtain as many prisoners of the Nephites from the Lamanites as it were possible" (Alma 54:3), though Moroni is eager for an advantageous exchange. Granted, Moroni's letter does set terms for a prisoner exchange; but unless Moroni expects to win the return of Nephite prisoners by driving Ammoron into a rage, the record is referring to a later stratagem and not to the letter.

Circuitous diplomacy is scarcely Moroni's style, nor are compromise and concession. He opens by warning Ammoron of "the justice of God, and the sword of his almighty wrath, which doth hang over you" (Alma 54:6), and he warms to the task by calling Ammoron "a child of hell" (Alma 54:11) and a murderer like his brother. This sort of language would indeed get Ammoron's attention, but it would hardly dispose him to arbitration. But then, Moroni knows his man only too well. Vowing that "we will retain our cities and our lands; yea, and we will maintain our religion and the cause of our God," even if it means arming women and children (54:10), he threatens Ammoron with ruin and death unless he pulls out of Nephite lands. Throughout his letter, he repeatedly goads Ammoron with taunting intimations that Ammoron is neither smart enough to take Moroni's advice nor wise enough to cease fighting "against the people of the Lord" (Alma 54:8). Moroni's epistle angers Ammoron all right, but it does not intimidate him. It may serve a subtler purpose, however, in leading Ammoron to underestimate Moroni's tactical skill and mental astuteness. In the end, Moroni defeats Ammoron not by temper, tongue, or physical force, but by intellectual prowess and finesse. Mormon obviously enjoys reporting the flamboozled enemy's lame attempts to fool the Nephites with their own strategies.

Even as Moroni is regaining lands that had been lost to the Lamanites, he receives the lengthy epistle (comprising chapters 56 through 58) from Helaman referred to above, a letter that is both encouraging and disheartening. Though in some respects resembling a military report to a superior officer, Helaman's letter is also the communication of a church leader to a beloved friend and colleague. In chapter 57, Helaman tells of having exchanged epistles with an over-confident Ammoron on the matter of prisoner releases. It appears that Ammoron is fishing in two streams. He tries negotiating to his advantage with both Helaman and Moroni, but neither bites on his tainted bait. The essence of Helaman's epistle is that in spite of dire food and supply shortages, and the rebellion and escape of a band of Lamanite prisoners, his forces have successfully retaken some Nephite cities.

As he reproduced, almost side by side, Helaman's long letter to Moroni and Moroni's reactive second letter to the Nephite chief judge Pahoran, Mormon must have seen the difference between Helaman's measured, understated prose and Moroni's explosive rhetoric. Helaman regrets even having to report that some time ago he begged Pahoran for men and provisions, and then waited "for the space of many months, even until we were about to perish for the want of food" (Alma 58:7), before the most meager assistance dribbled in. Helaman's diction and tone are very different from Moroni's. He flings no accusations at his countrymen, and he chooses non-combative words like "our embarrassments," and "grieved," and "fear" (Alma 58:9) to describe his situation. Furthermore, he generally assumes that there may have been a justifiable reason for his government's disregard of his need. Bolstered by faith, Helaman knows that even if human assistance fails him, he and his people can turn to heaven for aid.

One of the most difficult aspects of Helaman's situation is his isolation. He is ignorant of what is transpiring in other parts of the Nephite nation, and of why he has suffered neglect. For all he knows, Moroni, to whom he writes, has been "unsuccessful" and has no forces available to send. "If so," he says patiently, "we do not desire to murmur" (Alma 58:35). (Moroni's second letter to Pahoran leaves the chief judge no such latitude.) In the end, however, even the non-judgmental Helaman raises the possibility "that there is some faction in the government, that they do not send more men to our assistance" (Alma 58:36). It may be that his brief speculation about a possible government "faction" plants or reinforces suspicions in Moroni's mind, leading him to accuse Pahoran of betrayal. Then, as if catching himself in uncomfortable speculation, Helaman quickly drops that line of complaint: "But, behold, it mattereth not—we trust God will deliver us. . . " (Alma 58:37).

It suits Helaman better to count his blessings: the Nephites are again "in the possession of our lands; and the Lamanites have fled" (Alma 58:38). Moreover, the Lord has preserved Helaman's dear young warriors, in spite of their "many wounds" (Alma 58:40). Helaman's final paragraph is anything but a disgruntled statement of frustration and disappointment. It is, instead, an affidavit of spiritual stability and largess:

> And now, my beloved brother, Moroni, may the Lord our God, who has redeemed us and made us free, keep you continually in his presence; yea, and may he favor this people, even that ye may have success in obtaining the possession of all that which the Lamanites have taken from us, which was for our support. And now, behold, I close mine epistle. I am Helaman, the son of Alma. (Alma 58:41)

It is obvious from their letters that even though both Helaman and Moroni are engaged in military operations, their perspectives are very different. One is a church leader schooled in restraint; the other is a military commander trained in action. Nevertheless, it is only after his first letter to Pahoran appears to have been ignored that Moroni gets his dander up. In fact, he rejoices at the successes recounted in Helaman's letter, and he is optimistic about the future. Moroni's first request for support from Pahoran is not quoted, but it may have been quite congenial. When it goes unheeded, however, and when in the meantime troop deprivations multiply and the city of Nephihah is lost for lack of reinforcements, Moroni is fighting mad; his second epistle to Pahoran fairly seethes with fury. Mormon puts a mild cast on his summary: "And it came to pass that Moroni was angry with the government, because of their indifference concerning the freedom of their country" (Alma 59:13). But Mormon also elects to quote Moroni's scathing letter in its entirety; it comprises all thirty-six verses of chapter 60.

Even though a person of Helaman's temperament composes a different sort of letter, Moroni is certainly justified in his exasperation. The Nephite government has not sustained its fighting forces, and they have suffered severely. What rankles Moroni most is the Nephite governors' apparent desertion of the democratic ideal, even though, as he implies repeatedly, their only authority comes from those who elected them. "Can you think to sit upon your thrones in a state of thoughtless stupor, while your enemies are spreading the work of death around you?" (Alma 60:7) he demands. Helaman would not have accused anyone, much less his superiors, of reposing in a "thoughtless stupor," but Moroni uses inflammatory rhetoric with both his enemy and his magistrate. Impetuous in his wrath, he does not pause to consider that Pahoran might have been in desperate straits himself; he assumes, rather, that Pahoran and his consorts have negligently or willfully withheld assistance.

Moroni therefore lays the blame for the slaughter of faithful Nephites squarely on Pahoran and other elected officials, and he threatens vengeance and God's judgment. Curiously, he still addresses them as "my beloved brethren," though he adds a qualifier: "for ye ought to be beloved" (Alma 60:10). So much energy and life have been spent to preserve freedom and faith that to see his people forgotten and their cause set at naught nearly breaks Moroni's heart. He is not merely a hothead; he is a man driven past patience by suffering, by death on every hand, by the impending collapse of a beloved nation, and by the apparent dereliction of trusted leaders. He has already fought an exhausting civil war against the foolishly shortsighted king-men, a war that has left his army weak in the face of its external enemies. Now it appears that another segment of Nephite society is collapsing as well. Is it any wonder that he takes Pahoran to task? He is on the front lines, losing ground, and he thinks he has been abandoned.

Still, as I have suggested, Moroni's letter is not the letter Helaman would have written, and the text is revelatory in its juxtaposition of the two documents. Moroni's exposition takes a grave turn in Alma 60:18, where he suddenly accuses Pahoran and other elected leaders of more than neglect: "For we know not but what ye yourselves are seeking for authority. We know not but what ye are also traitors to your country." Ouch! Those words must have cut Pahoran to the quick. Moroni's biting insinuation arises from his own deep hurt and disappointment, from the conviction that trusted friends have betrayed the cause of freedom. Reproach mingles with anguish as Moroni presses his accusing questions.

In some respects Moroni's epistle is also a prophetic sermon, delivered to a congregation of one; he both quotes God ("remember that God has said that the inward vessel shall be cleansed first," Alma 60:23) and speaks for God ("Behold, the Lord saith unto me . . . ," Alma 60:33). Moroni fearlessly admonishes his file leader to "repent of that which ye have done, and begin to be up and doing, and send forth food and men unto us, and also unto Helaman." Otherwise, he vows to leave the Lamanite wars and commence the cleansing of the "inward vessel" (Alma 60:24). Here Moroni's epistle makes another pivot, from accusation and warning to specific threat. Unless Pahoran acts in "a true spirit of freedom" (Alma 60:25) and sends aid, Moroni vows to march on Zarahemla. If he finds "even a spark of freedom remaining," he swears to "stir up insurrections among you, even until those who have desires to usurp power and authority shall become extinct" (Alma 60:27).

Perhaps persuaded by his own argument and his sense of betrayal, Moroni half-believes he is addressing a despot and a traitor who has forsaken both his people and his God. Yet if Pahoran is such a man, only someone as courageous as Moroni would dare blame and accuse him openly. Moroni claims to fear only God, and I believe him. The conclusion to his letter—a conclusion in which, significantly, he still describes himself as Pahoran's captain—aptly characterizes the man and the principles for which he stands. It is his personal creed, and it is beautiful:

> Behold, I am Moroni, your chief captain. I seek not for power, but to pull it down. I seek not for honor of the world, but for the glory of my God, and the freedom and welfare of my country. (Alma 60:36)

In clean, pure prose, in balanced antithesis (I seek not this, but this), Moroni reveals his absolute integrity. He speaks the language of unconscious nobility, the philosophy of a saintly, earnest soldier who loves freedom more than life. Every now and then there arises among mortals one of those great souls for whom liberty is the very essence of being. Without such individuals, freedom could scarcely have been won and maintained in any country, including the United States. I consider Moroni to be the first great American patriot, of the same courageous and single-minded disposition as those who, many centuries later, also espoused the ideal of liberty and committed their lives to establishing a free society in the new world. There is no posturing when Moroni speaks. He means every word.

Moroni's integrity and valor are matched only by Pahoran's magnanimity; his response to Moroni's stinging indictment is simply incredible. It comprises chapter 61. Obviously, Pahoran knows his captain, and he knows himself. Moroni has misjudged him, but Pahoran denies himself the luxury of taking offense. Instead, he calmly but firmly explains that Nephite revolutionaries have overthrown him and claimed his judgment-seat. With a battery of loyal freemen he has taken flight, and from Gideon "sent a proclamation throughout this part of the land; and behold, they are flocking to us daily, to their arms, in the defence of their country and their freedom, and to avenge our wrongs" (Alma 61:6).

The dissenters dare not attack Pahoran and his expanding

forces, but they possess Zarahemla and have appointed Pachus king. In his lust for power, Pachus has allied himself with the Lamanites. Not wanting to shed Lamanite blood, and especially reluctant to fight his traitorous countrymen, the gentle Pahoran is heartened by Moroni's resolve to deal aggressively with these enemies of freedom. Equating "the Spirit of God" with "the spirit of freedom" (Alma 61:15), a now resolute Pahoran proposes that he and Moroni join forces.

But before proposing his plan, the generous Pahoran makes it clear that he bears no ill feelings toward Moroni for his unfair accusations and testy threats. I think I know how most of us, myself included, would have responded to Moroni's letter. Colloquial English offers a wealth of expressions for such moments—none of them suggesting tranquil composure—and I am sure Pahoran's language was equally endowed. But instead of exploring its rich possibilities for venting anger and wounded pride, Pahoran makes a response that is a classic in forgiveness: "And now, in your epistle you have censured me, but it mattereth not; I am not angry, but do rejoice in the greatness of your heart." A long pause is needed here for the reader to absorb that. Without censuring his accuser in the least, without becoming, as we say, defensive, Pahoran quietly and with great dignity adds a personal statement of his own creed: "I, Pahoran, do not seek for power, save only to retain my judgment-seat that I may preserve the rights and the liberty of my people. My soul standeth fast in that liberty in the which God hath made us free" (Alma 61:9). The wrong stops with Pahoran. He absorbs it; he does not send it on to others or return it to Moroni. And as with Moroni, there is no posturing. Pahoran also means every word.

Most assuredly, the Nephite nation is unusually blessed in this era to have three exceptional leaders in Helaman, Moroni, and Pahoran. Different as they are in their individual natures and assignments, all three love God and freedom above any considerations of convenience, safety, influence, or power. The word, as Pahoran says, is their preferred weapon of persuasion, but the price of religious freedom may be higher than that:

> Therefore, my beloved brother, Moroni, let us resist evil, and whatsoever evil we cannot resist with our words, yea, such as rebellions and dissensions, let us resist them with our swords, that we may retain our freedom, that we may rejoice in the great privilege of our church, and in the cause of our Redeemer and our God. (Alma 61:14)

Chapter 62 recounts the rallying of the Nephite peoples around a heartened Moroni as he rolls through the land raising "the standard of liberty" (Alma 62:4). Today we speak of the "charisma" of certain prominent personalities, but the word is too feeble to capture the irresistible energy of such a man as Moroni. The record says that "thousands did flock unto his standard, and did take up their swords in the defence of their freedom, that they might not come into bondage" (Alma 62:5). Together Moroni and Pahoran march into battle against the king-men, restoring Pahoran "to his judgment-seat" (Alma 62:8); but the internal rebellion has posed such a threat to both church and state that law enforcement is stepped up once more in an effort to preserve a democratic form of government. We are reminded again of the discomfiting truth that a free society must sometimes restore peace and preserve freedom by the swift application of stern justice. Above all, this fact offers emphatic testimony of trying times for the Nephite nation. It was most surely the Lord's wisdom that placed selfless and righteous men at the head of Nephite institutions—church, government, and armies—at this auspicious moment in history.

Internal matters being settled at last, Moroni and Pahoran turn their attention to their historic enemy, the Lamanites. Many of the Lamanite captives, however, want no more of war. They make a covenant of peace, "to join the people of Ammon and become a free people" (Alma 62:27). As a result, they "begin to labor exceedingly, tilling the ground, raising all manner of grain, and flocks and herds of every kind. . ." (Alma 62:29). As we have seen before, many Lamanites are more teachable and penitent, more amenable to peace and righteous living, than apostate Nephites. When the Nephite armies finally prevail, peace is re-established in the land, with Helaman returning to the preaching of the word, Pahoran returning to his civic duties, and Moroni turning over his military command to his son Moronihah and retiring to his home.

Readers of the Book of Mormon commonly infer that Nephite prosperity invariably leads to forgetfulness and pride. Some conclude, therefore, that austerity rather than abundance is the Lord's way, and that abundance is not really a blessing at all. I think they are wrong. The language in the closing verses of Alma 62 celebrates prosperity—which is entirely different from material indulgence—as a blessing that can and should coexist with humility and righteousness. The key to the Nephites' peace, in fact, is that very coexistence, for "notwithstanding their riches, or their strength, or their prosperity, they were not lifted up in the pride of their eyes; neither were they slow to remember the Lord their God; but they did humble themselves exceedingly before him" (Alma 62:49). Mormon stresses their constancy, noting that "they did pray unto the Lord their God continually, insomuch that the Lord did bless them, according to his word, so that they did wax strong and prosper in the land" (Alma 62:51). Soon thereafter, Helaman passes on.

Chapter 63, the concluding chapter of the book of Alma, is Mormon's summary of the next several years. He tells of Moroni's death and a minor uprising among Nephite malcontents and Lamanites. The most interesting information in Mormon's summary, however, receives only brief notice. I am helplessly intrigued by his statement that between 57 and 53 B.C., the period covered in this chapter, there are several exoduses from the area around Zarahemla—one large departure by land and several by sea. Fifty-four hundred families, a *huge* number of people, comprise the first group to migrate into the land northward, and later another group sets "forth into the west sea" (Alma 63:5). The first ship returns only to sail north again; it and other ships are "never heard of more" (Alma 63:8). Alma's son Corianton disappears with one of the ships that embark to take provisions to the northern emigrants. In these adventuresome journeys lies a tale I sorely long to read.

## 17

## Helaman 1-6: Helaman's Legacy in Troubled Times

The end of the book of Alma marks the close of an era. The leaders who had figured prominently in the establishment of strong, mutually supportive civil and church governments, and those who had seen the Nephites through major wars in the cause of religious and personal freedom, have, as Mormon frequently says, "gone the way of all the earth" (Helaman 1:2). It is significant that these men all died of natural causes. I sense a new somberness in Mormon's account, however, as he summarizes the concluding events of the period and reports the rapid-fire and sometimes highly disturbing events that mark the beginning of a new era.

Although the book of Helaman contains only sixteen chapters, it is packed with important events and doctrine. The book chronicles a period of political fluctuation and intrigue; but most important, it describes an unprecedented and, as it turns out, ruinous philosophical separation of church and state. When Nephite political leadership repudiates its religious legacy, greedy and ambitious judges and other civil authorities corrupt and change the law. Worse still, a conspiring band of murderers and thieves cunningly infiltrates Nephite society and government. The half-century preceding the coming of Christ, though blessed intermittently by repentance and peace, is by and large a dangerous time for the Nephite nation. It is as though Satan is working overtime to destroy this people before Jesus can teach them.

The period begins on a sinister note, with a divided populace, contested elections, assassinations, insurrection, and war. Then Helaman, a righteous son of the deceased prophet Helaman, is elected to succeed the two murdered sons of the first Pahoran as chief judge. Helaman himself narrowly escapes assassination, and the conspiring Gadianton makes his first appearance in the pages of the Book of Mormon. Nevertheless, several years of relative peace attend Helaman's rule, years marred only by "a little pride which was in the church" (Helaman 3:1) and some increasing internal contention. The latter, Mormon implies, produced major northward migrations of "an exceedingly great many" people "out of the land of Zarahemla" (Helaman 3:3), among them "many of the people of Ammon, who were Lamanites by birth" (Helaman 3:12).

Mormon's report also contains some rare bits of topical information. For example, we learn that because most of the timber in the north had been harvested by the now extinct Jaredite civilization, the emigrants became "expert in the working of cement" (Helaman 3:7), and they imported timber from the south. They also practiced conservation so that trees once again began to "spring up" (Helaman 3:9) and grow to maturity.

Being in an editorial mode, Mormon also offers some perspective on his task. It is impossible, he says, for a single abridgment to represent or encapsulate the countless books and records kept and passed from generation to generation. But in one sentence he provides a good laundry list of the times:

> ... a hundredth part of the proceedings of ... the Lamanites and of the Nephites, and their wars, and contentions, and dissensions, and their preaching, and their prophecies, and their shipping and their building of ships, and their building of temples, and of synagogues and their sanctuaries, and their righteousness, and their wickedness, and their murders, and their robbings, and their plundering, and all manner of abominations and whoredoms, cannot be contained in this work. (Helaman 3:14)

For the omission of abominations we should probably be grateful, though the histories would be fascinating.

Implicit in Mormon's statement is the fact that this was an enormous civilization, in spite of frighteningly effective, though inadvertent, "population control" practices such as murder and war. If the narrow neck of land Mormon mentions occasionally as a boundary between the land northward and the land southward is the area today breached by the Panama Canal, or even if the boundary was farther north, it is plain that both the Nephites and Lamanites had ample room for expansion. And surrounded by sea as they were, it was natural for them also to build and sail ships, both for commerce and exploration. With shipping activities on his mind, Mormon fittingly adopts a sailing metaphor to describe the safe journey of Christ's followers "across that everlasting gulf of misery" prepared for the wicked. The word of God, he says, will "land" the souls of the righteous in the heavenly kingdom (Helaman 3:29-30).

By this time, the Lehites had been on the American continent five and a half centuries—longer than the European habitation of North America if we begin counting with Columbus. Zarahemla alone must have been an immense population center with many suburbs. I smile at Mormon's remark that the church experienced such growth and prosperity "that even the high priests and the teachers were themselves astonished beyond measure" (Helaman 3:25).

Fortunately for the Nephites, when the second Helaman dies in 39 B.C., his eldest son Nephi succeeds him as chief judge. These are eventful years; but not choosing to dwell on secular matters, Mormon accelerates his account, moving swiftly through summaries of rather momentous events. Chapter 4 tells of dissenters again inciting the Lamanites to war. Were it not for the malcontents, the Nephites and Lamanites might well have been living rather amicably with their differences, each group having its own lands and its distinctive culture, and each respecting the other's borders. Time after time, the rebels undermine their own government and enlist the Lamanites in their greedy quest for territory and power. In fact, on this occasion, it is two years before the reluctant Lamanites are persuaded that they have old grievances to settle.

Throughout the see-sawing battle, Nephite lands are lost and retaken and lost again, and Mormon blames the Nephites' pride for their vulnerability. Pride is most effective at undermining character, for it leads to oppression of the poor, refusal of sustenance for the needy, mockery of the sacred, denial of prophecy and revelation, and participation in a broad assortment of popular vices (Helaman 4:12). Pride also leaves the Nephites to face their enemies without the Lord's sustaining power. Consequently, they are "smitten, and driven before the Lamanites, until" they lose "possession of almost all their lands" (Helaman 4:13). As it has ever been with fickle human nature, the threat of extinction is a rather effective catalyst for serious religious enthusiasm. Fictionist Flannery O'Connor puts it aptly: ". . . a taste for self-preservation can be readily combined with the missionary spirit."[1] The Nephites realize that their wickedness and disbelief have driven the Lord and his sustaining power out of their lives, leaving them on a physical par with the Lamanites "even man for man" (Helaman 4:26).

At last Nephi grows "weary because of their iniquity," and like Alma before him, he "yielded up the judgment-seat, and took it upon him to preach the word of God all the remainder of his days" (Helaman 5:4). His brother Lehi joins him. Mormon's commentary on the state of affairs is a reminder of the inescapable democratic dilemma—the risk of a corrupt, irresponsible electorate:

> For as their laws and their governments were established by the voice of the people, and they who chose evil were more numerous than they who chose good, therefore they were ripening for destruction, for the laws had become corrupted. (Helaman 5:2)

A man named Cezoram succeeds Nephi, but as we shall see, four years later he will be murdered in the judgment-seat, and so will the son who succeeds him (see Helaman 6:15). That makes four out of six chief judges assassinated in a few short years. A high-risk profession, indeed. Even worse than coaching.

---

[1] O'Connor is speaking of the grandmother's sudden zealousness when she finds herself staring down the barrel of the Misfit's pistol in "A Good Man Is Hard to Find." See *Mystery and Manners* (New York: Farrar, Straus & Giroux, 1969), p. 110.

For some time now, the record has been centrally absorbed by civil matters, struggles that have consumed the energies of both church and political leaders. Beginning with Helaman 5, however, when Nephi leaves the judgeship to become a full-time teacher, the record, like his life, revolves to religious matters. I also sense Mormon's conscious intent to restore that focus. Chapter 5 contains a representation of Helaman's counsel to his sons Nephi and Lehi, a discourse that establishes the link between repentance and the Atonement. Since it appears posthumously in the record, it may have been recorded by Nephi; or perhaps Mormon chose to interject Helaman's words as a preamble to Nephi's challenging and eventful ministry. In any case, Mormon indicates that Helaman taught Nephi and Lehi a great deal more, both "written" and "not written" (Helaman 5:13).

Helaman first reminds his sons who they are and whose names they bear. A skilled rhetorician, he deftly builds to his climactic idea by means of incremental repetition and parallel structures. I have endowed you with the "names of our first parents," he tells Nephi and Lehi, so

> that when you remember your names ye may remember them; and when ye remember them ye may remember their works; and when ye remember their works ye may know how that it is said, and also written, that they were good. (Helaman 5:6)

Clearly, the Nephites who have kept the faith are a history-conscious people, schooled in the treasured records they possess. In this short exposition, Helaman's allusion to Nephite teachings of the past suggests that the church regarded the religious utterances of Nephite prophets as scripture.

Helaman also anticipates Jesus' parable about building upon a rock rather than upon sand when he speaks of the Savior as our metaphorical rock: "And now, my sons, remember, remember that it is upon the rock of our Redeemer, who is Christ, the Son of God, that ye must build your foundation" (Helaman 5:12). Consistent with numerous other scriptures, in Matthew 16:18 the

Savior is probably also referring to himself, and not to Peter, as the rock upon which he will build his church. He is addressing Peter, but the subject of their discussion just then is the identity of Jesus as "the Christ, the Son of the living God" (Matthew 16:16). Through revelation from the Father, Peter knows the identity of the being who speaks to him. That is, he knows on whose foundation the church is to be established.[2]

The subsequent preaching of Nephi and Lehi leads many dissenting Nephites back to the faith. It also "astonish[es]" and "convinc[es]" 8,000 Lamanites in and around Zarahemla (Helaman 5:19). But when the brothers enter the land of Nephi (for many years, now, the center of the Lamanite nation), they are cast into prison. As if doubly highlighted by the contrastive dark setting, the events that follow are beyond description. The narrative suddenly bursts into an account of spiritual experiences the likes of which we have not seen in the abridged record for some time. Nephi and Lehi are encircled by a pillar of fire, and as they testify that God is manifesting his power, the earth ratifies their words by shaking mightily. A cloud of darkness overshadows all but Nephi and Lehi, filling the throng with what Mormon calls "an awful solemn fear" (Helaman 5:28). The phrase describes not fright, but terror that reaches deeper than fright, as suffering reaches deeper than physical pain. A solemn fear, an awful fear, signifies the presence of unfathomable power, and danger to the soul.

Out of the hush a voice speaks, commanding repentance. It is "not a voice of thunder," but "a still voice of perfect mildness, as if it had been a whisper, and it did pierce even to the very soul" (Helaman 5:30). The strength of that voice, though not expressed in decibels, causes the earth to rumble and the prison walls to tremble. In its third iteration, Mormon reverently reports, the voice speaks "marvelous words which cannot be uttered by man" (Helaman 5:33). An apostate Nephite named Aminadab becomes

---

[2] In Mormondom it is generally agreed that the rock to which the Savior refers in Matthew 16 is the "rock" of revelation. The preceding verses in Matthew 16, plus the corroborating testimony of Helaman, suggest additionally to me the interpretation I have offered here. Throughout scripture, the "rock" is almost invariably the Savior himself, and his gospel. In Jacob 4:16-17, as I noted earlier, the word "stone" is used rather than the customary "rock."

interpreter of the event, and he is permitted to see "through the cloud of darkness the faces of Nephi and Lehi" shining like "faces of angels" (Helaman 5:36). Aminadab describes the two encompassed in transcendent glory, "convers[ing] with the angels of God" (Helaman 5:39). He advises the questioning Lamanites to "repent, and cry unto the voice, even until ye shall have faith in Christ . . ." (Helaman 5:41). Caught up in the miracle, they, too, are "encircled about, yea every soul, by a pillar of fire" (Helaman 5:43).

In this resplendent moment, all present are "filled with that joy which is unspeakable and full of glory":

> And behold, the Holy Spirit of God did come down from heaven, and did enter into their hearts, and they were filled as if with fire, and they could speak forth marvelous words.
>
> And it came to pass that there came a voice unto them, yea, a pleasant voice, as if it were a whisper, saying:
>
> Peace, peace be unto you, because of your faith in my Well Beloved, who was from the foundation of the world.
>
> And now, when they heard this they cast up their eyes as if to behold from whence the voice came; and behold, they saw the heavens open; and angels came down out of heaven and ministered unto them. (Helaman 5:44-48)

The voice is that of the Father, and again, his quiet tones pierce the understanding with more force than a roar. It is not noise that makes us listen, it is a whisper in silence—something my mother learned early.

The three hundred Lamanites who see and hear these things become such powerful witnesses that many others believe also, forswearing "their hatred and the tradition of their fathers" (Helaman 5:51), forsaking their weapons of war, and returning Nephite lands they had seized. The beginning of chapter 6 recounts the happy results of these conversions just thirty years before the Savior's birth—the spread of the gospel, the opening of unrestricted commerce and travel among Lamanites and Nephites, and even the conversion of Nephites through the preaching of the steadier, more righteous Lamanites. For this charmed moment, they are one nation instead of two or three.

Unparalleled prosperity and peace accompany these developments. The land, rich in ore, yields precious stones as well as abundant crops and herds. Skilled women and men make exquisite works in gold and silver and fine cloths. But, as if on schedule, maybe even ahead of schedule, the mercurial Nephites somersault into pride and material appetite. They "grow in wickedness and abominations, while the Lamanites . . . grow exceedingly in the knowledge of their God" (Helaman 6:34). Satan grabs their hearts and coaxes them into a vile brotherhood of mutual protection, secret murders, robbings, plots, oaths, and abominable covenants with the rapidly-multiplying Gadianton thieves. The Gadiantons do not learn their oaths from the Jaredite record; they learn them from Satan. It is a telling distinction that the converted Lamanites rid themselves of the Gadianton robbers with great dispatch, while the inconstant Nephites welcome the villains with open arms.

"And thus," Mormon laments, the Gadiantons and their sympathizers "did obtain the sole management of the government, insomuch that they did trample under their feet and smite and rend and turn their backs upon the poor and the meek, and the humble followers of God" (Helaman 6:39). It strikes me again, as it has before, that throughout Book of Mormon times, apostate generations are invariably characterized by their uncharitable treatment of the poor and lowly. This chapter that had begun on such a happy note ends in gloom: "And thus we see that they were in an awful state, and ripening for an everlasting destruction" (Helaman 6:40).

## 18

## Helaman 7-16: The Warnings of Nephi and Samuel

The remainder of the book of Helaman, chapters 7 through 16, Mormon titles "The Prophecy of Nephi, the son of Helaman." He thus distinguishes it from the more general narrative "of Helaman and his sons" (Helaman 16:25) that precedes it, narrative that contains a good deal of social summary. It is 23 B.C. as chapter 7 begins, and Nephi returns to Zarahemla from a discouraging mission in the land northward to find Zarahemla mired in "awful wickedness, and those Gadianton robbers filling the judgment-seats" (Helaman 7:4). All semblance of decent and responsible government has vanished, and the judicial system is in shambles.

A broken-hearted Nephi climbs the tower in his garden, bows himself down, and pours out his soul to God, bewailing his ill-timed birth. How much better, he thinks, to have lived in the happier day of the first Nephi's exodus to the promised land from Jerusalem. He begins with a classic lament, a nostalgic yearning for a simpler past when, he supposes, people were "easy to be entreated, firm to keep the commandments of God, . . . slow to be led to do iniquity; and . . . quick to hearken unto the words of the Lord" (Helaman 7:7). Like many of us who enshrine the "good old days," Nephi conjectures that "if my days could have been in those days, then would my soul have had joy in the righteousness of my brethren" (Helaman 7:8). Surely, the first Nephi would have been amused at anyone's viewing his troubled time as something of a Golden Age.

In offering this agonized yet hardly private prayer, Nephi catches the attention of several passersby, and their report brings "multitudes" of curiosity seekers (Helaman 7:11). Mormon quotes from Nephi's prophecy to this gathering as well as from his touchingly personal, yet formal, opening lament. Seeing the expectant crowd, Nephi rises to the occasion. The reader is not quite prepared for the metamorphosis as the mournful man disappears and the fearless prophet steps forth. Gone is the troubled, nostalgic tone as Nephi reproves his listeners for marveling at him when they ought to be marveling at their own folly. From his high lectern, Nephi cries mightily the prophets' perennial refrain of repentance, seeming to concentrate all his pent-up anguish into this moment. His prophetic warning is gruesome: Repent, or the Lord "shall scatter you forth that ye shall become meat for dogs and wild beasts" (Helaman 7:19).

In some sense, Nephi and Samuel the Lamanite (whom we will discuss later in this chapter) function as textual alter egos. Representing two traditionally opposing cultures, they deliver essentially the same two-fold message, and from the tops of two high structures: (1) The Nephites, who have "sinned against that great knowledge," will be destroyed while the Lamanites will be preserved (Helaman 7:24); and (2) the redeeming Christ will soon be born. When speaking prophetically, many of the Lord's servants, Nephi included, exhibit great facility with language. Nephi attributes his words to "the Lord God" (Helaman 7:29), but his individual gifts prove him to be both a poet and an orator. There is poetry in his expression of personal grief, and there is oratory in his impassioned pleas, his rhetorical questions, and his parallel warnings.

Mormon does not record Nephi's entire discourse, but he includes enough to introduce the reader to a powerful new voice speaking for the Lord in the critical years preceding the Savior's birth. Taking heart in the fact that a few defend him, Nephi seeks to jog the memory of his listeners, and in the process to sting their collective conscience. He enlists God's ancient prophets as his confederates in warning, but the heart of his message is that the Christ who will come in the flesh is not a Nephite invention. He was known by the prophets from the beginning.

Scarcely pausing, Nephi informs the incredulous townspeople that even as he speaks, their chief judge, Seezoram,[1] has "been

---

[1] This must surely be an alternate spelling of "Cezoram," the name of another recent, and also ill-fated, chief judge.

murdered by his brother" (Helaman 8:27). Both men, he adds, are Gadianton conspirators. Chapter 9, which is largely narrative, chronicles the events that follow Nephi's shocking disclosure. True to form, the corrupt judges try to implicate Nephi in the slaying, but when he orchestrates the murderer's confession, some citizens are convinced that Nephi is indeed a prophet. Still others take an extreme view, asssuming him to be a god.[2]

Although Nephi's earlier experience in the Lamanite prison and his impromptu sermon from the garden tower certainly predict his emergence as one of the book's great men of God, it is probably not until chapter 10, when the Lord personally endows him with the very powers of heaven, that we become fully aware of the magnitude of his prophetic mission. As the chapter opens, Nephi's audience, both accusers and defenders, evaporates, "leaving Nephi alone" (Helaman 10:1) with his solitary meditations on what has occurred. Nephi is no stranger to the miraculous or to the guidance of the Spirit, but perhaps never before has he felt the Lord prompting him in such a specific and unusual way. Having been totally in the Lord's hands—acting as his instrument and his voice—Nephi seems to feel his aloneness all the more acutely when the event is over.

Three times in two verses Mormon uses the word "pondering" to describe Nephi's state of mind. Today, by contrast, as the accelerating quest for excitement, symbols, and pleasures absorbs us, we barricade our souls against quiet musing and inspiration. Not so Nephi. He is "much cast down because of the wickedness" of his people (Helaman 10:3), but his mind is focused and open to divine infusions. In his humbled state, Nephi can hear the Lord's voice, and it makes a remarkable promise:

> . . . I will bless thee forever; and I will make thee mighty in word and in deed, in faith and in works; yea, even that all things shall be done unto thee according to thy word, *for thou shalt not ask that which is contrary to my will.* (Helaman 10:5; emphasis added)

---

[2] I note in passing that these otherwise apostate people have apparently not abandoned certain of their religious practices. For example, they are said to observe the burial of their chief judge by "assembl[ing] themselves together" not only "to mourn," but also "to fast" (Helaman 9:10). It appears, however, that Lehite observance of the Law of Moses did not evolve into the detailed and strict practices that characterized the law in the old world.

Has the Lord ever trusted any mortal more? Whatever Nephi asks, barring nothing, will be done. Nephi is one of those rare beings whose will is in total harmony with the will of his God.

The Lord vows further that Nephi "shall have power over this people," including the astounding ability to "smite the earth with famine, and with pestilence, and destruction" (Helaman 10:6) if the wickedness of the people warrants it. Moreover, the Lord declares, "I give unto you power, that whatsoever ye shall seal on earth shall be sealed in heaven; and whatsoever ye shall loose on earth shall be loosed in heaven" (Helaman 10:7).[3] In a word, Nephi is empowered to act with God's might. I doubt that any mortal has ever carried more responsibility. Cognizance of the power within his grasp could have corrupted a lesser man.

Even before reaching home, Nephi turns in his tracks and begins preaching to the scattered multitudes. "Notwithstanding that great miracle" they have witnessed, the people "revile against him" (Helaman 10:13, 15), but they are unable to apprehend or imprison him because he is "taken by the Spirit and conveyed away out of the midst of them" (Helaman 10:16). We should pause for a moment on that statement. I read it to mean that the Spirit lifts Nephi bodily and removes him from harm's way. At the very least, the Spirit accompanies him from place to place throughout the Nephite nation, "from multitude to multitude" as he declares "the word of God" personally or sends it forth with other faithful teachers (see Helaman 10:17). Here is a man of such great faith and goodness that the Spirit attends, guards, and perhaps even transports him through space, that he might fulfill his calling. But it is to no avail; the people spurn Nephi's message and fall into violent contention among themselves.

We sometimes overlook this Nephi in our consideration of the great Nephite prophets, inconspicuous as he is initially in the

---

[3] The Savior was to make the same promise to Peter in Matthew 16:19, though the King James Bible uses the term "bind" instead of "seal." Perhaps these scriptural passages refer to the authority to perform sealing ordinances anciently.

book of Helaman, and presiding as he does over the church in a day when Satan owns the minds and hearts of citizenry and governors alike. We also might miss the implications of Mormon's passing remark that Nephi and his brother Lehi had "many revelations *daily*" (Helaman 11:23; emphasis added). Continuous communion with the Spirit must have been Nephi's arm of strength through one of the most unstable periods in the history of the Nephite nation, the decades just before the birth of Christ. The inconstancy of Nephi's people grieved him sorely as he watched them yo-yo in their pride, forsaking their God even as God prospered them.

Chapter 11 details thirteen years (from 20 B.C. to 7 B.C.) of just such vacillation, beginning with the famine Nephi asks the Lord to send in a last-ditch effort to divert his people from making war on each other. There are some splendid passages in Helaman 11, in the brief interludes of repentance. One such passage is Nephi's prayer to the Lord (quoted in verses 10 through 16) asking him to end the three-year famine, to "send forth rain upon the face of the earth, that she may bring forth her fruit, and her grain in the season of grain" (Helaman 11:13). The famine ends, and Mormon seems to celebrate along with Nephi's people, virtually singing of the rain and the earth's fertile renewal. More lovely still is the human renewal: "And behold, the people did rejoice and glorify God, and the whole face of the land was filled with rejoicing; and they did no more seek to destroy Nephi, but they did esteem him as a great prophet" (Helaman 11:18). Mormon is quick to add praise of Lehi, who is "not a whit behind" his brother in "righteousness" (Helaman 11:19).

Peace and prosperity abound, church influence spreads, "and the more part of the people, both the Nephites and the Lamanites, did belong to the church" (Helaman 11:21). This utopian period, however, is disappointingly brief. In less time than it takes to tell it, the Nephites forget the lessons so hard in the learning and plummet again into disbelief and chaos. I find it both disturbing and revealing that the first quarrels to crack the fragile peace concern "the points of doctrine which had been laid down by the prophets" (Helaman 11:22). The record does not specify which doctrines are the subjects of disagreement, but in any religious society, ancient or modern, some persons are eventually going to challenge the doctrines of orthodoxy, for the sake of argument and intellectual or social independence.

I find it disturbing, too, that the next round of conflict in the Book of Mormon has its impetus in the actions of Nephite dissenters who have "taken upon themselves the name of Lamanites" and then "stirred up" "a certain number" of others "who were real descendants of the Lamanites" (Helaman 11:24). We have come to respect the solemnity with which Lehite believers take upon them the name of Christ, and we shudder when former believers adopt a name that announces them to be avowed enemies of Christ. This band of dissenters becomes the nucleus for a new round of Gadianton activity, and fear of the robbers "stir[s] [the Nephites] up again in remembrance of the Lord their God" (Helaman 11:34). But, as usual, the stirring is short-lived.

As if unable to conclude this disheartening turn of events with only his customary editorial splice, Mormon momentarily leaves the narrative and produces a moving commentary on the matter at hand. At least chapter 12, which does not read like an abridgment, appears to belong to Mormon rather than Nephi. Mormon also ends the chapter with "Amen," signifying its function as a separate discourse in its own right. At the chapter's beginning, Mormon observes that it is one of the unfortunate truths of human nature that "ease" combined with "exceedingly great prosperity" (Helaman 12:2) can lead to forgetfulness; and "except the Lord doth chasten his people with many afflictions, yea, except he doth visit them with death and with terror, and with famine and with all manner of pestilence, they will not remember him" (Helaman 12:3).

Much of chapter 12 resembles a two-part antiphonic psalm, with verses 1-6 decrying human weakness and verses 9-21 contrastively praising the might of "our great and everlasting God" (Helaman 12:8). Verses 7 and 8 function neatly as a transition between the two parts as Mormon sets God's magnificence against the comparative "nothingness of the children of men" (Helaman 12:7). The reader can sense the shift in Helaman 12:4 to a more formal mode of discourse as Mormon introduces poetic repetitions and reversals. He has been speaking directly to the reader—"and thus we see"—but now he distances himself from both the reader and his own feelings with a highly rhetorical lament. The passage merits examination.

"O how foolish, and how vain, and how evil, and devilish," Mormon begins. Then he abruptly interjects a parallel reversal that continues the scheme but employs a play on the antonyms "quick" and "slow": ". . . how quick to do iniquity, and how slow to do good, are the children of men; yea, how quick to hearken unto the words of the evil one . . ." (Helaman 12:4). The alternating how quick/how slow/how quick pattern of verse 4 does a bit of doubling in verse 5 to how quick/how quick and how slow/how slow, with a distinct break in the middle:

> Yea, *how quick* to be lifted up in pride; yea, *how quick* to boast, and do all manner of that which is iniquity; [break] and *how slow* are they to remember the Lord their God, and to give ear unto his counsels, yea, *how slow* to walk in wisdom's paths! (Emphases added)

The final half of that verse catalogues, through the reproach of negative example, the things contrary mortals should do but do not. We might also note that Mormon speaks both metaphorically and alliteratively in that line—"*give ear* unto his counsels," and "*w*alk in *w*isdom's *p*aths."

In verse 7, a transitional verse, as I mentioned, Mormon returns to the exclamatory "O how," this time to introduce a construction resembling an oxymoron, a figure consisting of two contradictory parts or notions: "O how *great* is the *nothingness* of the children of men" (emphases added). Then with subtle craftsmanship, after declaring that mortals "are less than the dust of the earth" (verse 7), Mormon employs the "dust" image to illustrate, by contrast, God's power over dust and everything else (verse 8). With a play on one word, therefore, Mormon vaults

from an enumeration of mortal weaknesses and inconstancies to
a celebratory list of the mighty capabilities of God. He focuses
especially on God's controlling power, exercised through his
voice, over the earth (dust) he created and, by implication, over
humanity. There is power, too, in Mormon's words as he composes an anthem of praise in condensed, repetitious structures,
beginning with "Yea, behold at his voice do the hills and the
mountains tremble and quake" (see Helaman 12:9-18). This
hymn to God's power reminds us again of our immeasurable
debt to Mormon, who enriched his abridgment with personal
insights and testimony, and yes, even poetry.[4] The concluding
verses of chapter 12 turn smoothly into a short sermon teaching,
among other things, that repentance is the cement that binds
grace and works together.

Mormon resumes the narrative with the indomitable
Lamanite prophet Samuel, who hazards a journey to Zarahemla in
order to preach repentance to the imperious and inhospitable
Nephites. No surprise, the Nephites throw him out. Samuel starts
for home and the friendly environment of faithful Lamanites, but
the Lord promptly sends him back, as he had sent Alma back to
Ammonihah. The plucky and obedient Samuel mounts the city
wall and "with a loud voice" prophesies "whatsoever things the
Lord put into his heart" (Helaman 13:4). The topic that occupies
him first and longest is the imminent destruction of the Nephite
people—just the thing to win him oodles of friends in Zarahemla.
He minces no words, however; and unlike Alma, who had in
more hopeful days refrained from publicly announcing the specific time of Nephite destruction (see Alma 45:9-10), Samuel
broadcasts it from the wall: ". . . four hundred years pass not away
save the sword of justice falleth upon this people" (Helaman
13:5). Even now, he cries, Zarahemla is being spared only because
of the righteous. Samuel also makes specific and prolonged refer-

---

[4] Of particular interest for another reason are verses 14 and 15. I add verse 15 here as a footnote, for it resembles such in Mormon's text: "And thus, according to his word the earth goeth back, and it appeareth unto man
that the sun standeth still; yea, and behold, this is so; for surely it is the earth that moveth and not the sun." The
language here indicates rather clearly that the Nephites, at least in Mormon's time, understood the basic workings of the solar system and knew that it was the movement of the earth, and not of the sun, that brought day
and night. Visions of the Creation would have taught earlier prophets these things, too.

ence to the cursing of both the land and the treasures the Nephites have hidden in it. Your material goods, he tells them, will "become slippery, that ye cannot hold them" (Helaman 13:31).[5]

Samuel, who is obviously an orator of the first order, is also extremely courageous. The personal risk is incalculable for a lone missionary facing a hostile crowd, and the fact that he is a blunt, outspoken Lamanite compounds the danger. Still, at first his hearers seem spellbound by his diction and delivery, his incredible daring, and the compelling energy of his personality. But even he must wonder how long the Nephites will abide him. God has commanded him through an angel to deliver this particular message, he declares, and the Nephites are to hear him out. Although Mormon has recorded only a fraction of Samuel's words, repentance and doom are clearly not Samuel's only themes. He also issues the thrilling prophecy that in just five years, "then cometh the Son of God to redeem all those who shall believe on his name" (Helaman 14:2).

Supremely gifted in language as well as prophecy, Samuel describes lyrically the "many signs and wonders" (Helaman 14:6) that will announce the Savior's birth, among them a brilliant "new star" and a night that "shall not be darkened" (Helaman 14:3-5). At these and many other signs, Samuel promises, "ye shall all be amazed, and wonder, insomuch that ye shall fall to the earth" (Helaman 14:7); but "whosoever shall believe on the Son of God, the same shall have everlasting life" (Helaman 14:8). His earlier warning about the ultimate destruction of the Nephite nation foretells events 400 years distant, but the signs he prophesies now will be witnessed in just a few years by the very people gathered before him. Samuel's words pulse with immediacy as he cries repentance and prophesies "the coming of Jesus Christ, the Son of God, the Father of heaven and of earth, the Creator of all things from the beginning" (Helaman 14:12).

---

[5] This phenomenon is a curious one to me, the "slippery" disappearance of swords and tools and wealth. There were, of course, a number of unpleasant and befuddling curses visited upon the children of Israel in Moses' time, but this one presents a special brand of frustration.

I like Samuel, this gutsy, eloquent testifier of the word. What a sight he must have been, high on the wall proclaiming both terror and wonder. No one has spoken with more precision and authority on the advent of Christ and the doctrines of resurrection, repentance, and atonement, or with more understanding on the doctrine of the first and second deaths. There is to be, he says, a general resurrection from the first death, a death which is both spiritual and temporal—spiritual because Adam and his posterity are separated from God, temporal because they are mortal. Samuel also describes redemption from a later "spiritual death, yea, a second death" in which the knowledgeable unrepentant "are cut off again" and separated from God forever. Since no Nephites have been born without the law, redemption from the second death, Samuel insists, applies only on "condition of [their] repentance" in mortality (Helaman 14:18).

Having expounded the doctrines most pertinent to Christ's mission, Samuel turns now to a second set of signs, those that will signify his death. While no less marvelous than the first, they present a terrifying contrast to the luminous precursors of the Savior's birth. The prophetic juxtaposition of signs most certainly increases the drama surrounding Samuel and the ominous events he foretells from the towering wall around Zarahemla. The language in the first two verses of his prophecy is harsh and strong, like its subject. There are few polysyllables and many forced stops and hard sounds—t's, k's, d's, b's, and g's—sounds that suggest the earth's shrieking and splitting. The language of the second pair of verses is less violent but more grim, depicting the altered face of the once solid earth:

[1] Yea, at the time that he shall yield up the ghost there shall be thunderings and lightnings for the space of many hours, and the earth shall shake and tremble; and the rocks which are upon the face of this earth, . . .

Yea, they shall be rent in twain, and shall ever after be found in seams and in cracks, and in broken fragments upon the face of the whole earth. . . .

[2] And behold, there shall be great tempests, and there shall be many mountains laid low, like unto a valley, and there shall be many places which are now called valleys which shall become mountains, whose height is great.

And many highways shall be broken up, and many cities shall become desolate. (Helaman 14:21-24)

In fact, the modified language in verses 23 and 24 readies us for a happier turn of thought in verse 25. The Savior's death is both tragic and joyous, perhaps the most excruciating of religious paradoxes. It is not, therefore, a sacrilege to greet the signs of his death with gladness as well as sorrow. Indeed, some will join him in resurrection. The chaotic darkness, however, will persist three days. Samuel also foresees untold other events, more persuasive than tempests and darkness, and informs his listeners that the choice to perish or be saved is theirs. He thus echoes a perpetual theme in the Book of Mormon: without freedom to make choices, human experience would be meaningless. I note, too, that Samuel speaks of the relationship between restoration and redemption much as Alma had (in Alma 41): ". . . ye can do good and be restored unto that which is good, or have that which is good restored unto you; or ye can do evil, and have that which is evil restored unto you" (Helaman 14:31).

In chapter 15 Samuel gives major attention to a subject Nephi had broached earlier: the Lord's promises to Samuel's own people, the Lamanites. It is fitting, and hardly coincidental, that a faithful Lamanite prophet is designated to rehearse those promises among his faithless and estranged ancestral kin. The subject is obviously dear to him, and he addresses it with grace and feeling. After admonishing the Nephites still one more time to repent, he begins constructing a bridge between the two prongs of his prophecy, Nephite destruction and Lamanite preservation. At the same time, he sets the Lord's earlier displeasure with the Lamanites against his longstanding support of the Nephites. Having represented his own people as the traditional "wicked" counterparts to the "chosen" Nephites, Samuel proceeds to demonstrate that there remains a marked contrast between the two peoples. They have traded roles, however; the once "hated" Lamanites (Helaman 15:4) are righteous, and the once "loved" Nephites (Helaman 15:3) are not. The shoes, in other words, have changed feet.

The Lamanite fathers, in their ignorance, may have performed despicable deeds; but there is in the Lamanite character a stability and strength lacking in the Nephite character. Samuel declares that once the Lamanites accept the truth, ironically "through the preaching of the Nephites" (Helaman 15:4), they rarely waver. And "because of their firmness when they are once enlightened, behold, the Lord shall bless them and prolong their days," even until the prophesied "latter times" when they shall be restored "to the knowledge of the truth" and "numbered among [the true shepherd's] sheep" (Helaman 15:10-13).

As he leaves Samuel's prophesying and resumes his narrative, Mormon essentially summarizes events and conditions that close out the record designated as the book of Helaman. He observes that Samuel's words register in the hearts of some, and those few seek out Nephi. But predictably, the rest of his listeners are incensed. Evidently, they have not enjoyed the rehearsal of Lamanite virtues any more than they have relished the numeration of Nephite vices. They register their opinion by throwing stones and discharging arrows at Samuel as he stands above them on the city wall, "but the Spirit of the Lord was with him, insomuch that they could not hit him" (Helaman 16:2). When they try to seize him, he leaps from the wall and escapes to his people, "never [to be] heard of more among the Nephites" (Helaman 16:8). So ends a dramatic, even theatrical, episode in Book of Mormon history.

As Samuel has been holding forth from the wall, Nephi has been at work in the city, "baptizing, and prophesying, and preaching, crying repentance unto the people, showing signs and wonders, working miracles among the people, that they might know that the Christ must shortly come" (Helaman 16:4). Again, the highly condensed narrative barely touches events that would undoubtedly inspire us in the telling. What were those "signs and wonders"; what were those "miracles"?

Mormon next describes conditions in the five years preceding the birth of Christ. The only detectable change with the passing years is one of degree rather than kind: the faithful few are more diligent, but the greater number "began to be more hardened in iniquity" (Helaman 16:12). It perplexes me that the more numerous the signs and wonders, and the more vocal the angels in declaring the "glad tidings of great joy" (Helaman 16:14), the more stiffened the unbelievers become against the word. The fact that these people are unmoved by obvious and multiple miracles tells us how enamored they are of "their own wisdom" (Helaman 16:15) and how steeped they are in skeptical vanity. They condescendingly allow that the prophets "may have *guessed* right" on "*some* things," there being "so many" (Helaman 16:16; emphases added). That arrogant statement may be the most telling character disclosure of all.

Mormon reports the rationalists' self-serving dialogue as they begin "to reason and to contend among themselves" (Helaman 16:17). They excuse their faithlessness on the grounds that "it is not reasonable that such a being as a Christ shall come," but if he should, "why will he not show himself unto us as well as unto them who shall be at Jerusalem?" (Helaman 16:18). Then they impute deceitful motives to prophets and church leaders, arguing that the latter predict future events "in a land which is far distant" so that "they can keep us in ignorance, for we cannot witness with our own eyes that they are true" (Helaman 16:20). A deceptively persuasive argument, on the face of it. Furthermore, the doubters contend that in creating dependence on "their words," the prophets also relegate the people to lifelong servitude (Helaman 16:21).

This talk has a certain appeal, as irrationality posing as reason sometimes does, but it is just another face for pride. We know who the deceivers are, and they are not the prophets. Obviously impatient with such intellectual pandering, Mormon indicates that he has reported only a small part of the "foolish and vain" things that the people "imagine up in their hearts" (Helaman 16:22). As he regretfully observes, ". . . Satan did get great hold upon the hearts of the people upon all the face of the land" (Helaman 16:23).

The book of Helaman ends with the conclusion of "the ninetieth year of the reign of the judges over the people of Nephi" (Helaman 16:24). It is now 1 B.C.

# 3 Nephi 1-10: Turbulent Years Before Christ's Appearance

The book of 3 Nephi is a landmark chapter in Nephite history. It spans the years of Christ's birth, ministry, and crucifixion in the old world, and his ministry as a resurrected being in the new. Spectacular cosmic signs herald his birth and signify his death, fulfilling prophecies old and new.

As the book opens, there is a semblance of normalcy, for the chief judge and his military appointees are once more honorable men and faithful church members. Nevertheless, there is anything but peace and stability in the land. Helaman's son Nephi, who had succeeded his father as prophet and record keeper (having relinquished the chief judgeship in order to teach the gospel full-time), departs "out of the land of Zarahemla . . . and whither he went, no man knoweth" (3 Nephi 1:2-3). Although he does not return and is never found, Mormon does not speculate on the possibility of his translation into an immortal state.

Nephi's son, also named Nephi, is charged with care of the records. Mormon says little by way of specific praise or even description of this Nephi, who is the central human figure in 3 Nephi. The record speaks for itself, but it is easy to overlook the greatness of the man whose life and work are understandably eclipsed by the coming of the resurrected Lord and Savior to his people in the western hemisphere. However, every indication is that this Nephi was a spiritual giant, singled out by Jesus and undoubtedly foreordained to be his prophet and leader during the most auspicious period in Lehite history.

As the time of the Savior's birth approaches, the faithless Nephites take perverse pleasure in the believers' seemingly fruitless watch for the signs foretold by Samuel, the Lamanite prophet.

Insisting that the prophesied day has already come and gone, the doubters even set a deadline for the event and attach a death penalty if the signs fail to appear by the appointed day. A grieving Nephi bows "himself down upon the earth," crying "mightily to his God in behalf of his people" (3 Nephi 1:11). Like the early Nephite Enos, Nephi entreats the Lord "all that day" (3 Nephi 1:12), and at last he hears blessed news from the heavens:

> Lift up your head and be of good cheer; for behold, the time is at hand, and on this night shall the sign be given, and on the morrow come I into the world, to show unto the world that I will fulfill all that which I have caused to be spoken by the mouth of my holy prophets. (3 Nephi 1:13)

There are no more memorable words in scripture, and Nephi's heart must have sung to hear them. The next verse is also memorable, and more than a little challenging. The Lord says that he comes "to fulfill all things" decreed "from the foundation of the world, and to do the will, both of the Father and of the Son—of the Father because of me, and of the Son because of my flesh." I find the parenthetical statement puzzling, but read it as a declaration that the plan of salvation was authored by both Father and Son. Thus, in carrying out the plan in the flesh, the Savior is fulfilling his own divine will as well as the Father's.

At the signs of Christ's birth, the impressionable, if not persevering, Nephites fall to earth in fear and "astonish[ment]" (3 Nephi 1:15, 17). They know their sins and their ripeness for correction, and many who find themselves still drawing breath are "baptiz[ed] unto repentance" (3 Nephi 1:23). With their conversions, peace temporarily returns to the land, ruffled only by a dispute as to the status of the Law of Moses now that the Savior has been born. The point is clarified: the law will not be fulfilled until the Savior's mission is complete.

Peace or not, the Gadianton robbers are still entrenched in the mountains, and they continue to multiply and to molest civilized society. Nephite dissenters again begin consorting with the thieves, swiftly, incredibly, forgetting or discounting the wondrous signs they have witnessed. More surprising, some of the younger generation of Lamanites are led away by lies and flattery to join the Gadianton band. As the robbers grow in strength and numbers, life grows increasingly difficult for faithful Nephites and Lamanites. By the end of the fifteenth year—the Nephites now ✳ reckon time from the Savior's birth[1]—the Nephites are on the brink of destruction.

The Gadianton robbers are, as we say, "feeling their oats," and in this spirit their leader, Giddianhi, sends an insolent, swaggering epistle to the virtuous Nephite chief judge, Lachoneus. In that letter he pretends to praise Lachoneus and the Nephites for what he calls their "firmness" (3 Nephi 3:2) in defending their way of life. His real purpose, however, is intimidation. He glibly advises the Nephites to "yield up . . . your cities, your lands, and your possessions" (3 Nephi 3:6). Otherwise, his so-called "brave men" of "unconquerable spirit" (3 Nephi 3:3,4) will "visit you with the sword" (3 Nephi 3:6) "even until ye shall become extinct" (3 Nephi 3:8). The whole letter is a fascinating study in tone as it interweaves condescension, mockery, and threat.

Even as the hypocritical Giddianhi speaks seeming praise, his suppositional language betrays his disdain for the pitiable, misguided Nephites who are defending a hopeless and unjust cause. You are to be congratulated, he says, for firmly "maintaining that which *ye suppose* to be your right," and he grants that "ye do stand well, *as if* ye were supported by the hand of *a god*, in the defence of your liberty, and your property, and your country, *or that which ye do call so*" (3 Nephi 3:2; emphases added). I observe also his sly reduction of Christian deity by applying the indefinite article "a" and the lower case "g" to the word "god."

At one moment feigning concern, and obviously enjoying his duplicitous little game of rhetoric, Giddianhi says that it seems "a

---

[1] Mormon pauses in this chapter to establish the time of these events, by the several different ways his record keepers measured it. Originally, time in the record was reckoned from the year Lehi and his family left Jerusalem, and we learn here that the Savior's birth occurred 600 years after that date. The last hundred years in the record, however, have been counted from the beginning of the rule of judges in Nephite society. Mosiah, the last Nephite king, died only nine decades before the birth of Christ.

pity" to him that the "most noble Lachoneus" would "be so foolish and vain as to suppose" that he and his people "can stand
against" the Gadianton forces (3 Nephi 3:3). Then, with all the
subtlety of an axe murderer, he justifies his men's "everlasting
hatred" as a moral response to "the many wrongs . . . done unto
them" by the Nephites (3 Nephi 3:4). Moreover, he claims the
works of the secret Gadianton society "to be good," for "they have
been handed down" from an "ancient date" (3 Nephi 3:9).
Indeed, Satan's schooling of Cain in evil's dusky arts is about as
ancient as such instruction gets. If once engaged, Giddianhi
warns, these indignant worthies could not be restrained from
completely destroying their oppressors. His motive, he implies, is
benevolence. He claims to speak out of "feeling for your welfare,"
since the Nephites, who exhibit such a "noble spirit in the field of
battle," are only defending that which they mistakenly "believe to
be right" (3 Nephi 3:5).

Alternating between tones of conciliatory flattery and bold
malice, Giddianhi vows total destruction unless the Nephites
agree to unconditional surrender. In his next breath, however, he
shifts into verbal reverse with the phrase "in other words," grandly
inviting the Nephites to "unite with us . . . and become our
brethren that ye may be like unto us—not our slaves, but our
brethren and partners of all our substance" (3 Nephi 3:7). Now
there is a fine phrase, "*our* substance," since it is the Nephites who
own the substance which is to become "ours." Giddianhi follows
his two-faced overture with a virulent oath of annihilation for the
Nephites should they fail to meet his demands.

Lachoneus is, of course, flabbergasted at Giddianhi's auda-
cious epistle, and he responds by mustering his people and all that
they possess into the area around Zarahemla and Bountiful.
There, with God's help, and under the command of the faithful
Gidgiddoni, they can fortify and defend themselves. As in earlier
times, the Nephites are not to be aggressors, but are to fight only
in defense of their lives, land, and liberty. And soon enough, the
Gadiantons give them that terrifying opportunity. The attackers
look more like demons than soldiers, with blood-dyed "lamb-skin

about their loins" and shorn, helmeted heads. They quickly learn, however, that the Nephites fear their God more than they fear their enemies. A "great and terrible" (3 Nephi 4:11) battle ensues, perhaps the most deadly to date in Lehite history. Giddianhi is slain, and the robbers retreat.

Unfortunately, they do not stay in retreat, but in just a few years launch a new offensive, a "siege" to "hem" the Nephites "in on every side" and "cut them off from all their outward privileges" (3 Nephi 4:16). As it turns out, however, it is the Gadiantons, not the Nephites, who are cut off, and the narrative plays on that fact repeatedly. Mainly, the robbers are separated from food and supply sources because the Nephites have removed everything, leaving bare their deserted cities and lands. Severance from a food supply is not the only cutting off, however. To add to the Gadiantons' misery, the Nephite forces keep dogging them, "falling upon their armies and cutting them off by thousands and by tens of thousands" (3 Nephi 4:21). In desperation, the Gadianton leader, Zemnarihah, orders a retreat, but the Nephites anticipate it and "cut off the way of their retreat" (3 Nephi 4:24).

Zemnarihah is "taken and hanged upon a tree." When he is dead, the Nephites do not merely cut the rope by which he hangs; they "fell the tree to the earth" (3 Nephi 4:28) in a gesture of "cutting" that is symbolic of far more than one man's death. He represents the menace that has threatened the Nephites' very existence, and when he is gone they raise songs of praise so stirring that Mormon, obviously moved, records them. This conflict could well have meant the end of the Nephite nation, and the Nephites know it. A chastening experience, it has prompted every "living soul" (3 Nephi 5:1) to trust prophecy, to repent, and to serve God. The surviving Gadiantons, a genuinely *captive* audience, are taken prisoner and taught the truth. Any who covenant to cease their murderous practices are released. Furthermore, the chastened Lamanites among the Gadianton prisoners are not required to become Nephites. Instead, the victors grant those "who were desirous to remain Lamanites, lands, according to their numbers" (3 Nephi 6:3), of their own. The generosity of the victorious

Nephites sets a model for individuals as well as states.

At this point Mormon pauses in the narrative, as he has done before, to remind his readers who he is and to clarify matters pertaining to the records in his care. He regrets that he can recount so little of the last twenty-five years, the years since Christ's birth in the Holy Land, in his abridgment. I sense that in the beginning, when recorded Lehite history basically followed one family group, most of the significant spiritual events could be chronicled. And it was easy enough to include the whole of the first Nephi's sacred writings. By now, however, even with wars and other disasters regularly pruning the family tree, the Nephites comprise a huge populace with a complex story. Bearing this in mind, the reader should not be surprised to find that earlier accounts in Mormon's abridgment seem more detailed and complete than later ones. Furthermore, searching through stacks of records and trying to condense their contents is time-consuming work, as is fashioning metal plates and engraving characters on them. Then, too, the time and opportunity for Mormon to do the work most surely decreased as the political realities of his own day shackled and consumed him.

Lest any wonder about the identity and perspective of the connecting narrative voice in this record, "I am called Mormon" (3 Nephi 5:12), the abridger avows candidly, and "I am a disciple of Jesus Christ, the Son of God. I have been called of him to declare his word among his people, that they might have everlasting life" (3 Nephi 5:13). Mormon knows who he is, and what God expects him to do. He represents the truest and finest of the human race—strong, intelligent, forthright, eye singled to his task and his God. Before resuming his "account of the things which have been before me" (3 Nephi 5:19), he makes a simple but moving statement of faith, a declaration that is the measure of the man: "I am Mormon, and a pure descendant of Lehi. I have reason to bless my God and my Savior Jesus Christ. . ." (3 Nephi 5:20).

During the first few years following the Gadianton war, the Nephites return to their lands and rebuild their cities. Temporarily sobered by their brush with extinction, they are righteous, just, and orderly. But again, prosperity spawns pride, which in Nephite society invariably translates into neglect and mistreatment of the poor. Despite Book of Mormon emphasis on the matter, we today seldom make a personal mental connection between pride and disregard of the poor. Mormon and his predecessors, however, universally make that connection. They have seen the repeated evolutions of an egalitarian society into one in which people are "distinguished by ranks," classified and valued "according to their riches and their chances for learning; yea, some were ignorant because of their poverty, and others did receive great learning because of their riches" (3 Nephi 6:12).

Forever the undoing of the Nephite people, pride almost seems to have been a defect in the blood. Perhaps it is too easy for us, blind to our own pride, to decry it in these ancient peoples and to feel superior to them, especially when Mormon so frequently points it out and denounces it. I cannot help wondering, however, what an astute observer such as Mormon would see as the chief failing of turn-of-the-century America. Most critics rightly point to a decay of moral character; but taken a step further, that decay can usually be traced to a national absorption with self and pleasure. Call it pride, call it selfishness, call it greed, or call it moral decay; in both societies it originates in a preoccupation with things of the world. "Power, and authority, and riches" (3 Nephi 6:15) are worshiped instead of God, and the poor are all but forgotten. Education is valued not as a road to wisdom and understanding, but as a route to prestige, influence, worldly success, and material ease. In all honesty, I see in myself a troubling assortment of the failings that Mormon gathers under the canopy of pride.

Less than a decade after the costly defeat of the Gadianton armies, the "great inequality" in Nephite society shatters the church. As before, it is converted Lamanites, not Nephites, though only "a few" this time, who remain "firm, and steadfast, and immovable" (3 Nephi 6:14). Mormon uses oddly appropriate phraseology to describe the Nephites' wickedness. For "a long time," he says, they have been "carried about by the temptations of the devil whithersoever he desired to carry them" (3 Nephi

6:17). The words "carried about" suggest the surrender of personal volition, motivation, power, and choice. "Carried" implies a greater dependency than "led," and its implications are more damning. Mormon is quick to point out that the Nephites "did not sin ignorantly" (3 Nephi 6:18).

Apostasy cuts so deep that inspired teachers are secretly executed, and the perpetrators protected, through the collusion of corrupt judges, lawyers, and high priests. Enter once more the old Gadiantonism as the conspirators seek to dismantle the system that Moroni and the first Helaman had fought so valiantly to maintain. They intend "that the land should no more be at liberty but should be subject unto kings" (3 Nephi 6:30). These power-mongers succeed in murdering the chief judge and disrupting the government, but they are not able to establish a central monarchy. Instead, they splinter the domain "into tribes, every man according to his family and his kindred and friends" (3 Nephi 7:2).

Although each tribe has its own leader who dictates the law for that tribe, at least the individual tribes are united in their opposition to the secret combination that had wiped out the central Nephite government. Furthermore, they "establish very strict laws that one tribe should not trespass against another, insomuch that in some degree they had peace in the land" (3 Nephi 7:14). Mormon indicates that "there were no wars *as yet* among them" (3 Nephi 7:5; emphasis added), but obviously he is not holding his breath, for the people have renounced religious faith. Outnumbered by tribespeople, the conspirators flee into the north with their appointed monarch. There he hopes to establish a powerful kingdom and attract Nephite dissidents—which, given the Nephites' past performance, is almost a sure bet.

We should not underestimate the significance of these events. It is no small matter for a body politic to undergo a change of the magnitude experienced in Nephite society just before Christ's new-world ministry. The speed with which the Nephite nation turned a central democratic government into a diverse collection of individual tribes is, to use one of Mormon's favorite terms, astonishing. It is even possible, I suppose, that this tribal system, initiated in 31 A.D., is the genesis of the tribal system that has pre-vailed among Lamanite posterity into the present day. In any case, the natural calamities that soon disrupt civil order and every other kind of order, followed by the Savior's appearance and ministry, put a swift end to tribal laws and boundaries of the day.

Through this section of the narrative Mormon has scarcely mentioned the prophet Nephi, who succeeded his father Nephi as head of the church and principal record keeper. But now, in the latter half of chapter 7, Mormon offers a brief update. The record includes none of Nephi's discourses, and precious little of his expe-rience, preventing us from enjoying firsthand the quality of his mind and spirit. Given Mormon's responsibilities and time con-straints, his explanation for the brevity of his account is under-standable, but disappointing nonetheless: "And he [Nephi] did minister many things unto them; and all of them cannot be writ-ten, and a part of them would not suffice, therefore they are not written in this book. And Nephi did minister with power and with great authority" (3 Nephi 7:17). That teasing line, "a part of them would not suffice," tells us that we are missing something excep-tional. I am drawn to this last Nephi, though for the present I am denied access to his meditations and teachings. Surely, the Lord revered Nephi, or he would not have chosen him to serve at his side when he came.

The record indirectly alludes to Nephi's spiritual quality in passing comments about daily visits from angels and instructions from the Lord's own voice. This prophet has "had power given unto him that he might know concerning the ministry of Christ," but he is also the sorrowful "eye-witness to [the people's] quick return from righteousness unto their wickedness and abomina-tions" (3 Nephi 7:15). Mormon merely outlines in tantalizing abbreviation a few of Nephi's miraculous acts, which he continues to perform openly, "in the name of Jesus" (3 Nephi 7:20), despite the people's resentment. Nephi is no ordinary man, for "in the name of Jesus did he cast out devils and unclean spirits; and even his brother did he raise from the dead, after he had been stoned and suffered death by the people" (3 Nephi 7:19). There is a whole story in that one sentence about Nephi and his brother, one that either Nephi or Mormon elects not to tell. It is a sign of the times that most witnesses of the miracle are jealous rather than spiritually quickened. Even so, a good many people repent and are baptized.

There is also a story in chapter 8 that Mormon only briefly sketches—a story of death and mayhem and fear almost beyond human imagining. It appears to me that nature's response to the Savior's crucifixion was much more violent in the new world than in the old. The storms reported in the Bible seem mild by comparison with the destructive upheavals Nephi witnessed. Why this should be so is open to conjecture. Were the Lehites more wicked than their old-world counterparts? Was Jesus less real to them? Comparisons aside, "in the thirty and fourth year, in the first month, on the fourth day of the month, there arose a great storm, such an one as never had been known in all the land" (3 Nephi 8:5). Lightning, thunder, tempests, and earthquakes batter the earth, sinking some cities, burying others, setting fire to still others, and dropping some into the sea. Destruction is great in the land southward and even greater in the land northward as highways buckle, rocks split and plunge fragmented into great fissures in the earth, and people are "carried away in the whirlwind" (3 Nephi 8:16) and lost forever. Twice Mormon says that the "whole face of the land was changed," becoming "deformed" (3 Nephi 8:12, 17). In fact, so enormous are the upheavals and deformations that earlier geographic descriptions of the area may no longer apply in any strict sense.

The survivors of this three-hour cataclysm—to some it seemed aeons—and of the three days of "thick darkness" (3 Nephi 8:20) that follow, are frantic with fear and anguish. So dense is "the vapor of darkness" (3 Nephi 8:20) engulfing them that nothing will ignite. No glimmer of light penetrates "the mists of darkness which were upon the face of the land" (3 Nephi 8:22). We are not surprised that during this time, "there was great mourning and howling and weeping among all the people continually" (3 Nephi 8:23). (There was also some fast repenting, I might add.) Then suddenly, out of the darkness and in the midst of "great and terrible" lamentations (3 Nephi 8:25), a voice peals across the land. Its first words bring small comfort:

> Wo, wo, wo unto this people; wo unto the inhabitants of the whole earth except they shall repent; for the devil laugheth, and his angels rejoice, because of the slain of the fair sons and daughters of my people; and it is because of their iniquity and abominations that they are fallen! (3 Nephi 9:2)

I note that the Lord's first observation to his stricken people is that the devil laughs at the woes and destruction of those who have served him. By contrast, once the Lord has listed the fallen cities and described their individual fates, he appeals to the survivors to come to him and be healed. Unlike Satan, he sorrows in their sorrow, he suffers in their suffering, and he takes no pleasure in their anguish and death.

It is significant, I think, that the Lord calls each of the lost cities by name and describes the means of its destruction, proving that he is neither an indifferent nor a distant God, but rather a God who knows intimately what transpires on earth. Different cities meet different ends, but all are destroyed for the same reason: "to hide their iniquities and their abominations from before my face, that the blood of the prophets and the saints shall not come any more unto me against them" (3 Nephi 9:5, 7, 8, 9, 11). The Lord could no longer bear to watch the wickedness of mortals, nor to see them heap murder after murder of his beloved servants upon their already guilty heads.

When the survey of destroyed cities is complete, however, the tone changes; the Lord tells his trembling people that they "are spared because ye were more righteous than" the slain, and he implores them to "return unto me, and repent of your sins, and be converted, that I may heal you" (3 Nephi 9:13). He has stayed his hand again, even though over the years the hard-headed, stiff-necked Nephites have impressively demonstrated that they require a lot of convincing before they will change—consider the stimulus of slaughter, famine, and pestilence, for starters—and that they seldom stay convinced. And now, after severely correcting his still beloved people, the Lord offers mercy, forgiveness, and blessed healing. He is advocate, not adversary; salvation for God's children is his deepest desire.

With a majesty inimitable in mortals, the speaker formally announces himself and his redemptive mission. Godly power and love surge through his words; there is no more compelling attestation of divine Sonship anywhere:

> Behold, I am Jesus Christ the Son of God. I created the heavens and the earth, and all things that in them are. I was with the Father from the beginning. I am in the Father, and the Father in me; and in me hath the Father glorified his name.
>
> I came unto my own, and my own received me not. And the scriptures concerning my coming are fulfilled.
>
> And as many as have received me, to them have I given to become the sons of God; and even so will I to as many as shall believe on my name, for behold, by me redemption cometh, and in me is the law of Moses fulfilled.
>
> I am the light and the life of the world. I am Alpha and Omega, the beginning and the end. (3 Nephi 9:15-18)

When a little later the resurrected Savior walks and teaches among the Nephites, he reiterates many of the things he had taught among the Jews. Now, however, in his annunciatory discourse as a voice from the heavens—this is after his death and before his appearance as a resurrected being—the Lord makes a particular point of instructing the Nephites to cease making sacrificial blood offerings. His stress on the matter indicates that animal sacrifice was still a part of Nephite worship, along with other aspects of the Mosaic law. Blood offerings were instituted in Adam's time as precursory types of the Savior's atoning sacrifice; but with his infinite sacrifice, symbolic blood sacrifices are rendered unnecessary.

What the Lord requires now, his voice explains, is a higher sacrifice, that of "a broken heart and a contrite spirit" (3 Nephi

9:20). The concept has been introduced before, but it has new force now that the law is fulfilled. The required sacrifice is no longer the firstling of the flock, but the willing surrender of the stubborn human will to its Creator. It is the humble relinquishing of mortal sin and pride. Those who make that sweet sacrifice will experience a second baptism, not of water, but of spirit, or fire: "And whoso cometh unto me with a broken heart and a contrite spirit," the voice says, "him will I baptize with fire and with the Holy Ghost. . ." (3 Nephi 9:20). The Lord concludes the first segment of his discourse with a tender affirmation and invitation: ". . . whoso repenteth and cometh unto me as a little child, him will I receive, for of such is the kingdom of God" (3 Nephi 9:22).

Hours of dazed silence follow these words. Incapable of utterance, the people even "cease lamenting and howling for the loss of their kindred which had been slain" (3 Nephi 10:2). Indeed, as the poet Wordsworth observed, some things "lie too deep for tears" *(Ode to Duty)*. Then the voice speaks again, now in a familiar and loving simile, declaring four times that the Nephites are of the house of Israel and that the Lord seeks to gather them "as a hen gathereth her chickens under her wings" (3 Nephi 10:4, 5, 6; see Matthew 23:37 and Luke 13:34, where Jesus uses the same expression). I note that when addressing the surviving Nephites, the Lord varies the context of the phrase slightly, each time making a different point. The first time he reminds them that in the past he has often sheltered and cared for them, as members of the house of Israel:

> . . . how oft *have I gathered you* as a hen gathereth her chickens under her wings, and *have nourished you.* (3 Nephi 10:4)

The second and third times, he slightly alters the verb tense by adding the words "would" and "would not," indicating that his listeners have frequently rejected his offered protection:

> . . . how oft *would I have gathered you* as a hen gathereth her chickens

under her wings. . . . yea, how oft *would I have gathered you* as a hen
gathereth her chickens, and *ye would not.* (3 Nephi 10:5)

The fourth time he shifts to future tense, exchanging "would" for
"will" and promising that even now he is willing to draw those he
has spared into his sheltering embrace. In this, too, agency is oper-
ative; the Lord will not force mortals into spiritual safety:

. . . how oft *will I gather you* as a hen gathereth her chickens
under her wings, *if ye will repent and return* unto me with full purpose
of heart. (3 Nephi 10:6; all emphases added)

These, the Lord's final words, trigger a new round of weeping
and howling that continues for the three days of darkness, accompanied by the earth's sympathetic aftershocks, its rueful groanings
and wrenchings. Then a hush descends, the darkness is dispersed,
"and the mourning, and the weeping, and the wailing of the people who were spared alive did cease." The healing begins with the
earth itself, for it "did cleave together again"; then the people's
"mourning was turned into joy, and their lamentations into the
praise and thanksgiving unto the Lord Jesus Christ, their
Redeemer" (3 Nephi 10:10).

This section of the record refers pointedly to the Lord's love
for his people, and his particular love for the prophets. Here and
elsewhere, the Lord venerates the prophetic role, manifesting that
those who abuse the prophets offend God, and their offense cannot be overlooked. As we have just seen, the Lord wishes no more
spilling of his servants' blood. Mormon is certainly aware of the
Lord's views on the matter, for in his periodic tallies of Nephite
atrocities, he frequently mentions and harshly condemns the ston-
ing, banishing, and murdering of prophets. Moreover, in the
midst of the cataclysm, some guilty Nephites lament their conduct on precisely that point: "O that we had repented before this
great and terrible day, and had not killed and stoned the prophets,
and cast them out. . ." (3 Nephi 8:25).

In fact, it is their tolerance of the prophets that has won a reprieve for the guilt-stricken survivors. The saved, Mormon says unequivocally, are "the more righteous, . . . who received the prophets and stoned them not; . . . who had not shed the blood of the saints" (3 Nephi 10:12). This, too, holds wisdom for our day, even though verbal stones are more often our weapons of choice. Mormon then adds his personal testimony on the matter of prophets, speaking not as a record keeper, but as a prophet himself.

*20*

## 3 Nephi 11-16: Jesus' First Teachings

In his conclusion to 3 Nephi 10, Mormon introduces what may be the most important pages in the Book of Mormon. He appears to be temporarily signing off, and the summary note indicates that "chapters 11 to 26 inclusive" give an account of "Jesus Christ [who] did show himself unto the people of Nephi." The Savior's teachings continue into chapter 28, but the note suggests that chapters 11 to 26 constitute a segment of the record distinct from the surrounding sections. Very likely, Mormon quotes freely from the original record in these chapters, although, as he says later, "there cannot be written in this book even a hundredth part of the things which Jesus did truly teach unto the people" (3 Nephi 26:6). I am convinced that Nephi's eyewitness account profoundly affects Mormon's report here, even though Mormon does not directly attribute the actual words to Nephi.

The text itself offers several indicators that Mormon closely follows, and even excerpts, the later Nephi's record. For example, the first verse of chapter 11 begins, as English teachers like to say, *in medias res*, in the middle of things, rather than with Mormon's customary overture. Then, too, I detect the influence of a narrative style different from his. While Mormon typically writes in somewhat abrupt or clipped phrases, punctuating his thought with frequent pauses, the language in these chapters seems quite flowing and unbroken. More to the point, throughout the chapters describing the Savior's appearance and teachings, the record projects an immediacy, a presence, that it lacks when Mormon is solidly positioned between the primary record keeper and the reader. This is not to downplay Mormon's role in the least, but only to emphasize his personal involvement with the narrative he is reading as well as the narrative he is writing.

Mormon picks up the account a short time after the cataclysm, when it joins a large group of people—the more faithful, probably—who have gathered calmly around the temple in Bountiful to take stock of things, as people do following tragedy. Instead of counting their losses, however, they are "conversing about this Jesus Christ, of whom the sign had been given concerning his death" (3 Nephi 11:2). In the phrase just quoted, the word "this" before the Savior's name presents a variety of potential meanings. To test the possibilities, the reader might try speaking the phrase "this Jesus Christ" with several different inflections, and then speaking it without the word "this." In some contexts, and with some inflections, "this" can add stature to a noun. But in the passage at hand it seems to have the opposite effect, suggesting Christ's uncertain reputation in Bountiful.

The Savior's first physical appearance in the western hemisphere is obviously a more public event than either his birth or his resurrection in the old world. He comes to this far land neither as a tiny infant nor as an intimate friend. In what might suggest a preview of the second coming, Jesus arrives gloriously in his full identity as the living, resurrected Christ—announced in a soul-piercing voice by his Father, robed in white, "descending out of heaven" to stand "in the midst of them" (3 Nephi 11:8). The baffled Nephites, who do not "open their ears to hear" the Father's voice until the third repetition (3 Nephi 11:5) of "Behold my Beloved Son," at first take him for an angel. Then he stretches forth his hand and speaks: "Behold, I am Jesus Christ, whom the prophets testified shall come into the world" (3 Nephi 11:10-11).

Remembering, finally, the prophecies of Christ's coming to this land "after his ascension into heaven" (3 Nephi 11:12), the spellbound multitude sink to the earth. But it is in stepping "forth one by one" to feel the nail prints that they know him, and they shout in unison, "Hosanna! Blessed be the name of the Most High God!" They fall at his feet and "worship him" (3 Nephi 11:15-17). The Savior's appearance works the same miracle upon these destitute survivors that his spiritual arrival works upon individual lives in any age. It transforms despair into unspeakable joy.

Nephi is there, of course; Jesus knows him and singles him out as the leader of his church.

Two matters seem to require immediate attention, and Jesus takes them up with Nephi and the chosen disciples before addressing the general multitude. The first is the proper method of baptism; the second is the doctrine of unity as it is exemplified in the Father, Son, and Holy Ghost. We would do well to pay special heed to the Master's priorities in this, his first instructive discourse among the Nephites.

The fact that the church has been at odds rather than unified over how the baptismal ordinance is to be performed gives Jesus the opportunity to teach that in his church, form and principle are inseparable. The very syntax of his sentence joins the procedural ordinance of baptism and the doctrine of unity as he firmly declares that "there shall be no disputations among you, as there have hitherto been [on the method of baptism]; neither shall there be disputations among you concerning the points of my doctrine, as there have hitherto been" (3 Nephi 11:28). Then too, the fact that all three members of the Godhead are named in the baptismal prayer implicitly confirms their absolute unity—a unity which is obviously a oneness of intent and affection rather than of person. The Son, after all, stands before them as one being, speaking of the cherished relationship he enjoys with the other two personages in the Godhead: ". . . the Father, and the Son, and the Holy Ghost are one; and I am in the Father, and the Father in me, and the Father and I are one" (3 Nephi 11:27). Clearly, Jesus is teaching more than proper baptism procedure; he is also denouncing contention in the church body: ". . . he that hath the spirit of contention is not of me, but is of the devil, who is the father of contention, and he stirreth up the hearts of men to contend with anger, one with another" (3 Nephi 11:29).

Still another point can be made in the fact that here, as elsewhere, the admonition to repent is followed innumerable times by the directive to be baptized. Since, on some occasions, the audience for that directive is the church body, I can only assume that the admonition is not solely for the unbaptized. We often speak of the sacramental ordinance as one in which believers reconfirm their baptismal covenants. If the ordinance is in some sense, then, a symbolic rebaptism or renewal of baptism, repentance appropriately precedes the partaking of the sacramental emblems and is never an accomplished fact. Both repentance and baptism are, therefore, perpetual rather than one-time, discontinuous events; and the counsel to repent and to be baptized is applicable, even essential, throughout our lives. Then, too, in 3 Nephi 12:2 the Lord links *humility* and baptism in the same manner as he customarily links *repentance* and baptism: "Yea, blessed are they who shall believe in your words, and come down into the depths of humility and be baptized. . . ." In equating humility and repentance this way, he makes them synonyms.

Because his doctrine is the immutable foundation of mortal faith (see 3 Nephi 11:39), Jesus teaches much as he had taught in Jerusalem. Some might think it odd that he would so nearly repeat himself, and that the record keepers would prepare a duplicate account. We should remember, however, that the brass plates in the Nephites' possession contained only holy writings recorded prior to 600 B.C., and that the faithful Nephites still observed the Law of Moses. The new and fulfilling law the Savior brings with him must be the same for all his people. Moreover, Nephi and Mormon could not have anticipated the specific teachings that would be canonized in the New Testament; nor could they suppose that those teachings would be preserved unchanged.

We should remember, too, that while the Savior's words to the Nephites are not entirely new to twentieth century readers, they were new to the Nephites, at least as they came directly from the Savior's mouth. No doubt, Joseph Smith was influenced by the phrasing of the King James New Testament as he rendered in English the Savior's counsel; but where the Nephite record varied from the text already familiar to Joseph, he readily departed from King James. It seems to me that if someone were trying to perpetrate a hoax, he would scrupulously avoid appearing to copy existing scripture that is so easily identified and compared. Joseph certainly made no effort either to vary or to copy the text.

How complete a record the contemporary Nephi made of the Savior's teachings we cannot know; but, as Mormon observed earlier, there was obviously a great deal more than could be inscribed in an abridgment. Even so, the Savior's ministry in the western hemisphere can be counted in days rather than years. (In 3 Nephi 26:13, Mormon says that Jesus initially spent three days among the Nephites, but that subsequently "he did show himself unto them oft, and did break bread oft" and administer it to them.) In any case, the heart of Jesus' ministerial teachings to the Nephites, judging by Mormon's abridgment, is basically what we know in the New Testament as "The Sermon on the Mount." It comprises chapters 12, 13, and 14 of 3 Nephi. Since that remarkable sermon largely describes the gospel of salvation that fulfills and supplants the Law of Moses, we can appreciate why it would be repeated almost verbatim to the Lehite segment of the house of Israel. With some interjections intended for an exclusively new-world congregation, and some mostly minor variations, additions, and omissions, these three chapters essentially mirror Matthew 5, 6, and 7. Most of the textual variances and substituted verses—1-2, 19, 29-30, 46-47—occur in chapter 12.

It is enlightening to compare the language variances in the two texts. Verses 1 and 2 of 3 Nephi 12 are specific to the Nephites; they initiate the work of the church, introducing its appointed leaders and teaching the purpose and importance of baptism. Noteworthy is Christ's repeated prefatory use of the phrase "blessed are ye" or "blessed are they" to describe believers and those who will be taught by believers. With verse 3, the Savior launches into the "Beatitudes" as we know them. For me, however, the preliminary "blessed" phrases found only in the Book of Mormon provide a stirring introduction to both the message and the poetry of the familiar passage; and they underscore the happiness that accompanies belief.

The Savior's replacement in 3 Nephi 12:19 is also notable, for it returns to the theme of humility which he had stressed in verse 2. By contrast, the corresponding verse in Matthew 5:19 speaks of the consequences of breaking the "least commandments" and the blessing awaiting any who "do and teach them." Remembering that pride (the antithesis of "a broken heart and a contrite spirit") is a particular failing of the Nephites, we can understand Christ's alluding to it in connection with repentance, even as he reprises a previous message. Verse 20 in both texts has the same basic content, but it is adapted for the two cultures.

I find it especially interesting that the Book of Mormon does not replicate the two most sensational verses in the Matthew rendering of the sermon, those that figuratively advise the plucking out of an offending eye and the cutting off of an offending hand, lest the "whole body should be cast into hell" (Matthew 5:29, 30). On one level, the figure may apply to excising the wicked from the church body—a detail the cataclysm has already seen to among the Nephites. On another level, however, a reader privy to both texts could read 3 Nephi 12:29-30 as an interpretive gloss on the two displaced Matthew verses, one that suggests a highly personal application: the need to obstruct corrupting notions and feelings from the individual human heart. The offending "eye" and "hand" as Jesus describes them in the new world are anger, name-calling, grudge-bearing, contentiousness, and passive adultery. Moreover, blocking evil from the heart is better than trying to excise it after the fact.

The Savior's final substitutions in 3 Nephi 12 are in verses 46 and 47. The corresponding verses in Matthew allude to the publicans—a reference that would be anachronistic among the Nephites. In its place, Jesus restates his purpose to fulfill the law. Perhaps in teaching that in him "old things are done away, and all things have become new" (3 Nephi 12:47), Jesus means that our personal lives as well as our religious observances can be blessed by rebirth, higher consciousness, and changed emphasis. Prophets such as Benjamin and Alma had taught the importance of character and individual goodness, and they had certainly understood that the true gospel encompassed love and mercy as well as justice. But it remained for the Savior, in person, to articulate and accomplish the full gospel. Instead of rebuking his already chastened people, he teaches them how to live, how to act, how to treat each other, how to pray and worship and love. Along with authority to perform ordinances, he brings the keys to abundant, meaningful living, which are seen now to be virtually identical to the keys that lead to repentance and the soul's salvation. The doctrines of love, happiness, and humility are conjoined with the doctrines and ordinances of salvation—faith in the Lord Jesus Christ, repentance, and baptism by water and by the Holy Ghost. Temporal observances, Jesus also helps us realize, have direct bearing on the life of the spirit.

It is surely not by chance that the Savior's first sermon to a suffering people who have been stripped of pride, possessions, and countless loved ones essentially begins with these words:

> Yea, blessed are the poor in spirit who come unto me, for theirs is the kingdom of heaven.
> And again, blessed are all they that mourn, for they shall be comforted.
> And blessed are the meek, for they shall inherit the earth. (3 Nephi 12:3-5)

No one needs to hear such words more than they—they whose need is defined by the words. The New Testament, however, omits the words "who come unto me" in verse 3. An unfortunate omission, for certainly, the blessedness alluded to lies in coming to the Savior rather than in suffering poverty of spirit.

There is one other significant omission in the Matthew version of the Beatitudes. The Book of Mormon reads: "And blessed are all they who do hunger and thirst after righteousness, for they shall be filled with the Holy Ghost" (3 Nephi 12:6). Matthew 5:6 ends with the word "filled," before the vital reference to the Holy Ghost. I will not add further commentary to an already thoroughly explicated, but lovely, piece of scripture—a piece which includes the Lord's Prayer and other memorable teachings.

The "new gospel" the Savior brings leaves some of his Nephite listeners perplexed over "what he would concerning the law of Moses" (3 Nephi 15:2). After all, the law has been their behavioral standard for centuries, a firm socio-religious frame that has given order and stability to their lives; and now it seems to have been snatched away at the same moment that they have also lost their supporting physical and political structures. No wonder the Nephites are confused.

Jesus patiently explains that as author of the law, he and he alone can fulfill it, that is, *finish* it. Very possibly, the Nephites have not realized that the being now addressing them is "he that gave the law" (3 Nephi 15:5). He assures them that "I do not destroy the prophets," and any prophecies and covenants not yet fulfilled "shall all be fulfilled" (3 Nephi 15:6); nevertheless, "the law which was given unto Moses hath an end in me" (3 Nephi 15:8) because "I am the law, and the light" (3 Nephi 15:9). They simply must understand: the Law of Moses is no longer the principal governing code for the house of Israel, and that includes Nephite society.

At this juncture, Jesus turns from the multitude and addresses the twelve. I can see why Jesus does not attempt to lead the whole body of Nephites through a complex discourse on the various peoples whom the Lord calls his. Nevertheless, Mormon's decision to include such an exposition attests to its importance. Jesus wants his chosen disciples to see a larger picture than their experience provides. Perhaps he also wants to teach them (and us) an indirect lesson about the respect he offers the Father. Jesus explains that in the old world, the Father instructed him to say "that other sheep I have which are not of this fold; them also I must bring, and they shall hear my voice; and there shall be one fold, and one shepherd" (3 Nephi 15:17; see John 10:16). We know that Jesus was referring to the Nephites, though he was forbidden to elaborate. The stubbornly proud are separated from the believers by their failure to understand intentionally cryptic doctrines.

Jesus tells his Nephite disciples, too, of still "other sheep, which are not of this land" (3 Nephi 16:1). These are most likely the lost tribes, who must also learn how to advance beyond their old governing law to a higher order of understanding, faith, and responsibility. Of additional interest is Jesus' statement that if those who saw him at Jerusalem were specifically to "ask the

Father in my name" (3 Nephi 16:4), they could learn through the Holy Ghost of the Lehites and other branches of their family tree. It seems that special knowledge is available, but mortals must exercise faith enough to ask for it. Apparently, the Israelites in the old world have not inquired, and the written record must evidence independently what could have been known centuries earlier through revelation.

Despite earlier discussion of the subject in the Nephite record, the content of chapter 16 is no easier to grasp than that of chapter 15. The Savior speaks several times of his covenant to gather scattered Israel and to restore them to full gospel knowledge. He also foretells many latter-day events and conditions, including a general sellout to wickedness and a rejection of the gospel's fullness. Indeed, it is easier to live a partial law. The Gentiles, he says, will "be lifted up in the pride of their hearts above all nations, and above all the people of the whole earth" (3 Nephi 16:10). (Does that sound like any North Americans we know?) If the Gentiles fail to repent, Jesus warns, the house of Israel will be "suffer[ed]" to go "through among them, and tread them down." I am not sure what that means, but Jesus says it twice, in verses 14 and 15. Perhaps the house of Israel is to become a chastening agent or influence among the Gentiles, if in the last days they require chastening. Most of these things the prophets had foretold, and now the Savior underscores them, quoting Isaiah in a conscious allusion to scripture in the Nephites' possession. We should not miss the fact, however, that the passages Jesus chooses to quote from Isaiah are not grim forecasts of destruction, but joyous celebrations of his second coming:

> Thy watchmen shall lift up the voice; with the voice together shall they sing, for they shall see eye to eye when the Lord shall bring again Zion.
> Break forth into joy, sing together, ye waste places of Jerusalem; for the Lord hath comforted his people, he hath redeemed Jerusalem.
> The Lord hath made bare his holy arm in the eyes of all the nations; and all the ends of the earth shall see the salvation of God.
> (3 Nephi 16:18-20; see Isaiah 52:8-10)

## 21

## 3 Nephi 17-19: The Resplendent Presence of Christ

Chapter 17 of 3 Nephi may well be my favorite chapter in all of scripture; it reaches far deeper than mere understanding and appreciation. The chapter is given not to doctrinal teaching, but rather to a spontaneous outpouring of the Spirit, a manifestation of love between the Savior and the Nephite people that exceeds the imagination. Nonetheless, as Jesus concludes his first day of teaching among the Nephites and begins to take his leave, it is mental, not emotional, preparation he urges, instructing his listeners specifically to "ponder" his words, to seek understanding from the Father, and to "prepare your *minds* for the morrow" (3 Nephi 17:3; emphasis added). Seldom, I suspect, do we think to ready our *minds* for spiritual instruction and enlightenment. Personal experience teaches me that it is easier simply to enjoy the emotional aspects of spiritual events than it is to focus the intellect on the unfolding of such events.

Before leaving, the Savior "cast[s] his eyes round about again on the multitude," and he sees that the people are "in tears," looking "steadfastly upon him as if they would ask him to tarry a little longer with them" (3 Nephi 17:5). Deeply touched by their unfeigned yearning for his very presence, he lingers, beseeching them to bring him the afflicted that he might "heal them" (3 Nephi 17:7). In seeming paradox, the voice that recently spoke to the Nephites out of the darkness, solemnly detailing the frightful consequences of divine retribution, is in truth the same voice that in person now promises healing and mercy. He spoke then in his role as mighty God of the earth; he speaks now in his role as the Good Shepherd. The resurrected being who ministers to this suffering, chastened, and destitute people is not only the powerful King of Creation, he is also the Lord of Mercy who would heal the aching hearts and shoulder the burdens of his people. As readers, we are privileged to participate in an exquisite scriptural moment when the world stands still, when the Savior's limitless love for earth's children flows directly to them, unrestrained, from his magnificent heart.

That love is the more precious because its expression is overtly personal and particular rather than intuitive and general. The Nephites see their Savior's face as he voices his compassion for them. They also witness his gentle healing, his blessing of their little children, his prayers to the Father in their behalf, and his tears. Nothing in my reading experience equals this account for tenderness and pure feeling. Most certainly, Nephi's spiritual sensitivity informs this part of the record. The words themselves seem to ride on a current of elevated emotion, their simple beauty almost matching the transcendence they try to describe, their failed effort to express the inexpressible conveying a message of its own. No mere mortal could find language for the moment when everyone present, "both they who had been healed and they who were whole, [did] bow down at his feet, and did worship him; and as many as could come for the multitude did kiss his feet, insomuch that they did bathe his feet with their tears" (3 Nephi 17:10).

After gathering their little children about him, Jesus enjoins the multitude to "kneel down upon the ground" (3 Nephi 17:13). Then he, too, humbly kneels and utters a prayer to the Father, a prayer that defies duplication or description. In saying nothing, the record says everything: ". . . the things which he prayed cannot be written" (3 Nephi 17:15). The blessed witnesses can do no more than "bear record" that a holy event has occurred, but at least we have the concrete testimony of one who was there. The pronouns "we" and "us" confirm that Mormon is quoting from Nephi's original account:

> The eye hath never seen, neither hath the ear heard, before, so great and marvelous things as we saw and heard Jesus speak unto the Father;
>
> And no tongue can speak, neither can there be written by any

man, neither can the hearts of men conceive so great and marvelous things as we both saw and heard Jesus speak; and no one can conceive of the joy which filled our souls at the time we heard him pray for us unto the Father. (3 Nephi 17:16-17)

"So great was the joy of the multitude" at the end of the Savior's sublime prayer to the Father that they are literally "overcome" (3 Nephi 17:18). Jesus bids them to arise, saying, "Blessed are ye because of your faith. And now behold, my joy is full" (3 Nephi 17:20). And so is mine. I ask the reader to vocalize slowly with me the concluding verses of chapter 17, mentally recreating this indescribable scene:

> And when he had said these words, he wept, and the multitude bare record of it, and he took their little children, one by one, and blessed them, and prayed unto the Father for them.
> And when he had done this he wept again;
> And he spake unto the multitude, and said unto them: Behold your little ones.
> And as they looked to behold they cast their eyes towards heaven, and they saw the heavens open, and they saw angels descending out of heaven as it were in the midst of fire; and they came down and encircled those little ones about, and they were encircled about with fire; and the angels did minister unto them.
> And the multitude did see and hear and bear record; and they know that their record is true for they all of them did see and hear, every man for himself; and they were in number about two thousand and five hundred souls; and they did consist of men, women, and children. (3 Nephi 17:21-25)

A distinct tone shift and subject change mark the beginning of chapter 18, although it is still the first day of the Savior's ministry among the Nephites. Mormon may have omitted something transitional from Nephi's record, or perhaps Nephi did not indicate what transpired between the moving events described in chapter 17 and the more institutional matters that occupy chapter 18. However it was, Jesus now undertakes to instruct his disciples on procedures of considerable importance to him.

Directing his disciples to bring bread and wine, Jesus initiates the sacramental ordinance, first in specific detail with the disciples, then more generally with the multitude. All who partake are filled, having feasted spiritually as well as physically. The incident evokes not only the Last Supper described in the New Testament, but also the miraculous feeding of the multitude with five loaves of bread and two fish. On that occasion, too, which is described in all four gospels, and which was surely a symbolic prefiguring of the Last Supper, the multitude partook and were filled.

As Jesus stresses the matter of the authority requisite for acting in his name in the performance of such ordinances, we remember that the first ordinance he instituted in the new world was baptism. The second is the sacrament, and again Jesus connects the two in an interlocking that suggests why he instituted baptism first: covenants must be made before they can be remembered and renewed. The Savior's precise language is crucial, for he explains that the bread is to be eaten "in remembrance of my body, which I have shown unto you" (Nephi 18:7). Likewise, the wine is to be partaken "in remembrance of my blood, which I have shed for you" (3 Nephi 18:11). But in both instances, the Savior emphasizes that the partaker vows always to *remember* him.

Bearing in mind that the word "remembrance" or "remember" occurs four times in the corresponding passage in 3 Nephi, we can see why Matthew's account alone could lead to some confusion:

> And as they were eating, Jesus took bread, and blessed it, and brake it, and gave it to the disciples, and said, Take, eat; this is my body.
> And he took the cup, and gave thanks, and gave it to them, saying, Drink ye all of it;
> For this is my blood of the new testament, which is shed for many for the remission of sins. (Matthew 26:26-28)

Luke's account is closer to Nephi's in that it suggests something other than the physical reality of the emblems. Luke introduces the concept of "remembrance," which Matthew overlooks altogether:

> And he took bread, and gave thanks, and brake it, and gave unto them, saying, This is my body which is given for you: this do *in remembrance of me.*
>
> Likewise also the cup after supper, saying, This cup is the new testament in my blood, which is shed for you. (Luke 22:19-20; emphasis added)

While the accounts of Nephi and Matthew agree as to the emblems and their general significance, Matthew's account invites disputation when it quotes the Savior as having said only that "this is my body" and "this is my blood." Even though at the moment Jesus is obviously speaking symbolically—he does not give his actual flesh and blood to the disciples, but a representation of them in the bread and wine—some devout readers of Matthew have assumed that the sacramental bread and wine somehow become the Savior's flesh and blood. This view is especially difficult to accept when it is applied, as I think consistency demands it be, to the bread and wine Jesus offers to his apostles. Jesus is there with them, in the flesh; his blood has not yet been shed. At times, Jesus does speak figuratively of the emblems as his body and blood, even in the Book of Mormon. But the definitive passage in 3 Nephi where Jesus institutes the ordinance does not allow for a literal interpretation. It states unequivocally that the bread and wine are not the actual body and blood of Christ, but are eaten "in remembrance" of them. The sacramental prayers, which Jesus apparently introduces on this occasion, also stress remembrance. Mormon does not include the prayers, but his son Moroni adds them later, when he finds himself with time and space enough to insert materials he deems beneficial to future generations (see Moroni 4 and 5). It is specifically such remembrance that assures the partaker of the companionship of the Spirit of the Lord.

The Savior's language makes a further distinction: the bread signifies Christ's *body*, his being or his person, while the wine (or water) signifies his *blood*, his sacrifice. The ordinance, therefore, replaces the blood sacrifices that were previously required under Mosaic law as symbolic types of the sacrifice Jesus would make.

Once the infinite sacrifice is accomplished, temporal anticipatory sacrifices are unnecessary and inappropriate. What is needed now is a spiritual sacrifice—a broken heart and a contrite spirit, and a solemn pledge of faithful remembrance. Jesus also makes it clear that the ordinance is not optional in his church; it is commanded. The exactness of his instructions concerning the ordinance demonstrates its immense significance to him. His followers are to "do these things" always, just as he has shown them, not "more or less than these" (3 Nephi 18:12-13). Only then can they withstand the sore testing of the adversary.

Even as Jesus cautions his disciples against allowing unworthy participation in the sacramental ordinance, he warns that on no account is the church to ostracize or exclude anyone from congregational worship. In stating plainly the consequences of intolerance—". . . whosoever breaketh this commandment suffereth himself to be led into temptation" (3 Nephi 18:25)—Jesus also implies that the welcoming of sinners into church fellowship increases the saints' individual ability to withstand temptation. The connection between tolerance of other mortals and intolerance of Satan is heartening, if a bit puzzling. Perhaps it is the pride accompanying intolerance that opens the door to Satan's influence. The real subject here is charity; and charity, after all, is not a Sunday observance, but a way of life that renders the devil helpless. I think he finds charity bewildering, since he never experiences that emotion.

Speaking of emotion, it is an emotionally-charged moment when Jesus takes leave of the disciples to "go unto the Father for your sakes" (3 Nephi 18:35). I can scarcely imagine their awe as the Savior touches each "with his hand . . . , one by one," speaking "unto them as he touched them" (3 Nephi 18:36). The twelve "bear record that he ascended again into heaven" (3 Nephi 18:39) after giving "them power to give the Holy Ghost" (3 Nephi 18:37).

Earlier I confessed that 3 Nephi 17 was my favorite chapter in all scripture. A possible rival, however, is 3 Nephi 19, a tenderly affecting account of the disciples' receiving the Holy Ghost, followed by the Savior's reappearance to intercede with the Father in their behalf. After the Savior's ascent, which ends chapter 18, the multitude disperse to their homes. But they do not disperse with their lips closed, and news of their experience spreads like wildfire. As a result of this nightlong buzz, "an exceedingly great number, did labor exceedingly all that night, that they might be on the morrow in the place where Jesus should show himself unto the multitude" (3 Nephi 19:3). The disciples (among them Nephi's brother Timothy and his son Jonas[1]) go forth to meet an assembly so large that it is divided into twelve groups for instruction. Clearly, Jesus' words have been recorded, for with humble exactitude, the disciples teach "those same words which Jesus had spoken—nothing varying" (3 Nephi 19:8). Twice they kneel and pray "to the Father in the name of Jesus," asking "that the Holy Ghost should be given unto them" (3 Nephi 19:8-9) and enjoining the multitude to do the same. Then, with the multitude close behind, the disciples proceed to the water's edge for baptism.

Since baptisms had been performed among the Nephites throughout their history, I think it likely that the twelve had already been baptized according to their earlier practice. But once the Savior has made his atoning sacrifice, a new baptism is apparently required, just as a new kind of sacrifice (a broken heart and a contrite spirit) is required. To signify Christ's death, burial, and resurrection, Nephi and the other disciples go "down into the water" (3 Nephi 19:11) and "come up out of the water" (3 Nephi 19:12, 13). More glorious even than their baptism by water is the wondrous baptism by fire that follows, as they receive the Holy Ghost. Words do feeble justice to such an event, and Mormon's modest summary only hints at the moment's breath-taking splendor:

> . . . when [the disciples] were all baptized and had come up out of the water, the Holy Ghost did fall upon them, and they were filled with the Holy Ghost and with fire.

---

[1] It appears that five of the Nephite disciples were named after Old Testament (that is "brass plate") prophets. There were two Jonases, a Zedekiah, a Jeremiah, and an Isaiah. Perhaps these men descended from many generations of faithful believers.

And behold, they were encircled about as if it were by fire; and it came down from heaven, and the multitude did witness it, and did bear record; and angels did come down out of heaven and did minister unto them. (3 Nephi 19:13-14)

And then Jesus, too, "came and stood in the midst and ministered unto them" (3 Nephi 19:15), instructing all to kneel and the disciples to pray. Although the disciples have just prayed to the Father in Christ's name, they are so overwhelmed at his presence that they break precedent and "pray unto Jesus" rather than the Father, "calling him their Lord and their God" (3 Nephi 19:18). This is a departure from his instructions regarding prayer; but in a personal invocation to the Father, Jesus explains why, under the present circumstances, it is acceptable: ". . . they pray unto me because I am with them" (3 Nephi 19:22). By implication, were he not with them, they would pray only to the Father in his name as they had done previously.

Three times on this occasion the Savior separates himself from the multitude, "bow[s] himself to the earth" (3 Nephi 19:19), and prays fervently to the Father. It touches me profoundly that Jesus, himself a God, sinks to his knees when he prays, in an expression of worshipful humility. This particular prayer, or series of prayers, is reminiscent of Jesus' great intercessory prayer for his disciples recorded in John 17, where, as here, he pleads for unity. He asks fervently that he may be united with the Nephite believers even as he is united with the Father, "that I may be in them as thou, Father, art in me, that we may be one" (3 Nephi 19:23, 29). The equation also demonstrates a hierarchy of authority: in an ideal unity, Christ is to mortals as the Father is to him. Obviously, too, the oneness of the Father and Son cannot be a oneness of being, though it bespeaks, as in John, a perfect unity of intent and desire (see John 17:21-23).

Jesus' love and concern for his Nephite disciples is no less than the love he expressed for his disciples in Jerusalem. These blessed new-world apostles "still continue, without ceasing, to pray unto him; and they did not multiply many words, for it was given unto them what they should pray, and they were filled with desire" (3 Nephi 19:24). That passage truly describes the essence of spiritual listening—the exercise of vocal restraint to learn the subjects of our prayers as well as the answers. Too often we are so eager to talk that we fail to listen, so busy "multiplying" our words that we fail to consider that the Spirit, knowing us and our needs, might give us even the words we are to pray.

The brightness of the Savior's countenance is reflected in the faces of his Nephite disciples; it is the kind of moment that Shakespeare's eloquent observer, Enobarbus (in *Antony and Cleopatra*), would have said beggars description:

> . . . Jesus blessed them as they did pray unto him; and his countenance did smile upon them, and the light of his countenance did shine upon them, and behold they were as white as the countenance and also the garments of Jesus; and behold the whiteness thereof did exceed all the whiteness, yea, even there could be nothing upon earth so white as the whiteness thereof. (3 Nephi 19:25)

Jesus speaks of what has occurred (the "whiteness," or light, in their countenances) as evidence of purification, and he prays that others, hearing their words, will be purified as well. The passage also suggests what is meant when Jesus prays that he "may be glorified in" his disciples (3 Nephi 19:29). He is not expressing a desire to bask in glory as the world defines glory. Rather, he is acknowledging that he is glorified in mortals when they are one with him, when his image shines in their countenances, when they reflect the light of his holy being. We remember that Alma spoke of the phenomenon as an indication of the change of heart that signifies spiritual rebirth.

No record is made of Jesus' third prayer, a prayer heard and understood only "in their hearts" (3 Nephi 19:33), a prayer beyond human utterance or replication:

> And tongue cannot speak the words which he prayed, neither can be written by man the words which he prayed.
> And the multitude did hear and do bear record; and their hearts

were open and they did understand in their hearts the words which
he prayed.

Nevertheless, so great and marvelous were the words which he
prayed that they cannot be written, neither can they be uttered by
man. (3 Nephi 19:32-34)

I can only assume from this and similar statements in chapter 17
that one of the attributes of Deity is an exceptional gift for language—sometimes beyond representation in temporal words or
characters. That the apostle John was aware of this gift is obvious
in his dramatic introduction of the Immortal Son and Creator as
"the Word." Passages such as those quoted above, and the first
chapter of John, confirm what my English teacher's heart told me
long ago: language is a precious thing—not to be used carelessly
or in the service of deceit or prurience. Surely, in the matter of
language, too, we are to follow the Savior's example.

Chapter 19 ends as Jesus returns to the disciples and tells
them that no others, not even his followers in Jerusalem, have seen
or heard "so great things as ye have" (3 Nephi 19:36), for no others have shown "so great faith" (3 Nephi 19:35). Given Jesus'
much lengthier association with his old-world disciples, this is a
remarkable statement.

## 22

## 3 Nephi 20-23: Old Testament Prophecies

Chapters 20-23 of 3 Nephi are distinctly different, in tone and intensity, from the touching and instructive chapters just concluded. Except for their opening and closing verses, all four treat one subject and can be taken together. That subject is the fulfilling of God's promises to the house of Israel, his covenant people. So important are the prophecies regarding these promises that Jesus commits a significant portion of his short ministry in the new world to iteration and reiteration of them. Moreover, in several instances Jesus uses the language and oracular tone characteristic of Old Testament scripture, especially Isaiah.

There is a marked stylistic shift as Jesus departs from a familiar teaching and ministerial manner to a more formal poetic and prophetic mode. Having comforted and taught, he now seeks to sharpen the instruction and also to warn his people. They must know who they are; and latter-day readers, too, must know their role in the unfolding divine agenda. Jesus repeats several prophecies that appear in Isaiah, and at least twice instructs the Nephites specifically to "search these things diligently; for great are the words of Isaiah" (3 Nephi 23:1; see also 20:11). The Savior's emphasis on Isaiah more than justifies the first Nephi's veneration of that gifted prophet and his writings.

Most lay readers today, however, find Isaiah a bigger bite than they want to chew, and they settle for a little nibbling around the edges. Despite the fact that Isaiah's message is for latter-day Gentiles as well as covenant peoples, the scattering and gathering of Israel seem somewhat remote to most of us. We know that we are wrong in this, but what we know does not necessarily translate into a passion for reading Isaiah. By contrast, the scattering and gathering of Israel have arresting implications for the Savior's immediate listeners, who are themselves among the scattered. However individual latter-day readers see themselves, as Israelites or Gentiles, both groups play a role in the fulfillment of the Savior's prophetic utterances, as either gatherers or the gathered. Ultimately, membership in the house of Israel is not a matter of ethnic origin anyway; all who choose Christ and accept his doctrine become his covenant people.

Following the poignant experiences recorded in chapter 19, the Savior enjoins the multitude to cease praying verbally and arise, but not to cease praying "in their hearts" (3 Nephi 20:1). The spiritual feast continues as Jesus again administers the sacramental ordinance. This time, however, the record explicitly states that bread and wine are produced miraculously, not just multiplied, for "there had been no bread, neither wine, brought by the disciples, neither by the multitude" (3 Nephi 20:6). Those who eat the bread and drink the wine, Jesus says, eat of his body and drink of his blood to their souls; and their souls "shall never hunger nor thirst, but shall be filled" (3 Nephi 20:8). As if proving his words on the instant, a sublime scriptural moment unfolds. The people are "filled with the Spirit; and they did cry out with one voice, and gave glory to Jesus" (3 Nephi 20:9). From this point through verse 5 of chapter 23, Mormon ceases summary and quotes the words of Jesus exclusively.

The Savior's subject is the ongoing identity of the Israelites to whom he speaks, children of the covenant who are geographically, and perhaps emotionally, severed from their roots. Obviously, too, Jesus wants certain prophecies with distinct latter-day application to be forcefully restated in the Nephite record. His attention to these prophecies confirms their importance. The text is interwoven not only with major borrowings from prophecies recorded in Isaiah, but also with fragments from other Old Testament prophets and prophecies. Inherent in the promised land covenant is a warning that the latter-day Lamanites, "a remnant of the house of Jacob" (3 Nephi 20:16), will be a scourge to unrighteous and unrepentant Gentiles. Also inherent is a lovely millennial promise: this land "shall be a New Jerusalem," endowed with "the powers of heaven" and graced by the presence of the Son (3 Nephi 20:22). The Savior augments his already exalted rhetoric as he teaches these isolated people who they are and what lies ahead for their seed.

Jesus describes prophetic scatterings on two continents: (1) the scattering of those who had resided in Jerusalem in the past and those who would reside there in the future,[1] and (2) the scattering of the remnant seed (the Lamanites) by the Gentiles in the new world. Both prophecies have been fulfilled. The Savior's statements verify that what is now the American continent is indeed the site of the "New Jerusalem," the second promised land (3 Nephi 21:23-24) spoken of by earlier Book of Mormon prophets. It is a land of freedom in which the record might come forth and in which the Father's covenant might be fulfilled. One thing is certain from the Savior's repeated declarations on the subject: the destiny of the Gentiles is intertwined with that of the covenant peoples. Through the Gentiles, if they merit it, the Savior will restore his gospel and teach it to the house of Israel (Judaic and Lamanite peoples alike) in the last days. In fact, the teaching of the gospel and the sharing of the record will be indispensable in the gathering process. The truths of the gospel and the irresistible magnetism of the Nephite record will draw the covenant people home. "And then," Jesus promises, "shall the power of heaven come down among them; and I also will be in the midst" (3 Nephi 21:25). The Second Coming.

After repeating a passage from Isaiah that he had cited earlier, a passage that seems to foretell the conversion of monarchs (see 3 Nephi 20:45 and 21:8; Isaiah 52:15), Jesus quite pointedly describes the restoration of his gospel in the latter days through "a man" whom he does not name, but whom Mormons understand to be Joseph Smith. Jesus also foretells Joseph's persecution and martyrdom, and his final eternal safety (see 3 Nephi 21:9-10).

---

[1] In the Book of Mormon as in Isaiah, two old-world scatterings of Israel—one just after Lehi and his family leave Jerusalem, the other much later—are sometimes merged rhetorically into one event.

Verse 11 appears to foresee Joseph's translation and publication of the Book of Mormon and to warn against skepticism. On the matter of record-keeping, Jesus gives no quarter; he directs the Nephites to preserve "my words" for later generations. That the recorded words are to include prophetic teachings is obvious from his injunctions to "search the prophets" (3 Nephi 23:4-5) and from his diligence in "expound[ing]" scriptures in the Nephites' possession (3 Nephi 23:6).

Jesus also expresses displeasure with recent laxities in Nephite record-keeping: "Behold, other scriptures I would that ye should write, that ye have not" (3 Nephi 23:6). He actually examines the Nephite records and sees that Samuel's divinely-commissioned prophecy of the resurrection and ministering of "many saints" at the time of Christ's resurrection (3 Nephi 23:9) is missing. "Was it not so?" he insists, and his disciples answer, "Yea, Lord, Samuel did prophesy according to thy words, and they were all fulfilled" (3 Nephi 23:9-10).[2] The Master's withering reproach re-emphasizes the importance he attaches to the record and its contents. He demands, "How be it that ye have not written this thing, that many saints did arise and appear unto many and did minister unto them?" (3 Nephi 23:11). The record is to bear witness not only that resurrection is real and literal, for Jesus and mortals both, but also that prophets are revelators of his word. Nephi remembers "that this thing had not been written," and Jesus commands "that it should be written; therefore it was written according as he commanded" (3 Nephi 23:12-13). (See Helaman 14:25, where the prophecy in question now appears in the record.)

Still another matter has caught my attention as I have worked through these thorny chapters that treat latter-day fulfillment of the Lord's covenants with the house of Israel. Twice Jesus quotes at some length from the words given to Isaiah, who prophesied voluminously on the doctrine. The prophecies Jesus repeats

---

[2] The disciples' response indicates that there were resurrections in the new world as well as in the old.

appear mainly, though slightly reordered, in Isaiah 52 (see 3 Nephi 20:32-45 and Isaiah 52:1-2, 7-15) and Isaiah 54, which comprises all of 3 Nephi 22. Micah and others are cited as well. There are, as always when Old Testament passages are rendered in the Nephite record, minor variations. But one variation in particular seems very purposeful. It occurs only in the fragmented passages repeated from Isaiah 52, and not in the discourse which replicates Isaiah 54 in its entirety.

A comparison of similar verses in Isaiah 52 and 3 Nephi 20 reveals that early on, the Savior employs the word "Father" for the word that appears as "Lord" or "God" in Isaiah. In these passages, then, Jesus makes a careful distinction between the identities and roles of the Father and the Son—a distinction the ancient prophets normally bypass, unless they are talking specifically of the Messiah. I have also observed that most Christians, Mormons included, follow the practice of the prophets and do not specify Father or Son when referring to Deity generally. The term "Lord" or "God" often serves our purposes, as it has frequently served mine in this essay. Certainly, both terms can apply to either Father or Son, though "Lord" most often designates Jehovah, or the Son. Below, however, are instances in which Jesus uses the word "Father" where Isaiah had used the less specific term "Lord" or "God," instances in which the reader might have assumed that "Lord" and "God" refer to Jehovah (Jesus) rather than to the Father. I note, too, that in such references Jesus habitually defers to the Father as the First Cause, even when alluding to events in which he himself plays a prominent role:

*Isaiah:* . . . for they shall see eye to eye, when *the Lord* shall bring again Zion (52:8)
*3 Nephi:* . . . for they shall see eye to eye. Then will *the Father* gather them together again (20:32-33)

*Isaiah:* . . . for *the Lord* hath comforted his people, he hath redeemed Jerusalem (52:9)
*3 Nephi:* . . . for *the Father* hath comforted his people, he hath redeemed Jerusalem (20:34)

*Isaiah: The Lord* hath made bare his holy arm in the eyes of all the nations; and all the ends of the earth shall see the salvation of *our God* (52:10)

*3 Nephi: The Father* hath made bare his holy arm in the eyes of all the nations; and all the ends of the earth shall see the salvation of *the Father*, and *the Father* and I are one (20:35; emphases added)

Although it is possible that in some (but not all, see verse as just quoted) of Jesus' allusions to "the Father" he is referring to himself in his role as the Creator and "God of the whole earth" (see 3 Nephi 22:5; Isaiah 54:5), it seems to me that he does not usually apply the term "Father" to himself. Others, including Isaiah, do, however.

After 3 Nephi 20:35, in repeating Isaiah, Jesus uses the same terms as his prophet, not changing "Lord" and "God" to "Father." Perhaps in adding "and the Father and I are one" to his recital of the prophecy, Jesus signals that, since he and the Father are united and act as one, he will not continue to amend Isaiah's expression. But in his own discourse, when he is no longer citing words that have come previously through a prophet, Jesus refers constantly to "the Father." In fact, in the verse that follows the Isaiah citations he does so twice: ". . . all these things shall surely come, even as the Father hath commanded me. Then shall this covenant which the Father hath covenanted with his people be fulfilled. . ." (3 Nephi 20:46).

In chapter 21, too, as Jesus alludes repeatedly to the Father and his work, words, and covenant, he meticulously distinguishes between the Father and himself and clarifies their roles and relationship. On one occasion, he includes the Holy Ghost in that clarification: ". . . I shall declare unto you hereafter of myself, and by the power of the Holy Ghost which shall be given unto you of the Father. . ." (3 Nephi 21:2). Later, he names himself ("who am Jesus Christ") and speaks of "the Father" in the same context, but specifies a different function for him (see 3 Nephi 21:11).

The departures from Isaiah's words, and the subsequent distinguishing of divine roles, underscore a salient characteristic of the Savior's new-world teachings in their entirety, at least as recorded by Nephi and represented by Mormon. Jesus speaks unceasingly of the Father, almost invariably differentiating between himself and the Father in a way that accords honor and stature to the Father beyond what Jesus would claim for himself. Without question, before the Savior's appearance, the record focuses on Christ as Lord, Creator, and Redeemer of the earth. But when Jesus comes in person, he transfers attention from himself to his Father, whom he obeys in all things. The three members of the Godhead are wholly united and bear witness of each other; but the Father is clearly the highest of supreme beings, he whom the Son, though one with him in power and glory, honors as his head.

In his earliest words to the Nephites, immediately after announcing his name, Jesus made it unmistakably clear that the Father is in charge and that he is the Son who fulfills the Father's will. The Father is the source of all things, Jesus said, the great initiator; the Son, we conclude then, is the Father's creative agent, the one who enacts the Father's plans and ideas. This relationship in no way reduces the Son's status. In 3 Nephi 11:11, and earlier, when he was perceived only as a voice in the darkness (see 3 Nephi 9:15), the Savior articulated the role of divine Sonship, and the words he spoke characterize the whole of his discourse with the Nephite people. It could not be more plain; the Son responds to the Father's prerogative:

> . . . I am the light and the life of the world; and I have drunk out of that bitter cup which the Father hath given me, and have glorified the Father in taking upon me the sins of the world, in the which I have suffered the will of the Father in all things from the beginning.

Significantly, in all the preceding books and chapters in the Book of Mormon—that is, before the Savior's ministry in the new world—references specifically to "the Father" (meaning the Savior's Father and our Heavenly Father) occur only thirty-one times;[3] but chapters 11-21 in 3 Nephi, the chapters chronicling

---

[3] Of these thirty-one mentions, twelve occur in just one chapter—2 Nephi 31, where they are part of the first Nephi's closing testimony and counsel to readers of our day. Also, there are double mentions in eight verses, reducing total verses using the term to twenty-seven, before 3 Nephi. The term "the Father" is used several other times in the Book of Mormon to mean Christ in his role as Creator, hence "Father," of this earth.

Christ's teachings in the new world, quadruple that figure with at least 125 occurrences. Nevertheless, such distinguishing references are not unique to the Book of Mormon, for there are a number of allusions to "my Father" or "the Father" in the Sermon on the Mount and in other New Testament scriptures. But the fewest references to "the Father" in the pertinent section of 3 Nephi occur in chapters 12 and 14 (four mentions), which are basically rehearsals of teachings in Matthew 5 and 7 rather than teachings that originate in the Savior's Nephite ministry.

Regardless of the setting, whenever Jesus is personally present, he speaks of the Father and the Father's supreme authority; but the profusion of such references in his words to the Nephites is unmatched in other scriptural accounts. I cannot, of course, begin to cite all the instances, but below are a few examples from 3 Nephi. They are typical in that they indicate Jesus' scrupulous definition of his role as the divine Son who fulfills commandments given him by the Father:

> . . . not at any time hath the Father given me commandment that I should tell it unto your brethren at Jerusalem (15:14)
> Neither at any time hath the Father given me commandment that I should tell unto them concerning the other tribes of the house of Israel, whom the Father hath led away out of the land (15:15)
> This much did the Father command me, that I should tell unto them (15:16)
> . . . I was commanded to say no more of the Father concerning this thing unto them (15:18)
> . . . the Father hath commanded me (15:19)
> . . . I have received a commandment of the Father (16:3)
> And thus commandeth the Father that I should say unto you (16:10)
> . . . thus hath the Father commanded me (16:16)
> . . . then I must go unto my Father that I may fulfil other commandments which he hath given me (18:27)
> Behold now I finish the commandment which the Father hath commanded me concerning this people (20:10)
> . . . the Father hath commanded me that I should give unto you this land, for your inheritance (20:14)

Jesus also makes frequent reference to the Father's words and deeds, and on several occasions he prays to the Father before and in behalf of the Nephite people. Plainly, the Father is not only a separate being (God is not likely to pray to himself), but he is also the ultimate source of commandments and blessings alike. Just as plainly, the love and respect that flow between divine Father and Son are immeasurable and inexpressible in earthly terms. When in the Decalogue, Jesus as Jehovah commanded the children of Israel to honor their earthly parents, he himself stood, and still stands, as the prime exemplar of obedience to that commandment. With every breath and act he honors his holy and almighty Father, and his solicitude for his mother Mary is well documented. The text tells me that Jesus is determined to etch this truth indelibly in his listeners' minds: there is one divine personage who is Father over all, one to whom even he, Christ, owes obedience.

The extraordinary attention Jesus accords this instruction, and the specific directions the Father gives him regarding earthly matters, convince me that the Father is deeply involved in the affairs of mortals. Jesus does not portray the Father as a remote, aloof, impersonal administrator, though some have pictured him that way. Rather, as Father and Son labor together, it appears that the Son has particular responsibility in earthly matters. The Son's description of the Father's watchful interest in mortal concerns helps me understand why we pray to the Father rather than to the Son (except when the Son is personally present, as in 3 Nephi 19), and why we pray to the Father in the name of Jesus Christ, our intermediary.

I find it both comforting and heartening that again Jesus elects to repeat a prophecy from Isaiah (chapter 54 this time) that is replete with hope and even cheer. Perhaps the same inexplicable human perversity that draws us to horror films and to scenes of disaster leads us to focus a bit morbidly on the frightening prophecies of the last days, and to forget that there are also prophecies of comfort and peace for those times. Calling up the celebratory words he had voiced through Isaiah many centuries earlier, Jesus reminds the Nephites of his abiding love and lifts his voice to gladden them.

His listeners, present and future, are told to "break forth into singing," and to "fear not" (3 Nephi 22:1, 4; Isaiah 54:1, 4). He has forsaken them only "for a small moment," and will "with great mercies" gather them once again (3 Nephi 22:7; Isaiah 54:7). Below is a sampling of Christ's joyful promises, originally voiced through Isaiah and now delivered in person to an eager band of survivors in a distant land:

> For the mountains shall depart and the hills be removed, but my kindness shall not depart from thee, neither shall the covenant of my peace be removed, saith the Lord that hath mercy on thee.
> O thou afflicted, tossed with tempest, and not comforted! Behold, I will lay thy stones with fair colors, and lay thy foundations with sapphires.
> And I will make thy windows of agates, and thy gates of carbuncles, and all thy borders of pleasant stones.
> And all thy children shall be taught of the Lord; and great shall be the peace of thy children.
> In righteousness shalt thou be established; thou shalt be far from oppression for thou shalt not fear, and from terror for it shall not come near thee. (3 Nephi 22:10-14; Isaiah 54:10-14)

> No weapon that is formed against thee shall prosper; and every tongue that shall revile against thee in judgment thou shalt condemn. This is the heritage of the servants of the Lord, and their righteousness is of me, saith the Lord. (3 Nephi 22:17; Isaiah 54:17)

Surely these promises should strengthen the resolve and allay the fears of the latter-day faithful.

## 23

## 3 Nephi 24-30: Subsequent Ministrations and Miracles of Christ

These seven chapters are highly diverse and extremely important. We saw in 3 Nephi 23 the Savior's concern that the revelatory prophecies of Samuel, the Lamanite prophet, be written into the record. That same concern is evident in chapters 24 and 25 where, with minor variations, Jesus repeats for the Nephite people and the latter-day reader divine prophecies recorded in the Old Testament. Among them are words found in Malachi 3 and 4, which postdate the Lehite departure from Jerusalem by nearly two centuries.

Malachi's text first addresses specific doctrinal points— Christ's second coming, then judgment and the tithe. The scripture's next subject, however, is more abstract. In Malachi 3:13 (3 Nephi 24:13), the Lord accuses his people of speaking "words" that are "stout against" him, even though they plead innocence. (The reader might want to ponder the unusual use of the word "stout.") The error of the Israelites, it appears, lies in their wrongful questioning of God's justice, in their complaint that in this world the righteous often suffer while the wicked prosper. The answer to their charge? Ultimately, justice is always served.

Chapter 25 (Malachi 4) repeats a short but vital prophecy: Elijah will one day restore the keys for genealogical work and sealing ordinances. Joseph Smith, incidentally, once said that the word "turn" in the passage below "should be translated *bind* or *seal*" (Joseph Smith History 6:184). He, however, left it "turn."

Behold, I will send you Elijah the prophet before the coming of the great and dreadful day of the Lord;

And he shall turn the heart of the fathers to the children, and the heart of the children to their fathers, lest I come and smite the earth with a curse. (3 Nephi 25:5-6; see Malachi 4:5-6)

The literal fulfillment of this scripture is described in a vision witnessed by Joseph Smith and Oliver Cowdery in the Kirtland, Ohio, temple April 13, 1836:

> . . . Elijah the prophet, who was taken to heaven without tasting death, stood before us, and said:
>
> Behold, the time has fully come, which was spoken of by the mouth of Malachi—testifying that he [Elijah] should be sent, before the great and dreadful day of the Lord come—
>
> To turn the hearts of the fathers to the children, and the children to the fathers, lest the whole earth be smitten with a curse—
> (Doctrine and Covenants 110:13-15)

Thus, there are three scriptural versions of the Malachi prophecy, all essentially the same, two of them unmodified by either translation or scholarship.[1] Yet, the angel Moroni rendered the passage somewhat differently in the course of his instructions to young Joseph Smith (see Joseph Smith History 1:39). Using a striking horticultural metaphor to represent the planting, nurturing, and harvesting of an idea, Moroni focused on the turning of the children's hearts to their fathers. Elijah, he said, "shall plant in the hearts of the children the promises made to the fathers," and his language suggests that the obligation to one's ancestors is based on weighty pledges. Again, choosing different words from those in the Malachi prophecy, but retaining a semblance of his own metaphor, Moroni gave new meaning to the consequences of breaking the promises made to the fathers. He declared that without the planting he described, "the whole earth would be utterly wasted at [the Lord's] coming"; the very purposes of creation would be thwarted.

I see other possible meanings in the curse Malachi foresaw, too. Surely the disregard of ancestral, extended, and immediate family bonds and relationships is a failure of personal affection

---

[1] The word "heart," however, is singular in the Malachi and 3 Nephi versions, though plural in modern scripture. The singular form suggests a collective heart or consciousness of a people, while the plural form is more individual.

grievous enough, of itself, to be called a curse. Such failure, however, has other eternal implications, one of which is the neglect of the specific priesthood ordinance work that formally seals families—contemporaries and future generations as well as ancestors—into a lasting unit. I think, too, that Elijah's stated purpose, to turn hearts, applies on two levels. Eternal familial sealing is important, but so is familial *feeling*. Family members are to cherish and respect one another. In fact, family history and temple work seem linked to the fifth commandment of ten—to honor father and mother, lest one's days be shortened on the land (perhaps another way of stating the curse?).

Section 98 of the Doctrine and Covenants reveals further that the turning of hearts is a principle of affection applicable throughout the human family. In verse 16, the Lord commands the Saints to "renounce war and proclaim peace, and seek diligently to turn the hearts of the children to their fathers, and the hearts of the fathers to the children." The turning of hearts also refers to the spread of the gospel, particularly to the Jews, as verse 17 states. And if "the hearts of the Jews" are not turned "unto the prophets, and the prophets unto the Jews," the consequence is the same as Malachi had said—the smiting of "the whole earth with a curse" and additionally the consuming of "all flesh."

In all of this there is an implied caution against severing ties with the past and failing to learn its lessons, against devaluing the lives and contributions of our predecessors and forgetting our incalculable debt to them. In an epistle to the Church dated September 6, 1842, Joseph Smith offers additional insight into the Malachi passage. Speaking of the ordinance of baptism for the dead, he says that "unless there is a welding link of some kind or other between the fathers and the children," mortals "cannot be made perfect" (see Doctrine and Covenants 128:17-18). The implication is that we are not perfected in isolation, but as members of families that extend into both past and future. Then, too, the inability to "be made perfect" may be yet another characterization of the curse, one that nullifies the purpose of creation, as Moroni intimated.

When we think on it, Laman's and Lemuel's first despicable sin was turning their hearts from their father (and their fathers before Lehi) and from their brothers, Nephi and Sam. That early filial disaffection, multiplied among an entire people, became a curse against the whole land, and the Nephite nation was destroyed, in some degree, because of it. Moreover, the mighty Jaredite nation was incurably afflicted with filial enmity and sorely cursed thereby. Enmity and disloyalty have been the curse of many a family, and hence of many a country, through the ages, the history of English kings being a case in point. The turning of hearts, as an idea, has far-reaching implications.

We should not forget, either, that an angel speaks similar words to Zacharias concerning the mission of John the Baptist. John is destined to "go before [the Lord] in the spirit and power of Elias, to turn the hearts of the fathers to the children, and the disobedient [children?] to the wisdom of the just [fathers?]" (Luke 1:17), all to prepare a people for the first advent of their Lord. Joseph Smith distinguishes between the spirit of Elias and the office of Elijah, the former being seated in Christ's forerunners— John, for example, before Christ's first coming—and the latter being seated in priesthood keys and power, which Joseph himself received in preparation for Christ's second coming (see Joseph Smith History 6:249-54). It would appear, then, that Elias/Elijah[2] is the forerunner spoken of in both 3 Nephi 24 and 25 (and Malachi 3 and 4). The turning of hearts must occur  preparatory to the Lord's second coming, just as it was to occur before his first coming.

Although Moroni did not mention it, the turning described in Malachi (and 3 Nephi and the Doctrine and Covenants) is clearly in two directions, toward future as well as past generations. In fact, in the pertinent scriptural passages, the turning of the fathers' hearts to the children is mentioned first. And when Luke

---

[2] "Elias" is the Greek rendering of the Hebrew "Elijah."

describes "the spirit and power of Elias" (Luke 1:17), he speaks only of the turning of "the hearts of the fathers to the children" and not of the reverse. Moreover, in the Malachi and 3 Nephi passages, the definite article is used before "children" (*the* children), while the possessive pronoun is used before "fathers" (*their* fathers). I would not want to make too much of this, but the usage does imply a general application to *all* children of succeeding generations, not just to the fathers' own progeny. On the other hand, the usage suggests that the promises made by the children were specifically to *their* fathers, their personal ancestors. Taken together, the various "turning of hearts" passages give new meaning to the phrase, and at the same time enhance the Malachi prophecy and offer an expansive definition of Elijah's role.

I can take the possibilities farther still. Since each generation is the parent of future generations as well as the offspring of its own mothers and fathers, then one generation must turn its heart toward the next if life and meaning are to continue. I venture to suggest that the turning prescribed could apply not only in the performing and perpetuating of sealing ordinances, but also in the making of a sacred record and the tending and preserving of the earth for generations born and unborn. Indeed, the scripture uses the term "earth," perhaps alluding to the planet as well as its inhabitants. Malachi may be predicting that the *earth* itself will be "smitten with a curse" unless we look not only to the good of ancestors who preceded us, but also to the good of children who follow us. A literal reading of the passage suggests that in our unparalleled consumption of the earth's resources and our sometimes careless destruction and pollution of the natural environment, some of us are turning our hearts away from our children. In so doing, we are bringing an inevitable, perhaps irreversible, curse upon the land which God intended for us to use, care for, and, yes, replenish. The passage might also be making an allusion to child abuse.

Without question, the Savior is concerned for future generations. It is for them, too, and not just the "fathers," that Elijah is to come; it is also for them that a record must be kept. The preserving of a record is the turning of the fathers' hearts to the children, just as exercising a wise stewardship over the earth's resources is a turning. It seems no accident that the matter of record preservation is juxtaposed in 3 Nephi against the passage from Malachi regarding intergenerational affection. Jesus repeats: "These scriptures, which ye had not with you, the Father commanded that I should give unto you; for it was wisdom in him that they should be given unto future generations" (3 Nephi 26:2).

The Savior's teachings to the Nephites, however, cover a broad spectrum, "from the beginning until the time that he should come in his glory." He speaks, too, of the end of time, when "the elements should melt with fervent heat, and the earth should be wrapt together as a scroll, and the heavens and the earth should pass away" (3 Nephi 26:3). The scroll figure intrigues me, and it appears also in the writings of Mormon (Mormon 5:23), Moroni (Mormon 9:2), and John (Revelation 6:14). I have difficulty forming a mental image of the melting earth wrapping as a scroll, but I fear the allusion is to a cataclysmic event involving volcanoes (or some other kind of "fervent heat") and earthquakes of monumental proportions. Hardly a pleasant thing to contemplate, and yet of itself the scroll figure is neither threatening nor frightening. In fact, it suggests a finishing, a wrapping up, even a unifying and gathering. In that sense it calls to mind the Savior's promise that Israel will be gathered, and that there will be one fold and one shepherd.

Mormon plainly regrets that he cannot write more than a small fraction of the Savior's words in his abridgment. In some instances, the Lord has forbidden a more complete transcription, and Mormon dutifully writes "the things which have been commanded me" (3 Nephi 26:12). Nonetheless, his matter-of-fact explanations lead to what is, for me, one of the happiest revelations in the Book of Mormon. Many centuries earlier, the first Nephi had prophesied the eventual release of the sealed portion of the record (see 2 Nephi 27:10-11, 21-22). Mormon expands on that prophecy, disclosing that his chronicle is intentionally partial, to test our willingness to accept it on faith. But he also foresees that if our faith in the abridged record is sufficient, we will receive "the greater things" recorded on the large plates of Nephi:

> And when they shall have received this, which is expedient that they should have first, to try their faith, and if it shall so be that they shall believe these things then shall the greater things be made manifest unto them.
>
> And if it so be that they will not believe these things, then shall the greater things be withheld from them, unto their condemnation.
>
> Behold, I was about to write them, all which were engraven upon the plates of Nephi, but the Lord forbade it, saying: I will try the faith of my people. (3 Nephi 26:9-11)

The passage promises that if we truly study and embrace the book now in hand, if we allow it room in our hearts and our lives, then the large sealed portion of the record will also be brought forth, and perhaps other records as well. The potential impact of such a possibility on a media-driven world is beyond calculation.

That these are precious times, replete with rare spiritual experiences, is apparent by the fact that the Lord forbids the recording of some events in detail. Mormon provides a general description of one such occurrence—the Savior's miraculous works with and through the amazingly teachable Nephite children. On this occasion, Jesus not only "did teach and minister unto the children," but he also "did loose their tongues, and they did speak unto their fathers great and marvelous things, even greater than he had revealed unto the people" (3 Nephi 26:14). I urge the reader to take a second look at that passage. Even infants "did open their mouths and utter marvelous things," but it was "forbidden that . . . any man write them" (3 Nephi 26:16).

No verbal reconstruction could do justice to such an event. And this was just the beginning of an extraordinary series of such happenings. At the end of the Savior's initial three-day ministry, the newly-ordained disciples go forth teaching and baptizing, and those "baptized in the name of Jesus were filled with the Holy Ghost. And many of them saw and heard unspeakable things, which are not lawful to be written" (3 Nephi 26:17-18). These hallowed experiences mark the onset of a halcyon period in Nephite history, an age when the law of consecration was in full flower, an age without class distinctions or hoarding of private possessions, when people "taught, and did minister one to another; and they had all things common among them, every man dealing justly, one with another" (3 Nephi 26:19).

Into this blissful society Jesus makes subsequent visits, and the record chronicles his teachings to the disciples. Jesus knows, however, that the charmed moment will not endure beyond a few generations. He verifies what the first Nephi and succeeding prophets had foretold, that "the fourth generation from this" will be "led away captive by [Satan] even as was the son of perdition." Like their infamous predecessor, Judas Iscariot, who becomes a type for money lust that leads to betrayal, the faithless Nephites "will sell me for silver and for gold" (3 Nephi 27:32).

Even in the harmonious present, the people are at odds over a name for the church. Incredulous, Jesus asks, "Have they not read the scriptures, which say ye must take upon you the name of Christ . . . ?" (3 Nephi 27:5). He continues to press the matter:

> And how be it my church save it be called in my name? For if a church be called in Moses' name then it be Moses' church; or if it be called in the name of a man then it be the church of a man; but if it be called in my name then it is my church, if it so be that they are built upon my gospel. (3 Nephi 27:8)

The importance the Savior attaches to calling the church by his name and performing its offices in his name, and his requirement that the church "at the last day" (3 Nephi 27:5) also bear his name, leave no doubt as to why the restored church bears his name.

Although Jesus grants that churches based on mortal creeds may well "have joy in their works for a season" (3 Nephi 27:11), he warns that joy apart from him and his gospel passes swiftly. In verses 13-20 of 3 Nephi 27, he outlines deliberately and simply the elements of "the gospel which I have given unto you" (3 Nephi 27:13). Distilled to its essence, the Christian gospel as Jesus Christ taught it is contained in these three concepts:

> 1.The Father sent him, and he came to do the Father's will. (13-14)
> 2.He came to "be lifted up upon the cross," drawing all mortals to him, that they might be lifted by the Father to be judged by the Son "according to their works." (14-15)
> 3.They who repent "of all their sins," who are baptized in his name, who endure in faithfulness to the end, and who have been redeemed by his sacrifice and "sanctified" through the Holy Ghost, will "stand spotless [before Christ] . . . at the last day" and enter into his rest. They who do not will be subject to the Father's justice and "hewn down and cast into the fire." (16-20)

Jesus then turns once more to the matter of records and record-keeping. The record's very content justifies the record, for it is not mortally construed, but divinely inspired. It contains doctrine and commandments "written by the Father" by which "shall the world be judged" (3 Nephi 27:26). Without canonized requirements, judgment would not be just. As the appointed "judges of this people," the Nephite disciples face a soul-searching question: ". . . what manner of men ought ye to be?" The only acceptable answer, for us as for them, is a tall order: "Verily I say unto you, even as I am" (3 Nephi 27:27).

The occasion in chapter 28 is unchanged from that in chapter 27, but the tenor is far different. The rather dazzling event described does not strike seasoned Mormons as particularly odd, but it must surely surprise others to read of three Nephite disciples who, like John the beloved, are allowed to remain and serve on earth until the Savior's second coming. Granted immunity from death, these extraordinary individuals are transformed into extramortal beings on the spot. And Jesus keeps multiplying their blessings, promising that they will experience neither "[pain nor] sorrow save it be for the sins of the world" (3 Nephi 28:9, 38). Their "joy shall be full," Jesus vows, "even as the Father hath given me fulness of joy"; and they "shall be even as I am" (3 Nephi

28:10). If at times we find ourselves contemplating what we assume to be a perpetually disappointed, sorrowful God, it is well to remember that he who suffered the inconceivable burden of all our sins also experienced a "fulness of joy." The Father not only knows that same glad fullness, but is the source of the gift.

Before departing, Jesus touches "every one of them with his finger save it were the three who were to tarry" (3 Nephi 28:12). And then, the resplendent miracle occurs. The firmament suddenly splits open and the three are "caught up into heaven, and saw and heard unspeakable things" (3 Nephi 28:13) they were "forbidden" and even powerless to utter (3 Nephi 28:14). Apparently, however, the three are able to characterize the physical sensation of their incredible experience. Although told by Mormon in third person, the narration has the electrifying energy of a firsthand account. I cannot help wondering if Nephi himself, the prophet and record keeper, were not one of the three. The participants are so overwhelmed that "whether they were in the body or out of the body, they could not tell; for it did seem unto them like a transfiguration of them, that they were changed from this body of flesh into an immortal state, that they could behold the things of God" (3 Nephi 28:15).

Mormon is mystified by the "transfiguration" even as he reads of it and attempts to capture the event in his record. Later he learns from the Lord that "a change [had to be] wrought upon their bodies"; otherwise, "they must taste of death" (3 Nephi 28:37-38). The change, although "not equal to that which shall take place at the last day," was sanctifying and "holy" (3 Nephi 38:39). It shielded the three men from Satan, rendering him powerless to harm or even tempt them. In the meantime, Mormon says, the larger record confirms the three to be very much in evidence among the Nephites, actively teaching and baptizing. Without question, Mormon finds this a fascinating subject. He purports to end his account of the three in verse 24, but returns to it with renewed interest. The Lord forbids him to write the names of the three, though evidently, Mormon saw the names on records in his possession. His next statement (read it slowly) fairly shimmers with the miracle, confirming that the three remain and do not die with their generation: "But behold, I have seen them, and they have ministered unto me" (3 Nephi 28:26). There is a whole sermon in that one sentence, for Mormon lived in desperately troubled times, about three and a half centuries after the transformation of the three Nephite disciples.

In spite of their success in teaching their contemporaries, later on the three disciples experience a less than cordial reception in some quarters of the Lehite world. For example, "they were cast into prison by them who did not belong to the church," "they were cast down into the earth" in pits, "thrice they were cast into a furnace," and "twice were they cast into a den of wild beasts." Still, in all they are divinely shielded, for prisons are "rent in twain," pits cannot be dug "sufficient to hold them," furnaces can do them no harm, and they "play with the beasts as a child with a suckling lamb" (3 Nephi 28:19-22). And these are just the things of which Mormon is aware from his reading in the record. Given the lack of officially documented accounts of their activities in our day,[3] it is interesting that through the years the Nephite record keeper(s) apparently knew the whereabouts and activities of the three transformed apostles.

The final words of 3 Nephi appear as chapter 30, but they occupy only two relatively long verses. In them, Mormon continues to address his latter-day readers directly. The words are a powerful injunction, straight from the Lord, to turn from all manner of wickedness and come to him. It is a fitting conclusion to 3 Nephi, which is given largely to Christ's ministry and teachings among the Father's children in the western hemisphere.

---

[3] Unofficial accounts, however, abound. Contemporary LDS folklore is replete with faith-promoting "three Nephite" stories of mysterious strangers who rescue, assist, and instruct the faithful.

# 24

## 4 Nephi, Mormon: The End of a Nation

The book of 4 Nephi is a single, rather long chapter, but it summarizes nearly 300 years of Nephite history, from 34 A.D. to 321 A.D. Although Mormon may have been instructed to prepare only a brief encapsulation of these years, it is also possible that his demanding civic responsibilities in the waning days of the Nephite state made full representation of the lengthy period sketched in 4 Nephi simply out of the question. Furthermore, Mormon was prophet and historian for his own generation, a huge task in itself. In any case, this highly condensed summary contrasts sharply with some earlier accounts that include considerable detail and a good many contemporary discourses. A fuller account would have been especially gratifying because, except for a little trouble at the end, the first two centuries of this period were years of matchless tranquility initiated by the Savior's coming. Given the non-tranquil character of 200 years of American history, or almost any country's history, unruffled peace for two centuries seems nothing short of miraculous. And "miraculous" is the right word in another sense, too, for the gospel of Jesus Christ set the behavioral standard for an entire society. It was the city of Enoch on a grand scale.

I long to read the discourses and stories of these years, the sermons and miracles and ministerings of Nephi and the other disciples, and of Nephi's successors as record keepers—his son Amos (who kept the record of his people an astonishing eighty-four years), his grandson (also Amos), and Ammaron. Under normal circumstances, Mormon would likely have abridged books representing each of these prophet-scribes. As it is, he tells us just enough to whet our appetites for a good deal more:

> . . . the people were all converted unto the Lord, upon all the face of
> the land, both Nephites and Lamanites, and there were no con-
> tentions and disputations among them, and every man did deal justly
> one with another.
>
> And they had all things common among them; therefore there
> were not rich and poor, bond and free, but they were all made free,
> and partakers of the heavenly gift. (4 Nephi 1:2-3)

In those two verses, the word "all" appears four times, under-
lining the fact that every living soul participated in this community of saints, each enjoying the freedom and peace that accompany faith, unselfishness, classlessness, and sinlessness. These "par-
takers of the heavenly gift"—a lovely phrase—actually *lived* the
ideal that utopian societies have managed to achieve only in their
dreams, having "all things common among them" and reaping the
material benefits of mutual "prosperity in Christ" (4 Nephi 1:23).
Then, too, Mormon's summary of the "great and marvelous works
wrought by the disciples of Jesus" suggests a hundred (or a thousand) stories worthy of telling:

> . . . they did heal the sick, and raise the dead, and cause the lame to
> walk, and the blind to receive their sight, and the deaf to hear; and all
> manner of miracles did they work among the children of men . . . in
> the name of Jesus. (4 Nephi 1:5)

As Mormon aptly observes, ". . . surely there could not be a happier people among all the people who had been created by the
hand of God" (4 Nephi 1:16). The reason is simple. It was
"because of the love of God which did dwell in the hearts of the
people" (4 Nephi 1:15).

This state of blessedness gradually gives way to the old incli-
nations and vices, however, and by 231 A.D. a small rift has
become "a great division" (4 Nephi 1:35). Once again, the terms
"Nephite" and "Lamanite" (along with their several subgroups)
designate those who accept and those who reject the gospel of
Jesus Christ. As history repeats itself, the children of the neo-
Lamanites are "taught to hate the children of God, even as the

Lamanites were taught to hate the children of [the first] Nephi from the beginning" (4 Nephi 1:39). Early on, it is the insinuative evils of pride and materialism that undermine this amicable society. Mormon specifically mentions "the wearing of costly apparel, and all manner of fine pearls, and of the fine things of the world" (4 Nephi 1:24), with predictable results: ". . . they did have their goods and their substance no more common among them" (4 Nephi 1:25). Furthermore, "they began to be divided into classes; and they began to build up churches unto themselves to get gain, and began to deny the true church of Christ" (4 Nephi 1:26).

In time, the wicked outnumber the righteous, and the Gadianton conspiracy is resurrected. When the second Amos dies and his brother Ammaron becomes the record keeper, Ammaron is "constrained by the Holy Ghost" to "hide up the records which were sacred" (4 Nephi 1:48) to protect them. Maybe it is just as well that Mormon has spared us the disheartening details of a people who "did not dwindle in unbelief" merely, but rather "did wilfully rebel against the gospel of Christ" (4 Nephi 1:38). Why are years of unmatched righteousness, peace, and joy displaced by years of unmatched wickedness and woe? It is as if the far-swinging of the moral pendulum in one direction creates the force that sends it careening back the other way.

### Mormon's Book

Mormon, the son of Mormon and a descendant of the first Nephi, is born into perhaps the unhappiest century in Nephite history. His generation enjoys virtually none of the bliss that followed the Savior's ministry; worse still, he is witness to the final destruction of the Nephite people. In the end Mormon, too, is killed in the savagery that devours the combatants on both sides of the fated conflict. Fourth Nephi ends in 321 A.D., when Mormon is about ten years old. He begins his own account with that year, noting that Ammaron observed him to be a "sober child" who was "quick to observe" (Mormon 1:2), and appointed him at that tender age as the future Nephite annalist. Possibly,

Ammaron did not know that Mormon would also become the abridger of all writings on the large plates of Nephi.

In keeping with the latter assignment, Mormon adds an abridgment of the history he has kept of his own generation, titling it "The Book of Mormon." Mormon says he has made "a full account" of his people's "wickedness and abominations" on the large plates of Nephi, and he "forbear[s]" to detail the corruption in his abridgment. In this spiritually destitute land, "there were no gifts from the Lord, and the Holy Ghost did not come upon any" (Mormon 1:13-14). Witchcraft and other dusky sorceries abound, the Gadianton robbers "infest the land" (Mormon 1:18), and the Lord curses it against treasures as he had done in times past.

At age eleven, Mormon moves with his father to Zarahemla, and within four years he is preaching among the Nephites, burning their consciences. They respond by silencing him. Self-characterized as sober-minded, Mormon finds his young life shaped by responsibility; but even so, he "was visited of the Lord, and tasted and knew of the goodness of Jesus" (Mormon 1:15). If today we are inclined to question the seriousness of teenagers, we might think back on Mormon, who at age ten is selected to be the keeper of the sacred record, and at age fifteen is engaged in public preaching. Even more astounding, Mormon indicates that "in my sixteenth year I did go forth at the head of an army of the Nephites" (Mormon 2:2). Although he modestly attributes his youthful appointment to the fact that he was "large in stature" (Mormon 2:1), undoubtedly this particular teenager was a dynamic presence among his people. (Then, too, front-line duty would curtail his pesky preaching.)

The next chapters tell a grim story of a driven and morally bankrupt people. In their initial lamentations in the face of military destruction, the Nephites are not truly repenting, as Mormon had hoped, but are only expressing "the sorrowing of the damned" (Mormon 2:13). These grim pessimists, who weepingly "curse God, and wish to die" (Mormon 2:14), are the very opposite of the repentant Nephites of earlier eras. Deeply troubled, an adult

Mormon now sees "that the day of grace was passed with them, both temporally and spiritually; for I saw thousands of them hewn down in open rebellion against their God, and heaped up as dung upon the face of the land" (Mormon 2:15).

No longer does the threat of defeat lead to repentance, new strength, and victory. The only glimmer of hope in this disconsolate nation flickers across the horizon when Mormon's troops, stirred by his oratory to fight harder for homes and families, rally with enough success that a temporary treaty is negotiated. The Nephites are to occupy the land northward, the Lamanites the land southward. But, in spite of Mormon's exhortations, his people foolishly credit this and subsequent successes to their physical prowess rather than to God's mercy. Emboldened by their own boasting, they determine to march against the Lamanites and wreak vengeance, swearing "by all that had been forbidden them by our Lord and Savior Jesus Christ," that they would attack their enemies "and avenge themselves of the blood of their brethren" (Mormon 3:14). Much as he loves his people, and often as he has led them to battle, Mormon will have none of their vindictive barbarism: ". . . I, Mormon, did utterly refuse from this time forth to be a commander and a leader of this people" (Mormon 3:11). Nevertheless, he pours out his soul "all the day long" for them, though "it was without faith, because of the hardness of their hearts" (Mormon 3:12).

A measure of the man is the fact that Mormon does not cease to pray for his people, even after he has lost hope for them. He knows he is praying for the damned, but he still prays. The decision to count these people wholly lost is the Lord's alone; he, their brother, is obligated to love them and to pray for them. As the Lord says sharply, "Vengeance is mine, and I will repay" (Mormon 3:15). It might be assumed from such a phrase that the Lord is by nature a fearsome and vengeful God. The context of the passage in Mormon 4, however, disputes that characterization. As I read it, the Lord is not issuing threats, but rather is declaring that the prerogative of retribution is reserved exclusively for Deity. In effect, and consistent with past stipulations against Nephite

aggression in any form, the Lord forbids his prophet to be a party
to vengeful warfare.

The events described in chapter 4, spanning 363 to 375 A.D.,
are almost too gruesome to recount. The vainglorious Nephites
start the fracas this time, rashly quitting a position of relative
safety and venturing into Lamanite territory. The upshot of their
foolish enterprise "is impossible for the tongue to describe," so
"horrible" is the "scene of the blood and carnage." Mormon sadly
reports that "every heart was hardened, so that they delighted in
the shedding of blood continually" (Mormon 4:11). To delight in
the continual "shedding of blood" is to enter the last stages of
human degeneracy.

Reading Mormon's account, we are not entirely surprised to
learn that, in the Lord's reckoning, the wickedness of Mormon's
contemporaries, Nephites and Lamanites alike, exceeds that of
any peoples in the history of humankind. Our horror at the news
only increases when we consider the exorbitant depravity of the
Jaredites at the time of their destruction. The seesaw battles,
which drag through several years, are vicious enough; but during
two major conflicts, the Lamanites capture Nephite women and
children and "offer them up as sacrifices unto their idol gods"
(Mormon 4:14, 21).

In time, the vastly outnumbered Nephites permanently lose
any advantage they might have gained. "And from this time [375
A.D.] forth," Mormon says, "the Nephites gain[ed] no power over
the Lamanites, but began to be swept off by them even as a dew
before the sun" (Mormon 4:18). The placid figure of dew and sun
that Mormon evokes seems oddly incongruous with the subject of
national extermination. That very incongruity, however—the figure's benign image in shocking contrast to its terrible subject—
creates a tension that augments the phrase's emotional impact.
The effect builds as the reader stops on the figure, then allows its
implications to sink in. The advantage of figurative language is its
connotative richness, its ability to suggest more than the literal. I
can see at least two interpretive applications of Mormon's simile.
First, the figure aptly describes the plight of the Nephites: they are

as helpless before the legions of Lamanite warriors as the dew is helpless before the evaporative power of the sun. And second, dew, which is both inert and transparent, also characterizes the Nephites in a less obvious but more poignant way. Dew leaves in its passing no residue, no significant mark of its visit; with the rising sun, the dew's total substance disappears. Even its enlivening effect is transitory.

There is in Mormon's poetic figure, I think, an attempt to formalize his sorrow and despair, to distance himself from his anguish. After all, these vanquished souls are not unknown characters inhabiting the annals of ancient history. They are his contemporaries, some of them very likely family, neighbors, and friends. His exquisite pain invites an exquisite simile. It strikes me, too, that Mormon may have consciously used the indefinite article, *a* dew, rather than the definite article, *the* dew. *A* dew seems decidedly more circumscribed, inconsequential, and diminutive than *the* dew. Many centuries later, that most original and exacting of poets, Emily Dickinson, makes the same choice when she describes a bird drinking "a dew" from a convenient grass, and also when she whimsically finds the idleness of grass appealing enough to wish that she, too, were "a hay." Coincidentally, the English translation of the simile, with the indefinite article, adds a curious echo of its mood and meaning which Mormon could not have anticipated: "a dew" resonates in the ear as "adieu."

The erosion of the Nephite state prompts a heartsick Mormon to retrieve all the buried records before his nation skids into oblivion. He knows the prophecies, he sees no gestures toward a saving repentance, and he assumes that in due time this Godforsaken people will be dispensed to kingdom come. And indeed, twenty-five years hence, a once mighty nation is reduced to dust and bones. Even though Mormon knows his people are irretrievably lost, his affections lead him to "repent" of his earlier vow and to resume leadership of the Nephite armies. We should note, too, that the Nephites are no longer fighting to avenge themselves. They are fighting for their lives. In the end, Mormon cannot abandon his people, but neither does he share their vain hope that he can "deliver them from their afflictions" (Mormon 5:1). In full cognizance of the situation and "without hope" (Mormon 5:2), he stoically casts his mortal lot with his doomed people. He elects to participate in the human struggle. Surely, action is better than paralysis, even if hope is exhausted. With Mormon in command, the Nephites rally to deflect several Lamanite advances; but in 380 A.D. the Lamanites "come again," this time in such "great . . . numbers that they did tread the people of the Nephites under their feet" (Mormon 5:6). Mormon regrets having to record even a bare outline of these frightful events, but he realizes "that these things must surely be made known" (Mormon 5:8).

Mormon speaks again, in well-crafted prose, of the record and its purposes, of writings that must "be hid up" until the Lord "shall see fit, in his wisdom," to bring them forth ("wickedness will not bring them forth," Mormon 5:12-13). Before that time, however, the remnant who survive the last great conflicts between Nephites and Lamanites will degenerate even further, into "a dark, a filthy, and a loathsome people, beyond the description of that which ever hath been amongst us, . . . and this because of their unbelief and idolatry" (Mormon 5:15). Again, no one should suppose that this degeneracy is racial, or even inevitable, for these "were once a delightsome people, and they had Christ for their shepherd; yea, they were led even by God the Father" (Mormon 5:17). What Mormon pictures here is the awful decline of a people who have lost faith and surrendered themselves to the devil's dark influence, who have refused the Spirit's illumination and suffered its withdrawal. His very anguish lifts Mormon to new levels of eloquence and understanding, and poetic figures once more adorn his style as he describes the state of the remnant survivors: ". . . they are led about by Satan, even as chaff is driven before the wind, or as a vessel is tossed about upon the waves, without sail or anchor, or without anything wherewith to steer her. . ." (Mormon 5:18).

The blessings that might have been tendered to this people, Mormon says, will now be "reserved . . . for the Gentiles who shall possess the land" (Mormon 5:19) in a future day. As I observed earlier, some of us may need to adjust our doctrinal priorities to include promises made to the house of Israel. Those promises are, without question, a principal theme of the Book of Mormon. They are a major concern of several prophets from the first Nephi to Mormon, and of the Savior during his brief ministry in the western hemisphere. Over and over, the Nephite record testifies that, in concert with the Gentiles, the record is destined to figure prominently in the conversion of Israel to Christ. Mormon also reconfirms that the ancient prophets prayed for latter-day peoples, that the hearts of those fathers were unceasingly turned to the children. What is needful now is the turning of the children's hearts. When Mormon again employs the scroll figure in his conclusion to chapter 5, it seems especially to denote finality.

In the beginning of chapter 6, Mormon returns to more immediate concerns. The rhetoric reflects the heaviness of his heart as he prepares to "finish my record concerning the destruction of my people, the Nephites" (Mormon 6:1). The Lamanite king, who can afford to be generous, agrees to meet the combined Nephite forces in the land of Cumorah—"a land of many waters, rivers, and fountains" (Mormon 6:4)—for one last-gasp, all-or-nothing battle. (The contradiction of fighting to the death in a lovely landscape seems not to have been lost on Mormon.) The year is 385 A.D., and an aging Mormon takes precautions to save the sacred records of his people. He hides all but a few "in the hill Cumorah," giving the remainder to Moroni (Mormon 6:6).[1] This done, he faces with his terrified people the ominous approach of the Lamanite armies, which are legion.

The massacre commences, and in the end only twenty-four Nephites remain of a force of 230,000. A few escape into the south and a few desert, but the rest are slain—men, women, and children. Mormon and Moroni survive, though Mormon is wounded. Their feelings are beyond expression as with the break-

---

[1] Moroni must have had access to all the records, for he later addends his own abridgment of the record of the Jaredites (the book of Ether) to his father's abridged record.

ing daylight father and son survey, from the top of the hill Cumorah, the carnage of broken bodies below. Racked to the soul, Mormon allows his agony to break through his customary reserve:

> And my soul was rent with anguish, because of the slain of my people, and I cried:
> O ye fair ones, how could ye have departed from the ways of the Lord! O ye fair ones, how could ye have rejected that Jesus, who stood with open arms to receive you!
> Behold, if ye had not done this, ye would not have fallen. But behold, ye are fallen, and I mourn your loss.
> O ye fair sons and daughters, ye fathers and mothers, ye husbands and wives, ye fair ones, how is it that ye could have fallen!
> But behold, ye are gone, and my sorrows cannot bring your return. . . .
> O that ye had repented before this great destruction had come upon you. But behold, ye are gone, and the Father, yea, the Eternal Father of heaven, knoweth your state; and he doeth with you according to his justice and mercy. (Mormon 6:16-20, 22)

After the manner of a eulogist, Mormon channels his sorrow into a patterned lament for a people beloved, in spite of their stubborn refusal of Christ. Thus, a chapter that began in flat despair ends in unspeakable grief—grief that finds a voice only in poetry.

Mormon's last written words (those which Moroni adds later were written earlier) are, incredibly, directed with emphatic urgency to the posterity of the victorious Lamanites who have just erased the Nephite nation. Under such circumstances, a lesser man might have given vent to rage and malediction, but not Mormon. He tells these latter-day people who they are and what they must do, for their own salvation. Despite his broken body and wounded heart, Mormon is trying to prepare his enemy's children for the fulfillment of God's promises to them. For emphasis, he repeats his opening imperative, "know ye that ye," in four successive verses, teaching the core of the Christian gospel in the fourth:

> Know ye that ye are of the house of Israel.
>
> Know ye that ye must come unto repentance, or ye cannot be saved.
>
> Know ye that ye must lay down your weapons of war, and delight no more in the shedding of blood. . . .
>
> Know ye that ye must come to the knowledge of your fathers, and repent of all your sins and iniquities, and believe in Jesus Christ, that he is the Son of God, and that he was slain by the Jews, and by the power of the Father he hath risen again, whereby he hath gained the victory over the grave; and also in him is the sting of death swallowed up. (Mormon 7:2-5)

In this, his final exposition, Mormon briefly outlines the plan of salvation in terms that contrast the bliss of the redeemed with the shambles of his temporal world. Referring again to the complementary relationship between the Book of Mormon and the Bible, Mormon also sees the Nephite record as an instrument for turning the hearts of the Lamanite children to the fathers.

Here Mormon's record ends, and his son Moroni undertakes to "finish the record of my father, Mormon." Moroni explains that he has "but few things to write, which things I have been commanded by my father" (Mormon 8:1). If we find Moroni a little abrupt, we must remember his circumstances and his innate discomfort with a writing assignment. Since the finish of the great and final war, the Lamanites have entertained themselves by hunting down and killing any remaining Nephites, including Mormon. Apparently not satisfied with their victory over the Nephites, the frenzied Lamanites turn on each other, "and the whole face of this land is one continual round of murder and bloodshed" (Mormon 8:8). Writers and filmmakers have at times engaged in horrifying speculation about the aftermath of a nuclear holocaust. We can endure their fictions because we know them to be products of the mind. We are powerfully aware, however, that Moroni is no fictional hero, invented by an imaginative futurist. Moroni is, for all practical purposes, the only survivor of a vast populace that he has watched die, first *en masse* and later one by one. He has lived the nightmare of national slaughter, and he is still in great peril. The restraint of these few simple words engraved on metal plates touchingly conveys his suffering and his utter aloneness:

> And my father also was killed by [the Lamanites], and I even remain alone to write the sad tale of the destruction of my people. But behold, they are gone, and I fulfil the commandment of my father. And whether they will slay me, I know not. (Mormon 8:3)

By this time (c. 401 A.D.), Moroni has been a solitary fugitive for several years, and his words communicate his quiet despair: ". . . I will write and hide up the records in the earth; and whither I go it mattereth not" (Mormon 8:4). It is a sorrowful man who claims to lack "room upon the plates" even to reiterate the purpose of the record. Later on Moroni does lengthen the record, but he has no disposition now to make new plates. As he says, "ore I have none, for I am alone" (Mormon 8:5). Those last three words, "I am alone," speak volumes. Few of us, regardless of our circumstances, can fathom the emotion behind Moroni's statement: "My father hath been slain in battle, and all my kinsfolk, and I have not friends nor whither to go; and how long the Lord will suffer that I may live I know not" (Mormon 8:5). Even the disciples who tarried were removed from this hostile environment to some unnamed place, though earlier they ministered to Moroni and his father.

Beginning with verse 13, Moroni commences what he fully intends to be the final portion of his writing. The year is uncertain, but since his last chronological reference was to the passing of 400 years since Christ's birth, the time is between 401 and his subsequent sign-off in about 421. Almost ceremoniously, Moroni asserts his identity and the significance of the record he is burying, a record that will resurface when God wills it. And, he declares, those latter-day people who embrace the record and overlook its human imperfections "shall know of greater things than these" (Mormon 8:12). Moroni seems to be suggesting again what his father had indicated in 3 Nephi 26:9-11, that if the world accepts Mormon's abridgment, additional writings will be forthcoming. So speaking, Moroni seems to take heart, for the priceless record he holds harbors the hope of future generations.

Venerating his righteous predecessors, Moroni avows that "even from the dust will they cry unto the Lord" for "their brethren," the Lamanites, and for "him that the Lord should suffer to bring these things forth" (Mormon 8:23-25). It should come as no surprise (but who would have thought of it?) that through the centuries the makers of the record would pray for the latter-day prophet destined to bring their writings to light. And Moroni knows how much divine help that prophet will need. He composes in concrete detail a keenly accurate, highly disquieting description of our day (see Mormon 8:26-32). Of tangential interest is his prediction that things far away, in "foreign lands" and "divers places," would be "heard of," a prophecy that indirectly predicts global communication inconceivable in his day. However advanced the Nephite civilization, there was no electronic transmission of information from faraway lands, much less the atmospheric pollution foreseen in verses 29 and 31.

Envisioning the wickedness of our day, an anguished Moroni seeks to bring us to our senses through bold declarations and penetrating questions. He knows his audience only too well: "Behold, I speak unto you as if ye were present, and yet ye are not. But behold, Jesus Christ hath shown you unto me, and I know your doing" (Mormon 8:35). That phrase, "I know your doing," strikes home with piercing realism. It is also a reminder that Moroni experienced miraculous visions and other spiritual manifestations. Most certainly, Jesus himself and the Holy Spirit were Moroni's companions through many years of anxious, solitary wandering. Is it faithless of me to wonder why he was left to roam the earth such a long time?

As if reading not only our times, but also our very souls, Moroni rhetorically interrogates us: "O ye wicked and perverse and stiffnecked people, why have ye built up churches unto yourselves to get gain? Why have ye transfigured the holy word of God, that ye might bring damnation upon your souls?" (Mormon 8:33). Moroni sees pride as the definitive spiritual flaw of latter-day peoples and their churches, a failing that engenders "all manner of iniquities" (Mormon 8:36). Specifically, he charges that "ye do love money, and your substance, and your fine apparel, and the adorning of your churches, more than ye love the poor and the needy, the sick and the afflicted" (Mormon 8:37). Wishing to jar us out of our wasteful, self-satisfied complacency, he asks, "Why are ye ashamed to take upon you the name of Christ?" (Mormon 8:38). More pointedly still, "Why do ye adorn yourselves with that which hath no life, and yet suffer the hungry, and the needy, and the naked, and the sick and the afflicted to pass by you, and notice them not?" (Mormon 8:39). These are only some of the thorny, accusing questions Moroni puts to us. I think we should heed this man, even more than we would heed the sole survivor of a great nuclear disaster. Moroni is not merely a survivor; he is the bearer of tidings from across the sea whom we met in the beginning of this essay. He is God's oracle.

In what Moroni truly believes are his final words to future generations, he pulls no punches as he confronts the faithless. God is real, Moroni declares; will you deny him at judgment, to his face, even as you deny him now? Echoing earlier Nephite prophets, Moroni reasons that the wicked will find the Lord's presence unendurable, anyway, for they will be "racked with a consciousness of guilt" at having "abused his laws" (Mormon 9:3). In fact, he adds, it would be "more miserable" for such "to dwell with a holy and just God," knowing their guilt, than "to dwell with the damned souls in hell" (Mormon 9:4). Simply and profoundly, he describes the concept of hell as a condition of the soul: "For behold, when ye shall be brought to see your nakedness before God, and also the glory of God, and the holiness of Jesus Christ, it will kindle a flame of unquenchable fire upon you" (Mormon 9:5). No physical torment could exceed the unmitigated anguish of intense and everlasting regret.

Knowing the magnitude of the latter-day skepticism he is

confronting, Moroni is intent on establishing the truth that God is unchanging and a God of miracles, past, present, and future. A dearth of miracles can be imputed to a changed human race, not to a changed God. Moroni proves his point by chronologically outlining the whole inviolate framework of the Christian gospel, with each miraculous aspect giving rise to the next, from the creation to the spiritual redemption of the righteous.[2] We do not commonly think of the Creation and judgment as "miracles," *per se*; but for Moroni, these are among the mighty events that could not have occurred if God were not a God of miracles. In fact, the first of these miracles, the Creation, is indisputable proof of God's supernal powers:

> Who shall say that it was not a *miracle* that *by his word* the heaven and the earth should be; and *by the power of his word* man was created of the dust of the earth; and *by the power of his word* have miracles been wrought? (Mormon 9:17; emphases added)

As a bibliophile, I am captivated by the scriptural language frequently employed to describe the miraculous exercise of divine initiative, tuition, and might. If Moroni and the other holy scribes are speaking more than figuratively, much, if not all, miraculous achievement, including (or especially) the creation of worlds, is accomplished through "the power of his word." Since Jesus Christ, the agent of creation, is spoken of as "the Word," we can plausibly conjecture that in the divine verbal conception of a miracle lies the beginning of its inevitable realization. This idea is imaged brilliantly in the Lord's assurances to the brother of Jared—assurances of divine safekeeping through a lengthy sea journey. The Lord reminds his prophet that "the winds have gone forth out of my mouth, and also the rains and the floods have I sent forth" (Ether 2:24). God the Father speaks, and the creative act or miracle is initiated through the

---

[2] In describing the effects of judgment Moroni contends not only that the "filthy shall be filthy still" and the "righteous . . . righteous still," but also that the "happy shall be happy still" and the "unhappy . . . unhappy still" (Mormon 9:14). Moroni's words echo Alma's concept of restoration, and perhaps additionally relate to temperament, attitude, and life-view as well as to the verdict of judgment. I think that "righteousness" and "happiness," though they occur together, need not be merely repetitive synonyms in this context. The idea that a disposition toward happiness or unhappiness literally carries over into the next life may well be a subtext here. Such a reading suggests one more way in which mortals, to some extent, choose their own destinies.

"power of the word," the instrumentality of the Son.

To believe in Christ, Moroni reasons further, is to believe in miracles. If no miracles are in evidence, it is because "the children of men . . . dwindle in unbelief, and depart from the right way, and know not God" (Mormon 9:20). Among the believers, there will always be miracles in the form of answered prayers, and miraculous signs will accompany the preaching of the word (see Mormon 9:24-25 and Mark 16:17-18). The promise is restricted neither to prophets nor to covenant peoples, but extends "unto all, even unto the ends of the earth" (Mormon 9:21).

As Moroni prepares to conclude his record, he shifts to a distinctly oracular mode, challenging his latter-day readers in a series of sweeping rhetorical questions:

> . . . who can stand against the works of the Lord? Who can deny his sayings? Who will rise up against the almighty power of the Lord? Who will despise the works of the Lord? Who will despise the children of Christ? Behold, all ye who are despisers of the works of the Lord, for ye shall wonder and perish. (Mormon 9:26)

This is the voice of Old Testament prophecy, sounding a warning to a wicked and perverse generation. But instantly, the oracle gives way to the man, and Moroni pleads as loving brother and counselor that we humbly seek "the Lord with all [our] heart" (Mormon 9:27). Then, in another quick change of tone, Moroni addresses his reader with unguarded directness: "Behold, I speak unto you as though I spake from the dead; for I know that ye shall have my words" (Mormon 9:30). I have little doubt that after his people were destroyed, the record was Moroni's central temporal concern. He talks about it and worries verbally over it repeatedly, especially over its possible human imperfections. But even the expository deficiencies of Moroni or his predecessors can be beneficial, he says, if the reader will "give thanks unto God that he hath made manifest unto you our imperfections, that ye may learn to be more wise than we have been" (Mormon 9:31). That brief expression of personal counsel takes Moroni beyond concern for possible human errors in the record. As one mortal to another, he implores his latter-day reader to learn from the mistakes that brought his own people down.

Constraints of space, and the hardship of inscribing text on metal plates, dictated composition not in Hebrew but in "reformed Egyptian," which Moroni says was "handed down and altered by us, according to our manner of speech" (Mormon 9:32). (In any culture, written language gradually reflects inevitable changes in verbal usage.) Since Hebrew is known for its compactness, and yet would have required more space than "reformed Egyptian," then the latter must have been highly compact indeed. Despite these difficulties, accurate translation is assured, Moroni says, because "the Lord knoweth the things which we have written, and also that none other people knoweth our language; therefore he hath prepared means for the interpretation thereof" (Mormon 9:34). Moroni then officially closes the record. But he returns to it, as we shall see.

## Ether 1-2: The Ancient Jaredites

The book of Ether is an anachronism in the Book of Mormon, but a fascinating one. As I mentioned in discussing the books of Omni and Mosiah, Ether chronicles an earlier society—called "Jaredites" after one of their first leaders. The bones and record of these people were found by a group of King Limhi's people in about 121 B.C. (see Mosiah 21:25-28). Ether was their last prophet, and he prepared the record which consisted of twenty-four metal plates. Although Limhi was unable to translate the inscriptions, when he and his people escaped from Lamanite bondage and returned to Zarahemla, Mosiah prepared a translation with the aid of special instruments that accompanied the record.[1] Moroni, who found the Jaredite plates with the records and materials he received from his father, very likely consulted Mosiah's translation as he labored to prepare an abridgment. Moroni's summary is so brief (fifteen chapters) that it is easy to dismiss this early people as a small blip on the screen of religious history in the western hemisphere. To do so, however, is to underrate enormously their size and significance.

This group of immigrants left the Biblical world at the time of the tower of Babel and the confounding of tongues, about 2200 B.C., thereby initially preceding Lehi's group by 1,600 years. Surely by divine intent, the sole wandering Jaredite survivor was discovered sometime between 580 and 300 B.C. by a group of Mulekites from Zarahemla.[2] His name was Coriantumr, and

[1] In a revelation given to Joseph Smith in June 1829, the Lord promised to show him a number of relics preserved and hidden with the Book of Mormon plates, among them "the breastplate" worn by a translator, which apparently held the translating devices called "the Urim and Thummim." The apparatus, I presume, freed the hands of the translator. The Urim and Thummim, the Lord says, "were given to the brother of Jared upon the mount, when he talked with the Lord face to face" (Doctrine and Covenants 17:1). According to the Bible dictionary, the term comes from Hebrew and means "Lights and Perfections," an interesting and oddly appropriate designation for such instruments. The term appears a number of times in the Old Testament.

[2] The Mulekites, we remember, had left Jerusalem about a dozen years after Lehi's group. They established the city of Zarahemla and eventually merged with the Nephites. This single survivor and the record of his people (which he did not have, but which was found later) make a rather uncanny link among the three groups of people who were led independently to a land of promise in the western hemisphere long before the Vikings and Columbus pointed their ships west.

Ether had prophesied his solitary perpetuity. Imagine his astonishment when, in what he had assumed was an uninhabited land, he stumbled on people from his ancestral home; and imagine their reciprocal amazement when they encountered him. I will speak more of Coriantumr later, for he is the last king of the Jaredites, and a prominent figure in the closing chapters of the book of Ether.

In his abridgment of Ether's record, Moroni makes no references to dates and time, but he does trace Jaredite genealogy, which provides some sense, at least, of the passing generations and centuries. The group spent four years in the wilderness before embarking for the promised land, and they were nearly a year—344 days—at sea. By any accounting, however, the Jaredites outdistanced the Nephites by several centuries, spanning what may have been sixteen or seventeen hundred years. At most, the Nephite-Mulekite group survived a thousand years. Ether must have had access to historical records from which he wrote his account, but they probably perished in the inferno of hate and war that consumed the Jaredite nation. I suspect that only the records (the twenty-four metal plates) that Ether "hid . . . in a manner that the people of Limhi did find them" (Ether 15:33) were spared.

So what do we make of this isolated civilization that paralleled many centuries of Biblical history? It helps us to realize that, although the Jaredite nation had Hebraic origins and was contemporary with many Old Testament prophets, unlike the Nephite civilization it would not have had a substantial underpinning of Old Testament scripture to stabilize its language and religious practices. In fact, Noah was still alive when Jared and his family split off from the home territory and established themselves in the new world, totally isolated from the world of the Old Testament prophets which Lehi and his family inherited and, to a large extent, brought with them.

Even if the record the Jaredites carried to the new world (see Ether 8:9) contained scriptures, those scriptures would have been far different from the brass plates brought much later by the

Lehites. We should remember that the Jaredites were already in the western hemisphere when prophets such as Abraham, Isaac, Jacob, Joseph, Moses, Joshua, Saul, David, Solomon, Elijah, and Isaiah lived. Ether knew of these giants through revelation, but the Jaredites missed them. While they may have been tutored in a similar law of which we have no knowledge, the Jaredites most certainly missed the Law of Moses, which governed the Nephites until Christ's ministry. The Jaredites produced their own sacred writings, but we know virtually nothing about them. What a fascinating study their prophecies and sermons would make; very likely the twenty-four plates abridged by Moroni contain some of them.

To begin the book of Ether, then, is to leap backward in time, from the early fifth century A.D. when Moroni first closes his father's record, to the departure of Jared and his family for the wilderness and the new world. We are talking about a 2,600-year reversal, considerably longer than the time lapse between the birth of Christ and our own day. And, indeed, it does seem a strange world we are entering. Odd as some Lehite names register in the modern ear, they nevertheless have a "biblical" ring; and we have grown accustomed to them. Then suddenly we encounter, with some exceptions, names the likes of which we have never seen anywhere: Ethem, Com, Pagag, Amnigaddah, Hearthom, Lib, Kish, Corom, Shez, Morianton, Heth, Kib, Omer, Shule, and so on. Any that seem familiar may be reminiscent of early Old Testament nomenclature.

One other thing is disorienting to the modern reader: the first generations of these people lived a *long* time. Aged or young, they begat children right and left, and some did not stop with a mere twenty or thirty offspring. I assume that plural marriages were part of the culture, though the record does not specifically say so. As we gasp and turn to Ripley, we should remind ourselves that the typical mortal life span generally lengthens in obverse proportion to the age of the human race. Adam and Eve lived several centuries, and Methuselah had been dead only a century and a half before the Jaredite departure. The book of Ether, then, chronicles

an age of astounding longevity. Given their high birth rate and
lengthy lives, one can see why these people, who began as a sizeable
party anyway, grew to be a vast nation. On the other hand,
given their propensity for mutiny and murder, it is surprising that
any of the nobility lived to beget thirty or forty children.

One of the most disturbing aspects of the book of Ether is the
seeming scarcity of filial love, son for father and brother for
brother, among the ruling classes. Their villainous plots and
intrigues are reminiscent of the ambition-driven atrocities that
sully centuries of European royal history. Seeking power and personal
glory, son after son lops off the head of father after father—
or enlists someone else to do the foul deed. By contrast, rarely in
Lehite political history, at least as we have it, does a son turn murderously
against a father, or a brother against a brother. The most
glaring instance occurs in Lehi's own immediate family, in the
rebellion of his sons Laman and Lemuel.

It is obvious to me, then, even from our highly condensed
account of the Jaredites, that the two civilizations differed substantially
from each other. The peoples chronicled in the two
records first saw daylight in very different times indeed. Although
their primal origins are the same, their cultures developed along
different courses, and for many centuries in different hemispheres.
They were, however, equally proficient at wickedness and equally
quick to forget the Lord. Obviously, they shared many of the same
vices, being human like the rest of us, but their particular soft
spots seem different. For example, the most prevalent and
destructive vice among the Jaredite people, next to their thirst for
power, was seemingly not pride, as with the Nephites, but a fascination
with "secret combinations." Almost from the start, they are
captivated by the clandestine oaths and intrigues which Mormon's
record attributes to Satan and to the Jaredites' none-too-distant
countryman, Cain (see Helaman 6:27). Such insidious bands do
eventually subvert Nephite and Lamanite societies, but not until
relatively late. Nevertheless, they are responsible for the final
destruction of the Nephite nation, as Moroni points out in
Ether 8:21. The first Nephi warns against them in a general way

(see 2 Nephi 9:9), but it is not until the book of Helaman, in the years shortly before Christ's birth, that conspiracies become a serious threat. We remember that Alma instructed his son Helaman to conceal the Jaredite record lest the Nephites find attractive the abominations detailed in Ether's writings. Mosiah, too, was forbidden to publish and circulate his translation of the twenty-four plates because of the devilish utterances and practices they contained.

There are other differences between the two societies. The Jaredites, whose filial disaffection I have already noted, seem more politically ambitious and ruthless than the Nephites, perhaps partly because they maintained a monarchy continuously, while the Nephites eventually established a democracy, with a system of elected chief judges rather than kings. In the Jaredite monarchy, unfortunately, anyone who could displace a king, be he honorable or not, could assume the throne. The system directly rewarded and thus encouraged intrigue and murder. By contrast, although some Nephite chief judges were violently unseated, at least an assassin could not easily take the place of his victim because chief judges were elected by a vote of the people. The Jaredites may also have been more inclined toward concubines and whoredoms, if kings Riplakish and Morianton are not just the odd exceptions (see Ether 10:5, 11). Among the Lehites, however, marital fidelity was honored and expected, as Jacob's sermon on the subject attests.

I repeat, the weakest thread in the Nephite rug was, without question, *pride*. I am amazed that, given its frequency in the Nephite record, the word "pride" does not even appear in the book of Ether. We can probably assume, however, that any society that abides an unprincipled ruling class is likely to spawn a good deal of pride, at least among the privileged. The fact that pride is not mentioned in Ether may be partly attributable to the book's being doubly condensed, an abridgment of an abridgment. What the void cannot be ascribed to is a shifting focus in the second abridger, Moroni; for in his own writing, Moroni is as concerned about pride as were his Nephite predecessors. In my view, the absence of warnings against pride in the book of Ether confirms the book as the product of another people and time.

There are a few high points in the book of Ether, but most of Moroni's summary is blackly forbidding. Twice the Jaredite nation destroys itself, though the first time a few stragglers survive to start things up again. Not so the second time; only Coriantumr and Ether remain when the last rampages sputter out. The two civilizations differ greatly in cultural circumstances, but the Jaredite parallels with the Nephite experience are painfully, and fascinatingly, close. Two huge and relatively sophisticated civilizations that inhabited the greater American continent between 2200 B.C. and 400 A.D. literally wiped themselves off the face of the earth. A remnant of the later nation survived, but was scattered in a devastated land and never of itself reconstructed a centrally unified Christian civilization. When the dust clears, only Moroni is left of millions who called themselves Nephites, and only Coriantumr of the Jaredites. Undoubtedly, Moroni saw his own people prefigured in the Jaredites, and himself in Coriantumr. How it must have racked his soul to read of the depravity and destruction of still another nation in what had been set aside as a promised land for the Lord's covenant people. In the end, Coriantumr had offered his kingdom in exchange for the lives of the few who remained, but his enemy had refused any resolution short of death for the king. Like Moroni, Coriantumr became a lone wanderer in a wilderness of corpses and ruined cities, though as the last mortal (he thought), save a prophet, he did not fear hostile marauders as Moroni must have.

Moroni, who is condensing what reads like a nightmarish preview of his own people's story, plays a significant role as the narrative voice in much of the book of Ether. Sometimes he is openly present, as when he interjects commentary and discourse; other times he is simply a recording consciousness; but always he is there. And plainly, abridging Ether's record magnifies Moroni's own very personal anguish. Physical hardship is not his only reason for abbreviating Jaredite history. But, as is so often the case, what is left unsaid has a voice of its own. We must suppose that across sixteen or more centuries, three to four times the number of years stretching between Christopher Columbus and the present, countless doctrinal discourses were delivered. And behind these few short chapters lie thousands of splendid as well as sordid human dramas. Moroni begins detachedly enough, explaining simply the origin of the book of Ether, his omission of material available elsewhere, and his incomplete representation of Jaredite history. He first traces Ether's ancestry back through twenty-eight generations to Jared.

Despite Jared's apparent civil, and perhaps family, prominence early on, it is not Jared, but his unnamed brother who is the first prophet and spiritual leader of this band of castaways.[3] The roles and relationship of the two men are a fascinating study. Jared's brother is said to be "a large and mighty man, and a man highly favored of the Lord" (Ether 1:34); nevertheless (since Ether is a descendant of Jared), the line of record keepers, and of at least some prophets, may descend from Jared rather than his brother. Then, too, in the beginning, Jared is clearly the initiator in practical matters, and his brother the executor of his directives: ". . . the brother of Jared did cry unto the Lord according to that which had been spoken by the mouth of Jared" (Ether 1:39). But why does Jared not take his requests to the Lord himself? Perhaps he and his brother observe a strict division of labor. In any case, three times in the days of the confounding of tongues Jared sends his brother to the Lord with special requests, three times the brother complies, and three times the Lord consents.

It soon becomes apparent, however, that whatever the established social protocol between them, it is not Jared, but his brother, the prophet, who is to lead the group once they depart for the wilderness. Although the Lord twice mentions Jared, seeming to recognize that in worldly matters Jared indeed has held some authority over his brother, from now on this brother will take

---

[3] Joseph Smith was said to have indicated on one occasion that the man's name was later revealed to him as *Mahonri Moriancumer*. Either Joseph or Moroni apparently found it simpler just to call him "the brother of Jared." I note, however, that the Jaredites named their wilderness settlement, before their ocean crossing, Moriancumer (see Ether 2:13), apparently after their prophet, the brother of Jared.

instructions not from Jared, but from the Lord. Accordingly, the Lord directs the brother of Jared to gather flocks, seeds, friends, and family, and then to "go at the head of them down into the valley which is northward." He adds, "And there will I meet thee, and I will go before thee into a land which is choice above all the lands of the earth" (Ether 1:42). The Lord has high expectations for the nation that he will personally guide to the promised land:

> And there will I bless thee and thy seed, and raise up unto me of thy seed, and of the seed of thy brother, and they who shall go with thee, a great nation. And there shall be none greater than the nation which I will raise up unto me of thy seed, upon all the face of the earth. (Ether 1:43)

It is hardly a coincidence that the arrivals of Mulek's group and Lehi's group correspond with the decline of the Jaredite nation. True, the impending destruction of Jerusalem presented an auspicious opportunity for Lehi's and Mulek's evacuation; but we should not forget a longstanding divine resolve to establish a segment of the covenant people in a new land of promise. That the Lord's intentions not be thwarted, the failure of the first group made expedient the coming of others (two more should markedly improve the odds for success), and there was little delay in launching them. The subsequent failure of the combined later groups led, not to yet another attempt to send covenant people from Jerusalem, especially into a now hostile environment, but instead to preparation for the transfer of the gospel and its promises to the Gentiles who, centuries later, would inherit the land and accept Jesus Christ as their Lord and Savior.

Moroni skims much of Ether's record, but he gives unusual attention to the inauguration of the Jaredite enterprise, specifically to the Lord's dealings with the brother of Jared. In this, too, the Jaredites' story parallels that of the Lehites, whom God had likewise sent into the wilderness for spiritual humbling and physical toughening before dispatching them across the sea. Very likely, the people of Jared's day had fewer of the civilized comforts enjoyed by Lehi's family, and therefore required less preparatory time to build stamina and resourcefulness before they embarked for the new world. On the other hand, their civilization must have been less skilled at route finding and navigation than the Lehites and Mulekites, for the Lord would provide more personal assistance in their journey, initially going "before them and [talking] with them as he stood in a cloud" (Ether 2:5), much as he would lead Moses and the children of Israel. Lehi's group, however, coming from a more advanced culture, would not enjoy such intimate leadership. For them, the Lord would provide technical guidance in the form of a special compass whose degree of reliability was proportionate to the faith of the Lehites.

As Jared's group sojourn in the wilderness, the Lord instructs them to "build barges, in which they did cross many waters" (Ether 2:6) under his constant supervision—training runs, it appears, on the Mediterranean or the Red Sea. Eventually, they are brought to the ocean's edge. Explicit in the Lord's decree, regarding their ultimate destination in the "land of promise," is a warning as well as a blessing, and Moroni interrupts the narrative to underscore that point: ". . . whatsoever nation shall possess it shall serve God, or they shall be swept off . . . when they are ripened in iniquity" (Ether 2:9; see 2:8, 10, 11, 12). After four years in the wilderness, the Jaredite group needs a nudge. Approaching Jared's brother, the Lord "stood in a cloud and talked with him . . . for the space of three hours . . . , and chastened him because he remembered not to call upon the name of the Lord" (Ether 2:14). This seeming forgetfulness perplexes me, for earlier the Lord had told Jared's brother that he would bless this people "because this long time ye have cried unto me" (Ether 1:43). Although ignorant of the group's circumstances, I nonetheless find it odd that a prophet would "remember not" to call on the Lord in four years, and would need reminding that "my Spirit will not always strive with man" (Ether 2:15). However it was, three hours permit a long conversation, indeed, and Jared's brother gets the message. He repents of his dereliction and receives instructions for building and outfitting eight small, light-weight, water-tight barges. They are to be built "after the manner of barges which ye have hitherto built" (Ether 2:16), and the Lord will drive them across the sea before the winds.

It will be a rough passage, but these closed-in, tree-length barges[4] can withstand anything nature can contrive, including total submersion. The brother of Jared takes several practical concerns about the sealed, windowless vessels to the Lord—one for light, another for steering, and a third for air. The second and third the Lord solves for him, but as to the matter of light, the Lord forbids the use of fire and insists that his supplicant use his own ingenuity to devise a solution. When the brother of Jared has a workable idea, the Lord will entertain his request. Twice the Lord invites his prophet to make a specific request rather than simply present a general problem and expect instant accommodation. A good lesson in the proper interplay between self-reliance and God-reliance. For the voyage and their safety, however, and for their navigation, the group will be totally reliant on the Lord. His preparation and guidance notwithstanding, 344 days is a long time for mortals to endure tight, windowless quarters—not to mention each other.

---

[4] Since the barges were "the length of a tree" (Ether 2:17), they probably contained no vertical seams, except at the two ends. This undoubtedly contributed to their being water-tight. It appears to me that shipbuilding and seafaring skills had advanced considerably by the time Lehi's family embarked for the promised land because they traveled in a large, open sailing vessel. Nevertheless, the Jaredites had an opportunity to practice and develop both their shipbuilding and seafaring skills before they were required to negotiate the ocean.

## 26

## Ether 3-11: Bitter Fruits of an Auspicious Beginning

Although much of the book of Ether relates a morose tale of a people's headlong plunge into oblivion, there are some moments that almost knock the eyes out to read them, and chapter 3 recounts one of those. It begins where chapter 2 leaves off, with the brother of Jared trying to hit upon a means for illuminating the eight closed vessels that would carry his family and friends to the promised land. But before chapter 3 ends, he has conversed face to face with the Lord Jesus Christ and seen visions covering the whole of human history. Thus, a chapter that begins with a very practical matter evolves to a gloriously spiritual conclusion.

As chapter 3 opens, Jared's brother conceives a workable scheme for lighting the vessels. He prepares sixteen small white stones, "as transparent as glass," which he had "molten out of a rock" (Ether 3:1) on mount Shelem, and he carries them to the top of the mountain. There he asks the Lord to touch them and infuse them with radiant light. The whole tenor of his prayer suggests an attitude considerably altered since his first matter-of-fact petition seeking light and ventilation for the vessels. Jared's brother has learned that mere obedience to instructions and articulation of wants is not enough. The Lord expects both humility and initiative of his servants. Chastened by the experience, and newly taught his responsibility, Jared's brother is no longer an unimaginative laborer, burying his talent, methodically following instructions, and expecting to be "command[ed] in all things" (see Doctrine and Covenants 58:26). He still needs the Lord's help, but he has earnestly applied himself to the task. In the process, he has grown in faith, intellect, and ability. The mindset changes when we strive to solve a problem ourselves rather than merely take it to a superior for solution.

It truly is a different man who now approaches the Lord, and his opening words signal the change. He begs forgiveness, acknowledging the weakness and low state of mortals in comparison with the Lord's holy might and station. At the same time, he notes that mortals are required by "commandment" to ask for what they need (Ether 3:2). What he has learned is that the *manner* of the asking is all-important. Demonstrably humbled and contrite, Jared's brother turns to the next portion of his prayer, which combines a worshipful, celebratory tribute with a specific request for help. He presents the sixteen pieces of prepared ore with full faith in the Lord's ability to illuminate them perpetually and says:

> And I know, O Lord, that thou hast all power, and can do whatsoever thou wilt for the benefit of man; therefore touch these stones, O Lord, with thy finger, and prepare them that they may shine forth in darkness; and they shall shine forth unto us in the vessels which we have prepared, that we may have light while we shall cross the sea. (Ether 3:4)

Yet again, Jared's brother humbly affirms God's power ("Behold, O Lord, thou canst do this," Ether 3:5) and humanity's puny understanding of such power. It is clearly humility combined with faith that evokes the miracle:

> . . . when the brother of Jared had said these words, behold, the Lord stretched forth his hand and touched the stones one by one with his finger. And the veil was taken from off the eyes of the brother of Jared, and he saw the finger of the Lord; and it was as the finger of a man, like unto flesh and blood; and the brother of Jared fell down before the Lord, for he was struck with fear. (Ether 3:6)

Neither the reader nor Jared's brother is prepared for such an immediate and powerful manifestation. No wonder the prophet's knees buckle—and yet what he sees is precisely what he prayed for.

In reporting that the Lord asks "why hast thou fallen?" (Ether 3:7), the text might seem to suggest that the Lord does not know what his prophet has seen. I think we can rest assured, however, that the Lord knows and is merely testing the man's perception of the event. Even though Jared's brother protests that he "knew not that the Lord had flesh and blood" (Ether 3:8)—that is, a body, for the Lord does not have flesh and blood at this time—we remember that he had asked the Lord to touch the stones "with thy finger" (Ether 3:4). He must, therefore, have assumed that God was a defined personage. Still, the Lord clarifies what his prophet saw: a portion of his spirit body. Through his faith, the man has "seen that *I shall* take upon me flesh and blood" (Ether 3:9; emphasis added). Had the man's faith been less, he would not have seen any part of the Lord's being. In a later summary of the event, Moroni declares, as Alma had, that when faith is strong enough, it is transformed into sure knowledge, and miracles cannot be withheld:

> And because of the knowledge of this man he could not be kept from beholding within the veil; and he saw the finger of Jesus, which, when he saw, he fell with fear; for he knew that it was the finger of the Lord; and he had faith no longer, for he knew, nothing doubting.
> Wherefore, having this perfect knowledge of God, he could not be kept from within the veil; therefore he saw Jesus; and he did minister unto him. (Ether 3:19-20)

After Jared's brother acknowledges having seen the finger of the Lord, the Lord continues to question him, requiring him to verbalize the experience. Implicit in his question, "Sawest thou more than this?" (Ether 3:9) is the possibility that this mortal could have seen still more of the Lord's person. Christ was there in his full personage, but he awaited the opening of a man's spiritual eyes to his presence. The prophet's quick, confident answer to the Lord's question is a far cry from his first trembling response. He is ready to see more: "Nay; Lord, show thyself unto me" (Ether 3:10). The test continues: "Believest thou the words which I shall speak?" (Ether 3:11). And Jared's brother unhesitatingly answers, "Yea, Lord" (Ether 3:12). On the instant, the veil is lifted, and the brother of Jared beholds his God.

The Lord then makes an explicit connection between redemption and the faith that leads to sure knowledge. "Because thou knowest these things ye are redeemed from the fall," the Lord says; "therefore ye are brought back into my presence; therefore I show myself unto you" (Ether 3:13). The Lord also teaches his prophet just how, in addition to his role as Creator, he can be considered "Father" as well as "Son"—something Moroni would already know. This is basic schooling for a very early prophet. First, "In me," he says, "shall all mankind have life," and second, ". . . they who shall believe on my name . . . shall become my sons and my daughters" (Ether 3:14). Reason tells us that since mortal life derives through those we call our parents, Christ, from whom immortal life comes, can be called the Father of redeemed mortals. As Nephite prophets would also testify, the faithful are reborn spiritually, in mortality, as his children.

Christ's next statement, one of the dynamite passages I alluded to earlier, contains a grand four-part revelation: (1) Jared's brother (not the mortal Adam?) is apparently the first human being to have seen the Lord in his glorious premortal state; (2) the faith of Jared's brother exceeds that of any other who has lived to this time (including Adam? we must wonder again); (3) the Lord's mortal body will have the same form as his spirit being; and (4) mortals are created in the image and likeness of his spirit being. The Lord could not be more plain:

> And never have I showed myself unto man whom I have created, for never has man believed in me as thou hast. Seest thou that ye are created after mine own image? Yea, even all men were created in the beginning after mine own image.
>
> Behold, this body, which ye now behold, is the body of my spirit; and man have I created after the body of my spirit; and even as I appear unto thee to be in the spirit will I appear unto my people in the flesh. (Ether 3:15-16)

We can hardly overstate the significance of this early revelation regarding the nature of Christ's premortal being. Even though the Savior had not yet acquired mortal flesh and blood, his spirit body was substantial, having mass, form, and density. The premortal, mortal, and postmortal Jesus have the same identifiable features. But the surprise Jared's brother registers on seeing Christ's being reminds us again of the earliness of these events. The revelations do not stop here, either. Unable to "withhold anything from [the brother of Jared], for he knew that the Lord could show him all things," the Lord spreads before his dazed prophet's eyes a magnificent vision of "all the inhabitants of the earth which had been, and also all that would be" (Ether 3:25-26).

We can gauge the importance of this event and its implications by the fact that Moroni both summarizes what occurs and quotes from the transcendent conversation in his otherwise highly-condensed abridgment. And being a guardian of records himself, Moroni takes special account of the Lord's detailed instructions to the brother of Jared, instructions concerning the priceless account he is to inscribe of the things he has seen and heard on the mountain. By contrast, Moroni cursorily scans centuries upon centuries of Jaredite history in a text that reads like a royal census, a brief compendium of Jaredite kings and kingdoms. Obviously, the Lord is very particular about the Jaredite record, just as he will be particular about Nephite writings. He specifies what is to be written, how it is to be preserved, and when it is to be disclosed—or, more accurately, when it is *not* to be disclosed. More than once, Moroni repeats the Lord's directives forbidding that the record Jared's brother makes of this sacred event "come unto the children of men" until after the confirming evidence of Christ's earthly ministry (Ether 4:1; see also 3:21).

It appears from what Moroni says in Ether 4:2 that the Nephites to whom Jesus ministered did indeed see what the brother of Jared had written about his miraculous experience: "And after Christ truly had showed himself unto his people he commanded that they [the Jaredite records] should be made manifest" (Ether 4:2). But once the Nephite nation falls again into disbelief, these precious writings are understandably denied them. Moroni is instructed to "hide them up again in the earth" (Ether 4:3). It is also possible that, along with the marvelous writings of

Jared's brother, the Nephites saw the rest of the Jaredite record—the part especially forbidden earlier because of its Satanic content. Perhaps it conspired to undermine the Savior's legacy of tranquility and virtue. Moroni is somewhat ambiguous on the matter, saying only that "after that," the Nephites "dwindled in unbelief" (Ether 4:3). It is hard to imagine evil written oaths so alluring that even the righteous could not withstand them.

Whatever enigmas the multiple records present to the modern reader, Moroni is totally clear about his own assignment. And regardless of huge omissions and painfully spare condensations, the genesis of Jaredite history is at least represented in the Book of Mormon. Moroni also manages to insert some choice passages, such as verses 6-19 of Ether 4, which carry the Lord's counsel to our time. To faithful latter-day Gentiles, his splendid promise is sanctification and then a manifestation of "the things which the brother of Jared saw, even to the unfolding unto them all my revelations" (Ether 4:7). The language leaves little room for disputation; there will be visions—and *all*, literally *all*, his revelations are to be unfolded. There is a downside to the news, however, for the Lord also vows that when his revealed word issues forth, signifying that the Father's work is commencing (see Ether 4:17), any who deny it will "be accursed" and denied "greater things" (Ether 4:8). Reason tells me that the "accursing" refers less to punitive actions from above than to self-inflicted internal barriers against great spiritual and intellectual knowledge. Latter-day Gentiles and covenant peoples will realize their promises even as the revelations of John are "unfolded in the eyes of all" (Ether 4:16).[1]

Chapter 5 is mainly a short interjected set of instructions from Moroni to the latter-day translator of the record, but Moroni also

---

[1] It occurs to me, as I again read the word "unfolded" in this chapter, that there may be a link with earlier prophecies that in the last days the earth would be rolled up like a scroll (see 3 Nephi 26:3; Mormon 5:23; 9:2). Before, I had assumed a catastrophic interpretation of that figure. That may indeed be its intent, but in light of the "unfolded" figure here, I see another possibility, the ultimate unrolling of the scroll. A scroll contains writing—perhaps the divine word, revelation. I wonder if the figure suggests that the earth itself will be a revelation, a realization of God's word. Is this a way of describing the voluminous truth offered if mortal faith is sufficient, and the role of a celestialized earth in revealing such truth? Certainly, the idea is compatible with section 130 of the Doctrine and Covenants, which refers to the Revelations of John, and which describes the earth in its celestial state as "a Urim and Thummim to the inhabitants who dwell thereon" (v. 4).

issues a pithy challenge to the modern reader. If you do not believe me now, he says, you will when we stand together at judgment. Having experienced what he has, and knowing what he knows, Moroni is not one to mince words, nor to concern himself with the vagaries of diplomacy.

In chapter 6 Moroni returns to the Jaredite narrative, briefly describing the group's travel preparations, including the placing of two lighted stones at either end of each vessel, and the long voyage to the promised land. Jared and company, Moroni says, "set forth into the sea" with a will, "commending themselves unto the Lord their God" (Ether 6:4). I like that upbeat launching. Moroni's rather charming description of the group's abiding gratitude as they are driven before God's constant and "furious wind . . . towards the promised land" (Ether 6:5) suggests a happy conviviality very different from the social turbulence that would characterize the journey of Lehi and his family more than fifteen centuries later:

> And they did sing praises unto the Lord; yea, the brother of Jared did sing praises unto the Lord, and he did thank and praise the Lord all the day long; and when the night came, they did not cease to praise the Lord. (Ether 6:9)

The same prophet who earlier neglected to call on the Lord for four years is now in constant communication with his God. Then, too, having brothers at the helm who are in accord rather than at odds (contrast Jared and his brother against Nephi and his older brothers) makes a strenuous journey more agreeable. But surely, had these ancient voyagers not been secure in their sealed barges and in their faith, the mighty tempests and repeated submergings would have destroyed them emotionally as well as physically. Moroni's summary is concise, yet lyrical:

> And thus they were driven forth; and no monster of the sea could break them, neither whale that could mar them; and they did have light continually, whether it was above the water or under the water. (Ether 6:10)

The Jaredite arrival is similarly gladsome:

> And when they had set their feet upon the shores of the promised
> land they bowed themselves down upon the face of the land, and did
> humble themselves before the Lord, and did shed tears of joy before
> the Lord, because of the multitude of his tender mercies over them.
> (Ether 6:12)

The immigrants, even as they grow and flourish, are "taught to
walk humbly before the Lord; and they were also taught from on
high" (Ether 6:17). From the beginning, the Lord has kept unfailing watch over these beloved pilgrims.

All too soon, however, in fact by the time Jared and his
brother reach old age, the seeds for civil strife are planted.
Gathered to conduct a census of their rapidly increasing population, and to make their final requests of Jared and his brother, the
people ask that a son of one of the brothers be appointed king.
Both brothers oppose the idea, the prophet foreseeing that "this
thing leadeth into captivity" (Ether 6:23). More easily persuaded,
Jared at last acquiesces, and he enjoins his reluctant brother to
withdraw his objections. Only Orihah, of all the sons, can be pre-
vailed upon to accept the office. The next chapters sketch in rapid
order the reign of each king and his successor, rather candidly
assessing the behavior of each. They also describe wars among
fathers, sons, and brothers, and divisions of the kingdom into
opposing groups.[2]

As with the Nephites, there are periods of contrition which
lead to prosperity and peace, but they do not last. Will mortals
never learn that principle of cause and effect? Almost invariably,
some son of some king—or a son's daughter in one instance—sur-
renders to greedy ambition and rebels, or incites rebellion, against
his father and king. Sometimes wars erupt among siblings when
one betrays while another defends their father-king. In a word: a

---

[2] Moroni also makes occasional geographical links between Jaredite and Nephite civilizations, noting that
certain Jaredite events occur near what later became specific Nephite sites. (See, for example, Ether 7:6; 9:3, 31.)

number of kings are slain, and a good many others endure count-less years of captivity. One plot against a good king named Omer bears mentioning because it uncannily foreshadows the circum-stances surrounding the beheading of John the Baptist (see Ether 8 and 9). There are villains enough in the story, but the most despicable is probably Akish, who betrays first his friend, then his partner in crime, then his own son.

Such incidents, unhappily, are not atypical in Jaredite society, where ambition infects generation after generation. Moroni point-edly observes that Akish had sworn his followers into a bloody conspiracy with the same devilish "oaths which were given by them of old *who also sought power*, which had been handed down even from Cain, who was a murderer from the beginning" (Ether 8:15; emphasis added). And the initiator of the plot, the daughter of the dethroned usurper, justifies murder to "obtain kingdoms and great glory" (Ether 8:9). She finds precedence for such evil in ancient records, presumably those carried by the Jaredites to the new world. Desire for power is unquestionably the defining attribute of Cain's spiritual descendants, and secret combinations pledged to get it plague the Jaredites as they would plague later generations of Nephites and Lamanites. The threat of such com-binations is so real that Moroni interrupts his narrative to caution later readers and nations against them.

For Moroni, as for the valiant commander whose name he bears, human liberty is paramount, and he specifically warns latter-day Gentiles to "suffer not that these murderous combina-tions shall get above you" (Ether 8:23). Moroni's selection of the word "above" rather than "among" may have been purposeful. When such combinations achieve political supremacy, they are doubly dangerous. Their aim is "to overthrow the freedom of all lands, nations, and countries," and their allegiance is to "the devil, who is the father of all lies." With studied gravity, Moroni says that he is "commanded to write these things that evil may be done away" (Ether 8:25-26). If we think Moroni over-earnest on the matter, we should consider the informed perspective from which he writes. He has witnessed the ravaging of his own nation by

these evil influences, and he has studied the record of an earlier
people who met the same fate.

The "secret society" which cleaves to Akish, and which "corrupted the hearts of all the people" (Ether 9:6), initiates a cycle of
ambition, intrigue, and war that destroys "nearly all the people of
the kingdom, . . . save it were thirty souls, and they who fled with
the house of Omer" (Ether 9:12). So the Jaredite group teeters on
the brink of oblivion just three to four centuries after arriving in
the new world. Thoroughly chastened by their narrow ransom
from extinction, the survivors make a new start under Omer, and
several generations of peace and prosperity ensue.[3] One prophet-
king, who must have been a man of immense faith, "even saw the
Son of Righteousness, and did rejoice and glory in his day" (Ether
9:22). That is all we know of the man—no sermons, prayers, or
prophecies of this mortal who, like the brother of Jared, beheld
the very being of his God. Perhaps one day we will know more
about those joyful years following the new start of Jaredite society.

As the narrative continues, the perpetually fragile peace is
fractured once more when a wicked son named Heth "embrace[s]
the secret plans again of old" (Ether 9:26) and "dethrone[s] his
father," heartlessly slaying the king "with his own sword." An
appropriate slogan for this society might be "patricide is prof-
itable," for Heth, like other usurpers of other thrones, then "did
reign in his [father's] stead" (Ether 9:27). Prophetic warnings are
ignored, and prophets are "cast into pits and left . . . to perish"
(Ether 9:29). But enough is at last enough. The Lord curses the
land with drought, famine, and a scourge of serpents, and the
people prudently choose to repent rather than to die.

A number of years and a few righteous kings later, the serpents
are eradicated and the land to the south becomes a great resource
for edible wild game. Rather than settle that land, the people prudently make a huge wilderness game preserve of it and confine

---

[3] I mention as a sidenote that Moroni almost casually drops a number of interesting pieces of topical information into his summary. For example, well along in his narrative he says that the first Jaredites fashioned means
to bring fish and bees as well as domestic animals to the new land. (Imagine traveling in a closed barge with all
these braying, smelly beasts!) After arriving, however, they apparently also found and tamed wild animals: "And
they also had horses, and asses, and there were elephants and cureloms and cumoms; all of which were useful
unto man, and more especially the elephants and cureloms and cumoms" (Ether 9:19). Those curious and tantalizing "cureloms and cumoms" remain a puzzle to the modern reader, though seemingly not to Moroni.

their own habitation to the land northward. The Jaredites may have been the first framers of land use policy in the western hemisphere. The great south wilderness also served, I suspect, as a fortuitous barrier between the Jaredites and the Lehites during the period when their civilizations overlapped. Without it, they might have discovered each other, and the Lehites might have been infected early on by the conspiratorial virus. We know that the Jaredite cities were well north of contemporary Lehite sites, because the bones of the Jaredites were found "scattered in the land northward" (Omni 1:22).

The survivors of the famine and the scourge of serpents rebuild their lives, and a greedy king named Riplakish ascends to the throne. He not only enjoys "many wives and concubines" (Ether 10:5), but he also taxes his people heavily to support his expensive tastes, throwing them into prison if they cannot or will not pay. While in prison, the debtors labor for him, refining gold and working other precious materials. In one ironic pair of clauses, Moroni captures the man's nature and the focus of his life: "And he did erect him an exceedingly beautiful throne; and he did build many prisons. . . " (Ether 10:6). Prisons are necessary to support the king's lavish lifestyle, both for the free labor they provide and the taxes they generate from those who prefer not to go to prison.

After forty-two years, the people tire of Riplakish—I should think so—and eventually Morianton battles to power. In describing Morianton's complex ambivalence, Moroni again shows his aptitude for characterization: "And he did do justice unto the people, but not unto himself because of his many whoredoms. . ." (Ether 10:11). In a few well-chosen words, Moroni has captured a man whose lifestyle is unworthy of him, a man torn between good and evil instincts.

A quick count of named kings and probable kings from this era down to the time of Ether and the last Coriantumr[4] suggests

---

[4] One of the sons Omer fathered in captivity was also named Coriantumr (see Ether 8:4), and there were undoubtedly others.

that at least twenty-four different monarchs reign through these centuries, maybe eight or nine righteously and justly. Of those eight or nine, six rule in succession during the zenith of Jaredite civilization—a period of industry, prosperity, and artistic development.

I pause here for a related housekeeping matter. The record appears to follow the royal-prophetic line, but when a usurper is on the throne and the "rightful" king is in captivity, the latter's descendants are listed rather than the fraudulent successors to the throne. Then, when a subsequent generation overthrows an insurgent, the royal and prophetic lines merge once more. Following the period of prosperity just alluded to, the throne is again snatched from the royal line, and the king and his descendants are consigned to a life in captivity. Five generations later the throne is won back, but too late to reverse the powerful undertow. Two good kings and numerous prophets are not enough to lift the lumbering, sin-bloated machine of state onto a righteous path.

An aggrieved Moroni notes that there are again "robbers in the land; and they adopted the old plans, and administered oaths after the manner of the ancients, and sought again to destroy the kingdom" (Ether 10:33). The king fights against them, Moroni says, but he does not prevail. Several generations of Jaredite prophets predict the end of this people if they do not change their ways, and for their candor some end up fleeing for their lives. Others are executed for prophesying "a great curse" and unparalleled warfare that would strew bones in great "heaps" across the landscape (Ether 11:6). After many years of war, famine, and pestilence (see Ether 11:7), this prophecy is realized to the fullest, for Limhi's people would later report "having discovered a land which was covered with bones of men, . . . a land," they realized, "which had been peopled with a people who were as numerous as the hosts of Israel" (Mosiah 8:8). Apparently still hoping to avert disaster, Jaredite prophets reappear, only to withdraw in mourning.

As the kingship passes from one conqueror to another, prophets again cry repentance; and in the days of Ether's father, "many prophets" appear once more (Ether 11:20), not only to cry repentance but also to reveal the Mulekite and Lehite migrations to the land of promise (see Ether 11:21). Thus, while the Jaredites knew they would have successors in the new world, the Lehites seem uninformed of their predecessors until after the Jaredite ruin. The Lord had good reason to keep the two nations apart—the same reason that, in part, led him to forbid the publication of the Jaredite record before his appearance to the Lehites: the risk of moral contamination.

The end approaches, and there is no periodic restoration of a righteous king to the throne. Each succeeding king seems to surpass his predecessor in wickedness. Shiblom, who had slain the prophets, is himself slain; Ahah achieves the throne and does "all manner of iniquity in his days"—and, Moroni adds tellingly, "few were his days" (Ether 11:10); Ethem "execute[s] judgment in wickedness all his days"; and "Moron⁵ [does] that which was wicked before the Lord" (Ether 11:14). Moron is overthrown by "a mighty man among them in iniquity" (Ether 11:15), but he recovers the kingdom only to lose it to "another mighty man" who "was a descendant of the brother of Jared" (Ether 11:17). And so it goes until Moron fathers Coriantor in captivity, and Coriantor fathers Ether. Chapter 11 ends on a despairing note: "And it came to pass that Coriantor begat Ether, and he died, having dwelt in captivity all his days" (Ether 11:23).

---

⁵ The name "Moron" seems Jaredite, but add the -i suffix and it becomes decidedly Nephite.

## 27

## Ether 12-15: Moroni's Discourse on Faith, and the Jaredite Fall

I said earlier that in spite of the general gloom, there are a few high points in the book of Ether. Chapter 12 is one of those. Moved to write after reading of Ether's life and teachings, Moroni produces one of the finest discourses in the Book of Mormon. The narrative time frame is the last generation of the Jaredite people, Coriantumr is "king over all the land," and Ether is "a prophet of the Lord" (Ether 12:1-2). Amazingly, as his nation disintegrates and his people race toward extinction, Ether's ceaseless refrain is *faith* and *hope*, which "he did cry from the morning, even until the going down of the sun" (Ether 12:3). At this juncture, I suppose, it makes little sense to preach anything else.

The temporal world is doomed, but there is another, "happier far" (Milton, *Paradise Lost*), toward which Ether looks. Full of the Spirit, this indomitable oracle of faith and hope "could not be restrained" (Ether 12:2), and he taught that "whoso believeth in God might with surety hope for a better world, yea, even a place at the right hand of God, which hope cometh of faith, maketh an anchor to the souls of men" (Ether 12:4). (In his epistle to the Hebrews, Paul uses the same lovely metaphor of hope as the soul's anchor; see Hebrews 6:19.) Obviously touched by Ether's words, Moroni speaks to latter-day peoples on Ether's subject and Paul's, too, in the first epistle to the Corinthians. Although Moroni treats all three principles that occupy Paul—faith, hope, and charity— his emphasis is clearly on the first while Paul's is on the third. Moroni's recitation, too, is less composed, less consciously poetic, than Paul's, but his focus is clear. The word "faith," or a related word, such as "belief," occurs at least thirty-eight times in Ether 12. By contrast, the word "hope" occurs only seven times, and the word "charity," which the Lord rather than Moroni introduces, occurs six times.

We might assume, from the way Moroni begins telling of Ether and Coriantumr, that chapter 12 will be largely narrative summary. But as he attributes Ether's rejection to the people's lack of faith, the very matter Ether was addressing, Moroni makes an object lesson of the situation. Ether, he says, "did prophesy great and marvelous things," but the literalistic Jaredites "did not believe, because they saw them not" (Ether 12:5). That statement resounds in Moroni's consciousness and launches his discourse. For these ancient peoples as for many moderns, seeing, and only seeing, is believing. The faith that must precede seeing is left out of the equation, and Moroni will not have it. He argues against the skepticism that says, "Show me and I will believe," and he insists that to believe is to acquire the power to see. Seeing, which becomes knowing, requires no exercise of faith. No wonder Jesus corrected Thomas and condemned signseeking, which would transpose the necessary order and make believing dependent upon seeing.

In language reminiscent of Paul, Moroni speaks boldly to the point, conscious that his latter-day audience might be as slow to understand this principle as were the people in Ether's day:

> . . . I would show unto the world that faith is things which are hoped for and not seen; wherefore, dispute not because ye see not, for ye receive no witness until after the trial of your faith.
>
> For it was by faith that Christ showed himself unto our fathers, after he had risen from the dead; and *he showed not himself unto them until after they had faith in him*; wherefore, it must needs be that some had faith in him, for he showed himself not unto the world. (Ether 12:6-7; see Hebrews 11:1; emphasis added)

Moroni's statement reveals why, after the great cataclysm, the surviving Nephites heard the Lord's voice speak at length from the distant heavens before he descended and ministered among them. Faith had to be engendered first.

In addition, Moroni helps us to understand an aspect of Paul's

famous treatise on charity in 1 Corinthians 13. Paul introduces his
subject with a rather abstract reference to "a more excellent way"
in 1 Corinthians 12:31, but he only obscurely suggests late in
chapter 13 just what it is that is exceeded in excellence. In Ether
12:11, however, Moroni defines the source of the "more excellent
way," and additionally indicates what that way exceeds:
"Wherefore, by faith was the *law of Moses* [the less excellent way]
given. But in the *gift of his Son* hath God prepared a more excellent way" (emphases added). That Paul also intends his readers to
know that the law is the less excellent way—as he implies elsewhere, too—is suggested in verses 9 and 10, when he says that "we
know in part, and we prophesy in part. But when that which is
perfect is come, then that which is in part shall be done away."
Before the coming of "that which is perfect"—that is, the Savior—
we spoke and understood as children, seeing darkly and knowing
partially, having the elementary Law of Moses as a guide. With his
coming, however, the detailed code of restrictions is fulfilled and
"put away" (1 Corinthians 13:11).

Having received the full gospel of salvation through Christ's
ministry and sacrifice, we are prepared for spiritual adulthood;
rather than detailed behavioral codes, we are now taught principles—faith, hope, charity—that require the thoughtful exercise of
personal agency and responsibility. We can thereby progress into
knowing as we are known (see 1 Corinthians 13:12). Moroni also
stresses that faith was the key to the Savior's coming, to the fulfilling of the law. Faith in Jesus Christ, he says, has been the great
initiator and mover through the ages, the generator of miracles. In
fact, those able to see within the veil, such as Jared's brother, had
already perceived through faith what was there.

Thus reminded of the faith of his own forebears regarding the
destiny of the record they kept, Moroni breaks into his discourse
on faith (see verses 23-37) to interject a conversation between
himself and the Lord about the precious record and its writers.
Beset with anxiety over his self-adjudged deficiencies as a writer,
and the alleged deficiencies of his predecessors, Moroni fears that
faithless sophisticated readers centuries hence "will mock at these

things, because of our weakness in writing" (Ether 12:23). Clearly, he is expressing more than a passing concern, and he insists that the problem goes beyond practical writing skills. As Moroni sees it, the Lord has so enhanced his prophets' spoken words that mere mortals "cannot write them." In the attempt, "we behold our weakness, and stumble because of the placing of our words" (Ether 12:25).

Moroni seems to be alluding to the arrangement of words into appealing, effective sentences—what English teachers call *style*. But I can confidently say, as an English teacher who has read countless pages of writing at every skill level, that any mockery the record meets today stems from weakness in the reader, not weakness in the writer. Still, I can understand Moroni's self-doubt. Untrained in written exposition, and conscientious in the extreme, he is required to record doctrine and condense history for the ages. More than that, he is to engrave it on the original non-erasable bond: metal plates. Under the circumstances, who could revise and rewrite? As one who revises endlessly, typically plowing through six and seven (or more) drafts of every manuscript, I fully understand Moroni's consternation. A one-draft requirement would stop my heart. Then, too, a hunted fugitive in a wasted land is not likely to invest much energy in polishing his prose.

With tender reassurance, and no sign of reproach, the Lord answers Moroni's concern and articulates a vital concept in Christian doctrine. He also returns Moroni to his original subject: faith. The Lord's first phrase fairly explodes on the page, and the rest of the passage is no less compelling:

> Fools mock, but they shall mourn; and my grace is sufficient for the meek, that they shall take no advantage of your weakness;
> And if men come unto me I will show unto them their weakness. I give unto men weakness that they may be humble; and my grace is sufficient for all men that humble themselves before me; for if they humble themselves before me, and have faith in me, then will I make weak things become strong unto them. (Ether 12:26-27)

I ask the reader to repeat those two verses, giving them place in the mind. Nearly every line contains wisdom enough to steer a life by. "Fools mock" (but the wise and the meek do not). "My grace is sufficient for the meek" (and the meek need not fear the disfavor of the proud and the mocking). "If men come unto me I will show unto them their weakness." That statement, I think, holds the key to repentance, and the key is faith. Again we are taught that believing precedes seeing, which precedes changing. How can we repent of weaknesses that in our pride and self-delusion we do not see? Humility, therefore, leads to faith and repentance—"I give unto men weakness that they may be humble"— and ultimately to spiritual strength. Only through humility can such a book, prepared by inspired mortals in their weakness and their faith, "become strong" for the reader. I know from personal, undeniable experience that this is so.

Re-engaging his subject as he speaks to the Lord, Moroni remembers that the Lord proffers faith, hope, and charity as the three essentials to the soul's salvation—three traits of character that lead one to Christ. After confirming his understanding of faith, the first principle, he turns again to the second principle, hope, and then to charity, the third principle. The ultimate source of our hope for reaching a heavenly home, he says, is the Savior's charity, his boundless love.

Moroni's increased consciousness of the Lord's love leads him to reflect further on charity, the principle Paul elevates above the other two. Moroni knows now that faith and hope, though necessary, are not enough. Unless God's children "have charity they cannot inherit that place . . . prepared in the mansions of [the] Father" (Ether 12:34). Moroni seems to intend a double meaning for the phrase "have charity." Mortals not only "have" the charity that reaches from their own hearts toward others, they also "have" the charity Christ extends to them. In exercising human charity, we receive divine charity, Christ's pure love. Moroni then secures his earlier digression on the record to the main body of his discourse by expressing hope that his Gentile readers will be charitably inclined toward him and the faithful writers who have preceded him. The Lord patiently assures Moroni that if the latter-day Gentiles "have not charity it mattereth not unto thee, thou hast been faithful" (Ether 12:37). At issue is the condition of our own hearts, not others' lack of charity. Moreover, in seeing our weaknesses we are "made strong" (Ether 12:37).

As a side note, just before this, Moroni makes what may be a conscious allusion to the parable of the talents (see Matthew 25:14-30), a parable Moroni might have seen in the larger Nephite record. He says to the Lord:

> Wherefore, I *know by this thing which thou hast said,* that if the Gentiles have not charity, because of our weakness [in writing], that thou wilt prove them, *and take away their talent,* yea, even that which they have received, and *give unto them who shall have more abundantly.* (Ether 12:35; emphases added)

The passage also suggests additional meanings for the parable in Matthew. In Ether, the word "talent" appears to mean the capacity for charity and for spiritual understanding, rather than for initiative and industry. I had once too hastily assumed that Jesus did not teach the Nephites in parables. After all, the abridged record of the Savior's ministry contains no real parables, other than the easily-interpreted story of the wise man who builds his house upon a rock (see 3 Nephi 14:24-27). I had thought that perhaps parables were unnecessary in the new world because those who lacked ears to hear had died in the cataclysm and did not need to be screened out by parables. The allusion here, however, disputes my first assumption. Since only a fraction of the Savior's teachings were included in Mormon's abridgment, it is entirely possible that Jesus repeated certain parables among the Nephites. Assuredly, parables, which are short and complete in themselves, are easy to excise from a doctrinal narrative. Moreover, many New Testament parables are quite culture-specific in reference and terminology. Not so the parable of the talents, which has general application to almost any culture. Jesus may even have taught a few "new world" parables, too.

The chapter ends with a formulaic farewell (see Ether 12:38), indicating that Moroni assumes these to be his final words of personal address to the Gentiles and to his Lamanite "brethren," for whom, despite all he has suffered, he expresses love. He will finish abridging Ether's writings, and then he will hide away the records. Having made his valedictory gesture, he adds a fervent testimony that is anything but formulaic:

> And then shall ye know that I have seen Jesus, and that he hath talked with me face to face, and that he told me in plain humility, even as a man telleth another in mine own language, concerning these things. . . . (Ether 12:39)

Those few lines say a great deal: The postmortal Jesus has, in person, visited and spoken with Moroni, humbly and plainly in Moroni's own language. Moroni has needed no convincing, and the Lord has used neither commanding tone nor rhetorical riddles in addressing him. I am deeply impressed that this man and his Lord have at times conversed as respectful acquaintances.

Moroni's closing words in Ether 12 are sure, but they do not exude the triumph of his final parting in Moroni 10. They seem, rather, the benediction of a lone laborer beset with doubts concerning the latter-day reception of the record over which he and his predecessors have toiled. He has seen enough of human vanity and depravity to wonder if mortals in *any* era can consistently recognize and cherish truth. In this state of mind, Moroni merely "commend[s]" the latter-day reader "to seek this Jesus" (Ether 12:41). Later, however, he virtually commands it: "Yea, come unto Christ. . ." (Moroni 10:32). As we shall see, between his abridgment of the Jaredite record and the composition of his last challenges to the reader, the beleaguered and despairing man vanishes. A confident Moroni proclaims that one day the record in his care will not only be read, but will change the world.

As chapter 13 opens, Moroni indicates that he is about to finish his account of Ether's faithless people. If the task has been disheartening, Moroni manages now to grasp a bright new hope. For a brief moment, at least, he is caught up in the shining possibilities of the New Jerusalem which Ether foretells. Verses 2-12 of chapter 13 fairly sing with the glory of Ether's revelation. Beginning in poetry—"after the waters had receded from off the face of this land it became a choice land above all other lands, a chosen land of the Lord" (Ether 13:2)—Moroni links his own prophetic vision and understanding with that of Ether. The two oracles almost become one voice, envisioning this choice land, to which the Lord has brought both Ether's and Moroni's ancestors, as "the place of the New Jerusalem, which should come down out of heaven" (Ether 13:3), in complement to the resurrected holy city of the old land.

In verse 7, the merged voices of Ether and Moroni describe Joseph's bringing "his father down into the land of Egypt" as a type for the Lord's bringing "a remnant of the seed of Joseph [Lehi's family] out of the land of Jerusalem" (Ether 13:6-7), a parallel the reader might not have seen. In both instances, the preservation of a branch of Israel was at stake. For Ether and Moroni both, the building of the two Jerusalems is a subject of intense interest and joy, and their separate perspectives combine in dual witness to similar events. Absorbed in their vision of the kingdom's rebirth after unspeakable destruction, the two prophets mutually sing the glad news of "a new heaven and a new earth," when all will "become new" (Ether 13:9). Moroni had read these inspiriting words in the Nephite record,[1] too, but he is moved to declare them again.

Moroni expounds still further, introducing the paradoxical notion from earlier scripture that in the latter-day restoration process, the Jews, "they who were first, . . . shall be last; and" the Gentiles, "they who were last, . . . shall be first" (Ether 13:12.)[2] But, interestingly, the Spirit interrupts and instructs Moroni not to pursue this line of prophecy. We are not told why, but it is a

---

[1] In 3 Nephi 12:47, Jesus delivers this prophecy to the Nephites. See it also in Revelation 21:1.

[2] See 1 Nephi 13:42, where an angel speaks similarly to the first Nephi, and Jacob 5:63, where the passage appears in Zenos's allegory of the tame and wild olive trees.

cogent reminder that prophets know a good deal more than they are able to say. Thus diverted, Moroni turns quickly to Ether and the Jaredite narrative. An exiled Ether escapes to a cave, there to finish the record, while his countrymen go about systematically destroying each other.

In the second year of hostilities, the Lord instructs Ether to tell Coriantumr that if he and his household repent, the kingdom and its people will be spared. Even this late, the Jaredite nation could have been saved, but the warning is to no avail. Coriantumr alone lives to see prophecy fulfilled "concerning another people receiving the land for their inheritance" (Ether 13:21).[3] As the years wear on, anarchy reigns and war spreads until it covers "all the face of the land" (Ether 13:25). Coriantumr finally slays his most persistent foe, a rebel named Shared (the name a derivative of Jared?), in an "exceedingly sore" three-day battle (Ether 13:27-28). In that fatal contest, however, Shared so severely wounds Coriantumr that he is unable to fight "for the space of two years, in which time all the people upon the face of the land were shedding blood, and there was none to restrain them" (Ether 13:31). A chilling statement, like ice water in the veins.

Chapter 14 opens with a reference to the unusual curse that, as in Mormon's day (see Mormon 1:18), is marked by the inexplicable disappearance of material goods. People clutch their possessions to their bosoms, neither borrowing nor lending, "and every man kept the hilt of his sword in his right hand, in the defence of his property and his own life and of his wives and children" (Ether 14:2).[4] In any age it is an appropriate curse for a materialistic people, but it is especially so among the Jaredites, where warfare is now the norm and internal intrigue and death abound on both sides of the battle line.

In the years following Shared's death, at least four insurrectionists seek to overthrow Coriantumr. The last is the fiendish

---

[3] This passage leaves no doubt that Jaredite prophets foretold future migrations to the new world.

[4] "Wives" appears here as the plural form, suggesting either that plural marriage was still practiced in this society, or that the term "every man" is used in the plural sense, meaning "all men" kept "their" swords ready.

Shiz. In his despoiling pursuit of Coriantumr through the land, Shiz heedlessly slays women and children and burns their cities; and when Coriantumr's forces prevail, they return the favor. Our wildest imaginings can scarcely reconstruct scenes of terror and despair such as these.

The reader now senses the hovering menace of final destruction, for nothing seems in the offing to halt the awful momentum. "So swift and speedy," and so horribly efficient, is one major battle that by its conclusion "there was none left to bury the dead." Neither the advancing nor the retreating armies pause to perform that one last gesture of human civility. Instead, they "march forth from the shedding of blood to the shedding of blood, leaving the bodies of both men, women, and children strewed upon the face of the land, to become a prey to the worms of the flesh" (Ether 14:22). The stench of decaying bodies is insufferable, a repugnant symbol of an accursed land. The armies are whirling human cyclones, sweeping "off the inhabitants before them" (Ether 14:27).

Although Moroni's is a highly condensed account, and some individual battles are pursued in rapid fury, we should be aware that these wars are many years in the making. By the beginning of chapter 15, Coriantumr has had sufficient time to recover from his various wounds and to contemplate soberly the astronomical fatality figures of these wars, "two millions of mighty men, and also their wives and their children" (Ether 15:2). If the figures represent only male warriors, the total slain would number several million. Heavy-hearted, realizing that the prophecies are "fulfilled thus far, every whit," Coriantumr begins to repent of his evil deeds. He sees his mistake, "and his soul mourned and refused to be comforted" (Ether 15:3). Regret beyond reckoning.

A rueful Coriantumr offers Shiz the kingdom in exchange for the lives of his people, and Shiz agrees, so long as he is granted the pleasure of personally executing Coriantumr. Whether this incident or something else triggers their rage, Coriantumr's unrepentant people are once more "stirred up to anger" (Ether 15:6), and a new round of warfare ensues. Thus, another opportunity for peace is sacrificed to spleen. In a temporary cessation of hostilities, what is left of Coriantumr's army makes camp by the hill Ramah, the "same hill," Moroni adds, "where my father Mormon did hide up the records unto the Lord" (Ether 15:11).[5] Now both sides begin to collect their total strength, gathering into one place "all the people upon all the face of the land, who had not been slain, save it was Ether" (Ether 15:12). From his secluded vantage point, Ether watches the lurid drama. The conscription of every last living soul in preparation for a final war takes four years. Everyone is armed, "men, women and children" (Ether 15:15), as a nation methodically manufactures its own doom.

The Lord created the earth in seven "days," and the Jaredites dismantle their portion of it in just eight mortal days. The battle commences with white-hot fury, and after two days of blood-curdling horror, Coriantumr makes a second offer of the kingdom if Shiz will spare his people. It is too late, however, for "the Spirit of the Lord" has departed, and Satan has "full power over the hearts of the people." Hope and reason have fled; dumbly propelled toward annihilation, the people go "again to battle" (Ether 15:19). Days three, four, and five pass in crazed violence, and by nighttime the senseless combatants are "drunken with anger, even as a man who is drunken with wine" (Ether 15:22). The survivors have no inclination to seek peace or to forsake their terrible resolve.

By the end of day five, all have "fallen by the sword save it were fifty and two of the people of Coriantumr, and sixty and nine of the people of Shiz" (Ether 15:23). A civilization fifteen centuries in the making is reduced to just over a hundred people, and the killing is not finished yet. At the end of day six, Coriantumr's force numbers twenty-seven and Shiz's thirty-two. The contestants are no longer thinking victory; there is nothing

---

5 The hill Ramah is called Cumorah by the Nephites. There is some speculation about whether the Hill Cumorah in New York state, where the angel Moroni led Joseph Smith to buried records on gold plates, is the same hill, geographically, where Mormon had hidden the records and where Moroni may have buried them before he died. There are several mentions of Cumorah in the Book of Mormon. Cumorah/Ramah was near the final battle scenes of both the Nephite and the Jaredite nations, and it was close enough to Zarahemla that the wounded Coriantumr was discovered and taken there. It seems obvious to me that the two civilizations, though separated by wilderness, occupied the same general landscape. Very likely, then, the records were not originally buried in what is now New York state. It scarcely seems possible that Moroni, as a mortal, could have transported them all those miles. On the other hand, as a resurrected being, Moroni could readily have moved them.

left to be won. Grimly, they eat and sleep "and [prepare] for death on the morrow" (Ether 15:26). On day seven, the remaining warriors fight "for the space of three hours," until all faint "with the loss of blood" (Ether 15:27). Coriantumr's men revive first, and struggling to wobbly feet, they "flee for their lives" (Ether 15:28). But Shiz and his men revive also and give pursuit, with a maddened Shiz swearing to kill Coriantumr or die himself. On the eighth day, Shiz and his men overtake Coriantumr's retreating soldiers, and in the ensuing battle all but Shiz and Coriantumr are slain. Shiz is unconscious, and Coriantumr is so weak that he has to steady himself by leaning on his sword. He rests briefly and then whacks off the head of Shiz. Horror sometimes carries a perverse fascination, and Moroni inscribes the grisly details of this encounter in his abridgment.

Although we often speak of Coriantumr as the last survivor of the once mighty Jaredite nation, there is, of course, another— Ether, who, like Melville's Ishmael in *Moby Dick*, and Moroni himself, lives to write the story. The fate of Ether, the Lord's witness to the fulfilling of prophecy, remains a mystery. His last written words introduce the possibility that like Enoch and perhaps several Nephite prophets, he was translated and did not taste death: "Whether the Lord will that I be translated, or that I suffer the will of the Lord in the flesh, it mattereth not, if it so be that I am saved in the kingdom of God. Amen" (Ether 15:34). So ends the account of a great nation that was born before Abraham and perished several centuries before Christ—a nation whose birth and death were and are virtually unknown to the rest of the world. Like the larger part of the Nephite chronicle, the full record of Ether may one day be brought forth.

## 28

## Moroni: Final Testimonies of Truth

Finding that, against all odds, "I have not as yet perished" (Moroni 1:1), Moroni appends additional material to his father's abridged record before he secures it along with the other records left in his care. The final section in the Book of Mormon, therefore, is the book of Moroni. It includes Moroni's own admonitions to future generations and several fragments of the Savior's instructions to his Nephite disciples, which Moroni had apparently gleaned from the records. He also interjects three of his father's discourses, a sermon and two letters. These "few more things" he adds in the hope "that perhaps they may be of worth unto my brethren, the Lamanites, in some future day" (Moroni 1:4).

Here is a man besieged on every side, fearing to "make . . . myself known to the Lamanites lest they should destroy me" (Moroni 1:1), witnessing the wholesale dismantling of human reason and sensibility, and yet thinking still of the welfare of latter-day peoples. Safety is a mighty scarce commodity, for the Lamanites have begun "exceedingly fierce" warfare "among themselves" (Moroni 1:2). Moroni knows full well that if these "brethren" of his discover him, they will dispatch him to kingdom come on the spot. They are meting out death to "every Nephite that will not deny the Christ" (Moroni 1:2). For Moroni, of course, denial is unthinkable under any circumstances, and he is forced to "wander whithersoever I can for the safety of mine own life" (Moroni 1:3). Like the Savior, whose dying thought was concern for his murderers, Moroni seems to bear no malice toward his enemies. Rather than nourish vengeance, he preserves a record for the progeny of Lamanites who would happily destroy it if they found it.

I admire Moroni, but he remains something of a mystery to me. There is simply no autobiography in his work, perhaps because he lacks confidence in his writing abilities. Or perhaps he simply does not want to divert attention from the sacred writings of others to himself. For whatever reason, his fascinating story remains largely untold. We know nothing of how Moroni occupied his time after his people were destroyed, or where and how far he traveled. How did he subsist? Did he cultivate crops or make cloth? What did he use for shelter? What we do know is that he has immense faith and physical stamina, and a "survivor's" temperament. Steadfast to the end, he performs the assigned task and retains both his sanity and his humanity. Sincere, far-seeing, hopeful, and yet never naively optimistic, he fully comprehends the immediate and eternal consequences of events he has witnessed. He also knows that every other living person in this ravaged land would gladly tear his heart out.

Even more remarkable than Moroni's physical durability, however, is his emotional and spiritual stamina. Much as he suffered in the excruciating years of war, undoubtedly his greatest test came later. A lesser man would have cracked or crumbled through the long decades of danger, deprivation, and isolation he endured. Where did his comfort lie, except in his God? When I consider the extent to which my own happiness and health stem from my association with other human beings, I wonder that Moroni held on for even a year, much less a third of a century, without the companionship of another living mortal being. Countless lonely campfires must have held his thoughtful gaze; countless heartaches and fears must have troubled his sleep. Surely, he found solace in the Lord and the Holy Spirit, for there was certainly none to be had in the Jaredite record, nor in his memories of his own stubborn, hell-bent people. In trying to fathom such utter aloneness, I am reminded again that the Book of Mormon begins with a small band of castaways, and it ends with one lone man, as the chronicle of the birth, growth, and death of a nation comes full circle to a solitary closing.

Denied the luxury of an early death, Moroni is probably

required to safeguard the records until they are no longer at risk. Perhaps a generation has to pass away before they will be safe in any hiding place, or mercifully forgotten by his enemies. In the cherished record resides the spiritual salvation of covenant peoples and Gentiles alike. I used to wonder why it was the sturdy Moroni rather than the dynamic Mormon who visited and instructed young Joseph Smith regarding the record. I think I understand now why it was Moroni. Not only did he conclude and conceal the record, but he made of his very life a shield around it. Preserving it became perhaps the primary purpose of his existence. We cannot begin to contemplate its preciousness to him who had lost everything but his life and his resolute faith.

Chapters 2 through 6 of the book of Moroni are short. They detail, for the benefit of the latter-day church, a few forms, ordinances, and practices that the Savior instituted when he appointed apostles and formally established the church in the days of Nephi, grandson of Helaman. Chapter 2, for example, describes the manner in which Jesus gave his chosen disciples the power to confer the gift of the Holy Ghost upon others by the laying on of hands. Chapter 3 describes the manner in which the chosen "elders of the church, ordained priests and teachers" (Moroni 3:1), and it quotes the prayer of ordination. Chapters 4 and 5 describe the procedures for administering the emblems of the holy sacrament in the church, and again the actual prayers of blessing and sanctification are given in the text. The principal subjects of chapter 6 are baptism and the conduct of worship services. The presence of this material suggests that Moroni was familiar with the larger contents of the records in his possession, and that these practices were followed at least early on among the faithful in his day. Very likely, too, he pored over the various records during his long years of exile, especially those unabridged portions containing the Savior's teachings in the new world.

In a passage that refutes Moroni's own deprecating assessment of his writing skills, he feelingly describes the reception of members into the church during Christ's new-world ministry:

> . . . they were numbered among the people of the church of Christ;
> and their names were taken, that they might be remembered and
> nourished by the good word of God, to keep them in the right way,
> to keep them continually watchful unto prayer, relying alone upon
> the merits of Christ, who was the author and the finisher of their
> faith. (Moroni 6:4)

"Nourished by the good word of God," "watchful unto prayer,"
and "the author and the finisher of their faith" are well-wrought
phrases, to be sure. I think, too, that the comfortable informality
of Nephite worship services in better days, which suggested harmony and devotion, must have struck Moroni as a poignant contrast to the later dissonance of his time:

> And the church did meet together oft, to fast and to pray, and to
> speak to one another concerning the welfare of their souls. . . .
> And their meetings were conducted by the church after the man-
> ner of the workings of the Spirit, and by the power of the Holy Ghost;
> for as the power of the Holy Ghost led them whether to preach, or to
> exhort, or to pray, or to supplicate, or to sing, even so it was done.
> (Moroni 6:5, 9)

It should be evident, in consideration of this model, why LDS
worship services, although structured, are relatively simple and
informal rather than ceremonial.

The next three chapters contain Mormon's rather than
Moroni's writings, one sermon and two letters, none of which
Mormon had intended for the record. In choosing to include
them, Moroni may have seen the sermon's compatibility with
Ether's and his own recent subject—"faith, hope, and charity"
(Moroni 7:1). Faith is, however, Mormon's first and main concern, as it was Moroni's. In performing the mammoth task of
abridgment, Mormon added a fair amount of explanation,
entreaty, and editorial commentary. But if Moroni had not managed to supplement his father's work, the record would contain
little besides editorial exposition from the great commander-
prophet who prepared the whole parcel for latter-day restoration.

As it is, the offering is slim, these three pieces and the twelfth chapter of Helaman. Mormon's sermon, which occupies Moroni 7, may be a complete text, though Moroni's explanation of his own purposes—to write "a few words" of his father (Moroni 7:1)—could mean that he has pared the discourse.

Typically, Nephite sermons require close attention because they are doctrinally rich and textually dense, and this classic piece is no exception. A priceless sample of Mormon's concentrated thought, it provides a unique window into the quality and depth of his intellect. We do not know the date or occasion, only that Mormon is addressing members of the church in a Nephite synagogue. His introductory remarks suggest a special assembly of the faithful in uncertain times. Peaceableness being a scarce commodity in the promised land just now, Mormon appreciatively calls his listeners "peaceable followers of Christ" (Moroni 7:3). In declaring that those who walk "peaceabl[y] . . . with the children of men" are destined to dwell with God (Moroni 7:4), he implies that a contentious earth life disqualifies one for heaven's peace. In the early part of his sermon, he also deftly links peaceableness with right action, for the "peaceable walk" he envisions is full of good works. And good works come from God, while evil works originate with Satan. The light of Christ, universally available, aids mortals to discern one from the other.

In verse 20, Mormon phrases a rhetorical question that serves as a transition from his introductory thoughts to his central theme. How, having learned to distinguish between good and evil, can one then "lay hold upon every good thing?" he asks. By exercising *faith* in Jesus Christ, who is the source of "every good thing" (Moroni 7:22), he answers. If Christ had not come, Mormon explains, mortals would have remained in a fallen state, estranged from the good. Even before his coming, mortals were apprised of it and its meaning; and they were informed of the good and dissuaded from evil by angels and prophets who testified of Christ. Thus, both before and after the Savior came, it was faith in the source of goodness that enabled mortals to lay hold upon the good, and "faith in his name" that saved them (Moroni 7:26).

Pursuing his subject further, Mormon asks still another rhetorical question, obviously a favorite teaching device with him. The question is whether miracles have "ceased because Christ hath ascended into heaven" (Moroni 7:27). The answer is a resounding *no*. Miracles will persist because angels will continue ministering to mortals of "strong faith and a firm mind in every form of godliness" (Moroni 7:30). We should not miss Mormon's careful inclusion of godly firmness of mind as a condition for receiving angelic ministrations; he seems to exclude unstable fanaticism. Nor should we miss the importance he attaches to the role of angels in the faith-building process. "The office of their ministry," as he describes it, is twofold: "to call men unto repentance, and to fulfil and to do the work of the covenants of the Father" among his children (Moroni 7:31).

The call to repentance we readily understand; "the work of the covenants" may need explaining. That work, we assume, has been underway since the time of Joseph Smith; and Moroni, who writes his father's words about the services of angels, will himself, as an angelic messenger, play a major role in initiating the fulfillment of covenants. According to Mormon, angels teach prophets, and prophets testify so that "the residue of men[1] may have faith in Christ, that the Holy Ghost may have place in their hearts" (Moroni 7:32). Only if the Gentiles develop faith in Christ can God's covenants with the children of Israel be fulfilled, for the Gentiles, we remember, are to be the instruments through which the gospel is restored to Zion. Faith is the catalyst for miracles and for the ministering of angels.

Shifting to a more personal manner, Mormon turns now to the final section of his sermon, the three-pronged subject Moroni had identified in the beginning: faith, hope, and charity. Faith and hope are inextricably linked, Mormon says, because the hope he alludes to is not a general, abstract hope for a rosy, abstract future.

---

[1] I.e., the Gentiles. See Moses 7:20 in the Pearl of Great Price.

It is, rather, a solidly religious hope, tied specifically to faith in Christ's redemptive mission. Thus, as the Book of Mormon draws to a close, it presents us with three discourses, delivered by Ether, Moroni, and Mormon, on the relationship between faith and hope. Moroni, of course, is the one who elects to include these writings.

But there is another key to the faith-hope connection, one Mormon had mentioned before. Faith and hope are impossible, he says more than once, unless one is "meek and lowly of heart." Perhaps most important, this kind of humility (or peaceableness), accompanied by a divinely inspired confession "that Jesus is the Christ," leads to true charity, without which a person "is nothing" (Moroni 7:43-44). Beginning with the last of verse 44, and continuing into verse 46, Mormon caps his sermon with a lovely passage that echoes Paul's inspired discourse on charity in his first epistle to the Corinthians. The reader may want to compare verses 1-8 of 1 Corinthians 13 with verses 44 to 46 of Moroni 7.

Mormon reaches beyond Paul, however, and defines charity as "the pure love of Christ" that "endureth forever" (Moroni 7:47). Perhaps endurance distinguishes charity as much as love. Perhaps, too, more than one interpretation of the phrase "pure love of Christ" is intended. The phrase intimates that a pure and Christlike love should grace all human associations and dealings; we are to love as Christ loves. But it may also suggest a deeper, more powerful application—that we are to love *with* his love, that through us others can come to know his love for them. Mormon's concluding sentence opens wide the doors of blessedness to mortals whose humble faith leads them to feel and express this charity, which is more than a transitory emotion. It is the key to our understanding of the Savior's nature, and therefore to our following his example and becoming like him. It is also a gift we must pray for.

After repeated readings of this sermon, I am still awed by the quality of Mormon's mind. I have greatly admired his skill in the abridgment of records; but watching him think, coming head to head with the person whom the faithful Nephites knew as their spiritual as well as their military leader, has given me a new perspective on his life and on the book he so selflessly prepared. One thing is certain: this finely crafted sermon resonates with the power of Mormon's intellect as well as the strength of his integrity and belief. No wonder even the faithless Nephites wanted him to lead and inspire their armies.

Mormon's two epistles to his son Moroni, which appear as chapters 8 and 9 of the book of Moroni, are less formally rhetorical and less difficult to grasp than his sermon; but they, too, show the vigor of his mind and leadership as well as the tenderness of his love. He speaks as both prophet and father, and his reasons for writing the first epistle are both personal and administrative. Only after expressing great joy in Moroni's "calling to the ministry" (Moroni 8:1) does Mormon turn to institutional matters. We do not know if he has other children, but we do know from these two letters that he and his son Moroni share a warm filial love that sustains them in times trying beyond description. There are several instances in the Book of Mormon in which righteous fathers give counsel and blessings to their sons, but this is the only instance of a father's personal letters to his son. Quite different from a patriarchal blessing, a personal letter is a uniquely candid and spontaneous form of writing. Still, Mormon uses at least one letter in the manner of Paul, to give doctrinal instruction on a matter needing attention in Moroni's part of the land.

Mormon's specific concern on this occasion is the reprehensible practice of infant baptism in the church, which Mormon says constitutes "solemn mockery before God" (Moroni 8:9). Chronologically, the first letter would have to be later than the sermon just discussed, yet considerably earlier than the second letter. Mormon is apparently writing from the battle front, though at the moment there seems to be a lull in the fighting. He begins as any loving parent would to a dear son who has upheld the faith of his fathers:

> My beloved son, Moroni, I rejoice exceedingly that your Lord
> Jesus Christ hath been mindful of you, and hath called you to his

ministry, and to his holy work.

I am mindful of you always in my prayers, continually praying unto God the Father in the name of his Holy Child, Jesus, that he, through his infinite goodness and grace, will keep you through the endurance of faith on his name to the end. (Moroni 8:2-3)

In the phrase "his Holy Child" we sense not only Mormon's awareness of the Father's feelings for the beloved Son and Lord, but also of Mormon's feelings for Moroni, his own son. This small glimpse into the genuine familial affection of two prophets is a rare treasure, perhaps all the more so because Mormon's letters were not intended by their author to be part of any permanent record.

The lengthy middle section of Mormon's letter is heavily doctrinal as he categorically denies the need for infant baptism on the grounds that little children are incapable of sin and therefore "need no repentance, neither baptism" (Moroni 8:11). I suspect that Moroni includes this letter in the book at least partly because the doctrine regarding infant baptism does not appear elsewhere in the abridged record. We do not know if the Savior specifically taught it to the Nephites, but we do know that the issue has arisen in Mormon's day and that he has "inquired of the Lord concerning the matter" (Moroni 8:7). In answer, the Lord repeats the words he had spoken during his ministry in the old world: "Behold, I came into the world not to call the righteous but sinners to repentance; the whole need no physician, but they that are sick; wherefore, little children are whole, for they are not capable of committing sin. . ." (Moroni 8:8; see Mark 2:17).

Repentance and baptism, Mormon says, are for "those who are accountable and capable of committing sin," and not for small children and strangers to the law. Since it is impossible for those "that are without the law" to repent of breaking it, "the power of redemption" automatically applies to "all them that have no law" (Moroni 8:22). Appalled that little children, who cannot understand the concept of sin, could be thought guilty in God's eyes, Mormon declares that they "are alive in Christ, even from the foundation of the world" (Moroni 8:12). He is much exercised over this matter, and he does not soon drop the subject. He even inversely links charity as well as faith and hope to the practice of infant baptism, asserting that anyone who believes "little children need baptism . . . hath neither faith, hope, nor charity" and is destined for "hell" (Moroni 8:14). Mormon's voice seems to merge with the Lord's when he suggests that true charity forbids the practice:

> And I am filled with charity, which is everlasting love; wherefore, all children are alike unto me; wherefore, I love little children with a perfect love; and they are all alike and partakers of salvation. (Moroni 8:17)

To insist "that little children need baptism," he adds, is to set "at naught the atonement of [Christ] and the power of his redemption" (Moroni 8:20), making repentance and baptism a "mockery before God, denying the mercies of Christ" (Moroni 8:23). He also warns that to practice infant baptism is to put one's soul in jeopardy.

Mormon's conclusion to this extemporaneous exhortation on infant baptism demonstrates again his thorough and logical thinking on doctrinal subjects. In two long sentences, he deftly wraps up his argument against infant baptism by taking it beyond ordinary considerations of form and process to the eternal purposes and implications of baptism in general. He implies that an important element in the journey from repentance to eternal life is, again, always, "meekness and lowliness of heart." Such humility accompanies, perhaps even signifies, the remission of sins. Here is Mormon's conclusion, a strong and agile summary of the first principles and ordinances of the gospel of Jesus Christ— faith, repentance, baptism, and reception of the Holy Ghost— especially in relation to humility, hope, and charity:

> And the first fruits of repentance is baptism; and baptism cometh by faith unto the fulfilling the commandments; and the fulfilling the commandments bringeth remission of sins;

And the remission of sins bringeth meekness, and lowliness of heart; and because of meekness and lowliness of heart cometh the visitation of the Holy Ghost, which Comforter filleth with hope and perfect love, which love endureth by diligence unto prayer, until the end shall come, when all the saints shall dwell with God. (Moroni 8:25-26)

We should not miss the fact that Moroni links the four basic gospel principles and ordinances with the faith-hope-charity triad. Nor should we overlook the fact that faith is the cornerstone of both structures. We can learn something, too, from tracing Mormon's sequence of cause and effect in this passage. As he describes it, the process of the soul's salvation begins with faith and repentance, which lead to baptism and the fulfilling of the commandments, which in turn lead to the remission of sins. This is not the end of the sequence, however, for the remission of sins leads to further meekness and humility, which in turn open the heart to the Holy Ghost, who then blesses that mortal with hope and enduring love, which are sustained by prayer until she or he returns to God's presence.

After concluding his instructional discourse, Mormon addresses his son more personally, promising to "write unto you again if I go not out soon against the Lamanites" (Moroni 8:27). He acknowledges that at bottom it is the Nephites' pride that renders them vulnerable to Lamanite assaults, and therefore pride that will accomplish their destruction. It is as if the Lamanites, in their vindictive paganism, symbolize the prideful unbelief of their Nephite counterparts by imaging an insidious alter ego bent on destroying its own better self. Mormon urges Moroni to "pray for [the Nephites], my son, that repentance may come unto them," but he is certain that "after rejecting so great a knowledge, my son, they must perish soon," as has been prophesied (Moroni 8:28-29).

Mormon's second epistle to Moroni relates a woeful tale, a tale of wickedness and depravity that breaks the heart to tell it. The lateness of the letter is confirmed in its dismal contents, and in the fact that Mormon proffers no doctrinal instruction. Although

Mormon's faith in both Moroni and God remains unshaken, the peoples' minds are closed. At the time he writes the second letter, he has been in the thick of battle, but he wants his son to "know that I am yet alive" (Moroni 9:1). His letter reveals that he is beseiged on two sides, by his own people's constant wrangling as well as by the Lamanite threat. Especially frustrating are his futile efforts to talk sense to the Nephites, for they greet him with wrath when he "speak[s] the word of God with sharpness" (Moroni 9:4) and ignore him when he does not. He gravely describes a people in the last stages of degeneracy, a people so enslaved by hatred that they are incapable of humane behavior or sentiment: "For so exceedingly do they anger that . . . they have no fear of death; and they have lost their love, one towards another; and they thirst after blood and revenge continually" (Moroni 9:5). To put it simply, there has been a frightening decline in human feeling just in Mormon's lifetime.

Mormon's gloomy observation in this letter contrasts markedly with his sermon on charity which Moroni inserted into the abridged record just pages ago, a sermon which apparently was received sympathetically by a congregation who had not yet fallen into disaffection. At the time of the first letter, although the Nephites were at war, the church was at least functioning as an organization. Leaders were being called to the ministry, and members met for instruction and worship. Not so now, however. As Mormon rehearses the atrocities on both sides, he asks, how can a once "civil and a delightsome people" (Moroni 9:12) stoop to such barbaric acts? He asks, too, how anyone can "expect that God will stay his hand in judgment against us?" (Moroni 9:14). Mormon seems intentionally to use the term "us," granting his own fate to be inextricably enmeshed with that of his people; and he continues to strive with them even as he helplessly grieves over them. These elect people, who once fostered civilization and enjoyed its amenities, have surrendered to anarchy and abandoned every shred of decency. Individually, "they are without principle, and past feeling; and their wickedness doth exceed that of the Lamanites" (Moroni 9:20). Again we encounter the disheartening expression, "past feeling," to describe the vacuous spiritual condition of a fallen people.

In spite of all he has seen, Mormon cannot bring himself to abandon hope entirely. Perhaps seeing in the Nephites' extreme suffering a chance even this late for repentance and rescue, he tries to stop their plunge into physical oblivion and spiritual hell. I keep reminding myself that if the Nephite nation had repented and remained faithful, the gospel restoration contingency plan would not have been necessary. Even though the Lord foresaw destruction and a need for restoration, repentance was always the preferred option, and continuance was always a possibility. Why else would the Lord have begun the enterprise in the first place— twice, in fact—and then have labored so hard to maintain it?

Toward the end of his letter, Mormon anticipates a reunion with his son "soon; for I have sacred records that I would deliver up unto thee" (Moroni 9:24). He also asks Moroni to add some of his own words to the record "if thou art spared and I shall perish and not see thee" (Moroni 9:24). The transfer of the records did occur, and the faithful father and son were together in the final days of battle, as we saw earlier. And Moroni did, as we know, contribute to the record. Mormon's words to Moroni show the greatness of his heart and the magnitude of his faith. He has witnessed the moral collapse of his nation, he is in the thick of a losing military enterprise, and he abides, undaunted, in faith and hope and charity. His concern is not for himself, but for his son:

> My son, be faithful in Christ; and may not the things which I have written grieve thee, to weigh thee down unto death; but may Christ lift thee up, and may his sufferings and death, and the showing his body unto our fathers, and his mercy and long-suffering, and the hope of his glory and of eternal life, rest in your mind forever. (Moroni 9:25)

For whatever reason, perhaps out of awe for death itself, we attach uncommon significance to the last utterances of mortals. Thought to encapsulate the collective wisdom of a lifetime, they often reflect an assigning of ultimate priorities. Moroni's final words, which constitute chapter 10 of the book of Moroni, certainly merit our full attention. They arrange themselves into four categories: (1) Moroni's personal testimony that the record is authentic and divinely inspired; (2) a discussion of spiritual gifts; (3) a brief reiteration of the themes that had occupied his father's sermon—faith, hope, and charity; and (4) a repeated plea to his latter-day readers to "come unto Christ, and be perfected in him" (Moroni 10:32). These are the things Moroni most wanted the descendants of his Lamanite brothers, and surely the rest of us, to contemplate.

First, the record. Verses 1 through 23 of chapter 10 are directed especially to those whose ancestral history is chronicled in the book's pages, the remnant of the Lehite nation—in the main, descendants of Laman and Lemuel. But, I repeat, what Moroni says here and elsewhere applies to every reader of the Book of Mormon. In the introductory pages of this book, I quoted Moroni's challenge to the reader, of whatever background or persuasion, to put the matter of the book's truth and authenticity to the test of sincere personal prayer (see Moroni 10:4-5). There is no need to wonder about the book; every person can know for himself or herself. If it does nothing else, this book testifies, even as the Holy Ghost testifies, to the reality and divinity of Jesus Christ.

Moroni's next subject is perhaps the most neglected of the four in our personal musings: the presence, power, and importance of spiritual gifts. Yet again, Moroni, like Mormon and Ether, shows his spiritual, intellectual, and prophetic kinship with Paul, this time in attesting that God shows forth his power in spiritual gifts among the faithful. Although variances in the Paul and Moroni texts are plentiful, verses 8 through 17 of Moroni 10 are essentially the same as verses 5 through 11 of 1 Corinthians 12. Among the individual gifts that Moroni inventories are the separate abilities to teach wisdom and to teach knowledge. In delineating them as distinct and different gifts, both Paul and Moroni seem to imply that although ideally the two are found together, and enhance each other, they may also be found apart. That is, the ability to acquire and dispense knowledge does not guarantee the companion ability to acquire and convey wisdom.

That Moroni chooses, in his final discourse, to write of spiritual gifts and their presence where faith flourishes, underlines their importance. Heirs to an empirical age (which Moroni undoubtedly foresaw) of reliance on scientific testing and investigation, we are conditioned to be skeptical of such gifts, to discredit anything we cannot explain through human logic or laboratory analysis. On the other hand, it is all too easy for the imaginations of the unstable and fanatical, who lack the firmness of mind alluded to by Alma and Mormon, to simulate such gifts and attribute them to God. I can see why, in his sermon, Mormon meticulously stressed the need for discernment. Spiritual gifts that originate with God are to be sought and cherished; spurious counterfeits of them must be rejected.

Moroni turns to his third subject—the principles of faith, hope, and charity—with almost an implied supposition of their natural link with the subject of spiritual gifts. Mormon had related them and Paul seemed to connect them, too, sandwiching his famous discourse on faith, hope, and charity (chapter 13 of 1 Corinthians) between two discourses devoted to discussion of spiritual gifts (chapters 12 and 14). In truth, perhaps only the gifts of life and the Atonement—the "more excellent way"—exceed the gifts of faith, hope, and charity. How often, indeed, do we even think of faith, or hope, or charity as spiritual gifts? Like his predecessors, Moroni relates the three, with faith giving rise to hope, and hope to charity. He then adds a rather profound afterthought that may have its genesis in his own experience with the Nephites and with the Jaredite record: "And if ye have no hope ye must needs be in despair; and despair cometh because of iniquity" (Moroni 10:22). To paraphrase: the unrepentant sinner considers himself beyond redemption. Indeed, the history of the Jaredite and Nephite nations proves Moroni's conclusion—iniquity without repentance produces despair.

In my introduction, I also quoted some of Moroni's next statement, which is preparatory to his final plea to his readers. Frank and ingenuous, almost disarmingly direct, Moroni writes as though he were looking us straight in the eye. He speaks, he says, "according to the words of Christ; and I lie not" (Moroni 10:26), and the time will come when the reader "shall know that I lie not" (Moroni 10:27). Subtlety is not Moroni's forte. When we meet him at the judgment seat, he declares, "the Lord God" will also meet us face to face, and pointing to Moroni, will say to us, "Did I not declare my words unto you, which were written by this man, like as one crying from the dead, yea, even as one speaking out of the dust?" (Moroni 10:27). This passage, echoing Isaiah, is powerful testimony—not the sort of thing a dissembler in any age could convincingly invent. Very simply, Moroni knows what he knows.

Having once more borne personal witness, Moroni momentarily appropriates language from Isaiah 52:1-2 and 54:2 to frame his concluding exhortation to the reader. But his own entreaty is more compelling still, with its promise of ultimate sanctification:

> Yea, come unto Christ, and be perfected in him, and deny your-selves of all ungodliness; and if ye shall deny yourselves of all ungod-liness and love God with all your might, mind and strength, then is his grace sufficient for you, that by his grace ye may be perfect in Christ; and if by the grace of God ye are perfect in Christ, ye can in nowise deny the power of God. (Moroni 10:32)

I note that the major syntactic turn in this one-sentence passage, at the word "then," comes very nearly at the midpoint. The first half of the sentence loops back on itself as it spells out the conditions for redemption; and the second half, casting back the same way, confirms the blessings and surety that follow the fulfilling of these conditions. As I have contended all along, Moroni has rhetorical abilities that he does not give himself credit for. Balance, antithesis, and repetition, for example, are tools he uses well. Moroni's skill is apparent also in verse 33, where he takes the conclusion of verse 32 as his premise and repeats the "if . . . then" construction from that sentence to chart the remainder of the course to sanctification:

> And again, if ye by the grace of God are perfect in Christ, and deny not his power, then are ye sanctified in Christ by the grace of God, through the shedding of the blood of Christ, which is in the covenant of the Father unto the remission of your sins, that ye become holy, without spot. (Moroni 10:33)

It impresses me that after all Moroni has seen and suffered, his concluding message can be so decidedly upbeat, optimistic, and absolute. Without question, this aging, solitary prophet knows that the Lord loves him and that eternal life in God's presence awaits him. His greatest desire is for all humankind to enjoy that same knowledge and inherit that same redemption. Below are the words that conclude not only Moroni's section of the record, but also the entire abridgment prepared by his father Mormon. I rejoice that Moroni's final words are wonderfully celebratory, and that he joyfully anticipates meeting us (me!), the very individuals for whom he and his ancestors have prepared the record, at "the pleasing bar" of Christ. How good of him to assume that judgment might be a happy occasion for us, too:

> And now I bid unto all, farewell. I soon go to rest in the paradise of God, until my spirit and body shall again reunite, and I am brought forth triumphant through the air, to meet you before the pleasing bar of the great Jehovah, the Eternal Judge of both quick and dead. Amen. (Moroni 10:34)

A book ending in this manner cannot be lightly dismissed. Even as I write these last sentences, I am overpowered by a sense of gratitude I cannot begin to describe. Gratitude for the lives and sacrifices anciently that made and preserved this record and the writings from which it derives. Gratitude for a loving Father and a loving Savior. Gratitude for the faith of a boy named Joseph Smith, who became the instrument of the record's translation. Gratitude for the faith of parents who knew long before I did that the book is true. Gratitude for my own sure faith, now, that this is indeed a holy work, priceless, saving, comforting, lifting, and immeasurably dear. To read it is to find a still center of truth in a world spinning with confusion. To study it is to be blessed by the choicest gifts of heaven. To write about it has been to discover the illuminated chambers in my own soul.

Sweet, indeed, is the word. And none sweeter than this word.

# Index

## About the Author

Marilyn Arnold brings to the publication of this book a rich background of scholarship, teaching, writing, and gospel study. She graduated from Brigham Young University with highest honors, and earned her Ph.D. in American Literature from the University of Wisconsin at Madison. Her distinguished career has included tenure at BYU as a Professor of English, Assistant to the President, Dean of Graduate Studies, and Director of the Center for the Study of Christian Values in Literature. A nationally recognized scholar on the works of author Willa Cather and other American writers, she has written four books on Cather and has published widely in scholarly journals and Church publications.

Reflecting on her own experience in writing *Sweet Is the Word*, the author recalls that "I was compelled to write this book. I find that writing about a text is the best way for me to come to understand it. More important, perhaps, is that I wanted somehow to turn whatever small gifts I have back to the Lord. Until a few years ago, my life was pretty much focused on my career. That needed to change. Beyond that, however, I earnestly hope that the manuscript will take readers, new and old, to the Book of Mormon with enthusiasm, vigor, and love."

A resident of St. George, Utah, Marilyn Arnold is an avid skier, hiker, and tennis player. She has served on the Sunday School General Board and on several Church curriculum committees. Currently she is a Spiritual Living teacher in her ward Relief Society, and also serves as her ward's teacher development leader.